REGULATED LIVES:

LIFE INSURANCE AND BRITISH SOCIETY, 1800–1914

In *Regulated Lives*, Timothy Alborn explores the transformation of different concepts of human life in the British life insurance industry between 1800 and 1914. Alborn describes how ideas of life, as they passed into an era of statistical thinking, medicalization, and capitalist bureaucracy, altered to accommodate modernity. As the ideas adapted to changing circumstances, Victorian life insurance companies continually reconceived their customers' lives as both consuming subjects and objectified abstractions. As consumers, policyholders were 'sympathetic lives,' whose hopes and fears for the future and responsibilities to family and society were anticipated, dramatized, and manipulated by the companies. Their lives were more purely conceived in abstract, objectified terms when they were analysed numerically and medically. As 'risks' bearing calculable economic values, policyholders were also 'commodified lives,' simultaneously acting as inalienable subjects and being acted upon as financial instruments. By examining the formulation of these different meanings of life by salesmen, actuaries, and doctors who worked for life insurance offices, Alborn suggests that the complexity of modern commercial and social institutions diminished the capacity of any one of those institutions to govern the people under their influence.

Based on extensive, previously untapped archival records, *Regulating Lives* is the first industry-wide history of life insurance during the Victorian period. It makes a major contribution to historical and sociological accounts of risk, modernization, rationalization, and the rise of consumer culture, and also provides rich new contexts for the history of Victorian medicine and science.

TIMOTHY ALBORN is a professor in the Department of History at Lehman College, City University of New York.

TIMOTHY ALBORN

Regulated Lives

Life Insurance and British Society, 1800–1914

UNIVERSITY OF TORONTO PRESS
Toronto Buffalo London

© University of Toronto Press Incorporated 2009
Toronto Buffalo London
www.utppublishing.com
Printed in Canada

ISBN 978-1-4426-3996-6

Printed on acid-free paper

Library and Archives Canada Cataloguing in Publication

Alborn, Timothy L., 1964–
Regulated lives: life insurance and British society, 1800–1914 / Timothy Alborn.

Includes bibliographical references and index.
ISBN 978-1-4426-3996-6

1. Life insurance – Social aspects – Great Britain – History – 19th century.
2. Life insurance – Great Britain – History – 19th century.   3. Great Britain –
Social conditions – 19th century.   4. Great Britain – Civilization – 19th century.
I. Title.

HG9057.A53 2009   368.32'0094109034   C2009-901863-2

University of Toronto Press acknowledges the financial assistance to
its publishing program of the Canada Council for the Arts and Ontario
Arts Council.

University of Toronto Press acknowledges the financial support for its
publishing activities of the Government of Canada through the Book
Publishing Industry Development Program (BPIDP).

Contents

vi   Contents

Tables and Figures

Tables

Figures

Acknowledgments

I first got the idea to work on life insurance as a graduate student at Harvard in 1987, in a seminar taught by Barbara Rosenkrantz and Allan Brandt. Barbara later advised my dissertation, part of which focused on British actuaries, and she invited Peter Buck to join my committee. As this book has evolved since then, it has gained immeasurably from conversations with Peter and Barbara, and Peter provided his usual wise feedback on the manuscript. While I was at Harvard, Christine Kim, Amy Speckart, Amy Cerrito, and Julie Torrie performed research that found its way into the book.

Although this book germinated at Harvard, most of my work went into it while I have been teaching at Lehman College, the Bronx campus of the City University of New York, and at the CUNY Graduate Center. Colleagues, staff, and administrators at CUNY have made this work possible and pleasurable: in particular, Andy Robertson, Evelyn Ackerman, Duane Tananbaum, Irene Pizzolongo, and Marlene Gottlieb at Lehman, and Randy Trumbach and Josh Freeman at the Graduate Center. Two CUNY graduate students, Ben Tyner and Nick Fokas, also assisted in compiling databases.

CUNY, together with the American Council of Learned Societies and the National Endowment of the Humanities, generously funded many research trips to Great Britain, and (in the case of the ACLS and NEH) provided me with time away from teaching to conceive and start writing the manuscript. In Britain, I was indebted to the hard work and good will of many archivists, including Sheree Leeds and Margaret Saunders at Aviva, Isabel Syed at Zurich Financial Services, Jennie Campbell and Clare Bunkham at Prudential, Dorothy Todd at Scottish Amicable, Simon Passco and Sian Yates at Clerical Medical/HBOS,

David Steel at Standard Life, Chris Morgan at the Faculty of Actuaries, Sally Grover and David Raymont at the Institute of Actuaries, Deborah Wilson at the Chartered Insurance Institute, Sally Harrower at the National Library of Scotland, and Allison Armour at Strathclyde University.

Above all, Stephen Freeth, Matthew Payne, and the rest of the staff at the Guildhall Library reliably provided me with countless reports and minute books from their rich collection. Materials deposited at the Guildhall Library relating to the Legal & General are used by kind permission of the Legal & General Group plc; those relating to the Atlas, Caledonian, and Guardian companies are used by kind permission of AXA UK; and those relating to the Economic, Alliance, Church of England, Provident, Rock, and Royal Farmers companies are used by kind permission of Royal & SunAlliance Group plc. Stateside, Ismael Rivera-Sierra at the Davis Library (St John's University) and Dot Christiansen in Special Collections and Archives (SUNY Albany) offered their valuable help; and when I was a graduate student the Whiting Foundation enabled me to use the archives at the Institute of Actuaries under the watchful eye of its then-librarian, Roy Park.

When I wasn't trying the patience of archivists, I was trying out ideas on colleagues, who were kind enough to invite me to conferences, consent to insurance-themed meals, recommend reading, and comment on drafts. Among many others, I would especially like to thank Greg Anderson, Will Ashworth, Geoff Clark, Deborah Cohen, Brian Cooper, Roger Cooter, Martin Daunton, Julie Early, Maria Farland, Margot Finn, Walter Friedman, Pamela Gilbert, Elsbeth Heaman, Nancy Henry, Anne Humpherys, Aeron Hunt, Michael Lobban, Donna Loftus, Peter Logan, Peter Mandler, Liz McFall, Bob Morris, Michael Moss, Sharon Murphy, Maura O'Connor, Robin Pearson, Steve Pincus, Mary Poovey, Joan Richards, George Robb, Eve Rosenhaft, Rebecca Stern, Chuck Upchurch, Deborah Valenze, Andy Warwick, Carl Wennerlind, Tammy Whitlock, and Felice Whittum.

A final set of colleagues stand out as co-conspirators in the production of this book: this is the New England Insurance and Society Study Group at the University of Connecticut Law School (recently relocated to the University of Pennsylvania), which I joined at the invitation of the indomitable and inimitable Tom Baker. This group gave me more ideas than I would care to admit and provided wonderful feedback on my work on numerous occasions. Besides Tom, Barry Cohen, Brian Glenn, David Moss, Geeta Patel, Adam Scales, Susan Silbey, and Carol

Weisbrod have become friends and colleagues over the past decade. Shortly before leaving Hartford, Tom also arranged through the Insurance Law Center for assistance in meeting publication costs, a commitment that Kurt Strasser and Peter Kochenburger have subsequently both honoured and supplemented.

Aaron Doyle, whose work on the sociology of insurance has been an inspiration, encouraged me to send my manuscript to Virgil Duff at the University of Toronto Press. Virgil has been a great editor: supportive, straightforward, and efficient. The two referees that he chose to read the manuscript also provided valuable feedback. I also owe thanks to the journal editors who have assisted in earlier incarnations of parts of this book. Portions of chapter 6 were previously published in *Victorian Studies* 45/1 (2002): 65–92, © 2002 by the Indiana University Press, and portions of the conclusion were previously published in Romanticism and Victorianism on the Net, no. 49 (February 2008).

Since I began working on this book in earnest ten years ago, I have shared my life with Alix Cooper and our cats Squash and Hermione. It has been a complicated decade, but thanks to Alix's love, patience, and good humour, it has never been lacking in mutual support. I dedicate this book to Alix, who is even happier than I am that it's done.

REGULATED LIVES:

LIFE INSURANCE AND BRITISH SOCIETY, 1800–1914

Introduction

A great change is gradually coming over the world. Adventure, sport, enterprise, are giving way to caution and the calculation of averages. Men do not take the risks they used to. The modern man is surrounded by police constables, sanitary inspectors, and insurance agents.
  – Norwood Young, *Badminton Magazine*, 1896[1]

This book explores the transformation of different conceptions of human life in the British life insurance industry between 1800 and 1914, as well as in the more general context of Victorian culture. Through this history, I demonstrate how ideas of life, as they passed into an era of statistical thinking, medicalization, and capitalist bureaucracy, altered to accommodate modernity, while also showing many signs of defying its totalizing promise. The result suggests that the complexity of modern commercial and social institutions diminished the capacity of any one of those institutions to govern the people under their influence. Although insurance companies may have shared responsibility with policemen and health inspectors for a rise in what one mid-Victorian called a tendency to become 'shockingly safe in all the relations of life and death,' they did so in ways that competed rather than converged with the efforts of others who specialized in minimizing risks to people's lives, health, and property.[2] Because of this, the 'great change' under way at the end of the nineteenth century failed to transform society as fully as contemporaries either hoped or feared it would. Gambling and enterprise survived the domestication of risk, and life insurance customers transcended the statistical averages, medical categories, and policy registers into which companies placed them.

As they adapted to changing circumstances, Victorian life insurance companies recurrently reconceived their customers' lives as both consuming subjects and objectified abstractions. As consumers, policyholders were *sympathetic* lives, whose hopes and fears for the future and whose responsibilities to family and society were anticipated, dramatized, and manipulated by the companies. Their lives were more purely conceived in abstract, objectified terms when they were analysed *numerically* (to determine their place in the office's lawlike mortality curves) and *medically* (to identify any special risks they might pose). Finally, as 'risks' bearing calculable economic values, policyholders were *commodified* lives, simultaneously acting as inalienable subjects and being acted upon as financial instruments. This book examines each of these four different meanings of life as they appeared in British life insurance, primarily by tracking their formulation by three different groups of people who worked for life offices, and who represented distinct but overlapping modes of thinking within the industry: agents, actuaries, and doctors.

Companies and People

Although British life insurance underwent a fascinating early history during the four decades after 1688 (which has been well recounted by Geoffrey Clark), it may be said without too much exaggeration that its history started anew after 1760 and that it did not begin fully to re-invent itself until after 1800.[3] That year the life insurance market in Britain was limited to around ten thousand customers, who held a little more than £10 million in coverage – half of which was provided by a single firm, the Equitable. Over the next forty years, the volume of business grew fifteen-fold, and the number of life insurance offices increased from just five (all based in London) to nearly ninety, including fifteen in Scotland and twelve in provincial England.[4] As the market grew, niches emerged. Many of the older firms, including the Pelican, Globe, and Royal Exchange, catered mainly to aristocratic customers who insured their lives as collateral when their need for credit exceeded what their property was worth. Several newer companies formed as 'class' offices, catering to specific professions or religious groups.

One thing these 'class' offices discovered was that it was possible to market life insurance as a means of family provision and not just as a crutch for staying in debt. Since such customers' income was 'solely dependent upon their own exertions,' the National Mercantile's actuary observed in 1847, it was possible to persuade them of their duty 'to provide a competency for their families in the event of their own premature death.' They also learned how to build on Britain's pre-existing class distinctions and use the bonds of community that these engendered as a means of selling life insurance. As an early Clerical Medical shareholder hoped in a letter to its founder: 'blending as many as possible of these two learned professions together ... shall necessarily create & stir up in it, that true *Esprit du Corps* which is in all large societies, the Life – the Main Spring – and Pivot on which all its energies depend.'[5] By mid-century a few life offices, including the Provident Clerks' Mutual and Marine & General, had extended the same model lower down the class scale, and others appealed to a more diffuse lower-middle-class market with aggressive sales tactics and innovative approaches to help such people keep their policies in force.

Even after life insurance had reached this far into British society, the vast majority of the population remained uninsured. From the 1850s a new type of company emerged, called 'industrial' offices, which mainly sold small policies to cover working families' funeral expenses. Pioneered by the Prudential and successfully copied by the Pearl and Refuge, industrial insurance was qualitatively different from 'ordinary' life insurance in almost every regard. Sales almost always involved door-to-door canvassing by heavily supervised full-time agents who were cut from the same working-class cloth as their customers. Actuarially, the incidence of working-class death (including infant mortality) and high lapse rates made industrial insurance more akin to fire insurance than to ordinary life insurance.[6] Medical examinations were rare or non-existent on the ground of cost; instead, gatekeepimg focused on red-lining insalubrious neighbourhoods.[7] For all these reasons, industrial insurance built on and contributed to very different meanings of life and death during its growth in the last half of the nineteenth century, placing it beyond the scope of this book. Its main impact on ordinary life insurance occurred after 1875, when the Prudential and other offices began competing successfully for a lower-middle-class market that became underserved after many earlier providers went bankrupt.

The Peopling of Life Insurance in the Nineteenth Century

As different classes of customers insured their lives with different offices, the offices themselves evolved complex networks of salesmen, managers, clerks, directors, and professional consultants. Some of these people had frequent and direct contact with policyholders: salesmen conversed with them on matters of life, death, domesticity, and money, while doctors made intimate inquiries regarding their health and came into physical contact with their bodies. Mostly removed from such forms of close personal interaction with customers were managers and clerks, who processed the immense quantity of paperwork that salesmen and doctors generated, and directors, who acted as arbiters among the various experts they had appointed. At an even further remove were lawyers, who investigated insurance companies' deeds and securities, and surveyors, who assessed the property that they required as collateral for the growing volume of loans they made using their reserve funds.

Insurance agents specialized in sympathizing with a wide range of calamities that might befall their clients at some time in the future. To facilitate these sympathetic encounters, life insurance offices tried to appoint agents who had an extensive circle of acquaintances or (failing that) with a talent to simulate intimacy: most often these agents were lawyers, bankers, merchants, or shopkeepers who sold insurance as a side-line to their profession or trade. As such, most of them were well versed in the various property relations resting in part on human mortality, and hence abetted the commodification of their customers' lives. To accomplish this, they reached from a wide assortment of arguments and chose the ones they thought would be most persuasive to each individual they encountered. Starting in the 1870s life insurance offices began appointing branch secretaries, agency superintendents, and inspectors, who educated and energized agents into making new friends or finding new opportunities to convince old ones to insure.

Life insurance offices called on actuaries and their clerical staffs to count and classify lives. Early in the nineteenth century, most of the men who did this were trained mathematicians who turned to insurance after making their reputation elsewhere. Later in the century, companies trained their own calculators, who rose through the clerical ranks and received certification from the Institute of Actuaries in London (which was established in 1848) or the Faculty of Actuaries in Edinburgh (established in 1856). They handed over their mortality data to these professional bodies, which painstakingly processed them to manufacture premium and valuation tables. Finally, life insurance offices called on doctors to certify that applicants were healthy enough to render premature claims less likely. Initially, they entrusted this task to a loose combination of head office directors, provincial surrogates, and customers' medical attendants. After 1820 most firms began appointing salaried medical advisers, mainly elite London or Edinburgh physicians; then at mid-century they also started appointing provincial medical examiners. Once insurance companies made this shift, the head office medical adviser's job changed from being solely that of examining candidates to constructing and evaluating the forms sent in by provincial examiners.

Salesmen, actuaries, and doctors all contributed to the ceaseless regulation of human life through the creation of markets, statistical categories, and 'biopower,' each of which has been identified with the rise of modernity. Salesmen who created a market for life insurance did so by convincing people of its primary role in the regulation of credit, saving, and domestic economy; actuaries used the statistics they generated on insured lives to convince people to accept their location in categories based on age, health, and behaviour; and doctors coaxed prognostic information out of prospective policyholders, both verbally and from the physical interrogation of their bodies. More broadly, and in keeping with much recent work on the sociology of insurance, the various people who worked for life insurance offices engaged in what Michel Foucault defined as 'governmentality': the diffuse exercise of power by non-state institutions.[8] Yet the regulated lives who bought insurance policies always resisted complete commodification, enumeration, or medicalization, by holding life insurance offices to their initial promise of sympathy and by playing these different manifestations of modernity against one another. As James Vernon has recently argued, 'the always already fractured nature of the techno-political interventions of experts' and 'the ways in which they were invariably frustrated by contingencies beyond their control' should teach us that 'governmentality' needs to be handled with care in application to real-world institutions and people.[9]

Meanings of Life

In the course of insuring people's lives, insurance companies invariably attached numerous, and not always consistent, meanings to those lives. Four such meanings, as indicated above, were the sympathetic life, the numbered life, the medicalized life, and the commodified life. None of these were original to life insurance. The sympathy-inducing melodrama of the deathbed, as invoked in an insurance agent's sales pitch, was (like all successful marketing techniques) not newly cut out of whole cloth, but rather an agile adaptation to existing customs.[10] 'Political arithmeticians' in the 1650s were numbering lives a century before life insurance companies started to do so, and the medicalized life originated, as Foucault and others have argued, with the birth of the clinic, not the insurance examination.[11] Nor did insurance companies originate an equivalence between life and property; rather they prospered by attracting attention to the many such connections (and accompanying risks) already embedded in landed, professional, and mercantile society.[12] What insurance companies accomplished was to bring these four meanings of life into a single institution. Their commercial success came from knowing how to combine these different perspectives in the most profitable fashion – resulting in a constant series of compromises that affected the pace of change within the insurance industry, and that often also led to more general reconceptions of human life in popular and academic discourse.

THE SYMPATHETIC LIFE

For many Victorians, their first taste of life insurance appeared as an invitation to imagine, like Scrooge in *A Christmas Carol*, the haunting spectre of their future mortality. Salesmen combined plaintive scenes of the uninsured's deathbed with sensational threats of premature death, which in their foretelling invariably struck without warning. They appealed (in the words of one Victorian wag) 'to all the *softer* feelings' of their customers, by asking how they could 'be so inhuman as to run the risk of leaving our wives helpless widows' and by promising that an insurance policy would fully absorb 'that drop of gall in our death-cup – the conviction that a young family is left destitute!' Beyond trying to evoke sympathy in prospective customers, agents acted out sympathy in the course of selling life insurance. Few commodities in Victorian Britain depended as much for their sale on the art of conversation. As the author of *'How to Become a Successful Agent'* explained in 1876, to sell life insurance required 'the patience that will be able to deal with ignorance as if it were intelligence, with rudeness as if it were politeness, and with multitudinous replies as if they were encouragement.'[13]

Besides presenting enough pathos to qualify as an archetype of early Victorian melodrama, life insurance stories taught wider moral lessons that inserted the life office into a web connecting the individual to his or her family and community. The most common of these was the husband's duty to provide for his wife and children, which the life insurance office reinforced by offering to act as a surrogate breadwinner following the husband's death. By taking the place of the husband in that scenario, life insurance also promised to diminish the individual's reliance on alternative social networks in the event of need – hence setting itself up in opposition to 'cold charity' or the even colder clutches of the poorhouse. Such stylized 'others' acted as crucial foils against which agents hoped they could convert the resolutely impersonal technology of insurance into a personification of caring sympathy.

By sympathetically juxtaposing imagined futures of poverty and prosperity, life insurance branded itself as 'one of the happiest contrivances of modern times.' Central to its 'highly cultivated' status, according to Standard Life's 1839 prospectus, was that it supplied every man with the power 'to decide whether he shall leave to his family the legacy of penury or independence'; another company's *Pocket Diary* identified life insurance with the 'projectile power of the mind, acting internally by anticipating the arrival of the personal Future.'[14] This emphasis on 'the personal future' repeated evangelical religion's reconception of salvation as a personal choice, which (as Callum Brown has argued) 'broke the mental chains of the ancien regime in Britain.' It also replayed one of the central devices of the Victorian novel, which traded on characters' futures by way of generating suspense and resolving plots.[15] More generally, the deathbed, sudden death, and descent into destitution were all common furnishings in Victorian religious and literary spaces, which shared with life insurance a self-consciously modern stance.

THE NUMBERED LIFE

Actuaries numbered lives so that they could sort insurance customers into different groups. Their most precisely calculated lines of discrimination concerned the relationship between age and expected mortality, as gleaned from mortality statistics that yielded laws 'regulating the existence of every human being' (in the words of the Legal & General's actuary).[16] Over time actuaries evolved a set of standard tables that varied little from office to office and which most policyholders accepted as equitable – nobody accused life insurance offices of 'ageism' when they charged higher rates for older entrants. They began in the 1780s by using tables derived from local birth and death registers, then in 1869 they collected information from twenty life offices, updating this thirty years later with a new collection from sixty firms. The only resulting tables that entered into general use concerned the 'healthy males' who comprised the large majority of the insured population. The rest, including women, people in high-risk occupations, and people who travelled abroad, occupied a statistical limbo: they were either treated as if they were 'normal' men, or they were subjected to arbitrary extra charges.

This same result occurred from the 1850s, when actuaries (often in conjunction with medical advisers) extended their notions of differential risk groups to prior medical conditions, 'hereditary taint,' and hazardous habits. In each of these cases they had less success at finding precise data and consequently produced highly variable premium scales. Insurers had spent the first half of the nineteenth century either rejecting these lives outright or charging a minimal extra premium without any pretense to precise risk-rating. A handful of offices that specialized in accepting higher-risk lives led others to re-examine their practice, and by the 1870s several surveys appeared that ranked 'survivancy' rates by cause of death. Around the same time, consumption hospitals were yielding data that indicated a clear correlation between family history and tuberculosis. Despite all these new data, however, actuaries faced an uphill battle converting them into meaningful risk groups – and it was a battle they only half-heartedly fought, since accurately underwriting these marginal lives made little difference to their bottom line.

THE MEDICALIZED LIFE

The reason medical certificates were necessary in life insurance underscores the diversity of ways in which its participants thought of life. Customers who feared premature death were most likely to insure their lives without being pressured into doing so. To the extent that their foreboding bore any relation to their future mortality, this disparity in perceived risk threatened to create an imbalance of unsound lives, and it linked profitability with the ability to select only 'first class' cases. 'But for the careful medical scrutiny which is generally made use of,' observed one mid-century medical adviser, 'we should ... have a class of Lives far below the average; a class which would include many that might almost be regarded as selected by themselves expressly for their badness.'[17] Implicit in this defence of the medical examination was that life insurance was both non-compulsory and subject to market forces. Since long lives were under no obligation to subsidize short ones, they always threatened to exercise their option of patronizing a company that was more careful in screening risks, surrendering their policy before it became a claim, or simply not insuring in the first place.

To address this problem of 'adverse selection,' life insurance offices turned to state-of-the-art medical techniques, which they hoped would help them determine the extent to which lives deviated from the norm. The unique circumstances of the insurance exam, including the need to perform it quickly and the emphasis it placed on accurate diagnosis, privileged the use of technology to an extent that had few parallels in Victorian medicine. A different sense in which the exam signified governmentality was in its emphasis on routinized interrogation, whereby examiners triangulated risk by checking off answers on a printed form. Doctors often spoke of the exam in prosecutorial terms and 'sentenced' unhealthy candidates to surcharges or rejection. The latter judgment could forbid a man from providing for his family or from borrowing money: this was the fate of Robert Louis Stevenson, whose self-described 'crazy health' meant his life was 'of no purchase in an insurance office.' Conversely, the evolving set of norms accompanying the insurance exam offered grounds for self-satisfaction among the majority of candidates who did make the grade. One magazine writer, after reporting the risks deriving from flat or barrel-shaped chests, invited his readers to 'retire forthwith to their bedrooms in the company of a measuring-tape,' where he hoped they would make the 'wonderfully reassuring' discovery that 'their chests come up to the required standard.'[18]

When doctors ventured to identify a defect, many rejected lives either protested (often successfully, and with support from their agents) or turned to another company with a more lenient doctor. Other potential customers simply did not show up, owing to their anxiety (warranted or not) about undergoing a medical examination. To address the first issue, life insurance offices negotiated with customers to arrive at acceptable extra premiums; to address the second, actuaries altered the insurance contract to protect profits without forcing customers to submit to medical exams. At the turn of the century, for instance, several firms introduced exam-free 'double endowment' policies, which combined a term life policy with an annuity worth twice as much when the term ended; this placed a sufficient incentive to live through the term to counteract selection against the office. By the mid-twentieth century insurance companies were subjecting fewer than half their customers to medical exams, preferring instead to protect themselves by contracting risky cases out to reinsurance companies or by submerging them in group plans.

THE COMMODIFIED LIFE

More directly than any other enterprise apart from slavery, life insurance set a price on human life. As it evolved in Britain during the nineteenth century, the insurance industry introduced a dizzying number of variations on this theme. For the individual purchasing an insurance policy, the value of life was translated into the sum required to care for dependents; loss of access to a wife's inheritance should she die before her father; the sum lost to a creditor in the event of death occurring prior to repayment; and the loss of livelihood suffered by a tenant whose lease ended with the life of a third party. As one advert concluded, there was 'scarcely a person in existence who is not interested in the happiness or well-being of others whose fortunes depend on his life, or is himself dependent on the lives of others for his own fortune, or some portion of his property.'[19] All these reasons for buying insurance established an equivalence between mortality and monetary value – a death nexus that precisely and morbidly expressed the cash nexus that Thomas Carlyle derided as the moral failing of British society. Even before 1800 Parliament had tried to restrict the more sordid aspects of this equation, by outlawing the sale of policies to third parties who could not demonstrate a material interest in the life insured. But this law had no reference to the many ways in which Victorians attached financial stakes to the contingency of living through the next year.

Besides drawing attention to the many links between life and property, life insurance taught consumers to connect the prospect of living with the growth of capital. By the 1830s 'reversionary bonuses' were common among most life insurance offices, whereby they passed along all or part of their surplus profits to the beneficiaries of their policyholders. In addition to popularizing the practice of investment among its customers, life insurance directly contributed to the enormous growth of investment over the course of the nineteenth century. Salesmen loudly proclaimed its role in this process, as when the Royal Exchange's Irish manager praised its contribution to 'the great foundation of credit, and mutual dependence, on which the vast superstructure of modern industrial and commercial life is reared.'[20] Life insurance also taught policyholders to think of the accumulation of capital as a lifelong, as opposed to sporadic, process. In the first half of the nineteenth century, life insurance offices proudly contrasted their potential for assisting customers to save for the long term with the easy access to money that savings banks provided. Although this message was well attuned to some varieties of early Victorian self-help, it limited the expansion of the market by ignoring the large number of people whose income was too irregular to pay regular premiums. To address this problem, companies liberalized some features of the insurance contract without altering its primary emphasis on the careful regulation of their customers' personal finance.

Sources and Plan of This Book

This book sits between business and cultural history. Put another way, the book as a whole should be of interest to readers who are interested in the intersection of business and culture in Victorian Britain, while different parts of it will be more interesting than others to readers whose interests lie more thoroughly in one camp or another. It opens with three chapters that trace the history of British life insurance using sources and methods that will be familiar to the business historian. The rest of the book is more broadly cultural, focusing (as the above introduction indicates) on issues as diverse as mathematics, literature, religion, medicine, and commodification. The point in these sections is not just to provide a cultural context for the development of British life insurance, although that is part of the goal. It is also, more importantly, to identify life insurance as itself a creator of culture: of new ways of telling stories, counting people, and examining bodies. I take it as a given that life insurance was largely successful as a financial undertaking – and although I provide much evidence to this end in the first three chapters and elsewhere in the book, I have mostly left it to others to quantify that success as a primary focus of their scholarship.

Historiography and Sources

The main reason I devote as much time as I do to a narrative history of life insurance in the opening chapters is because such an industry-wide history for the nineteenth century does not exist. Several scholarly company histories have appeared over the years, most notably Barry Supple's study of the Royal Exchange, Roger Ryan's dissertation on the Norwich Union, and Clive Trebilcock's two-volume history of the Phoenix and its affiliated companies.[21] Along with dozens of other insurance company histories, these books provide a vast repository of information.[22] Even taken together, however, they leave out huge parts of what should belong in even a conventional narrative history of British life insurance, let alone in a more broadly conceived study. By relegating the majority of Victorian life offices to the margins, the existing supply of company histories leaves out many of the most successful firms and all of the many failures. A more general problem that nearly all company histories share is the 'view from the boardroom,' which assumes that the perspective of company directors was the most important, if not the only relevant, aspect of a company's performance

– and more generally, that a company's performance is the only reason it should be interesting to the historian.[23]

I have tried to fill some of the gaps in the existing secondary sources in the pages that follow, by consulting records from nearly forty insurance companies that did business in Britain during the nineteenth century, including representative samples from each distinctive category of life insurance office. I have used archives from seven Scottish offices (the Scottish Amicable, Scottish Provincial, Caledonian, Edinburgh, Scottish National, Scottish Union, and Standard Life), two provincial firms (the Norwich Union and Yorkshire), three 'legal' offices (the Legal & General, English & Scottish Law, and Law Union), two other 'professional' firms (the Clerical Medical and University), two 'religious' offices (the Star and Church of England), and two firms specializing in overseas business (the Gresham and Standard Life). Among London firms I have drawn more from the records of those specializing in life insurance (the Crown, Eagle, Economic, London Life, National Mutual, National Provident, and Rock) than from those engaged in fire as well as life business (the Alliance, Atlas, Guardian, and Royal Farmers), since the latter type of firm is better represented in published company histories.

To pay the same sort of attention to all of these archives as Supple or Trebilcock paid to the archives of their respective companies would have been impossible. What I decided to do instead was to select minute books for study at crucial times in the company's or the industry's history and to pay special attention to manuscript reports on areas of the insurance business that a primary focus on board minutes is likely to miss. From the Norwich Union archive I found a cache of papers accompanying provincial medical examinations; from the Clerical Medical and the Legal & General, extensive correspondence with provincial agents; from the Crown and the National Provident, detailed actuarial reports; and from the Gresham and Standard Life, reports on foreign business. Policy registers, agents' lists, and salary books also enabled me to add to what remains a sketchy quantitative record on such issues as the occupations of agents and customers; salaries of actuaries and medical advisers; and rejection rates and extra premiums charged to 'under-average' lives.

On top of this foundation of archival research, I have examined tens of thousands of pages from insurance trade journals, medical and actuarial journals, general circulation newspapers and periodicals, government documents, pamphlets and prospectuses, treatises, and novels. I also made extensive use of trade and medical directories to discover what insurance agents and doctors did when they were not working for life insurance offices. Much more than is the case for the archives, I can say with some certainty (and my bibliography will back this up) that relatively few printed pages concerning nineteenth-century British life insurance have been left unturned or un-downloaded in the course of researching this book. This kind of all-out approach is really the only way to gain a full picture of how a product like life insurance – which so many people bought but so few people thought about – performed its crucial economic and cultural work. Among all this printed matter, trade journals were especially useful as a quasi-archive of reports of shareholder and policyholder meetings, published correspondence, and information on the large number of companies that failed and left no manuscripts behind. Finally, Cornelius Walford's compendious *Insurance Cyclopaedia*, together with his notes for the unpublished volumes on the letters I through Z, is a gloriously shabby museum of insurance ephemera that I have been visiting frequently since the early 1990s.

This combination of sources has enabled a perspective on nineteenth-century British life insurance that is both broader and deeper than anything that has yet been written. This is a topic that is just beginning to attract the interest of general economic historians, has drawn some attention from labour historians and historians of science and medicine, and remains largely ignored by everyone else.[24] Substantially more work has been done on the development of American life insurance in the nineteenth century, dating back to Morton Keller's *Life Insurance Enterprise* (1963) and Viviana Zelizer's historical sociology of life insurance, *Morals and Markets* (1983). Sharon Murphy's history of antebellum life insurance enables rich comparison with many of the themes discussed in the following chapters, at least up through 1870.[25] In addition to these insurance-specific studies, much additional work in American business history has included life insurance as an important case study.[26]

Plan of Book

As mentioned above, the first three chapters that follow offer different slices of a conventional narrative history of British life insurance in the nineteenth century. The first chapter recounts its expansion from London to Scotland, provincial England, and Ireland, and from there abroad to the United States, continental Europe, and the British Empire. Chapter 1 also discusses the spread of life insurance to different social classes, starting with the aristocracy and extending through the social scale to professional and other middle-class groups and to lower-income customers, as well as the introduction of new types of business organization that accompanied this extension. Chapter 2 shifts from the geographical and demographic impact of life insurance to its evolving business dynamic, focusing on the waves of competition and consolidation that recurred through the nineteenth century and including a longer look at failed life insurance offices than appears in most company histories. Instead of regulated lives, the focus in this chapter is regulated insurance companies, including government supervision (with a primary emphasis on the Life Assurance Companies Act of 1870) and efforts by the industry to regulate itself through trade and professional associations. Chapter 3 introduces the dramatis personae of the rest of the book, who have already been briefly described above.

Chapters 4 and 5 take up, in turn, the actuarial and melodramatic meanings of life and death that informed life insurance during the nineteenth century. Through a detailed survey of the construction of various mortality tables, I pry open the black box out of which emerged the industry's dizzying array of age-specific premiums and valuation methods. By revealing the changing modes of thought and practice that formed the basis of these essential components of life insurance practice, chapter 4 shows how companies got customers to trust in their numbers, but also suggests that these numbers were both limited in their application and subject to negotiation. Turning from numbers to stories of death and destitution, chapter 5 indicates that life insurance offices always appealed to their customers' hearts as well as their minds and that the goal of such appeals – to get husbands to allow life insurance offices to act as surrogate breadwinners in the event of their untimely demise – often jarred with the reality facing a widow who received what was often an insufficient insurance claim. Chapter 5 also emphasizes that only some insurance customers ever encountered this side of the business, since those who bought insurance as collateral had sufficient incentive to do so (the desire for a loan) without requiring to be stirred by plaintive references to the hereafter.

The next two chapters turn from the pricing and marketing of life insurance to its financial aspects: first in an account of the linking of fund management to life insurance, through the rise of the bonus, and second in an account of the changing ways life offices provided customers with mechanisms for saving their money. Chapter 6 opens with an overview of how insurers turned their premium income into interest-generating assets, building on existing work on this topic with a new analysis of Board of Trade returns for the period 1870 to 1914; and the chapter closes, after a survey of the different bonus schemes that appeared, with observations on the bonus as a type of Victorian spectacle, as an instrument of accountability, and as a catalyst for debates about distributive justice. Chapter 7 discusses the companies' efforts to market life insurance as a distinctively disciplinary form of saving, followed by a longer discussion of the various ways they eased the burden of this form of regulation on the many customers who were unwilling or unable to subject themselves to it. It concludes with a discussion of endowment insurance, which combined a term life policy with a deferred annuity and comprised the most popular form of life insurance sold in Britain after 1890.

The final three chapters of this book concern what economic historians generally refer to as the underwriting side of life insurance. This topic has received especially short shrift from business historians, whose singular focus on technical innovation has precluded any systematic inquiry into what was by all accounts a haphazard set of practices.[27] As the above discussion should indicate, it is precisely the haphazard manner in which life insurance offices developed their underwriting methods that makes it such an interesting topic for the purpose of this book. Following a broad survey of these evolving methods in chapter 8 (including proposal and referee forms, interviews with directors and medical advisers, disputed claims, and the appointment of provincial medical examiners), chapter 9 discusses the life insurance medical examination as a site of new forms of interaction between doctors and (typically healthy) bodies. Chapter 10 then addresses what life offices did with the results of their gatekeeping efforts, which changed over the course of the century from a simple choice of accepting or rejecting candidates to a much more complicated process of 'rating up' customers by adding years to their lives – often followed by a prolonged negotiation to arrive at a premium that both parties could accept.

A final remark is in order regarding this book's chronological sweep, which runs from the early nineteenth century up to 1914. This sets it apart from other British insurance histories (with the exception of Clark's on the eighteenth century), which track an individual company up to the present, and also from general histories of American life insurance, which either start or stop in the 1860s. In Britain that decade did not produce the same watershed as in the American case (or in American history more generally); but more importantly, the longer sweep is necessary in order to assess the salient transitions at the heart of this book. By 1914 the statistical and medical significations of life insurance had developed to a point that would remain relatively constant well into the twentieth century, as had its basic organizational structure and its place in a diversified global insurance market. For this reason as well, I have spent no time discussing the fortunes and misfortunes of British life insurance during the First World War. Not only would such a discussion have made a long book longer still, the actual impact of the war was relatively minor – both in actuarial terms and in its impact on business organization.[28] Instead of examining the war years as an epilogue to the long nineteenth century, I have ended several chapters with brief surveys beyond 1918, to indicate some of the longer-term legacies of British life insurance.[29]

1 Insuring Britain

Our risks are distributed amongst all classes of the community: amongst the aristocracy we have the Duke, the Lord, the Baronet, the Member of Parliament; amongst the clergy we have the Bishop, the Prebend, the Vicar, the Curate, the University Student; we have the Judge, the Barrister, the Solicitor, the Solicitor's Clerk; we have the Physician, the Surgeon, the Apothecary; we have also assured the merchant, the mariner, the shopkeeper, the assistant ... The risks are distributed over all parts of England, Wales and Scotland, and I am glad to say we have but very few in Ireland.
    – Alfred Smee, Gresham Life director and medical adviser, 1850[1]

From a narrow basis in London, British life insurance after 1800 expanded in several different aspects. Geographical expansion occurred first in provincial England, then in Scotland, and finally in Ireland, Europe, and overseas. Socially, life insurance offices first added new levels of specialization within an already existing aristocratic market, then they spread out from there. Some forged strong ties to the legal profession, which they used to identify prospective aristocratic customers. Other 'class offices' built on existing bonds of occupational solidarity or catered to specific religious denominations. With less success, a set of companies after 1830 started reaching beyond these groups to the lower- middle classes, then after 1850 a handful tapped the much larger working-class market by competing with local burial clubs. These latter 'industrial' firms, led by the giant Prudential Assurance Company, ultimately captured the lion's share of lower-middle-class policyholders as well by setting up 'ordinary' branches for that purpose. Many life insurers had long offered fire coverage from the same office, and by the end of the nineteenth century most successful firms added new types of coverage (including accident, fidelity, and marine) to this mix.

As life insurance spread to more regions and to less-wealthy classes, and formed part of increasingly diversified companies, the total volume of business increased while the average size of individual policies diminished. Total coverage rose from around £10 million in 1800 to £150 million in 1852, and stood at £676 million in 1900: a per capita increase over the course of the century from just under £1 to more than £16.[2] In the decade after the Napoleonic Wars, 57 per cent of all life insurance policies issued in the United Kingdom were for sums of £500 or more, and 36 per cent covered at least £1,000. Fifty years later the percentage of policies for £500 and up had dropped to 23 per cent, and only 11 per cent of policies covered £1,000 or more – not including millions of industrial policies covering less than £25.[3] Average policy size, estimated at over £1,000 from 1800 into the 1830s, fell to £481 by 1890 (not including industrial policies), by which point nearly a million people in Britain held 'ordinary' policies of £50 or more and an additional 9.9 million people held smaller policies – roughly 30 per cent of the population in all, and a clear majority of male breadwinners.[4]

These continual additions to the life offices' customer base inevitably altered and diversified both the products they sold and how they sold them. To sate middle-class demand after 1800, most offices either reduced their premiums (once it had been proven actuarially safe to do so) or returned substantial surpluses to beneficiaries when claims fell due. The mid-nineteenth century also saw significant modifications to the insurance contract, ranging from payment schedules to protection against disputed claims; these culminated with the endowment policy in the 1880s, which converted to an annuity if the insured survived to a predetermined age. The methods of selling this expanded range of products also changed dramatically over the course of the nineteenth century. Instead of relying mainly on directors, shareholders, or policyholders to convince their friends to insure, life offices from the 1840s established branches in large provincial towns, where resident secretaries appointed and monitored the progress of thousands of part-time salesmen. Industrial offices went even further, appointing full-time agents who collected premiums each week at the customer's doorstep.

Expanding Outward from London

Until after 1800 British life insurance was exclusively a London operation. Although the vast majority of life insurance offices continued to operate out of London, over the course of the nineteenth century many of the most successful firms appeared in Scotland and (to a lesser extent) in provincial centres like Norwich and Liverpool. Provincial firms succeeded by combining life insurance with strong fire branches or affiliated fire offices, and Scottish firms grew through innovative marketing and aggressive sales efforts. Scottish offices also succeeded by casting their net widely in search of policyholders: they had the necessary connections to catch wealthy clients, but were not too proud to go after lower-income customers as well. Finally, they were able to limit the number of new entrants into their market, which greatly increased the stability of the original dozen or so firms that appeared between 1815 and 1840.

London, in contrast, bred wave after wave of new life insurance companies, starting with the stock market boom of 1824–25 and continuing in spurts through the 1860s. Although the first set of companies added to a strong and stable market, most of those that followed failed to survive more than a few years, and they hindered the success of other London firms by diverting new business and tarnishing the industry's reputation. Many of the earlier London companies formed as 'class' offices, cultivating self-limiting occupational or religious groups; most of the later ones angled for the more diffuse lower-income market, but failed to discover how to reach such customers without spending too much. It was not until after 1880, when most mid-century London firms had disappeared, that the survivors began to give their Scottish and provincial rivals a run for their money. They did this by successfully imitating Scottish innovations, but also by leading the trend of diversifying into new forms of insurance.

In this section I trace the geographical dispersion of British life insurance, starting with its eighteenth-century origins in London and moving on to the provinces and Scotland. I then discuss how firms from all three of these regions exported life insurance – first across the Irish Sea and then to Europe, North America, and the British Empire. Following this survey, I return in later sections to the matter of 'class' offices – which expanded the overall market for life insurance while limiting the potential for individual firms to grow; to the marketing advantages that Scottish firms cultivated in the mid-nineteenth century; and finally to the rise after 1880 of the composite office, which built on a long-standing tradition in both London and the provinces of combining fire and life insurance in the same firm.

London Life Insurance

For more than a century after they first appeared in the mid-1690s, London life insurance offices catered to only a small sliver of the population. Most were mutual societies that capped membership and operated as 'mortuary tontines,' annually dividing available funds among beneficiaries of members who had died during the year. Two firms, the Royal Exchange Assurance and the London Assurance, charged customers up-front premiums to cover the chance of future death and dipped into share capital if their rates did not cover the risk.[5] All these firms found themselves constantly tugged between communitarian and speculative impulses. The mutuals might have been, as their most recent historian has claimed, 'miniature civil societies' that nurtured 'equity, mutuality, amicability, and paternal care,' but their popularity often hinged on the extent to which investments could leaven death benefits. A second form of speculation supplemented the stock market variety on the many occasions when life insurers collected premiums against the chance that a third party would die within a stipulated term. Until Parliament intervened in 1774 by requiring all policyholders to demonstrate a legitimate financial interest in the lives they insured, the Hanoverian gentry preferred this type of gambling over nearly all others.[6]

The balance between self-help and speculation shifted closer to its nineteenth-century pattern with the establishment in 1762 of the Society for Equitable Assurances on Lives. Within two decades after forming, this mutual office introduced two new wrinkles that would each cast a long shadow over British life insurance: the periodic division of a portion of surplus funds (or bonus, as it soon came to be called) starting in 1776 and a reduction of premiums in 1781 based on the Northampton bills of mortality. These two features greatly added to its popularity, convinced the Royal Exchange to issue lower-priced whole life policies, and spurred the formation of several new offices. The Northampton table would remain the industry standard for decades to come, until giving way in the 1820s to new tables predicting even lower mortality. By pinning premiums to the secure foundation of carefully tabulated vital statistics, these tables provided a powerful counterweight to life insurance's speculative side – although the latter persisted, owing both to the uncertainty of individual survival and the variable bonus.[7]

Despite these innovations an Englishman seeking to buy life insurance in 1800 still had only five firms to choose from, all located in London. In the two decades that followed, fifteen more London firms opened, including many that would endure well into the twentieth century. The first to form in the new century was the Globe, which its founder Frederick Morton Eden envisioned as a savings bank and

'Insurer to Friendly Societies'; when this failed, he settled for selling insurance to the aristocracy. Although the Globe would not survive the nineteenth century, many other early firms did, including the Rock, Provident, London Life, Eagle, and Atlas (all established between 1806 and 1808), and Sun Life, which formed in 1810 as an affiliate of the ancient Sun Fire. After a slow decade another wave of enduring offices formed in the 1820s, including the Guardian, Economic, Alliance, and Crown, as well as several of the most important 'class' offices discussed below. This set of insurers recruited some of London's most prominent capitalists to be their directors, including Moses Montefiore, Francis Baring and Samuel Gurney (Alliance), George Carr Glyn and Isaac Goldsmid (Globe), and Samuel Bosanquet (Palladium).[8]

Besides being the original centre of British life insurance, London was the main breeding ground for new companies during the busy mid-century decades: over four-fifths of all the life offices that formed between 1836 and 1870 were London-based (see Figure 1.1). Although the large majority of these were fly-by-night operations fuelled by a buoyant stock market, some held their own against their older neighbours. These included the Commercial Union (established in 1861), which mainly formed in response to a demand for lower fire premiums but soon built a strong life department; the Gresham (established in 1848), which emerged after 1860 as England's leading exporter of life insurance; and the Prudential (established in 1848) which built on its initial dominance of the industrial market to become Britain's leading ordinary insurer as well by 1900. On the debit side of the ledger, all the scandalous failures that darkened British life insurance during this period occurred in London, including those of the Independent & West Middlesex in 1840, the Sea Fire & Life in 1850, the Albert in 1869, and the European in 1871, and nearly all of the companies absorbed by the latter two had also been based in London. London was also home to the Briton Medical & General and the Great Britain Mutual, which suffered disastrous failures in the 1880s.[9]

New London life insurance offices were less likely to remain huddled in the City than had been the case with older firms. In 1825 all but two of London's twenty-eight life offices were based either in the City or nearby in Blackfriars, and nineteen crowded onto just four streets. In 1845 the majority remained in these two locales, although new clusters had appeared on King William Street (which had been built in 1830 as a link between the City and London Bridge) and the Strand. By 1855 a clear migration was under way, with more than half of the sixty life offices that

Figure 1.1
Number of new life insurance offices per decade, by location
of head office, 1801–1900.

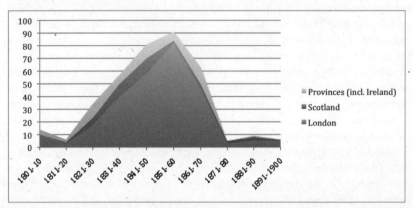

Sources: Insurance Directory and Yearbook (1987): 199–221; *Return* 1845; *Abstract Return* 1856 and 1863; *Return of Names* 1864–97; Walford I–VI *passim*; CWP *passim*; *Post Magazine* 46 (1885): 38, 50, 62–3, 74, 86; Hutchison 1846: 75–80; Bridges 1842: 23.

had formed since 1850 located in the West End, Cannon Street, or Cheapside (which linked St Paul's Cathedral to the Bank of England). The Prudential moved northwest from the City to Holborn Bars in 1876, and the Eagle moved to Pall Mall in 1868 after a new railway station forced it from Blackfriars.[10] Most of the older London life offices, though, stood firm in the small space between Cornhill and the Thames, preferring to make their existing offices taller when they needed more room instead of fleeing the City. The result was a late-century line of 'imposing and magnificent establishments' from Cornhill and Cheapside down to Blackfriars and the London Bridge, which vied with neighbouring banks in their 'palatial' exteriors and marble-strewn halls.[11]

The Provinces, Scotland, and Ireland

When the Exeter-based West of England Fire & Life Insurance Company opened in 1807, it became the first English firm to sell life insurance from a head office somewhere other than London. By 1820 life insurance offices had also formed in Norwich, Birmingham, and Bristol, and others soon followed in Leeds, York, and Manchester. These new companies followed a path that had been blazed by fire offices, which had grown thick on the ground in the provinces in the late eighteenth century. Few of the original provincial fire insurance offices survived once London offices noticed their success: five London firms gobbled up twenty-six provincial rivals between 1826 and 1850.[12] In general, London life offices responded even more effectively to provincial competition than their counterparts in fire insurance did. Instead of waiting for local concerns to flourish before acquiring them, life offices in the metropolis appointed provincial agents to sate the apparent demand before too many local firms could gain a foothold. Only 15 per cent of English life insurance offices that formed between 1800 and 1850 were based outside of London, compared with 57 per cent of English fire insurance offices established during that period.[13]

Among the few exceptional provincial success stories were the Yorkshire and the Norwich Union, which more than held their own in their respective counties, and a succession of Liverpool-based insurers. Although most of the latter firms specialized in fire insurance, all offered life insurance as well, and their sheer size guaranteed a major impact even when that side of their business was not a high priority. The Liverpool and London Fire & Life Insurance Company was established after the original Liverpool company added a London branch in 1846 and then in 1862 inherited a substantial life insurance business upon acquiring the Globe (in the process changing its name to the Liverpool & London & Globe). The Royal and the Queen also developed competitive life insurance divisions to supplement their export-oriented fire insurance business.[14] After building strong local markets, these firms slowly but surely found their way to London. The Norwich Union set up a London agency in 1815, based its actuary there for much of the century, and transacted a large share of its business out of that office. In addition to the Liverpool & London and the Royal, a third Liverpool-based insurance company with a strong London presence was the London & Lancashire Insurance Company, which formed in 1861 with a board in each city.[15]

In Scotland home-grown life insurance made up for its relatively late arrival by building up a disproportionate market share by the middle of the century. After the Scottish Widows' Fund formed as the first Scottish life insurance office in 1815, six firms appeared between 1823 and 1826, and some twenty more by 1848. Of equal significance for the future of British life insurance, new life office formation virtually ceased in Scotland during the two succeeding decades, while English firms continued to form at a rate of more than ten per year. Enabled in large part by the establishment in 1840 of a trade association, the Associated Scottish Life Offices, this allowed for stable growth at a time when many older English firms were losing ground, and most new ones were heading towards financial ruin. From this position of strength, many Scottish offices continued to grow for the rest of the century. As of 1883 seven of the top ten British offices in new business were Scottish (and twice as many people per capita insured their lives in Scotland compared with England), and by 1895 the sixteen Scottish life offices held a third of all life insurance funds in Great Britain (see Table 1.1).[16]

The Scottish Widows', which consistently ranked among the top five British firms after 1850, emerged from a uniquely Scottish context for life insurance: the many widows' funds that catered to the country's professions, which paid pensions to wives after members had died. It dropped its focus on pensions by the time it formed, and instead modelled itself after the Equitable, as did the Scottish Equitable, which emerged as a leading rival in 1831.[17] After a decade-long lull, the company boom of the mid-1820s generated the Scottish Union, Scottish Amicable, Standard Life, North British, and Aberdeen; and another burst of new company formation followed a decade later, with the Northern, Scottish Provident, City of Glasgow, and Life Association of Scotland appearing between 1836 and 1838 (see Figure 1.1). From their Scottish bases, these life insurance offices advanced across the border, with most establishing a presence in northern England by the 1830s and in London by the 1840s. In a typical pattern, Standard Life appointed local boards in Aberdeen and Perth in 1831, in Manchester and Liverpool in 1838, and in London in 1840.[18] By the mid-1850s eight Scottish firms had London branches, and their position there was further strengthened in 1862 when the North British merged with the London-based Mercantile Fire Insurance Company.

Irish life insurers first appeared in 1799, earlier than in the English provinces or in Scotland, but they never succeeded in protecting the market from British interlopers. With the exception of the 1820s, when as many as eight Irish-based life insurance offices existed, through the rest of the century no more than three were open for business at any one time. Both of the two original Dublin-based companies failed in the mid-1820s and were succeeded by the National and the Patriotic, heavily capitalized fire and life offices that survived the nineteenth century and even made inroads into England.[19] This still left much room for English and Scottish firms to sell life insurance, and they did so in

Table 1.1
Top ten British life insurers by premium income, 1871, 1890, 1910 (premium income; market share; proportion of foreign to total business)

Year	Life office	Premium income (£)	Market share (%)	Foreign business (%)
1871	Standard Life	504,786	5.7	
	Scottish Widows' Fund	424,180	4.8	
	Gresham	347,026	4.0	
	Eagle	290,851	3.3	
	Law Life	271,186	3.1	
	North British & Mercantile	268,184	3.1	
	London Life	267,792	3.0	
	Liverpool & London & Globe	254,805	2.9	
	National Provident	236,798	2.7	
	Life Association of Scotland	235,910	2.7	
1890	Prudential[a]	904,916	6.4	
	Scottish Widows' Fund	803,819	5.7	
	Standard Life	682,131	4.8	
	Gresham	620,036	4.4	
	Scottish Provident	496,050	3.5	
	North British & Mercantile	377,714	2.7	
	Life Association of Scotland	361,890	2.5	
	U.K. Temperance & General	345,153	2.4	
	National Provident	340,962	2.4	
	London Life	328,440	2.3	
1910	Prudential[a]	4,806,121	16.6	0
	Scottish Widows' Fund	1,258,509	4.3	0.4

Table 1.1 (Continued)

Year	Life office	Premium income (£)	Market share (%)	Foreign business (%)
	Norwich Union	1,230,746	4.2	30.4
	North British & Mercantile	1,114,174	3.8	7.9
	Commercial Union	1,012,866	3.5	23.8
	Standard Life	999,406	3.4	61.4
	Alliance	898,883	3.1	3.7
	Refuge[a]	880,893	3.0	0
	Sun Life	795,060	2.7	5.0

Source: Statements 1872: passim, 1873: 208; 1891: 372–6; 1911: 810, 812.
[a] Ordinary branch only.

large volume: a survey of seventeen mostly London life offices through 1837 revealed that nearly a quarter of their policies (close to 20,000) were on Irish lives.[20] Among the most successful of these early entrants into Ireland were the Atlas, Norwich Union, and Royal Exchange, and their apparent success prompted a further burst of interest in Ireland in the 1830s.[21]

Even before this second wave of British offices began to appear in Ireland, many of the original entrants were starting to have second thoughts about their presence there, owing both to suspicion of fraud and the (possibly related) discovery of higher Irish mortality rates among insured lives. The Atlas Assurance Company suspended its agency in Tralee after a round of frauds there, and the exposure of a fraud ring in Limerick in 1827 prompted several London offices either to scale back their Irish business or leave the island altogether.[22] By 1840 life insurance offices were confronting even worse news: hard evidence that Irish policyholders, who paid the same premiums as other customers, died at alarmingly higher rates.[23] Many new companies responded to their predecessors' experience either by postponing entry into Ireland or hedging their Irish business with extra regulations.[24] Despite such qualms, however, the proportion of British insurers with Irish agencies actually increased slightly during the 1840s, and for the rest of the century new English and Scottish life offices – including the Crown, Standard Life, and the English & Scottish Law – proved willing to step in when others retreated.[25]

The Rest of the World

The export of British life insurance abroad was neither as rapid nor as thorough as its spread at home. Few companies formed as specialist foreign insurers, and only a handful of British firms established more than a cursory presence in any given foreign country or colony. Taken together, though, foreign and colonial business formed a substantial share of the life offices' market, and by the early 1900s some of Britain's largest firms, including the Star, Standard Life, Norwich Union, and Gresham, sold more policies abroad than at home (see Table 1.1).[26] In all cases, the presence of British life insurance offices abroad prompted the establishment of local competitors, which typically received the shelter of legislative protection within a few decades of forming. The result was a pattern of early dominance by British life offices in a foreign or colonial market, followed by a partial or total retreat by all but a few of those firms. By the 1870s life offices from the United States were trying their luck in Great Britain and competing with British firms in most colonial markets. By 1920 life offices from Canada, Australia, and South Africa had opened for business in Britain as well.

One of the first parts of the world where British life insurance offices succeeded in finding customers was continental Europe, but success grew harder to come by after 1830. British business in central Europe started to dry up after several U.K. firms refused to pay a claim on the life of a German duke in 1825; a messy trial led to the formation of the Gotha Life Insurance Bank, which grew to become the largest continental life insurance office.[27] Fair-to-poor results marked British insurers' efforts to compete in most other European markets after 1850.[28] An exception to this general lack of success was the Gresham Life Assurance Society, which became 'a power throughout the continent of Europe' within a decade of opening a branch in Paris in 1854. Austria and Hungary anchored the Gresham's European business through the end of the century, but the company also maintained a healthy presence in Germany and Belgium, ventured into Spain in 1882, and opened an Egyptian branch in 1902. One of its secrets to European success was the Gresham's willingness to adapt to local demand: an emphasis on annuities in France, for instance. Another was geographical breadth: its branches in Spain and Egypt provided the

Gresham with new business when the Great War all but eliminated France and central Europe as markets.[29]

In the United States, British life insurance offices arrived later than in Europe and succeeded for an even shorter period of time. A dozen British firms established American branches (mostly in New York) between 1844 and 1854, but their market share fell from 7 per cent in 1855 to less than 2 per cent in 1865. British firms stood little chance of competing after local insurers started sharing surplus profits among customers in the mid-1840s. These firms made the most of their access to higher-yielding American investments, with the result that home-grown life insurance business increased from $160 million in new policies sold in 1862 to $1.14 billion in 1870.[30] By that year three U.S. insurers – the Equitable, New York Life, and Continental – had set up branches in London, and the Mutual of New York followed in 1886. Although British insurance managers decried their 'lavish outlay and unscrupulous assertion,' these 'invaders' never secured more than 2 per cent of that market, and most of them departed in the wake of revelations of financial scandals by the New York state legislature in 1906.[31]

The American pattern was repeated, although less thoroughly and more gradually, in Britain's colonies, where white settlers initially purchased life insurance from British firms but then eventually set up offices of their own – frequently with the help of protective legislation. More often than not, the British firm that blazed the trail for subsequent insurers was the Edinburgh-based Colonial, which formed in 1845 as an affiliate of Standard Life. Its sales pitch combined the pride and fear that coexisted in the minds of British settlers abroad. In one breath, an early prospectus praised 'our vast and widely-extended colonial possessions, daily becoming more and more densely populated by emigrants,' and in the next it promised financial security to families who would otherwise be 'left unprovided for, in a strange land, by the death of friends or relatives.'[32]

The Colonial's most lucrative overseas market was Canada, which generated nearly a quarter of its business in 1864; after it absorbed the Colonial in 1866, Standard Life earned up to 20 per cent of its income there. Most other British life offices, in contrast, insured Canadians in brief spurts. Between 1865 and 1875 five different Scottish firms prospered in Canada: the Reliance Mutual Life Assurance Society led all British insurers in Canada in the late-1870s, and the British Empire Mutual Assurance Company made a splash in the 1880s.[33] The Hamilton-based Canada Life took over from the Colonial as the market leader in

1866, a position it held well into the next century, and 1869 was the last year that U.K. life insurance offices had more Canadian insurance in force than companies from either the United States or Canada. By 1906 five Canadian life insurance offices had branches in Britain, where they took advantage of their higher-yielding investments to turn the sale of annuities into a special niche.[34]

As in Canada, British life insurance offices in Australia went from pioneers to also-rans over the course of several decades, owing to fierce competition from local firms. By 1870 the Liverpool & London & Globe had around £1 million insured there, and was joined by the Northern, Standard Life, and Church of England Fire & Life as market leaders.[35] When the Colonial arrived in 1863, its advance scout reported that the Sydney-based Australian Mutual Provident had taken control of the New South Wales market, but he anticipated 'a fair amount of business' in Victoria. Such openings were short-lived. Easier access to a booming land market and cash-starved colonial governments translated into higher yields on investments, which meant that local firms could afford to pay higher bonuses and charge lower premiums than foreign rivals. The Mutual Provident went from being 'the special pride of Sydney' in 1879 to being 'the first Colonial Life office that has made its way to the great central point of the British Empire' seven years later, and by 1901 four other firms also established London branches.[36]

British firms had more success at retaining stakes in South Africa and the West Indies. In South Africa only a single local company formed before 1890, leaving the way open for British insurers to fill the gap – which they did, in waves, into the 1910s. Life insurance markets in South Africa peaked in the 1890s as part of the more general economic boom spurred by the Transvaal gold discoveries, and by 1897 twenty-one British firms had South African branches. By 1910 these firms faced active competition from local life insurance offices, three of which followed other colonial firms to London after 1918.[37] In the West Indies the Colonial was an early market leader, as was the Scottish Amicable, which set up a Jamaican agency in 1845 to take advantage of the 'intimate connection of Glasgow with the West Indies.' Only two local West Indian life offices formed before 1890: the Barbados Mutual in 1840 and the Jamaica Mutual in 1844. The merchant elites who ran the Barbados Mutual established a strong branch network throughout the West Indies and kept the home island's business to themselves. The Jamaica Mutual was smaller, restricted its business to that island, and was less able to fend off competition from stronger British branches.[38]

Of all British colonists, white settlers in India remained loyal to British life insurance offices for the longest period of time. From the arrival of the Universal Life Assurance Society in 1834 until the end of the nineteenth century, only a single local firm (the Oriental, which formed in Bombay in 1874) had any success. Four more British companies joined the Universal in the 1840s, of which the Family Endowment and Medical Invalid soon dominated by charging the lowest rates. In the wake of the Sepoi Rebellion of 1857, both transferred their business to the Albert, which held on as the leading Indian insurer until its failure in 1869.[39] Several British companies rushed in to fill the ensuing vacuum, nearly all of which focused on British customers residing in India. The one exception was the Oriental Government Security Life Assurance Company, which made the unprecedented move of charging native and white customers the same rates. As more natives took the place of Britons in civil service and commercial posts after 1900, British-based life insurance offices needed to compete for this market if they wanted to stay in India at all. A few did so to varying extents; but these were exceptions, and the failure of most British life offices to pursue native risks was one of a number of factors that led Indian people increasingly to open their own insurance societies in competition with the available British offerings.[40]

Regardless of where in the world British firms tried to sell life insurance, their efforts were recurrently frustrated by local regulations and high expenses. Competition and regulation often (though not always) went hand in hand, since the aim of many insurance laws was to encourage local firms at the expense of foreigners. Austria, France, and Russia imposed temporary bans on foreign life insurers in the midnineteenth century, and taxes and deposit requirements had comparable effects in Canada and South Africa.[41] Regulations in the United States and central Europe had even more impact on British companies, mainly because of the proliferation of rules for different jurisdictions. Most directly, the New Zealand legislature in 1869 empowered the country's Post Office to sell life insurance to middle-class customers, with no cap on policy size and a provision for paid canvassers.[42]

An even more discouraging aspect of foreign business than protectionist laws was its high cost, owing to larger agency commissions, greater mortality, and higher overhead. In Europe and in most British colonies the standard practice was to pay salesmen a much larger commission on the first year's premiums, then less on renewals; since lapse rates were higher abroad, this translated into up to twice the commission than was paid in Britain.[43] A second source of expense abroad was higher mortality, often owing to the challenge of screening proposals at a distance. The only way to deal with this problem, though, was to pay inspectors to keep track of incoming business, which increased costs from a different direction.[44] In the sparsely populated colonies of South Africa and Australia, a final expense was the cost of canvassing for business. A 'Cape cart and a pair of horses' was standard issue for a South African insurance agent, and Australian salesmen brought medical examiners along on lengthy tours of the bush.[45]

The uneven record of success experienced by British life insurers abroad contrasted sharply with the spectacular success of British fire insurance in foreign and colonial climes. Unlike life insurance, where only a handful of companies earned most of their income from abroad, nearly all of the major fire insurance offices got most of their business from those sources by 1900.[46] Several causes lay behind these opposite fortunes. First, to the extent that life insurance offices marketed themselves as mutual funds (which was not an option in fire insurance), the higher yields available in North America and Australia favoured local firms there. Second, life risks were easier to calculate than fire risks, which meant that American firms could grow their business without requiring large capital reserves; the more heavily capitalized British fire insurance offices, in contrast, withstood major fires that wiped out dozens of American firms at a time. Finally, the availability of reinsurance treaties in fire insurance made access much easier. Whereas local life insurance offices often waged all-out war against British interlopers, their fire insurance counterparts saw the wisdom in striking treaties with British firms. They gained from the British offices' ability to pay heavy claims, while their treaty partners took advantage of the local firms' superior underwriting ability.[47]

Classes and Masses

As they extended their market outward from London, life insurers expanded the range of social classes they targeted as potential customers. The way they did this depended on where they were based. Many English offices engaged in market segmentation, targeting specific professions or religious denominations, and a later set of offices targeted lower-middle-class customers. This stood in contrast to most Scottish firms, which used their larger branch networks to attract customers from all walks of life. One index of this more diffuse customer base is average coverage, which for the top ten Scottish offices in 1888 ranged between £430 and £710. Only two of the top ten English firms fell in this range, with the rest either averaging over £1,000 or under £400.[48]

These two strategies for growing a market for life insurance were comparably successful in terms of overall volume of business, but the Scottish model was far more successful at growing individual companies. The social or religious solidarity that many English offices tapped into often created a prior commitment to collective self-help, which made it easier to sell insurance to such customers. But communitarianism cut both ways: to be an effective generator of solidarity, the community needed to be relatively small – which established a built-in ceiling on growth. An office that built its market share by appealing to a single group risked alienating that group if it sought to expand its market, or at the very least, it diluted the sense of community that had made it attractive to its original customers. Offices that cast their net more widely from the outset, in contrast, did not face this problem. Those that succeeded figured out how to generate alternative forms of solidarity – including brand loyalty and the bonds of friendship between an agent and his client – or how to compensate by seeking business more aggressively.[49]

The one social frontier in British life insurance that almost no company (English or Scottish) crossed was the huge population of workers earning less than £100 a year. These customers could only afford to spend a few shillings a year on a policy and typically bought just enough insurance to bury their dead. Until 1850 voluntary burial clubs ineffectively supplied this demand. After that point a combination of 'industrial' life offices and 'collecting' friendly societies emerged to turn burial insurance into a major business. The Prudential dominated this market into the late 1890s, by which point two other industrial offices (the Refuge, based in Manchester, and the London-based Pearl) and three collecting societies also established a significant presence. The success of these companies at insuring Britain's poorest wage earners was ultimately a blessing in disguise for lower-middle-class customers as well, since (starting with the Prudential) they all eventually set up 'ordinary' branches to cater to that market. The massive sales force and clerical staff they already had in place for the industrial side of business meant they could process this branch more efficiently than the many companies that had struggled to do so prior to 1870.

Class Offices

Several dozen English insurers that formed between 1820 and 1870 took on the appellation 'class office,' taking advantage of what one American journalist called 'the more thorough organisation of English society, and the sharpness with which class distinctions are drawn.' Their appeal to specific groups built on a long-standing tradition in voluntary insurance institutions, which had often formed in the past by adding an insurance feature to pre-existing guild associations.[50] The first move towards a more segmented market was the doing of lawyers, who were quick to recognize their central importance to life insurance once new offices started to compete for their custom. In response, they formed 'legal' offices that raised share capital either wholly or mainly from lawyers, then relied heavily on these shareholders to secure any insurance-related business that might come their way. The modus operandi was aptly described by David Deuchar in 1874: 'The borrower asks his solicitor to find him a sum of money on a certain security, and the solicitor, as agent and as shareholder, has a double interest in sending his client to his own company.' Who these lawyers' clients were was implied in the Equity & Law's 1844 prospectus, which noted that life insurance 'was now generally adopted in marriage settlements, charges upon life estates, and as auxiliaries to other securities, a very large proportion of [which] are necessarily effected through the legal profession.'[51]

The first legal office was the Law Life, which upon forming in 1823 restricted its proprietary to 'members of the profession of law.' When the Legal & General first formed, as the New Law Life in 1836, it had a similar restriction on shareholders; a week later it decided to add 'General' to its name and allot a third of its shares to non-lawyers.[52] In 1839 the English & Scottish Law formed with the novel plan of having dual boards in London and Edinburgh. Finally, with the appearance of the Equity & Law five years later, the market for legal life offices came close to reaching its limit. Of the three additional companies to form along these lines after 1844, only the Law Union survived the turn of the century. It was a testament to the relative success of this business formula, though, that even the two 'failures' – the Solicitors' & General and the London & Provincial Law – found healthy companies to purchase their business (the Eagle and the Guardian, respectively, in 1866 and 1883) and never came close to insolvency.

Among class offices, the legal firms were unique in that they targeted an occupational group to assist in selling insurance to other customers, as well as courting the legal profession per se. The other customers in question were, as often as not, landed elites. Over 40 per cent of the new policies issued by the Legal & General from 1870 to 1885 covered military officers and gentlemen, nearly half in connection with loans. Legal offices generated business mainly through their directors and share-holders or through appointed agents who were nearly always lawyers.[53] Although the legal offices' main reason for existence was to take advantage of lawyers' 'connection' with aristocratic clients, they incidentally secured a large amount of business from lawyers as well. Both the Law Life and the Legal & General insured more 'professional' men than gentry, and of the 1,048 such men on the latter's policy register in 1870, nearly half were lawyers.[54]

Starting with the company boom of 1824–25, new class offices appeared that looked beyond lawyers to the three remaining 'traditional' professions: clerical, medical, and military. The time was ripe for appealing to each of these groups. The decades leading up to 1825 had brought more comfortable conditions to many clergymen, a stronger sense of professional identity to doctors, and (during the long Napoleonic Wars) prosperity as well as awareness of the risk of premature death to military men.[55] First in line were the Clerical Medical, which equally courted clergymen and doctors, and the University, which less directly pursued the same class by insuring only Oxbridge alums. A final entrant in the 'clerical' market was the Clergy Mutual, which opened within a stone's throw of Westminster Abbey and limited its membership to ordained Anglicans and Presbyterians and their 'wives, widows, and relatives.' All three endured: the Clerical Medical until 2001 and the other two until 1919. Less enduring was the Royal Naval, Military & Honourable East India Company, which transferred its business to the soon-to-be insolvent European thirty years after forming in 1837.[56]

In the fifteen years after 1840 more than twenty life insurance offices were promoted that signalled a trade or profession in their name. Architects, artists, auctioneers, bankers, brewers, builders, civil servants, clerks, commercial travellers, doctors, engineers, farmers, gas proprietors, landlords, licensed victuallers, mariners, merchants, miners, pawnbrokers, preceptors, schoolmasters, and solicitors all received special appeals at this time from at least one (and usually several) new projects claiming to meet their specific insurance needs.[57] Many of these promised to divert funds to assist their target group, as when the Farmers & General earmarked a tenth of its profits to 'a provision for decayed farmers, an aid in the formation of Farmers' Clubs, and the distribution of prizes among agricultural labourers.' By 1854 this form of market segmentation had reached the point where the Diadem Life could announce in its prospectus that it was 'formed to meet the wants of those who do not possess a society calculated to promote their special interests.'[58]

A final variety of 'class' office catered to religious denominations. The first of these, founded in Bradford in 1832, was the Friends' Provident, which took advantage of the socially tight-knit, economically prosperous, and long-lived Quaker community. The next fifteen years brought out the Protestant Dissenters & General, the Church of England, the Star (a Methodist office), and the Catholic Law & General.[59] Although not with the single-mindedness of offices like the Clergy Mutual, denominational insurers spent a great deal of effort on ordained customers. They drew attention to the high proportion of life policies they issued to the clergy, offered reduced premiums to clerics, and lent money to ministers and their churches.[60] As much as possible, they also inserted themselves into customers' lives as quasi-ministers, who upheld Christian principles as they collected premium payments. This was the clear message of the first annual report of the Protestant Dissenters & General, which promised policyholders that it would 'minister to the comfort of those whom you dearly love; visiting your domestic hearth ... with the tone of kindness, and the supplies of a provident foresight.'[61]

By the end of the nineteenth century all three varieties of 'class' life office – legal, professional, and denominational – had seen better days. Even the relatively successful 'legal' formula was starting to sputter by the 1880s, owing both to a decline in aristocratic indebtedness and increased competition from non-legal offices for lawyers' services.[62] Other specialist companies discovered by 1900 that their target customers preferred not to insure exclusively with other members of the same profession. The proportion of doctors and clergy insured by the Clerical Medical fell from 28 per cent in its first seven years to 14 per cent in the 1880s, and to stay afloat the Clergy Mutual and the University needed to liberalize their entrance requirements after 1880.[63] A similar fate met most denominational life insurance offices. The Protestant Dissenters & General changed its name to the General in 1847, the Star insisted in 1900 that it had 'long since ceased to appeal *exclusively* to the Wesleyan body,' and in 1914 the Friends' Provident started admitting non-Quakers.[64]

The Lower-Middle- and Working-Class Market

Despite the social diversity encouraged by 'class' offices, British life insurance remained at mid-century largely a middle- and upper-class affair. In a sample of a hundred life insurance offices active between 1850 and 1870, fully 95 per cent of those established before 1840 insured (on average) at least £400 per policy, which would have been beyond the reach of nearly all working-class customers.[65] Most of these older life offices forbade agents from selling policies worth less than £50, and some had much higher cut-offs.[66] Older companies also either forbade customers from paying premiums in quarterly or half-yearly instalments, or discouraged this by imposing a surcharge to compensate the extra clerical labour.[67] This did not mean, however, that the market for working-class self-help was completely open. To appeal to 'struggling self-dependent men,' new companies needed to compete with savings banks and friendly societies, both of which thrived under laws that enabled them to offer secure and substantial yields.[68]

Prior to the 1830s only a handful of company promoters had turned their attention to this market. The London-based General Benefit Society (established in 1820) provided sick pay and medical attendance as well as life insurance to more than five hundred new working-class customers a year before failing in 1854. More successful was the National Provident, which formed in 1835 as a secular offshoot of the Friends' Provident. Along with a handful of smaller mutuals, the National Provident enrolled under the Friendly Societies Act of 1830, which enabled it to offer guaranteed interest on investments and exemption from stamp and probate duties. These privileges, which were revoked in 1854 after other insurers complained, helped the National Provident sell nearly 14,000 policies over its first fifteen years and earn over £150,000 in annual income during the 1850s. Mostly, though, its success stemmed from its widespread agency network, which carried life insurance (in the words of one defender) 'to the masses of the people, in the same way that cheap literature has been carried with effect to the masses.'[69]

The trickle of lower-middle-class life offices turned into a flood between 1840 and 1870, when a large majority of the hundreds of newly formed companies directed at least part of their attention to that sector. In the sample mentioned above, 79 per cent of the companies that formed after 1839 averaged less than £400 per policy issued, and 49 per cent averaged less than £300 – which meant that most of their customers paid under £10 a year in premiums. To succeed in this market, life insurance offices needed to modify their product to address their customers' uneven income stream. They responded with such innovations as half-credit policies (in which customers could pay premiums by borrowing on the security of the policy), 'deposit insurance' (in which customers could withdraw some of the premiums they had paid in exchange for a reduced claim), guaranteed surrender values, non-forfeiture clauses, and endowment insurance. They also adapted their marketing efforts to a broader audience through lectures, meetings, almanacs, diaries, and insurance-themed novellas.[70]

A very rough sense of the impact this new marketing strategy had on market share can be gained by comparing the available annual averages of new premium income of 'old' as opposed to 'new' life offices in England while the boom was under way. Based on a sample of twenty companies that formed before 1844 and sixty that formed between 1844 and 1861, these were £6,558 for the first set and £3,452 for the second. One can then extrapolate from these samples to the smaller number of 'old' than 'new' companies that did business during this period and factor in the shorter duration of new ones. This yields an annual new premium income of £219,570 in any given year for English life insurance offices that formed after 1844, and £546,793 for those formed before 1844, or a 71 per cent market share for the older firms. Measuring the number of customers instead of premium income paints a different picture, since older firms typically issued much larger policies: half of new English customers patronized the newer offices, although these were spread across more than twice as many firms.[71]

Two new lower-income offices, the Provident Clerks' and the Marine & General, succeeded by extending to this new customer base the same occupational model that had worked for higher-income customers. The Provident Clerks' formed in 1841 amid calls for a 'mutual benefit association' for clerks, and by the mid-1860s it was issuing more than a thousand policies annually for an average of £200 each. It enjoyed the patronage of prominent City financiers, who staffed its board, donated to a supplementary charity fund, and spread the word among employees. The Marine & General, which formed in 1852, was the brainchild of directors from the Peninsular & Oriental and Royal Mail shipping firms, who rotated as chairs of the new company and subsidized their employees' premium payments. Both firms survived by evolving beyond their original clientele – the first dropped 'Clerks' from its name in 1917, and the second branched out into baggage insurance for travellers.[72]

A variant extension of the class office model to lower-income customers was the United Kingdom Temperance & General (established in 1840), which turned temperance reform into a niche market for life insurance. Initially restricted to strict abstainers, the society opened a 'general' section in 1847 and hit on the idea of paying separate bonuses to each section (and allowing customers to move back and forth as they fell off and got back on the wagon). This move allowed the Temperance & General to broadcast the benefits of abstinence, by advertising the higher bonuses received by non-drinkers – which built a loyal following among the largely lower-middle-class customer base that turned temperance into a national campaign by the 1870s.[73] Although many other firms copied the Temperance & General's model, most of these failed by 1900; and as the larger movement waned, so did the fortunes of the surviving offices that had tapped into its energy. The Abstainers' & General became the Beacon in 1933, the Scottish Temperance changed its name to the Scottish Mutual in 1952, and the Temperance & General advertised itself as UK Provident from the late 1960s.[74]

Although the Provident Clerks', Marine & General, and United Kingdom Temperance & General were sturdy survivors in the lower-income market, by the 1860s they paled before a new breed of flashier offices that made it their business to break sales records. A few of these stood above the rest, and at least in volume of new business ranked among the leading offices in Britain. These included the Briton Medical & General, the British Equitable, and the European, each of which issued more than three thousand policies a year in the late-1860s. The first two faced insolvency by the 1880s, and the European crashed even sooner. Their problems (and those of dozens of smaller companies that failed to survive) began with the fact that it was expensive to attract and maintain business in this market, since smaller policies required as much processing as larger ones. Adding to the troubles of the many failed companies in this cohort were basic management problems like paying too much for transferred policies, excessive salaries, and a failure to monitor dishonest staff. At root, however, most of these firms failed because they overestimated the demand for their product, which remained a high-priced luxury for most people. Only 10 per cent of the British population in the 1860s earned £100 a year or more, and for anyone earning less it would cost at least a month's pay to buy a medium-sized policy worth £300.[75]

As disenchantment with failed bubble companies spread after 1870, lower-middle-class customers increasingly turned to the Prudential, which by that point had established itself as the nation's leading industrial insurer and was starting to build the 'ordinary' side of its business. In 1868 the Prudential issued its first 'middle-class table,' and within two years had 10,700 of these policies in force (compared with 670,000 'industrial' policies). By 1901 it was issuing more than seventy thousand ordinary policies a year, and it earned £4.8 million in premium income from that source by 1910 – more than the combined total of its four closest competitors. The ordinary business of two other industrial offices paled only in comparison to the Prudential: the Pearl issued more than ten thousand ordinary policies in 1901, and the Refuge passed the twenty thousand mark the same year (see Table 1.1). In 1911, 163,000 customers insured their lives through industrial companies' ordinary branches for an average of £72 per policy – far more than the £10 average for industrial policies, but only a sixth of what other firms covered. Overall premium income from ordinary policies in force comprised 36 per cent of these firms' total business.[76] These companies succeeded by teaching their vast army of salesmen how to sell policies in houses 'rather better than the others,' maintaining working-class customers' loyalty when their circumstances improved, using profits from their industrial branches to subsidize bonus payments, and being able to handle efficiently the high volume of incoming business – much of which was paid in monthly or quarterly instalments.[77]

Only a handful of traditional life insurance offices went out of their way to court the same class of 'ordinary' customers targeted by the Prudential, Pearl, and Refuge. Sun Life introduced a monthly payment scheme in 1901 and established branches in working-class London neighbourhoods. An army of more than two hundred salaried agents sold policies for as little as two shillings a month, covering sums as low as £20, and produced an immediate 50 per cent increase in the company's premium income. Although Sun Life's experiment paid off, other forays into working-class insurance were less successful. When the National Life set up 'monthly' branches with special canvassers late in 1889, the result was a 44 per cent surge in new premium income for 1890, but this fell back to the 1889 level in a single year. More troubling, expense levels in 1890–91 were more than twice as high as they had been in the early 1880s.[78] In 1891 the National's actuary warned its board that their detour into 'monthly' business was 'cutting off its traditions,' and he accurately predicted 'a serious hole in the Society's funds within the next few years.' This clash between 'traditional' methods of procuring life insurance and the aggressive pursuit of working-class business using 'troublesome' agents was apparently enough to keep most life offices out of the latter market until well after the First World War.[79]

The only major exceptions to the industrial offices' lock on lower-middle-class business were group schemes that were arranged through large employers. The pioneer in this sector was the Provident Clerks', which insured more than 400,000 railway workers in this way between 1860 and 1940. Two other group plans before 1850 involved the Northern Lighthouse Office, which paid for its lighthouse keepers to buy small Edinburgh Life policies, and the Excise Office, which generated 43 per cent of new Atlas policies between 1844 and 1852 through a subsidized plan for revenue officers.[80] After 1850 large employers and employee groups moved from arranging deals with individual companies to inviting competition among an array of firms. The first to do so was the Post Office, which between 1854 and 1859 convinced twenty-six firms to shave between 5 per cent and 20 per cent from premiums that were deducted from employees' weekly wages. The postal official Frank Scudamore was sufficiently encouraged to suggest in a pamphlet that 'large employers of labour ... would do well to consider whether they might not introduce the Post Office plan into their factories, mills, workshops, or counting houses.' A company that did so, he concluded, would 'gain a stronger hold on [employees'] good will, and bind them more firmly to its service.'[81]

Although most employers were slow to heed Scudamore's advice, by the end of the nineteenth century many employee groups actively sought concessions from life insurance offices for group plans. The biggest breakthrough came in 1890, when the Association of Civil Servants convinced the North British & Mercantile to offer them a 15 per cent reduction in premiums and quarterly payments at no extra charge – netting the company 3,667 policies in just four months. Later that decade the National Union of Teachers and the Irish National Teachers' Organization took bids for 'exceptional terms for assurances upon their lives,' as did the Local Government Mutual Guarantee Society, the National Poor Law Officers' Association, and the London County Council Insurance Society.[82] The only major British employers to take the initiative in buying group coverage prior to 1900 were banks, and as late as 1919 actuaries still lumped such plans among 'those superficially attractive schemes' that had sold well in North America but were less likely to fly in Britain. The handful of companies that did start pursuing group coverage more aggressively after 1920 dominated the market through the interwar period, once large British employers began to warm up to the idea.[83]

Business Organization

As much as any sector in the nineteenth-century economy, life insurance business organization and marketing went hand in hand. The structure of an office – the size of its branch network, whether it was mutual or joint stock, and whether it sold other products in addition to life insurance – directly affected its ability to attract customers. All these connections between structure and sales had much to do with the fact that most insurers after 1820 doubled as fund managers. Branch networks were obvious generators of new business, but their expense needed to be monitored lest it diminish an office's ability to pay large bonuses. A mutual firm had the distinct advantage of being able to divide all its surplus profit among policyholders, instead of reserving some for shareholders, while a joint stock company could counter that its share capital rendered it more secure. Finally, composite insurance had a clear appeal from a marketing perspective, both because it offered customers 'one-stop shopping' and because companies could leaven their bonus with profits from other divisions.

As in the matter of their choice of customers, English and Scottish firms varied significantly in business organization. Scottish insurers turned branch networks into a common practice, and although provincial English rivals soon copied them it took many London firms decades to catch up. Among the handful of life insurance offices that formed without shareholders, some of the most successful were Scottish, and this pressured other Scottish firms to start paying bonuses before that practice took hold in England. Conversely, it was in England that composite insurance was most common – both early in the nineteenth century, when many more English firms divided their energy between selling fire and life insurance, and at the century's end, when England dominated the new trend of offices that combined fire and life with accident, marine, and other forms of insurance. This innovation went a long way towards helping English firms narrow the gaps in marketing and performance that their Scottish counterparts had opened up since 1830.[84]

Branch Networks

For the first half of the nineteenth century, the basic model for selling life insurance was to open an office in a large city and appoint agents in outlying towns. Directors and staff processed customers who showed up at the head office, while agents, in exchange for a commission, sent in business from the provinces. After 1850 Scottish insurers built on this system by appointing full-time branch secretaries and inspectors, who in turn appointed agents and monitored their performance. Although provincial English firms were quick to copy this innovation, most

Figure 1.2
Percentage of life insurance offices with branches in selected British cities, 1880–1910.

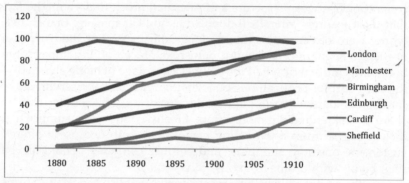

Source: *Post Magazine Almanack*, 1880–1910.

London companies waited until the 1880s before realizing that branches were vital to the maintenance of new business, and the extent of their networks lagged behind their northern neighbours until after 1900. By that point, however, reasonably large towns like Sheffield and Nottingham had at least a dozen life insurance branch offices on their high streets, and large cities like Manchester and Birmingham had more than fifty. Industry-wide the average number of branches per head office rose from just over four in 1885 to fourteen in 1910 (see Figures 1.2 and 1.3).[85]

To succeed in this environment, life insurance offices needed to keep close track of the benefits as well as the costs of acquiring new business, by distinguishing profitable branches from losing propositions. That strategy, which had long been pursued in Scotland, reached its height under J.J.W. Deuchar at the Norwich Union in the 1890s. By breaking down the relative cost, volume, and geographical distribution of his firm's existing and newly acquired business, Deuchar combined extraordinary growth with a low enough expense ratio to enable the maintenance of high bonuses – which itself was a prerequisite of continued growth. Actuaries continued to hone this side of the life insurance business into the twentieth century, adding layer upon layer of travel vouchers, expense accounts, and progress reports to deal with what Standard Life's manager called 'the crying need for economy in all directions.'[86]

Besides bringing a life office's organizational muscle closer to its hoped-for customers, an extensive branch network also made it easier

Figure 1.3
Branches per head office, 1870–1910 (by region in which head office
is located).

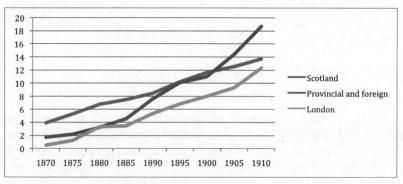

Source: Post Magazine Almanack, 1880–1910.

for directors to learn what those customers wanted out of the product
they were asked to buy. As a result, Scottish firms consistently stayed a
step ahead of public demand for new products and services, most notably protection against disputed claims and more liberal conditions for
travelling abroad.[87] Their success in this regard, combined with similar
innovations by newer London firms after 1840, generated a combination of dismay and denial from the older London offices. Upon being
taunted by a Lancashire policyholder who contrasted the Scottish
Widows' six-fold increase in business with the Equitable's steady decline, Arthur Morgan lashed out against the Scottish offices' 'gigantic
system of puffing, in which they do not scruple to deviate from the
usual courtesies observed between life offices.'[88]

When English firms finally began to copy the Scottish model of
branch formation, their branch secretaries actively prodded them to offer competitive products. The result was an explosion of 'fancy schemes'
after 1880, including convertible term policies, mortgage-linked policies, limited payment plans, partnership policies, charitable bequests,
supplemental disability coverage, and guaranteed surrender values.[89]
A common theme was to provide 'something sound and secure to suit
the changing taste of the public,' in one manager's words. By 1900
many onlookers thought the rage for 'fancy schemes' had reached
pathological proportions, and correctly pointed out that many had
either been available (if not widely promoted) for decades or combined

long-available offerings in one package.[90] Neither this perception, nor
the fact that relatively few people actually bought such policies, deterred most life insurance offices from trying to sell them – at least in
part because they guaranteed free publicity. As the National Mutual's
actuary observed in 1905, its 'new schemes were widely noticed in the
Press during the year, of course without payment.'[91]

Mutuals and Joint Stock Companies

If branch networks emerged as an essential structural feature of life insurance by the end of the nineteenth century, another organizational question
dated back before 1800: whether to form with or without shareholders.
Forming as a mutual came with the distinct advantage, demonstrated in
full force by the Equitable, of being able to divide all their surplus profits
among policyholders, and a succession of leading mutuals made the most
of this opportunity. At the beginning of the century, joint stock companies
countered that their share capital formed an added security against the
possibility that claims would exceed premium income; it was with this in
mind that Augustus De Morgan called life office shareholders 'ignorance-
insurers,' whose necessity would diminish as knowledge of vital statistics
improved. Once that day came to pass, joint stock insurers typically started buying back at least some of their shares, once it was clear that these
represented a 'dead weight upon [their] prosperity.'[92]

The vast majority of offices chose to raise share capital. Only twenty
of ninety offices formed as mutuals between 1800 and 1840, and fewer
than 10 per cent did so from 1840 to the end of the century. Although
London was home to the Equitable, which had proven beyond a doubt
that life insurance could succeed without shareholders, only one major
London office (the London Life) followed its example into the 1820s.
Part of the reason for this was that actuaries were not yet convinced of
the security of their life tables. Part of it had to do with the capital market, which up to 1820 was enormously elastic. Rising share prices meant
that life insurance stock traded briskly; ample investment opportunities gave companies a second income stream on top of their underwriting profits, enabling them to pay large dividends on their capital.
This trend temporarily altered between 1828 and 1835, when half of the
new London insurers were mutuals, including such major players as
the National Provident, National, and Provident Clerks'. After 1840,
however, most of the handful of mutuals that formed in London were
friendly societies that sold life insurance on the side.[93]

Mutuals were more common in Scotland, where six of the first six-teen life insurance offices formed without shareholders; four of these (the Scottish Widows' Fund, Scottish Provident, Scottish Amicable, and Scottish Equitable) attracted 35 per cent of sums insured among Scottish offices in 1870 and 41 per cent of premium income by 1892. One reason for this disparity was Scottish offices mostly formed in the same period (1828–35) that was the height of mutual formation in England – which, not coincidentally, was also a period when there was a lull in an otherwise buoyant stock market. Another reason was that fewer Scottish firms sold fire insurance, the riskier nature of which required at least some share capital. The only leading mutual in provincial England, the Norwich Union, had the best of both worlds, by forming in close affiliation with a joint stock fire office. The rest of the major provincial firms formed as heavily capitalized fire and life offices: with £2 million being the nominal share issue at the Liverpool, Royal, and Lancashire.[94]

Companies that did raise share capital raised much more of it prior to 1830. Proprietary offices that formed through the company boom of 1825 averaged more than £1 million in nominal capital. This average was padded by fire and life offices like the Alliance, which issued a whop-ping £5 million in nominal shares (£550,000 of which was paid up as of 1848), and companies that did a large annuity or loan business (to which end the European collected £1 million in paid-up shares when it formed in 1819). Large share denominations (usually in excess of £100) point to the type of proprietor that life insurance offices courted. In contrast, companies that formed between 1844 and 1870 pledged less than a quar-ter as much capital as earlier life offices and issued their shares in much smaller denominations (see Figure 1.4). The Professional, which formed in 1847 with £19,460 in paid-up capital held by 1,400 shareholders (and failed fourteen years later), criticized the 'unnecessary, unwieldy, and suicidal capital' held by older firms.[95]

Composite Insurance

For most of the nineteenth century, the only conceivable type of com-posite office was one that combined fire and life insurance: most other forms of insurance were not invented until after 1850, and the triumvir-ate of Lloyd's, the London Assurance, and Royal Exchange prevented any marine insurance rivals until the 1860s. The proportion of life in-surance offices that also covered against fires peaked at 32 per cent in

Figure 1.4
Nominal share capital, 1792–1894.

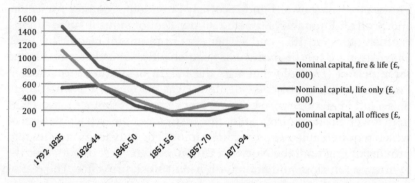

Sources: Brown 1849: 99; Dickson, *Sun Life* 1960: 12; *Economist* 38 (1880): 644;
ExMB; *First Report* 1844: 334, 343; *Hand Book* 1856: 112–41; Harrison 1992: 13,
15–16; Hogg 1837: 388; Magnusson 1983: 34; Moss 2000: 22; Pocock 1842: 99,
120; *Policy-Holder* 3 (1885): 193; *Post Magazine* 9 March 1850; 42 (1881): 440;
Raynes 1948: 138–9, 232, 234–5, 277; Schooling 1924: 3; Tarn and Byles 1921:
52; *Times* 13 March 1863, 14 Feb 1902; UlMB; Walford I–VI; CWP (Hope,
Palladium, People's Provident, Scottish Life, United Deposit, United Empire,
United Kingdom Life, Unity General, Victoria Life, Western, Whittington);
Worland and Paterson 1976: 10; *Return of Names* 1864, 1868–69.

the 1820s, hovered around 15 per cent from 1830 through the 1850s,
then rose again to 23 per cent in the 1860s. In terms of sales, fire and life
offices occupied a middle tier: all but two of the top twenty firms in
premium income as of 1870 sold life insurance exclusively, but so did
the vast majority of the bubble companies that formed and failed between 1840 and 1870. On the other hand, a customer in the 1870s was
far more likely to encounter an agent who sold fire as well as life insurance. Nearly two-thirds of Scottish agents in 1878 who sold life insurance worked for a fire and life office (often in addition to working for a
life insurance specialist), and another 11 per cent combined their life
office work with a specialist fire office.[96]

In London fire and life offices gave the Equitable a run for its money
into the 1820s. The Royal Exchange started focusing on life as well as
fire and marine insurance in the mid-1780s, as did the comparably ancient Union and London Assurance offices shortly after 1800. The

Imperial, which formed in 1803 as a fire-only office, added life in 1820, and the Globe, Albion, Atlas, and Guardian all offered both fire and life insurance from the outset. Britain's leading fire insurance office, the Sun, formed a spin-off life office in 1810, as did the Phoenix in 1797 (called the Pelican) and the County in 1806 (called the Provident). This pattern abruptly reversed in the company boom of 1823–26, when (with the key exception of the Alliance), most London-based insurers limited themselves to life insurance, and as class offices took centre-stage in succeeding decades this trend continued. The only major London offices to offer fire and life coverage after 1830 were the Law Union in 1854 and the Commercial Union in 1861.[97]

In contrast to the London scene, Scottish offices remained focused on life insurance throughout the nineteenth century, starting with the Scottish Widows' Fund in 1815. Although most other important Scottish firms either added life insurance to an already existing fire insurance business or began as fire and life companies, life insurance took precedence at most of them. The North British survived almost entirely on its life income in the 1830s and only became a fire insurance force in the 1860s. The Caledonian, Scottish Union, and Scottish National earned from three to eight times more revenue from their life than from their fire business as of 1871. Two other Scottish offices, Standard Life and the Scottish Amicable, shed their original fire insurance business soon after forming, and the Scottish Provident joined the Scottish Widows' and Scottish Equitable as a life insurance specialist in 1837. As mentioned above, provincial English offices took the opposite course, almost invariably subordinating life to fire insurance.[98]

After 1880 the fire and life office, and with it the life insurance specialist, gave way to the composite office that might include as well accident, marine, fidelity, or burglary coverage. This development continued the trend within life insurance to offer customers a wider choice of products and services; it also accomplished economies of scale, since it was more efficient for a single agent or branch office to sell several types of coverage. Finally, many life offices hoped to increase bonus payments by skimming from 'the profits of the new classes of business.' Although some firms diversified internally, most companies that became composites did so by purchasing the business of firms that specialized in other forms of insurance.[99]

To do so, it was necessary for such firms to exist; and conveniently, just as new fire and life office formation was starting to slow down after 1860 a proliferation of companies offering other types of insurance was under way. Most specialized in different types of accidents, involving railways, employers' liability, boilers, and plate glass. Like the early fire insurance offices, the large majority of these were local outfits that typically earned less than £10,000 a year in premium income. A few came to dominate their respective sectors of this market by setting up national agency networks, often gobbling up local firms along the way.[100] In addition to accident insurance, new companies offered guarantee insurance (indemnifying employers against dishonest clerks), livestock insurance, and insurance against hailstorms and burglary. Among the last new insurance companies on the scene were the marine offices, which carved out a significant share of the market from Lloyd's by 1870.[101]

Although accident, guarantee, and marine insurance offices were firmly established by the 1870s, combining them with each other or with a fire and life office was not. One main reason this soon changed was the rising prominence of the insurance broker in the industry. Originally, most brokers belonged to Lloyd's or worked closely with a Lloyd's member, and focused mainly on selling marine insurance. In the 1880s these brokers began to branch out into other types of insurance, collecting commission from different specialist offices; and a new breed of independent broker also appeared with few ties to the marine sector. At the same time, many fire and/or life offices found themselves sharing their agents' services with accident insurance offices, which often brought in at least as much business as the more traditional branches of insurance. To wrest control away from the brokers (who could not be relied on to steer customers to a single company) and to tap into the success of the accident insurance sector, many firms turned themselves into what the *Times* aptly called 'stores at whose counters all kinds of insurance are retailed.'[102]

Nearly all companies that ended up as composites began as English fire and life offices, which tended to be more heavily capitalized than fire or life specialists and had experience selling two distinct forms of insurance. All of the fifteen top composites in 1911 sold life as well as fire insurance or worked with a sister company that did; only three were Scottish. Sufficient share capital was crucial, either to cover new labour costs (when a company diversified from scratch) or acquisition fees (when it added new divisions by buying other firms).[103] The one major exception to the tendency for composites to originate as fire and life offices was the British Dominions Marine Insurance Company, founded in 1904 by a Lloyd's broker named Edward Mountain. After diversifying into fire, motor, accident, and fidelity coverage between

1910 and 1914, Mountain used wartime marine profits to purchase four life insurance offices between 1916 and 1918. Newly christened as the Eagle, Star, & British Dominions, Mountain's company emerged from the Great War as one of Britain's leading insurers.[104]

By 1930 composite insurance had left a deep imprint on life insurance employees, customers, and the few surviving specialist life offices. Excluding industrial offices like the Prudential and the Pearl, composite companies sold 63 per cent of all British life insurance in 1938. Since composites usually kept their life insurance funds separate, the day-to-day experience of actuaries and life clerks remained more or less the same; but their relative status and chances for promotion within the company diminished as the variety of non-life divisions increased. The composites' impact on customers was less ambiguous: they got the convenience of one-stop shopping for other varieties of insurance, and they were also more likely to receive large and stable bonuses – since many composites shored up bonuses with earnings from other divisions. The only specialist life insurance offices that could hold their own against these advantages were mutuals, which did not divert any of their profits to shareholders. This was the saving grace of the Scottish Widows', Scottish Equitable, and Scottish Provident, and the new competitive logic led Standard Life to mutualize in 1925. Even mutuals, however, felt the pinch: as a Scottish Equitable branch secretary complained in 1913, 'the loss of support formerly given by accident and by fire representatives, free to give help reciprocally, has meant much.'[105]

Conclusion

By all accounts life insurance flourished in Britain long before it began to take off in any other country, and it continued to be a uniquely British product well into the nineteenth century. As of 1859 more than half of all life insurance companies in the world were based in Britain, holding 59 per cent of all policies in force. A decade later, British firms still held 37 per cent of the £913 million in worldwide coverage (not including industrial policies) – and although this slightly trailed American firms (which held policies worth £406 million, or 44 per cent of the total), insurance per capita (£11.23) was still slightly higher in the United Kingdom. As these figures indicate, Britain and its American cousins far outstripped the rest of the world in the matter of life insurance at this time. France was a distant third with £62 million insured by sixteen firms, followed by Germany with £24 million, and per capita coverage in those countries was just £1.64 and £1.39 respectively – still far in excess of the £0.17 per head in the rest of Europe and £0.4 in the rest of the world. By 1925 British life insurance offices still came in second to American firms in total coverage, but the gap had ballooned to a staggering £10 billion: with Britain accounting for £1.8 billion of the world's total of £18 billion, compared with £12 billion held in the United States. Americans had also surpassed Britons in per capita coverage by this point, with £109 per head compared with just £39.[106]

As Americans took over as the world's leading insurers, Britons responded with a large helping of sour grapes but also a willingness to learn from the American firms' success. British actuaries sniffed at their 'showy bids for business,' worried that they catered to the 'accumulative, and ... speculative instinct of man,' and faulted the 'extraordinary generosity with other people's money' that they displayed by mixing good and bad lives in the same pool. Not everyone was so quick to condemn, however. The London secretary for the Friends' Provident argued in 1897 that British life insurance offices had much to learn from the Americans, who had 'made a thorough study of people as *they are*, and not as they *ought to be*.' A later *Times* correspondent recalled that 'when the big life offices of the United States first invaded Great Britain with their attractive and varied schemes of life assurance ... they gave, through their hustling tactics and astute methods of advertising, such an impetus to insurance business generally that British life offices were also the gainers.'[107] This mixture of conservatism and enterprise typified the steady growth of life insurance in Britain from the early nineteenth century up to 1914, which was marked by the life offices' periodic willingness to loosen their regulation of people's behaviour in order to increase the number of regulated lives who joined them.

2 Regulated Insurance Offices

The life assurance field seems capable, by ordinary culture, of giving only a certain crop of new business; if a larger return is wished from the soil than the amount it naturally yields, it can only be had at a cost to the policyholder in manure, at least as great as the return is worth to him.
– James Macfadyen, Legal & General assistant actuary, 1874[1]

In England life insurance grew in fits and starts over the course of the nineteenth century, and efforts to regulate it were similarly sporadic. A rush of heavily capitalized companies formed in the mid-1820s, followed by a stream of more than four hundred in the next four decades. Efforts to regulate growth were mostly ineffectual until 1870, when a wave of mergers was in the process of initiating a tsunami of insolvency. New publicity requirements appeared in 1844, but only for new companies, and neither the press nor a nascent actuarial profession could impose much order on the wayward mid-century market. It took renewed government involvement to effect real change in how English life insurance offices did business. The Life Assurance Companies Act of 1870 imposed unprecedented levels of accountability on life offices, monitored future mergers, and made it harder to start up new companies. Existing companies embraced the new law, which immediately helped to stabilize the market and, in the process, transformed the way life insurance was sold. The flood of new information concerning life insurance engendered a new form of comparison shopping among policyholders, mediated by a maturing insurance press and by brokers who offered themselves as guides to the annual government returns.

In stark contrast to their English counterparts, the Scottish insurance sector accomplished near-perfect levels of stability. Eleven of the thirteen Scottish life insurance offices that formed before 1840 survived the nineteenth century, and only fourteen more companies formed over the next three decades. In all, only one Scottish firm failed, and only one sold its business to a company that later failed. For customers of English life offices, there was at least the silver lining that their experience of market instability was usually less trying than in other corners of the financial sector. In contrast to stock market speculators, who suffered liabilities far in excess of their investments in the event of a crash, policyholders only lost their premiums if a company failed.[2] Although more than half of all English life offices that formed between 1800 and 1870 either failed or were acquired by a firm that later failed (see Figure 2.1), only a minority of policyholders in these firms lost anything close to the proportion of their savings that their counterparts stood to lose in a failed bank.[3] The reason for this was simple: relatively recent customers (a majority in most failed life offices, which failed because they spent too much on new business) had only been paying premiums into the company for a few years, usually less than £50. On the other hand, failure in a life office was cruelly inequitable: the oldest and most vulnerable customers lost disproportionately, reversing the usual redistributive functions of insurance.

Unsupervised Growth, 1800–1870

Until 1870 there were sharp differences between the pattern of growth in England and that in Scotland. Prior to that time growth in England was largely an unregulated affair, despite the best intentions of legislators, actuaries, and the press to restrain competition. Into the 1830s life insurance received no sustained scrutiny either in the press or in Parliament, and actuaries generally stayed out of other companies' affairs. It was not until the Independent & West Middlesex abruptly shut its doors in 1840 that people seriously considered the question of accountability as it applied to life insurance. That scandalous failure set in motion the Joint Stock Companies Act of 1844, which required all new companies (including life insurance offices) to register a profit and loss account with the Board of Trade. A newly active insurance press also emerged in the 1840s, attracted by advertising prospects but also committed (in at least some cases) to protecting the public against abuses. Finally, the company boom kindled a sense among English actuaries that active cooperation was

Figure 2.1
Number and duration of life insurance offices based on decade
formed ('successful offices' = surviving or absorbed by an office that
survived as of 1900).

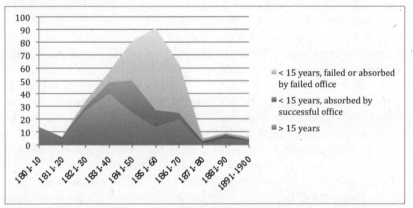

Sources: *Insurance Directory and Yearbook* (1987): 199–221; *Return* 1845; *Abstract*
Return 1856 and 1863; *Return of Names* 1864–97; Walford I–VI *passim*; CWP
passim; *Post Magazine* 46 (1885): 38, 50, 62–3, 74, 86; Hutchison 1846: 75–80;
Bridges 1842: 23; Drew 1928: 52–4.

needed to inhibit excessive competition – something they learned a decade later than their Scottish counterparts, whose prior success at self-
regulation remained an elusive goal in England for several decades.
None of these responses were sufficient to stabilize a market that was
well on its way to implosion by the 1860s. The titanic collapse of the
Albert in 1869, followed by the disastrous failure of the European two
years later, capped a decade punctuated by ill-conceived mergers.

From Cozy to Competitive, 1800–1860

What passed for outside regulation before 1830 mainly took the form of
entry barriers. The Bubble Act, which had accompanied the charters
acquired by the Royal Exchange and London Assurance in 1720, required any new company (including all life insurance offices) to get a
charter prior to formation or risk forming under a settlement or trust
deed that rendered it illegal under common law. Each charter application led to an outcry among existing life insurance offices – starting

with the Equitable's petition for a charter in 1757, which the Amicable, London Assurance, and Royal Exchange successfully opposed. Similar opposition greeted charter applications by the Westminster, Kent, Albion, and Globe between 1789 and 1807.[4] In all these cases, the companies instead formed under deeds of settlement, and by the 1820s most new life offices formed this way without bothering to apply for a charter. As was the case with the aristocratic marriage settlements on which they were based, the challenge in these deeds was to protect the disposition of a company's assets from the whims of future recipients of income (shareholders, in this case), without being so rigid as to prevent adaptation to a changing market.[5] The typical deed featured dozens of clauses, took up to two years to finalize, and needed to be amended by a private act of Parliament at least once before the century was over.[6]

Once a life insurance company got off the ground prior to 1844, it faced little by way of formal accountability. Disgruntled shareholders sometimes vented in pamphlets or letters to the editor, as when John Parry rebuked the Eagle's 'self-appointed Directors and self-voted-in Auditors,' and such agitation occasionally did lead to substantive change.[7] Only a few outside critics called for the government to require published accounts in order to prevent (in the words of the *Times* City editor in 1838) 'possible projects of unprincipled adventurers.'[8] For the most part, customers mainly relied on agents to learn how to distinguish among different insurers, as well as treatises written by actuaries on behalf of the life insurance office that employed them.[9] A handful of legal and actuarial textbooks provided some information, but their lack of appreciation for practical business matters hindered their usefulness.[10]

This insular environment altered in 1840, with the failure of the Independent & West Middlesex. Got up by a physician, a smuggler, and two lawyers, this company opened its doors in 1836 and collected nearly £250,000 in insurance premiums and annuity deposits by December 1840, when its partners divided the company's assets and fled the country. It appointed to its board tradesmen whose names conveniently resembled those of eminent gentlemen; matched the lowest premiums available while burning through a quarter of them in agency commissions; and granted annuities at impossibly generous rates – which was a quicker method of getting ignorant investors to part with their money than the gradual accretion of insurance premiums would have allowed.[11] Peter Mackenzie devoted the March 1839 issue of his *Scottish Reformers' Gazette* to exposing the Independent & West Middlesex as 'a quack company, got up for the premeditated purpose of imposing on the public in matters of fire and life,' then spent the next two years defending himself against a libel suit. He handed his campaign over to the London solicitor Sir Peter Laurie, who spurred a parliamentary inquiry. Chaired by William Gladstone, the committee spent half its time focusing on the Independent & West Middlesex and other 'remarkable cases of miscarriage' and the rest gathering evidence about the status of company accounts more generally.[12]

The primary outcome of Gladstone's committee was the Joint Stock Companies Act of 1844, which required all new companies to provide a registrar with annual balance sheets, a list of shareholders, and the amount of shares that had been subscribed and paid up. The requisite balance sheet was defined a year later to be 'a true statement of the capital stock, credits and property of every description belonging to the company ... and a distinct view of the profit and loss.' This may have been adequate for a brewery, but it was too vague to offer a meaningful check on a life insurance office, which could show an apparent profit for many years before claims started to fall due. Actuaries from older firms attacked the returns as 'grievously defective' and predicted that the new law would 'open the door to still worse doctoring and cooking of accounts' than were committed before 1844. It was impossible, however, for any such critic to avoid the countercharge that few older offices published any accounts at all and that none were required to do so. When Robert Christie of the Scottish Equitable saw fit to publish a sampling of offending accounts in 1852, a Manchester actuary called it 'a good canvassing squib' from an actuary whose employer was 'not under parliamentary *surveillance*.'[13]

A growing sense of dissatisfaction on all sides prompted a second parliamentary inquiry in 1853, but this failed to deliver any new legislation. Tangible reform was stymied by actuaries' inability to agree on a standard method of valuing liabilities, paired with prevalent laissez-faire attitudes in Parliament.[14] While reformers wrung their hands, new life insurance offices increasingly ignored even the imperfect provisions of the 1844 statute. Fewer than half of all insurers that formed between 1851 and 1860 bothered to report their paid-up capital, and less than a third of all registered offices made any returns at all between 1856 and 1863. All this was ample evidence of the 'contempt and neglect' into which the 1844 act had fallen, as the author of *The Balance Sheets of Insurance Companies* complained in 1863; and still, he added, there remained 'no proof of a public nature' that life offices predating 1844 were sound. By 1870 most people involved with life insurance

would have agreed with Samuel Smiles's assessment that 'a more stu-
pid and worthless measure never became law.'[15]

Although he was not very effective at regulating them, the Joint Stock
Companies Registrar had no shortage of newly established English life
insurance offices to look after – but virtually no Scottish ones. The lack
of new start-ups in Scotland had almost nothing to do with the 1844
statute and almost everything to do with the formation of the Associated
Scottish Life Offices four years earlier. This group originated when a few
Edinburgh managers decided to hold quarterly meetings as a means of
'keeping up the good understanding which at present prevailed among
the Offices'; by 1845 it expanded to include Glasgow and Aberdeen managers, and through the end of the century its dozen or so members lobbied Parliament, restrained overly aggressive competition, and established effective entry barriers against would-be rivals.[16] Since many
Scottish managers were lawyers and accountants as well as actuaries,
they were able to influence access to the investment capital and customers that start-ups would have required. Member offices also innovated in
tandem, which pre-empted the introduction of competitive products that
were giving many of the new English offices a leg up on older firms.

English actuaries took steps to regulate their increasingly chaotic
market by looking to Scotland for inspiration and advice. The upshot
was the establishment of the Institute of Actuaries in 1848, which included representatives from all the Scottish firms and aimed to moderate competition by certifying actuaries from new companies who could
be taught to behave in a suitably professional manner.[17] Although it
soon succeeded at the narrower task of qualifying actuaries, the Institute
failed to bring order to the insurance boom. Before it even opened, thirteen actuaries from some of the oldest companies in London broke
away to form the Actuaries' Club, which spurned scientific papers at
public meetings in favour of the trade association model that had originally been pursued in Scotland – a model that was wholly inadequate
in the context of London in 1848.[18] Besides being unable to prevent this
defection, the Institute lost its Scottish contingent in 1856 owing to a
combination of logistics and a disagreement about what professional-
ism meant in practice. The Scots, already annoyed at having to troop to
London for meetings, resigned from the Institute's council after an
English member had certified the accounts of one of the firms that
Robert Christie had singled out as insolvent. They formed their own
society in Edinburgh, the Faculty of Actuaries, which was effectively an
educational arm of the Associated Scottish Life Offices.[19]

In their efforts to raise the tone of mid-Victorian life insurance, actuaries found uneasy allies among the swelling ranks of free-lance writers and magazine editors who viewed the burst in company formation as a splendid business opportunity. Dozens of books with titles like *A Popular View of Life Assurance* and *What Is Life Assurance?* provided nutshell histories, brief discussions of vital statistics, anodyne injunctions to insure, summaries of the unique features of each life office, and tabular comparisons of premiums. Their authors offered these guides as substitutes 'for the mysteries of the Actuary, or the studied labour of the Partial Advocate' – although many of them were in fact actuaries who worked for newly formed life offices.[20] Despite their many faults, they did provide a clear and reasonably balanced (if flowery) survey of what had become an incredibly complicated market, at little or no expense to the consumer. And by the 1860s, when a backlash had set in against the newer companies, a wave of more critical guides appeared that mirrored the newfound lack of consumer trust, using what they could from Board of Trade returns to help customers make safe decisions.[21]

The 1840s also witnessed the rise of a thriving insurance press, pioneered by Hooper Hartnoll's *Post Magazine*. Initially a general news outlet with a few insurance advertisements, within a decade the *Post Magazine* focused exclusively on insurance. Although Hartnoll shared the guidebook writers' missionary zeal, he had a fiercely independent streak and heedlessly butted heads with people if he thought their actions were bad for the reputation of insurance. His coverage of the dismal failure of the Sea Fire & Life in 1850 resulted in a libel suit, and he reported with relish on company promoters' antics.[22] Hartnoll also edited the *Post Magazine Almanack* annually from 1841, which provided (in his words) 'a full and carefully arranged collection of details respecting the Assurance offices in Great Britain' and which remains to this day a trusted reference work.[23] Both the magazine and the almanac had their share of imitators, most of which lasted only a year or two and were more obviously beholden to advertisers than Hartnoll was.[24] With some exceptions, the new insurance press supported the Institute of Actuary's aims. A bias in favour of professional standards was especially evident in the *Insurance Record*, which first appeared in 1864 and became a leading rival of the *Post Magazine*.[25]

Amalgamation and Failure, 1860–1870

The merger movement of the 1850s and 1860s was either a good or a bad thing depending on which company did the absorbing. Standard

Life and the Liverpool both grew stronger by means of an energetic acquisitions policy.[26] Most successful of all was the Eagle, which by 1866 had on its books policies originally issued by twenty different life insurance offices. As early as 1826 it purchased the United Empire as a means of facing 'the daily increasing competition in Life assurance,' and starting in 1846 its directors fended off what they called a 'vortex of an extravagant and dangerous competition' with a strategy of aggressive acquisition. When its bid to buy Pelican Life that year failed, it acquired the Protector, which came with the actuary Charles Jellicoe – a sworn enemy of 'old-fogeyism.'[27] Under his guidance, the Eagle acquired three other established firms in the next decade. From there it went after newer companies that could pass Jellicoe's rigorous actuarial tests, including the City of London in 1859 and the National Mercantile in 1866. Besides gaining renewal income from already purchased policies, the Eagle absorbed agents from many of its acquisitions, with the result that its new premium income increased five-fold between 1846 and 1866.[28]

Despite these success stories naysayers argued that amalgamation could seldom undo the absorbed offices' excessive expenditure and that it usually added to a company's costs by burdening the absorbing firm with extra legal fees and compensation packages for redundant directors and staff.[29] This perspective soon received ringing confirmation when the Albert failed in 1869 and the European followed suit in 1871. Between them, these two firms had purchased the business of sixty-nine different offices by the time they failed, and seven smaller firms failed between 1867 and 1874 after absorbing nineteen more companies.[30] The *Economist* greeted the Albert's failure by warning that amalgamation was 'in the last degree dangerous; you are buying what is insolvent, and what is sold because it is insolvent, and in all likelihood you will lose.' Four years earlier a disgruntled European director accurately described his company as a combination of insolvent companies rolled 'into one temporary structure of gigantic dimensions,' which would 'fall with a more disastrous crash when the time of its dissolution comes.'[31]

The history of the Albert and the European illustrates why they fell disastrously short of the Eagle's successful acquisition strategy. The Albert began as the Freemasons & General, one of two new companies in the late 1830s that catered specially to masons. After changing its name in 1849, it purchased ten life insurance offices between 1854 and 1865 and expanded into fire and marine coverage in 1864. The main difference between the Albert's acquisitions and the Eagle's concerned the financial health of the companies it absorbed and what it paid for their business. Two of the Albert's three largest purchases, the Family Endowment and the Medical Invalid, faced imminent insolvency when it stepped in with offers that enriched the two companies' shareholders and staff by nearly £100,000. Especially revealing was the £91,642 the Albert paid in 1858 as goodwill to the Bank of London, which boasted a large premium income but was saddled with an expensive branch network. When the Eagle bought the similarly constituted City of London the following year, it sweetened the deal by only £12,000, and quickly sold off its expensive industrial insurance branch to the Prudential. In all, the Albert spent £274,152 as compensation to the shareholders and staff of its absorbed firms, which was roughly equivalent to the deficit revealed by its 1866 valuation.[32]

Like the Albert, the European prefaced its meteoric rise and fall in the 1860s with several decades of unremarkable progress. Founded in 1819 with a healthy annuity business, in 1858 the European became the seventh life insurance office to amalgamate with the People's Provident over the five years that the latter firm had been in existence. Although the combined office had some strong suits, it was also saddled with an expensive branch network and more directors than it could afford. A year after buying the European's business, the People's Provident took its name, as well, and then went back to shopping for additional companies. Its first mistake was to accept the transfer of policies from the Professional, which failed in 1861 more than £200,000 in the red. Its second mistake was to absorb the British Nation, which had purchased eight life offices in its own right (representing twenty-eight distinct companies) between 1858 and 1863. The European spent more than £200,000 for all this business, and squandered an additional £50,000 in managers' salaries and commission fees between 1865 and 1869.[33]

The response of the financial press, the actuarial profession, and especially the legal system to these fiascos made it clear that the regulatory environment of English life insurance needed reform. Efforts by journalists to blow the whistle were substantially muted by the threat of litigation: the European charged three London papers with contempt of court for commenting adversely on its case before it had gone to trial, and the Albert sued a Calcutta newspaper for libel.[34] Actuaries hesitated to speak out for the same reason, and their authority was further weakened by the fact that both the Albert and the European had been able to find leading actuaries to certify the methods and results of their valuations shortly before failing.[35] Even if criticisms by journalists and actuaries had been more effective, however, they would have faced the problem that the Chancery judge who was assigned the European case in October 1869, Sir William James, refused to admit that a life insurance office's long-term liabilities called for a special definition of insolvency. This allowed the European to stay in business for two more years until another judge finally agreed to wind it up. Besides being wrong about the European, James was also inconsistent: although the Albert was in better shape at the time, litigants convinced him in August 1869 to order its liquidation.[36]

For both the Albert and the European, a winding up order was only the beginning of a long series of lawsuits that would cast a pall over British life insurance for another decade. The Albert spent two futile years trying to find a company willing to pay reduced claims out of its uncalled share capital, and prospective buyers spurned the European's similar proposals late in 1871.[37] That year began the decade-long process of getting shareholders from the two companies to pay their calls. Most of these arbitration hearings pitted policyholders against shareholders from acquired companies, who claimed that they had been improperly informed of or had never consented to the transfer of their business. Judges mainly sided with the shareholders in these cases, further eroding the capital that was available for paying the companies' claims.[38] When all was said and done, the only real winners were the lawyers, who emerged more than £360,000 richer from the carcasses of the failed companies.[39]

How much Albert and European policyholders suffered depended on how long they had held their policies and on the availability of share capital. People who bought their insurance directly from the European received less than 5s in the pound; they fared better if they had bought their policies from the several companies that paid in full. On the other hand, 'paid in full' in these cases did not mean what it usually did for a creditor of an insolvent company. Only annuitants and beneficiaries of claims that had fallen due during liquidation actually received the face value of the policy; the rest got a surrender value, which was seldom more than half of the premiums they had paid. In practice, younger customers barely suffered at all from the failure, since they typically lost only £10 or £20 in premiums and could easily buy a new policy somewhere else at just slightly higher rates. Older or unhealthy customers, in contrast, might lose more than £100 in premiums, and even if they could find another company to insure them it might be more than twice as expensive on account of their age or health.[40] In other words, the failures reversed the usual function of life insurance, whereby the more fortunate in a group subsidize the less fortunate.

Life Insurance after the Life Assurance Companies Act

In 1870, when the boom was turning into a bust, Parliament intervened by passing the Life Assurance Companies Act. The law's unprecedented publicity requirements for all life insurance offices made it easier for regulators, journalists, and policyholders to distinguish strong from shaky insurers, and its restrictions on company formation and amalgamation helped to stabilize an industry that was already in the process of weeding out its unhealthiest firms. For several generations after its passage, virtually everyone associated with British life insurance embraced the new law as a watershed. Insurance directors and actuaries referred to the decades prior to 1870 as 'the era of unwritten history' and 'the "dark ages,"' and they called the subsequent period 'a new era,' ushering in 'the most important epoch in the history of life insurance.'[41] Most such references focused on the newly available information the law enabled: 'a flood of light' in contrast to 'operations ... very much more in the dark' prior to 1870. The counterweight to this better publicity was 'the absolute liberty of action' that the law allowed firms regarding their internal management, which British insurance men were quick to contrast with similar laws in North America and continental Europe. As far as they were concerned, the British had perfected regulation by aligning the forces of the state with the market instead of pitting one against the other.[42]

In practical terms, the law's most significant impact concerned the marketing of bonuses. Before 1870 new life insurance offices frequently promised unrealistically high surpluses, based on overly optimistic projections of future investment yields and low mortality. By enforcing a much clearer statement of liabilities, the Life Assurance Companies Act almost immediately put a stop to this practice and over time created an incentive for companies to hold back more of their funds for the payment of bonuses in future generations. A less frequently mentioned aspect of the new legislative framework, but at least as important, was that for the first time since the eighteenth century effective entry barriers were in place. As a result, English life insurance companies after 1870 began to act much more like their Scottish counterparts had been acting since 1840. Working through the Associated Scottish Life Offices, insurance managers north of the Tweed had long liberalized in tandem, had cautiously reserved their funds to be able to pay future bonuses, and above all had been extremely effective at restricting the formation of new companies. The Life Assurance Companies Act, together with the weeding out that had taken place in the 1860s, brought about similar results in England.

The Life Assurance Companies Act

In March 1869, five months before the Albert failed, a Bristol banker named Stephen Cave introduced a bill into Parliament 'requiring the registration and publication of the Accounts and valuations of Life Assurance Companies.' The Associated Scottish Life Offices expressed their 'general support' of the bill, as did a meeting of London managers; the Guardian's actuary spoke for the majority when he hoped that a new law would quell 'a very uneasy feeling out of doors ... that assurance companies were not in that sound condition in which they ought to be.' Cave, who had been vice president of the Board of Trade under the Conservatives in 1866, worked closely with these managers through the summer, but had to withdraw his bill in July when he fell ill.[43] When he reintroduced the bill the following February, the intervening scandals (together with the companies' continued support) guaranteed its passage. In addition to the annual accounts already required under the 1844 statute, the Life Assurance Companies Act imposed a £20,000 deposit on all newly projected companies, outlined clearer rules for the winding up of companies, made it easier for policyholders to block a company's amalgamation, and forced all companies to publish a valuation of assets and liabilities every five years.[44]

The valuation requirement was by far the most important, since it came closest to addressing the root cause of the recent failures. Although the law did not prescribe a valuation method, the fact that it required companies to state their method focused discussion on this topic as never before. The key issue concerned how actuaries treated expenses. Most valuations in the first half of the nineteenth century (using the 'gross premium' method) had enabled life insurance offices to fudge on this point, by deducting the estimated future premium income from the liabilities and then adding the estimated future expenses. This had allowed the Albert, for instance, to look much healthier than it actually was, by wishing away the expensive agency network that it had acquired over the previous decade. Actuaries who had testified at the Albert's winding-up trial promoted 'net premium' valuations instead:

these assumed no future income or expenditure and instead simply deducted expected claims from the present assets and anticipated interest. The upshot of this method was to require a larger reserve fund; and within a decade of 1870, almost all British actuaries stood behind the net premium valuation as the best way to estimate liabilities.[45]

While Cave's proposed legislation worked its way through Parliament, not everyone was convinced that more publicity was the answer to the problems besetting British life insurance. Outcries appeared regarding 'the mephitic influence of red-tape regulations' and the bill's 'inquisitorial' schedules; and, as the *Economist* noted in 1869, 'the European did give a good many figures, which actuaries fought over till the public were confused.'[46] Others complained that the bill did not go far enough: Gladstone's Chancellor of the Exchequer, Robert Lowe, likened it to 'the stringent laws that have been passed in Massachusetts and New York ... with the sting taken out.' What counted most, though, given the Board of Trade's poor success at enforcing prior laws, was that life insurance offices were squarely behind this one. Thomas Sprague of the Scottish Equitable articulated what would be an enduring consensus among actuaries when he praised the act in 1872 as 'a happy mean between the old system of leaving the public to make unaided their own enquiries ... and the American system of State supervision.'[47]

The only sticking point, and it was resolved fairly quickly, concerned whether the Board of Trade would accept returns 'simply because they could not make head or tail [of] them' (in Sprague's words) or force all firms to render their accounts intelligible. The two officials responsible for receiving the returns, W.R. Malcolm and R.G.C. Hamilton, initially assumed the latter. To this end, they issued a report in which they ranked companies by the proportion of expenses to premium income, described the merits of different mortality tables, and scolded companies that assumed that a future reduction in expenses would offset large liabilities. Actuaries and directors from older London firms, which tended to spend less on new business and hence did well in such comparisons, praised Malcolm and Hamilton for their 'remarkable ability' and bragged about their ranking. Actuaries from companies with more aggressive (and expensive) marketing strategies, which included most of the Scottish firms, protested that the officials had gone too far. The Scots won this battle: an Associated Scottish Life Offices delegation emerged from a meeting in 1875 with the news that Board of Trade officials had decided that bringing an end to such reports would 'relieve them of much difficulty and anxiety.'[48]

The compromise that the Board of Trade settled on for the next quarter century was to write letters to companies that appeared to be evading the law, then publish the correspondence if the company refused to bend. Although those companies that were on the receiving end of this treatment reproached the Board's 'sneering, discourteous manner,' the system generally worked well. The red flags, which included heavy expense rates and poor valuation methods, mainly echoed those raised in the 1874 report; but since most of the firms that the Board singled out for comment were either industrial offices or on the verge of insolvency, few mainstream actuaries bemoaned this form of interference. And from the Board's perspective, its procedure had the salutary advantage of giving its officials something useful to do. As the *Bankers' Magazine* commented in 1890: 'The official mole throws up earth to show us that he has been burrowing underneath some account whose workings he is striving to discover, and then bring into harmony with the Board of Trade ways.'[49]

At first the new Board of Trade returns trickled down to customers through relatively narrow channels. A few companies recycled their Board-mandated accounts in special circulars, and in 1875 a Bristol firm distilled the manuscript returns into a chart, 'carefully revised and checked by the Offices themselves.' Most commentators agreed, however, that the new returns by themselves were next to useless: as one trade journal put it, they possessed 'all the characteristics of a proverbially uninviting Blue Book.'[50] The real breakthrough came from a new genre of insurance guides that began to appear in the late 1870s. Initially compiled by clerks or branch secretaries in their spare time, then later by full-time brokers, these arranged the new official returns in forms that were easier for would-be policyholders to digest. Bearing titles like *Where Shall I Get the Most for My Money* (1883) and *Where to Insure* (1890), these guides initially focused on the ratio of expenses to premium income, which was all that could be gleaned from the Board of Trade returns in the 1870s. After 1880 they started to 'deal exhaustively with the subject of the *Bonus Additions to Life Policies*': a typical table showed 'what £25 a Year Will Yield' at different ages over various periods of time.[51]

During the two decades when the Life Assurance Companies Act was starting to make an impact, managers built on the common ground they had achieved in 1869–70 to forge more coherent strategies for self-regulation. The Institute of Actuaries wore down the Actuaries' Club (and the Privy Council) to force a merger in 1884, in the process acquiring a royal charter. English managers also moved closer to the Scottish trade association model, forming the Life Offices' Association in 1889 to promote common interests through 'consultation and combined action.' Although the larger number of English firms restricted the association's effectiveness, it was reasonably successful at lobbying Parliament, and at the very least it provided a forum where managers could compare notes.[52] In Scotland cooperation continued apace. The Faculty of Actuaries received a charter in 1868, and it worked closely with the Institute on major mortality investigations in the 1860s and 1890s. After 1890 the Associated Scottish Life Offices regularly prodded the Life Offices' Association to follow its more proactive example in forming a common front.[53]

The confluence of more effective government supervision, better sources of information for consumers, and emerging standards of self-regulation among life insurance offices improved the chances for a stable and profitable life insurance industry after 1870. For several companies that had entered the 1870s in a shaky financial condition, however, the new framework was unable to prevent their failure – and in some cases may have assisted in their downfall. The two largest of these, the Great Britain Mutual and the Briton Medical & General, had grown in the same decade as the Albert and the European, and fell for similar reasons.[54] A brief description of the BMG's rise and fall reveals the limits of the Life Assurance Companies Act as a damage control mechanism and provides further insight into the complicated nature of insolvency as applied to life insurance.

With over twenty-six thousand policyholders as of 1874, the growth of the Briton Medical & General in the 1860s had mirrored that of the Albert and the European. After several unremarkable decades as the Briton, in 1862 the company purchased the shaky business of the Unity General and the New Equitable. With these transfers came a name change, followed by the aggressive establishment of a branch network. One last acquisition, of the Scottish Indisputable in 1866, made the BMG an overnight presence in Scotland as well.[55] What happened to the company between 1874 and its demise in 1886 was subject to two different interpretations. Its defenders held that its days of costly expansion were behind it and that it was looking forward to the profitable consolidation of the lower-middle-class market that it had built up. Its detractors countered that its past profligacy was an irreversible burden on its ability to meet its claims – and this view ended up being taken seriously enough to become a self-fulfilling prophecy. From July 1874, when the first alarm sounded, until the end of that year, nearly 30 per cent of the

BMG's policyholders lapsed or transferred their business to another company, drastically increasing an already high ratio of fixed costs to premium income.[56]

Adding to the company's troubles was the unique course that it pursued to survive its crisis. Spurning both liquidation and the transfer of its business to a caretaker office, the Briton Medical & General spun off a new company, the Briton, under the same management as the existing office and with the same branch network, which would accept new business while administering premium collection and claims payment for the moribund BMG. This plan looked good enough on paper to win the approval of leading actuaries, with the proviso that the new company would refuse to pay surrender values on BMG policies and would pay no dividends to shareholders until the old company was out of the red. It stood little chance of succeeding for the simple reason that that its directors ignored both provisos. Between 1875 and 1884 the Briton paid out more than £100,000 on surrendered policies, and it paid an average of 9.5 per cent on its capital through 1880. The directors' promises that the Briton's costs would diminish under the new scheme proved to be equally off the mark. The final blow came in 1885, when its manager died before completing an overdue valuation. The accountants who came in to finish the job discovered that he had fleeced the company of more than £100,000, in addition to masking £400,000 in unreported liabilities. In February 1886 the BMG was wound up, and a year later the Briton's policies were transferred to another company.[57]

Although most of the Briton Medical & General's wounds were self-inflicted, the new regulatory regime after 1870 rendered its final decade rockier than might have otherwise been the case. Thomas Bond Sprague, who was one of the most vocal advocates of the Life Assurance Companies Act, led the charge against the BMG in 1874 – claiming the high ground of actuarial standards, without mentioning the threat posed by the firm's new Edinburgh branch to his own quest for new business at the Scottish Equitable. While Sprague blanketed the insurance press with excerpts from Board of Trade returns that were designed to prove the company's insolvency, the Board spent the summer finding fault with its valuation, then published the ensuing correspondence. When a defender of the BMG claimed that the company 'had been bullied by the Board of Trade, and most unfairly,' Sprague responded on its behalf that it was only doing its job. It was with at least some justification that a Nottingham policyholder later argued that 'alarmists' in the insurance press, combined with 'vulture like' salesmen from rival companies, made the BMG's bad situation worse by scaring so many customers into dropping their policies.[58]

A silver lining in this story of reckless management and ineffectual regulation concerned the thirteen thousand policyholders who had stuck with the Briton Medical & General through its travails, and who fared better in the end than their counterparts in the Albert and the European. Their directors' blunders and its manager's crimes had left BMG in even worse financial shape than either of those firms: only £282,000 in assets against £1.15 million in liabilities. The difference, from the customers' perspective, was that the Life Assurance Companies Act provided clearer instructions to the Chancery judge to find a healthy life insurance office to take over the BMG's policies if at all possible. After the policyholders approved of this course, the judge deputed a consulting actuary to run the firm for five more years until Sun Life finally stepped in. By continuing to collect premiums and investing them at compound interest, Sun Life was able to pay between 50 per cent and 90 per cent of the face value of the policies – a vast improvement over liquidation, which would have netted policyholders less than a third of their paid-in premiums minus huge legal costs. Ten years earlier, members of the Great Britain Mutual (worth four shillings in the pound when it failed in 1881) agreed to a similar arrangement with the National of Ireland, which paid between 44 per cent and 95 per cent of the policies' face value over the next several decades.[59]

Settling Down, 1880–1914

As the nineteenth century came to an end most British life insurance offices could afford to dismiss the Briton Medical & General and similar failures as exceptional hangovers from an earlier era – and the Board of Trade agreed, after briefly considering further reform in response to outside criticism of the industry in the 1880s. Business grew steadily, with sums insured rising from £293 million in 1870 to £870 million in 1914, and with this enormous growth the nature of competition altered.[60] Above all, and most directly attributable to the Life Assurance Companies Act, life offices newly vied with each other to provide the greatest long-term security, claiming that they could offer higher bonuses in thirty years' time, rather than lower prices or higher yields in the present. As one actuary told the House of Lords in 1906: 'Our companies ... make enormously stronger reserves than any others. There is competition between them to stand well.'[61]

In contrast to previous laws, which encouraged the formation of new companies without holding them sufficiently accountable, the 1870 statute shifted the balance in favour of companies with strong reserves and a long history of paying claims. The easiest measure of strength, in this regard, was the level of interest life insurance offices assumed in its valuation, since (under the net premium method) a firm's future yield was the only variable with a significant margin of error. Assumed interest reached as low as 2.5 per cent in some cases by 1900, and it was often at least a full percentage point below a company's actual yields. As the Norwich Union announced in 1901, its conservative valuation had placed the firm 'in the very front rank as regards the strength of its reserves, and in doing so secures the maintenance of large future bonuses.' Life insurance offices achieved further distance from the prior generation's mushroom companies by drawing attention to their long history, which often spanned a century or more by the 1920s. The Rock's centenary celebration in 1906 of its 'venerable "Age, Wealth, Security and Stability"' typified this trend.[62]

The official publication of expense ratios initially appeared to prove that the best way to build strong reserves was to keep costs at a minimum. As the Royal Exchange's actuary advised in 1885, 'the very soundest offices ... should simply endeavour to hold their own for a time, and trust to the public being educated, as they assuredly soon will be, through the Board of Trade returns.'[63] The problem with this way of thinking was that low costs would only produce a large reserve if a steady stream of new customers showed up to replace those who died off – otherwise, claims would increase as the company collectively aged and reserves would decline.[64] As discussed in the previous chapter, after 1880 figuring out how to spend enough money to attract new customers without detracting from the bonus was the central question facing any company with a large branch network.

Another strategy for squaring increased costs with the need for stronger reserves was to take advantage of the economies of scale that came from amalgamation. Although this would eventually be a very popular option, it took time for most life insurance offices to get past the tendency (in the wake of the Albert and the European failures) to identify amalgamation with insolvency. Just twenty mergers took place in the first two decades after 1872, and many of those were clean-up operations. Revealingly, the two exceptions involved Scottish firms, which were mostly immune from guilt by association with the scandals of the late 1860s.[65] In England, most companies took pains to advertise

that amalgamation was the last thing on their agenda. A Sceptre director reminded shareholders in 1878, for instance, that the company had
always 'refused to entertain a proposal to amalgamate with another office long before the evil of amalgamations had been made manifest by
subsequent failures.'[66]

After 1889, however, life insurance mergers migrated south from
Scotland. Although they held steady at around one per year in the 1890s,
most involved London firms; then fifty mergers transpired in the next
two decades. In all, twenty-four of the twenty-seven life insurance offices that acquired another life office's business between 1890 and 1920
were English. The Alliance, after building a branch network by means of
provincial purchases in the 1880s, bought four struggling London rivals
between 1888 and 1911; Pelican Life acquired the British Empire Mutual
in 1902 and then in 1910 formalized its long association with Phoenix
Fire; and the Law Union picked up the Crown in 1891 and the Rock in
1909. The Liverpool-based Royal, meanwhile, acquired five provincial
rivals between 1891 and 1919, and the Norwich Union added to its presence in London by purchasing the Reliance and the Victoria Mutual, and
in Scotland by absorbing the Scottish Imperial. Although the Commercial
Union ventured into the working-class market by acquiring the Liverpool
Victoria Legal in 1913, consolidation among industrial firms generally
went on without the involvement of 'ordinary' offices.[67]

Augustus Hendriks of the Liverpool & London & Globe captured the
primary incentive for most late Victorian life insurance mergers, when
he observed in 1892 that amalgamation provided 'a haven of safety and
of good results to the assured, arising out of the economy of expenditure and the concentration of energy upon a condensed field of operation.' Most tangibly, it equipped a life insurance office with 'a new
army of agents and officials for its aggressive work' (as the *Economist*
noted in 1909) at little or no cost. Mergers could also enhance the appearance of safety through the acquisition of another office's antiquity.
In a third of all mergers between 1890 and 1920 involving firms of comparable stature, an older office transferred its business to a younger
one, and in another third the transferring firm was at least fifty years
old. The Norwich Union, which bought the Amicable in 1866, tacked a
lengthy bicentenary history of the latter onto its own centenary in 1908;
the Commercial Union, which had formed in 1861, bought the oldest
provincial English life office (the West of England) in 1894 and the two
oldest surviving London insurers (the Union and the Hand-in-Hand) in
1905 and 1907.[68]

By reducing the overall number of firms, the merger movement made self-regulation through bodies like the Life Offices' Association and the Associated Scottish Life Offices more effective. Self-regulation also gained from the rise of composites after 1880, since this brought a strong tradition of self-regulation among fire insurance offices into clearer focus as a model for the rest of the industry. Dating back to 1860 (and before that, through less formal tariff treaties), members of the Fire Offices' Committee had effectively regulated prices, salvage operations, and policy conditions.[69] Most of these tactics equally applied to accident coverage, and in 1906 the Accident Offices Association formed on the model of the Fire Offices' Committee. Both of these organizations boasted higher levels of cooperation than even the Associated Scottish Life Offices had ever exercised, and certainly were more effective than the Life Offices' Association. The establishment in 1917 of an umbrella organization, the British Insurance Association, extended the new multidivisional structure of insurance to the realm of self-regulation.[70]

If the rise of composites prompted self-regulation along the lines of fire and accident insurance, it extended to fire and accident coverage the model of state supervision that had originally been limited to life offices. After nearly forty years with no major insurance-related regulation, Parliament passed a new Assurance Companies Act in 1909 that included all branches of the industry except for marine and motor insurance. Although the new law owed more to recent scandals involving American life insurance offices than to the composite movement, its primary effect was (in the words of the *Times*) 'to protect the interests of nearly all classes of policyholders.' It extended many features of the 1870 act to other branches of insurance, including a £20,000 deposit (now required for all companies, not just start-ups) and annual returns of assets and premium income. Life insurance managers had significant input in drafting the 1909 statute, with the result that few new wrinkles applied to them. Its major innovations were to require insurers to state the principles by which they valued assets as well as liabilities, and to clarify the meaning of 'insurable interest' in industrial policies. In general, actuaries received the new law in the same positive manner as they had the old one. Henry Andras of the Alliance was typical in his prediction that it would 'still further purge Life Assurance business from well-known imperfections without checking its healthy development.'[71]

Conclusion

The mantra of 'freedom with publicity,' which managers repeated with near-religious fervour in the decades after 1870, continued to inform British insurance regulation well into the twentieth century. A new insurance law in 1946 introduced new capital requirements, but otherwise confirmed the status quo. The simple reason for this relative lack of legislative activity was the sector's impressive record of stability: after the failure of the Briton Medical & General in 1886, nearly nine decades passed before another British life insurance company went into liquidation. When Nation Life failed in 1974, after linking much of its coverage to disastrous property bond speculations, the impact on the industry was comparable to the Albert's failure a century earlier. The upshot was the Policyholders Protection Act of 1975, which replaced 'freedom with disclosure' with 'freedom with responsibility' – requiring all life insurance offices to contribute to a fund that would guarantee at least 90 per cent of the liabilities in any future insolvency. Although managers grumbled at the time that this law would encourage 'irresponsibility among policyholders and disreputable insurers,' it has continued to govern life insurance in Britain ever since.[72]

When the regulatory regime of 'freedom with publicity' first appeared in Britain in 1870, it was generally viewed as an example of uniquely strict state intervention. Its accounting provisions far exceeded those required by the similar Regulation of Railways Act (1868) or Gas Works Clauses Act (1871), which only called for simple balance sheets, and these in turn exceeded the regulations facing most other companies into the twentieth century. Although the immediate context for this heightened state supervision was the disarray into which life insurance had plunged during the 1860s, it owed at least as much to policyholders' alleged status as exceptionally deserving of financial protection. Many contemporaries assumed that encouragers of a uniquely disciplinary form of thrift should themselves be subject to a higher standard of government control: as a legal treatise put it in 1875, the provisions of the 1870 act were justified on the grounds of 'the vital interest which the most quiet, industrious, and unspeculative part of the community has in their stability.'[73]

For most British life insurance offices, increased transparency was a price they were more than willing to pay for being able to reclaim the moral high ground and economic stability that the events of the 1860s had endangered. From the perspective of English offices, an additional payoff of the 1870 act was the new entry barriers it erected. Together with the further weeding out of the market in the 1880s and the new wave of mergers after 1890, the result was a pronounced consolidation of business relative to the dispersion that had taken place among English offices at mid-century. The ten largest English non-industrial firms in 1910 earned 38 per cent of total U.K. premium income, compared with just 26 per cent in 1872. The five largest Scottish life offices, in contrast, fell in market share from 19 per cent in 1872 to 15 per cent four decades later. English offices built from this stronger foundation to catch and surpass their Scottish counterparts in the work of branch formation: they went from administering less than half to nearly three-fourths of British branch offices (leaving out foreign and colonial firms) between 1870 and 1910.[74]

Partly as a result of this consolidation, and partly because of parallel changes within the industry, both 'freedom' and 'publicity' meant very different things than what they had meant prior to the passage of the 1870 act. Before 1870 lack of government regulation translated into an enormous diversity in practice among English firms, which collectively worked to the advantage of the Scottish firms with their far more coherent set of industry norms. While older London firms resisted change into the 1860s, they let Scottish (and a few northern English) insurance offices achieve a monopoly in the ability to combine novel marketing methods with an assurance of financial stability. Despite the fact that the government preserved much of this freedom after 1870, consolidation, the rise of branch networks, and stronger self-regulation among English firms led to a decline in this diversity. By 1910 policyholders had much less to choose from among different life insurance offices, and many more options within any individual company, as menus of 'fancy schemes' became the norm.

'Publicity,' finally, did not evolve in quite the direction that many insurance reformers had assumed would be the case in the immediate wake of the Life Assurance Companies Act. In theory, that law greatly increased customers' access to trustworthy facts about financial performance and valuation methods: in contrast to the complete absence of any such data for most companies that had formed prior to 1844, and the random and unreliable nature of returns by companies that had formed since then, in the decades after 1870 the Board of Trade produced hundreds of pages of increasingly reliable and intelligible accounts. In practice, this access was mostly mediated by actuaries, brokers, and branch managers, who took it on themselves to explain the significance of a mass of figures that provided more detail than most customers had time to digest and required more technical knowledge than most customers possessed. The number of brokers who were willing and able (for a price) to perform this job increased to meet the growing demand; and unlike in 1870, when insurance customers outside of London or Edinburgh would have been hard pressed to find more than a handful of people capable of helping them pick a life insurance office, by 1910 prospective policyholders from Aberdeen to Cardiff could compare notes with dozens of trained branch managers before settling on where to insure.[75] As will be discussed in the next chapter, publicity in this sense of the word had a profound impact on employees at all levels of the industry. As will be discussed in chapter 4, this was also a type of publicity that improved the level of trust in the numbers that life insurance offices produced while altering the meaning of that trust.

3 Doing Business

Actuaries have their sphere in the scientific department of life assurance – seeing to the soundness of the principles upon which its complex machinery revolves ... But all that work, as interesting as it is necessary, would be uncalled for were it not for those who are out on the highways compelling proposers to come in.

— Archibald Hewat, Edinburgh Life secretary,
at Manchester Insurance Institute, 1899[1]

Describing 'the characteristic movement' of a Dickens novel, the literary critic Raymond Williams referred to people who 'speak at or past each other, each intent above all on defining through his words his own identity and reality,' in the course of developing the 'profound and decisive connections' that 'are the real and inevitable relationships ... of any human society.' Although the society Williams had in mind was the Victorian city (and a fictional one at that), his depiction of the 'rush and noise and miscellaneity of this new and complex social order' in many ways captures the profusion of human interaction that was necessary for life insurance to work in Victorian culture.[2] By the end of the nineteenth century, nearly every life insurance office depended on a network of directors, actuaries, secretaries, clerks, branch managers, and inspectors, not to mention the salesmen, doctors, lawyers, and surveyors who contributed their services on a free-lance basis. All these different people, each with subtly different conceptions of themselves and of life insurance, joined together to alter, in their turn, the way policyholders viewed themselves in relation to those who depended on them financially.

On paper, the people who kept the life office's complex social order moving more or less in tandem were the directors, elected by shareholders or (in a mutual office) by policyholders. These men either appointed or delegated the appointment of the rest of the people who worked under them. In practice, directors had a great deal of control over only some aspects of the business. From the early nineteenth century they ceded much authority to actuaries, in calculating premiums and valuing policies; to secretaries and clerks, in keeping track of an exponentially increasing volume of paperwork; and to lawyers and surveyors, in navigating the treacherous landscape that came with writing deeds and lending money on property. From mid-century they ceded additional authority to branch secretaries and inspectors, who appointed and monitored agents in hundreds of towns; and to medical advisers, who determined whether candidates for insurance deviated from an evolving set of standards for health and behaviour.

Out of this assemblage of people emerged the business of life insurance. Through a series of short surveys of directors, managers, branch secretaries, and salesmen, this chapter provides some basic context for how most of these people assembled themselves over the course of the nineteenth century.[3] One thing that immediately becomes clear from such an overview is how many different walks of life needed to come together to develop a market and deliver life insurance to that market. It would be a mistake to imagine that such a heterogeneous mix of people could work together seamlessly. Instead, they worked together when and how it suited them, and they usually managed to give the impression that a single corporate strategy guided their combined efforts. Directors preached profits, actuaries preached caution, branch secretaries preached energy, and salesmen preached whatever they thought would convince a prospective customer to buy insurance. In their various ways, they were all reciting the changing ground rules of a modern society.

Managers

The financial writer John Francis could think of no other sector 'in which subordinates are so respectfully regarded' than life insurance, since the actuary was 'master of a science in which the director is generally deficient.' Although this dynamic played out differently in Scotland and England, it left its mark on the evolution of managerial hierarchies in life insurance. There were certainly other sectors in the Victorian economy in which salaried managers rose to prominence, most notably banking and railways. Yet bank directors, for instance, usually knew more about loans and discounted bills than insurance directors knew about vital statistics and compound interest. For this reason, actuaries assiduously taught directors 'the various processes [they] employed' in order to convince them of the wisdom in acting on their advice, and directors usually heeded what their managers had to say.[4]

Shareholders and Directors

For most of the nineteenth century British life insurance offices mainly governed themselves, which meant different things depending on the presence or absence of shareholders. A joint stock insurance company promised financial security to policyholders in the event of insolvency, but restricted governance to its investors. A mutual office, at least in theory, extended governance to policyholders, who elected a board of management. In practice, directors in either type of office tended to govern with little input from their constituents and a great deal of input from their salaried officials. The only thing most shareholders were expected to do was to buy insurance and get their friends to do so, too. Many pre-Victorian companies required their shareholders to take out a minimum level of insurance or sell an equivalent amount to a friend; at the Rock, this netted over a third of its premium income during its first decade.[5] Although most companies dropped such rules by 1850, they continued to urge 'the co-operation of the Shareholders in extending the Business of the Company ... by recommending their friends to insure' into the 1880s.[6]

In mutual offices, policyholders voted for their directors, but like shareholders in joint stock companies they only took part in governance in exceptional circumstances.[7] Like shareholders, policyholders in mutual firms received constant reminders that they would indirectly gain by encouraging friends to insure. The National Mutual stocked local 'boards of reference' with 'well known men who are policy holders,' and the Provident Clerks' sent each customer a proposal form and a request 'to prevail on some one of your friends to fill it up.' Such tactics were equally available to joint stock life insurance offices that paid bonuses and began to appear in their marketing after 1850. The Briton urged customers to ask after uninsured 'friends formerly forgotten, or with whom they may have since formed an acquaintance,' and a Provident circular in 1892 proposed that since it was 'practically a mutual office,' it was 'to the interest of every Policyholder to introduce new assured to the office, and thus help to increase the profits to be divided.'[8]

Life insurance shares were generally viewed as 'safe' investments, which attracted a large proportion of women and gentry. According to a list of Atlas share transfers from 1814 to 1840, of those selling stock 51 per cent were 'gentlemen' or nobility, 20 per cent were widows or spinsters, and 11 per cent were manufacturers, merchants, or financiers; another list of the same company's shareholders over its first sixty years gives a higher proportion of women (33.6 per cent), indicating that women were more likely than men to hold on to their stock. 'Class' offices featured higher concentrations of professional men among their proprietary: 27 per cent of the Clerical Medical's original shareholders were clergy and doctors, and most legal offices (either by rule or preference) attracted mostly lawyers as investors.[9]

Regardless of specific governance structures, shareholders or policyholders were nearly always content to cede the day-to-day running of a typical life insurance company to their directors and to the staff that directors appointed. Early in the nineteenth century most life office boards featured between fifteen and twenty-five directors, with the large number at least partly related to the expectation that these men sell insurance to their friends and business contacts. Scottish life insurance offices had smaller boards (averaging fourteen in number in 1841), and most English boards had diminished in size to twelve or fewer by the 1850s. By that point directors had mostly ceded the job of selling insurance to paid agents, and long strings of 'names ... attached to companies' had come to be associated with shams like the Independent & West Middlesex.[10]

Most boards drew from many different occupations, with trade, finance, and the law at the fore. Merchants and bankers, especially those with contacts abroad, were especially common in fire and life offices, which often focused on commercial and overseas risks. Lawyers formed the single largest share (37 per cent) of directors from six Edinburgh life offices in 1841; over half of the life insurance directors in Glasgow in 1842, in contrast, were merchants.[11] As in other sectors, politicians and members of the aristocracy featured prominently on life insurance boards, more for their political and social contacts than their business acumen. The large number of such men made them a 'subject open to any novelist or satirist': a typical caricature was Lord Carlton in George Sala's novel Quite Alone, who 'went to sleep with commendable regularity at church, at the Opera, in the House ... and at the board meetings of the Elephant Life Assurance Association.'[12]

Despite novelists' barbs to the contrary, being an insurance director was not (as the Prudential's chairman insisted) a simple matter of 'coming in just before the board and having a glass of wine and some biscuits.' Especially early in the century, when many tasks had yet to be delegated to actuaries or outside consultants, and when business had yet to settle into a routine, directors had more than enough to keep them occupied. One director of the Rock grumbled in 1812 that he 'spent & used ... constant attention, great pains, & continual exertion' carrying out his duties, which included appointing clerks, investing funds, interviewing candidates, monitoring salesmen, auditing accounts, and signing correspondence. Over the course of the century, boards allotted some of these tasks to smaller subcommittees and hived off the rest to other men, including physicians, agency superintendents, and professional accountants. Although late Victorian directors still signed off on recommendations from this latter array of people, their role in the company increasingly became that of setting its long-term policy as opposed to running its day-to-day affairs.[13]

Investment, either by the full board or a subcommittee, endured as a primary responsibility of insurance directors throughout the nineteenth century. By the 1860s they mostly made these decisions in smaller finance committees, which assessed surveyors' reports on prospective mortgages (or personally inspected the property), picked new stocks and bonds, and tracked the value of investments over time.[14] The subcommittee structure enabled directors with special legal, surveying, or stock market experience to focus on what they knew best, and it also protected debtors from having 'their state made public to all.' This, at least, was the theory. John Maynard Keynes, who managed the National Mutual's portfolio after becoming a director in 1919, scoffed at the notion that a handful of directors picking their favourite stocks qualified as 'risk diversification.'[15]

In England, into the 1890s, a subset of life insurance directors also served as auditors. The most common arrangement was for two directors to perform a weekly audit of receipts, which was then checked annually by a separate set of shareholder-elected auditors. Some variation on this plan was, in fact, the only legal option for English life insurance offices until 1845, when the Companies Clauses Consolidation Act first enabled directors to hand over audit work to outside consultants. In Scotland, in contrast, where accountants often acted as insurance directors and managers, outside professionals performed these audits throughout the nineteenth century. The English & Scottish Law's

Edinburgh manager took sixteen years to convince his London board to adopt *'a continuous audit* by a professional accountant, conducted at regular intervals during the year'; by the time he finally succeeded in 1889, many other London companies were making the same transition. By 1898, according to one report, 'the greater portion' of English life offices was being 'audited by professional auditors, either entirely or in association with amateur auditors.'[16]

Finally, many insurance directors personally advanced their office's business by signing up new policyholders, or at the very least bought large policies themselves.[17] Many firms additionally appointed provincial boards, for which selling insurance was their primary reason for existing. Most Scottish life insurance offices set up local boards early and often, both in other Scottish towns and in England and Ireland, and many of the fly-by-night English companies of the 1850s were fond of local boards. Although later supplemented by branch offices, many insurance companies continued to maintain or newly set up local boards into the twentieth century. The Economic's 'committee of reference' in Edinburgh, first established in 1828, was still going strong in 1893, when its actuary sent each member several pocket diaries to 'hand ... to your friends as occasion offers, with a few words of recommendation of the Society from yourself.'[18]

For the hour or two per week that directors attended a life office board, they earned anywhere from £15 to £300 a year, with additional remuneration for executive duties or extra committee work.[19] Directors' fees were smaller and farther between at provincial boards, members of which earned from five shillings to £2 for each meeting they attended, and they met anywhere from weekly to every two or three months. Most boards only paid directors for the meetings they attended and fined those who showed up late or left early 'without leave from the chair.'[20] Fees and fines were not necessarily enough to guarantee regular attendance by directors, who often had many other irons in the fire. The factory inspector James Stuart, despite being chairman of the United Kingdom Life, only attended board meetings 'above 20 times' in 1839; as he told a Parliamentary committee, 'I need never go from January to December to their meetings, except I choose ... I go when I am in town.'[21]

Actuaries

One of the first orders of business for any board of directors was to appoint the man or men who would supervise the work of the office on a day-to-day basis. The first 'modern' life insurance office, the Equitable, was also the first to refer to its salaried manager as an actuary. Deriving from *actuarius*, the Latin term for a stenographer at the Roman Senate, the actuary debuted in the Equitable's 1761 deed of settlement, with duties that roughly matched those of the life office secretary in later years. The Equitable contracted the framing of its tables and valuations out to various mathematicians, most notably the philosopher Richard Price. It was not until 1774, when Price urged the board to appoint his nephew William Morgan to be assistant actuary, that clerical and mathematical skill came together in a new definition of the job. Only twenty-four years old at the time, Morgan would set the standard for an actuary's qualifications over the course of the next half-century, on account of the stature of the Equitable, his own status as a mathematician, and his personal intervention in the careers of many would-be actuaries.[22]

Neither the actuary's title nor duties would stabilize until after the first third of the nineteenth century, and significant diversity in form and function remained long after that. Most members of the Faculty of Actuaries in Scotland were called managers by their directors, and some English offices used the terms 'registrar' or 'mathematical inspector' into the 1830s. Although job descriptions also varied, a good early working definition was Augustus De Morgan's from 1831: 'An actuary combines with the duties of a secretary those of a scientific adviser to the board ... in all matters involving calculation.' Certainly compared with later in the century, the typical actuary prior to 1840 was expected to perform a broad combination of managerial, clerical, and mathematical tasks, with an extra burden of providing new premium tables in the case of start-up firms. When the Universal formed in 1834, its directors asked Robert Christie to take minutes at all their meetings, to produce 'rates, calculations, and other matters of computation,' to 'keep the accounts of the Society,' to 'prepare and issue proposals and prospectuses for the public,' and to provide 'all necessary information and advice relating to assurance.'[23]

Throughout the nineteenth century, a leading task of most actuaries was to train and supervise clerks. Their role as educators was especially important up to the 1850s, when the Institute of Actuaries and the Faculty of Actuaries took over many of those functions. A few actuaries (including William Thomson at Standard Life and Charles Jellicoe at the Eagle) gained renown as master educators: when B.H. Todd accepted a job as the Crown's actuary in 1853, he wrote to thank Thomson for assisting in 'the formation of my business character.' Although Todd doubtless also learned a good deal of mathematics, an emphasis on character formation was not unique to Standard Life. Actuaries presided over small staffs (typically ranging from five to ten clerks) with 'almost fatherly supervision.' After 1880 this included promotion of and participation in a whole host of leisure activities, including staff magazines, performing arts, and above all, athletics. Such opportunities offered a welcome respite from increasingly routinized clerical work at the end of the nineteenth century, with the onset of addressographs, card ledgers, and formal performance reviews.[24]

English and Scottish life insurance offices pursued different methods in appointing actuaries. In a sample of English companies that formed before 1840, 17 per cent hired men with university degrees, 20 per cent hired Royal Society fellows, and fully half hired men who had published academic papers or mixed with men who did so. In contrast, only one of fourteen Scottish actuaries appointed before 1840 had a university degree, none belonged to the Royal Society, and all but two had trained to be an accountant, merchant, or solicitor. A combination of practical and social factors lay behind these divergent appointment patterns. Since most of the early English offices formed when the technical basis of life insurance was still under construction, mathematical skill counted for more than was the case in most Scottish offices, which were mainly content to borrow tables and valuation methods that had been pioneered in England. Socially, businessmen and scientists interacted more closely in London than in Edinburgh, where accountants and lawyers dominated the professional and business scene.[25]

To find mathematically qualified actuaries, English firms recruited from universities and the civil service. Thomas Galloway moved from Sandhurst to the Amicable, Joseph Sylvester went from the University of Virginia to the Equity & Law, and W.S.B. Woolhouse joined the National Loan Fund after falling out with his boss at the Nautical Almanac Office. Although Benjamin Gompertz was self-taught, he had already made a name for himself at the Royal Society by the time the Alliance appointed him in 1824, and the Cambridge-educated Thomas Edmonds had published books on political economy and vital statistics when the Legal & General tapped him to be their actuary in 1837. Such men came with the downsides of commercial ignorance and lack of commitment. Gompertz oversaw a slow erosion of available assets in the Alliance's life fund during his two-decade career as its actuary, leading to a shareholder revolt, and Woolhouse consulted for two different life insurance offices that failed in the 1870s.[26] Even academic actuaries who did better at the business side of their job regretted the time it took from their avocations. Sylvester worried a year into his job that 'my mind is being frittered away on inferior objects' (and went back to teaching mathematics within a decade), William Frend lamented that his work at the Rock kept him from astronomical observations, and Joshua Milne took early retirement from Sun Life as soon as he could afford to do so.[27]

These downsides led most English life insurance offices to depart quickly from their initial pattern of recruiting managers with no business experience: less than 10 per cent of English actuaries appointed between 1850 and 1914 lacked prior insurance training, and only 15 per cent had university degrees. In large part, companies could do this without sacrificing technical knowledge because by that time the Institute of Actuaries had emerged as an efficient system for teaching all the requisite skills to clerks. In this context, a new breed of actuary appeared on the scene, combining a Cambridge degree with on-the-job training in a manner that provided key leadership to the nascent profession. Thomas Bond Sprague, the long-time editor of the Institute's journal and one of its leading contributors, was a senior wrangler at St John's College in Cambridge before clerking for six years at the Eagle; he moved on to the Equity & Law for twelve years before ending his career at the Scottish Equitable. Francis Colenso clerked at the Norwich Union for nine years before attending Cambridge, shortly after which he became the English & Scottish Law's actuary.[28]

If the Institute of Actuaries supplied English life insurance offices with a steady supply of freshly honed experts, its emphasis on the technical side of life insurance threatened to paint actuaries into a corner. Early leaders of the Institute had worked hard to define themselves broadly as 'practically acquainted with the business of life assurance in all its details,' and they worried when politicians tried to define their job more narrowly in order to facilitate state supervision. This fear receded by the 1880s, when the Life Assurance Companies Act and a royal charter provided a clear enough sign that the government was happy to let actuaries call their own shots. What the state was willing to give, however, the evolving business environment took away. As competition intensified, and as branch networks emerged to help life offices generate demand, the 'outdoor' labour of the branch secretary and agency superintendent rose in status at the expense of the actuary's 'indoor' work – leaving the latter open to the faint praise that he was good at math but not much else. This was the gist of an 1893

Bankers' Magazine definition of the actuary, as 'an indoor officer who knows logarithms and the differential calculus and all the algebraic signs and symbols.'[29]

The English actuary's status faced a second blow after 1890 as more life insurance offices added fire or accident branches, which further diluted his authority within the office. Most composite offices featured a general manager, who literally needed to think about insurance *in general*, and not just as it applied to a single type of risk – a task that actuaries were not necessarily well equipped to do. As the *Economist* remarked in 1910, the merger movement meant that 'the quiet student busying himself with mathematical formulae will be out of date, or at best a subordinate, and the chief place given to the administrator who takes the formulae at second hand and adds to them a practical knowledge of his own.' Only in isolated cases did this sort of administrator rise through the actuarial ranks; most general managers instead had previously worked as branch secretaries or as head of a fire insurance department.[30]

In contrast to their English counterparts, Scottish actuaries seldom scaled comparable heights of technical achievement, but neither were they ever in as much danger of losing status within the office. Part of this was simply because life insurance was so dominant in Scotland: all but five of fourteen Scottish life insurance offices in 1914 exclusively sold that product. Part of the contrast, though, derived from what in 1906 the Edinburgh Life's manager called his profession's 'mixed ancestry,' which included 'the accountant, the lawyer, the banker, the insurance official, the schoolmaster, and the professional mathematician.' When the Scottish Amicable hired a new manager in 1839, the debate was whether he would be 'a well educated experienced Merchant' or 'a thorough accountant.' In 1858 the North British picked as its manager David Smith, a leading Edinburgh solicitor who sat on several bank and railway boards, over three men with more insurance experience.[31] Such cases were far from unique. In all, 37 per cent of a sample of fifty-four Scottish actuaries hired in the nineteenth century had no prior insurance experience.

This pattern persisted into the twentieth century, despite the fact that actuaries in Scotland acquired formal professional status (through the Faculty of Actuaries) roughly at the same time as they did in England. One reason for this was that the Faculty, unlike the Institute, was almost entirely educational in its focus: its only publications until 1900 were student lectures, and only a few Faculty graduates had what James McCandlish of the Scottish Union & National called 'any pretensions at all to a scientific knowledge of actuaryship.' The leaders of the profession in Scotland – including McCandlish and William Thomson at Standard Life, mainly left their mark as innovators in marketing rather than actuarial science. Thomas Marr of the Scottish Amicable could honestly say in 1883 that the Scottish actuary had little time for mere 'abstruse calculations,' but instead had 'work of a more practical kind to engage his attention.' When Marr retired eight years later, his board replaced him with an accountant, Robert Blyth, who was 'well known in Mercantile circles as an able man who has had large and varied experience in general business.'[32]

Compared with that of the actuary or manager, the secretary's job was less taxing and came with significantly less professional status. An obituary in 1890 described 'a typical secretary' (the Scottish Provident's J.S. Morton) as 'genial, efficient and popular.' In contrast to the actuary, the primary consideration in hiring a secretary was gentlemanly bearing – since he was the person with whom most customers came into contact. When the astronomer John Herschel asked John William Lubbock, a Royal Exchange director, about his son's chances to become secretary there, Lubbock responded positively, since the younger Herschel was 'a superior person by education and social position.' It was also more important for the secretary to get along with the directors, since he (and not always the actuary) attended every board meeting. Nor did it hurt to get along with the actuary or manager. Charles Prentice lost his job as the Scottish Amicable's secretary in 1870 after 'making some foolish remarks' about his boss, and the directors refused him any severance pay.[33]

Before 1850 the average starting salary for an actuary was around £500 per annum, although these rates varied widely. Mid-career, actuaries in 1850 could hope to earn around £1,100, often with subsidized housing, compared with £900 for the average insurance secretary. Actuaries working for a company that combined fire and life insurance made about £300 a year more than those working for specialist life offices, a disparity that jumped to £500 for secretaries. Only the highest-paid actuaries earned as much as mid-century bank and railway managers.[34] Actuaries' starting salaries increased significantly after 1850, topping £1,000 more often than not – still substantially less than most bank managers made, and usually less than half what their general managers earned in those firms where such a position existed.[35] As with banks and railways, life insurance offices regularly padded their actuaries' base pay with bonuses; uniquely, these bonuses came in much larger lump sums every several years rather than smaller annual additions. The reason for the difference was the tremendous amount of the extra work that actuaries (together with their staff) put in to calculate the surplus that life offices periodically divided. The average bonus paid to a sample of fifty actuaries was £579, working out to just over 10 per cent added to annual wages if spread over five years.[36]

On top of paying a salary and bonus, most life insurance offices also permitted their actuaries to pad their earnings by acting as consultants. The unique character of life insurance work, in which the mad rush of the valuation punctuated years of dull routine, freed up large amounts of time for other projects without interfering too much with their 'regular' job. Close to half of all nineteenth-century actuaries did at least some paid consulting, most commonly for another insurance office, for pension funds, or for friendly societies.[37] The nature of consultants' work for life offices shifted over time, from helping new companies get off the ground to assisting industrial or colonial firms. Pension work moved from private funds set up by Scottish professions and the East India Company to government superannuation schemes, and friendly society work became routinized after 1875, when a new law certified a set of public valuers – all but two of whom, in 1887, worked for a life insurance office.[38] Consulting opportunities were far from evenly distributed. Some actuaries, like Charles Ansell, earned consulting fees that dwarfed what they made at their life office, and they employed a staff of clerks to handle this side of their job. On top of the £1,250 plus bonus that Ansell earned annually from the Atlas, his consulting work enabled him to buy a twenty-six-acre Welsh estate in 1852 worth £3,000 a year in rental income.[39]

A final perquisite of being an actuary or secretary was job security. In a sample of 176 actuarial appointments before 1900, 74 per cent remained with the same office until they retired or died, with the former receiving paid-up life policies or pensions that ranged from half to 100 per cent of their retiring salary.[40] More than a few companies permitted their actuaries to remain employed after their usefulness had run out. When the Legal & General appointed a new actuary in 1865, they literally kicked Thomas Edmonds upstairs, requiring him to attend twice a week on the second floor; the board finally pensioned him off five years later in the interest of 'the efficient conduct of the business of the Society.' The Royal Farmers, similarly, allowed its 'frigid, and almost repellent' actuary to persist in regaling the board with outmoded advice for a dozen years after he officially retired.[41] Job security also extended into future generations: in eight different companies a son replaced his father as actuary, and several others employed one or more of an actuary's offspring as clerks.[42]

Salesmen

When in 1861 Thomas Winser of the Royal Exchange remarked that the only way to sell life insurance was through the 'personal exertion of men of intelligence, position, and local influence,' he was repeating a truth that would have been self-evident to most insurance officials a half-century earlier. What had changed since 1810 was that such men of 'local influence' were far more likely to be appointed agents, working on a commission. By one estimate the total number of British life insurance agents increased from six thousand in 1837 to a hundred thousand fifty years later, which enabled life insurance offices to tap into markets that were all but impervious to the influence of metropolitan directors and shareholders.[43] At first these agents more or less passed as proxy directors: most were lawyers, merchants, and professional men who won friends and influenced people in Britain's larger provincial centres. Further expansion into smaller market towns, together with an increased number of firms chasing after a finite number of influential townsmen, required companies to turn to people like estate agents, grocers, drapers, and chemists, who would have stuck out like a sore thumb in a London boardroom.

   Another thing that had changed since 1810 was that unsolicited life insurance had become the exception rather than the rule. Thomas Marr at the Scottish Amicable was not alone in lamenting in 1886 that the average man 'takes less pains in his endeavours to provide for the future welfare of his family than he does in ordering his coat from his tailor.' To solve this problem, life insurance offices relied more heavily on advertisements and other promotional material than ever before, and they also intensified their search for agents who could bring the force of their personality to bear on uninsured breadwinners. As Geoffrey Marks of the National Mutual explained it, 'systematic and extensive' advertising in newspapers and magazines created name recognition for a specific office, whence came 'occasional inquiries which are followed by personal canvassing.'[44] And, from the 1870s, the key to effective canvassing was a well-organized network of branches, with inspectors to appoint and monitor agents and secretaries to keep track of the incoming business.

Appointing Agents

Into the 1850s life insurance offices entrusted the task of appointing agents to directors or actuaries. Bartholomew Bidder at the Royal Exchange frequently visited and corresponded with agents, as did John Reddish at the Royal Farmers, among several others. The experience of actuaries in this role was mixed. Bidder thought his time away from London was well spent, remarking that 'a few hours of personal communication with the agent would inform him much more of the nature of assurance and of the duties that he has undertaken, than could possibly be accomplished by correspondence.' Reddish was not as sanguine. 'The task of visiting Agents is very far from agreeable particularly to a person who has travelled so much as to find no new scenes,' he complained in 1857, and he thought the benefits were meagre when balanced against 'the grumbling of some, the indifference of others, the absence of many even when advised of the intention to call upon them, and the discomfort of some of the places which he has to make his temporary home.'[45]

Reddish was likely being more candid than some of his colleagues about what must have been an inconvenient absence from his day-to-day supervision of business. Some companies got around this by convincing officials to canvass while on holiday, as when the Royal Farmers' accountant spent the week he 'usually devote[d] to angling in the Lakes of Ireland' visiting the company's English agents. Others delegated the work to clerks, who were less likely to be missed, and the Edinburgh Life's directors divided the task of contacting potential agents among themselves in order to save their manager the trouble.[46] An exception to the early pattern of 'indoor men' doubling as inspectors was the Clerical Medical, which used special-purpose travellers to appoint agents and attract shareholders for three years after forming in 1824. It picked men who were sufficiently down-at-heel to be willing to accept as little as a pound a week for their efforts, but well enough connected to mix with the classes who comprised the firm's target market. Their recruiting methods ranged from buying port and grog for Oxford's 'young dogs' to attending a Sunday school inspection with a Chelmsford rector.[47]

It took twenty-five years for another company, Standard Life, to appoint a full-time inspector, when it named William White to that position in 1849. This time other insurers quickly followed suit. The job of the inspector or agency manager, according to one Royal Exchange actuary,

was 'to appoint, *instruct*, and be in *constant communication* with agents.'
Of these three tasks, the first and foremost was (in the words of the *Post
Magazine* in 1880) 'securing new agents of pushing character and local
influence.' Inspectors' appointment tours could generate dozens of new
agents in a short period of time: an Irish inspector netted the Edinburgh
Life 114 new agents in 1868, and between 1865 and 1870 the Crown's
South of England inspector appointed two hundred agents.[48]

Once he had appointed new agents, the inspector needed to impart
information concerning the company and answer any questions they
might have. Samuel Pipkin at the Atlas urged in 1884 that inspectors
should teach agents 'how to get business' by providing them with 'racy,
telling and forcible pamphlets' and showing them 'how to answer objections and to meet adverse criticisms.' This educative function was
especially important earlier in the nineteenth century, when knowledge
of life insurance was poorly diffused. Although the Epping agent appointed in 1849 by Edward Koch was 'busy and bustling withal,' he
warned the Scottish Amicable that the new man would require 'showing *how* to do business, to do a large one.' To assist, most life insurance
offices provided agents with well-indexed instruction manuals, filled
with information about how to arrange their receipts, guidelines for
steering candidates through the application process, and extracts 'from
the productions of various writers on the subject.'[49]

Besides telling agents how to do their jobs, inspectors also relent-
lessly prodded them, in order to maintain interest in what for most was
part-time work. Without constant visits from the head or branch office,
concluded the National Provident's E.C. Browne, the agent 'works only
spasmodically, or possibly does not work at all, but rests content with
just such fish as may find their way to his net.' For the inspector, this
translated into a life of ceaseless travel: 'paying a short visit to a town
and living at an hotel' was a typical day's work. Especially in a recently
opened district, appointment tours remained both the primary focus
and the most challenging aspect of his job. Not only 'all his time but all
his thoughts' (according to the Edinburgh Life's London secretary)
needed to be spent 'keeping regular lists of the persons he has begun
with, and taking his regular rounds.' Thomas Marr similarly regaled
his Manchester inspector with 'the necessity of calling occasionally
upon all the Agents to stir them up if possible.'[50]

Through the mid-nineteenth century most inspectors either worked
at the head office or for a local board in a large city. At Standard Life,
William White used Liverpool as his base, and his successor operated

out of London. By the 1870s local boards were giving way to branch offices, under the supervision of resident secretaries who reported directly to the head office. Their job, according to one secretary, was to be 'a constructor, superintendent, and feeder of machinery,' which in practice meant canvassing for new business, reporting on agency applications, and keeping accounts. Although the office management part of this list was important enough by 1900 to warrant the appointment of several clerks at most branches, it did not count for much if new business declined. When this occurred in the Law Union & Crown's Manchester district, its general manager told the branch secretary that he was mistaken if he thought that his main duties were 'administrative and centre in his Branch Office.' Instead, his 'primary duty' was 'to see that his Company is fully represented in the district ... through the continued infusion of new blood into that organization.'[51]

At mid-century, when most resident secretaries worked under local boards, their jobs were comparable to those of a head office secretary. The median tenure of branch secretaries appointed before 1875 was seventeen years, and many London secretaries for Scottish or provincial offices could legitimately claim to have as much as anyone to do with their companies' success. As the number of branches proliferated, and as the influence of local boards waned, head office managers came to view branch secretaries more as interchangeable parts than as long-serving office managers. Median job tenure declined to four years for secretaries appointed in the decade after 1900. Their careers were stable only in comparison with inspectors, just 21 per cent of whom stayed at the same position more than five years.[52] Late Victorian branch secretaries earned a base salary of around £300 a year, less than half of what their head office counterparts were paid, and they often made up at least part of the difference with commissions. Inspectors averaged an annual base salary of just under £200, with commission looming even larger in their take-home pay.[53]

Job instability did not necessarily mean insecurity. More than a third of all secretaries who left a branch stayed with the same company, in most cases moving to a larger district or a plum head office job, and nearly three-fifths of secretaries and inspectors who switched firms stayed in the same town. A typical example of in-house promotion was Sidney Dixon of the National Mutual, who starting in 1898 spent four years as an inspector (first in Nottingham, then in London), then three years as secretary in Cardiff, three more in Liverpool, and ended his career in 1920 as the office's Leeds secretary. One secretary who moved through a succession of firms, Ralph Cook Watson, started as the Provident's Newcastle inspector in the mid-1880s; moved in 1887 to be a Guardian inspector, first in Manchester and then in London; stayed in London from 1892 to 1897 as inspector for the City of Glasgow, English & Scottish Law, and Royal in succession; served as the Scottish Equitable's Newcastle secretary from 1897 to 1902; and finished his career in Newcastle in 1913 as secretary for Standard Life.[54]

Agents

In appointing agents, life insurance offices looked for 'gentlemen of active business habits, of good address, and of respectable and extensive connexions,' in the words of the Universal Life's first annual report. Beyond the basic task of selling insurance, they asked such men to provide an initial assessment of customers' health and behaviour, to insure their own lives, and (in some cases) to insert 'Paragraphs and Advertisements' in the local papers.[55] They also required people who could be trusted to handle large sums of money. The most typical arrangement before 1850 was for an agent to keep an open account and remit the balance every quarter. After 1850 better banking facilities prompted many life offices to require agents to send in premiums as they came in. Failure to remit payments in a timely fashion was one of the only sins that guaranteed an agency's cancellation (lack of new business only sometimes carried that penalty), and most company minute books include at least a few examples of such dismissals.[56]

The most sought-after qualification in a life insurance agent was a wide circle of friends. In 1843 the Aberdeen Fire & Life's Glasgow board appointed Hugh McTavish, a local wine merchant, on account of 'his acquaintance & friends being numerous,' and in 1844 the Scottish National's canvassing committee appointed a young Wakefield lawyer who appeared to be 'working his way forward, and to be making friends.' The only problem with appointing agents based on their supply of friends was that it took such men relatively little time to exhaust their 'connexion,' however extended it might be. Standard Life's Newcastle agent, whose banking contacts yielded an annual average of £5,828 in new coverage during his first seven years, sent in only £300 a year in the following four. The Crown experienced similarly sharp declines in new business acquired by agents after they went through their initial list of contacts. Its 169 English agents appointed between 1873 and 1879 (not counting its top six men) averaged £1,001 worth of new business their first year, £371 in their second, £224 in their third, and £115 in the years that followed.[57]

One solution to the problem of the diminishing returns of friendship was to keep hiring new agents when the old ones' usefulness had run out. The Crown's English sales staff grew from 501 to 564 between 1873 and 1880 despite nearly four hundred resignations, and the National Mutual needed to hire 2,778 agents between 1900 and 1911 to increase the size of its sales force by 425. Much of this turnover was anticipated at the outset. When Koch presented the Scottish Amicable with an inventory of newly appointed agents in 1849, it came with the proviso that 'the list now presented will require from time to time weeding out to a considerable extent, and the ground reoccupying by more efficient auxiliaries.' Viewed in this light, agency appointment was a lottery: out of hundreds of tries, only a handful of 'keepers' might emerge. Three such keepers at the Economic were John Maitland, T.C. Cooper, and George Smith (from Edinburgh, Liverpool, and Salisbury, respectively), who between 1835 and 1841 produced 40 per cent of its agency sales; 11 per cent of the Crown's English agents who sold any insurance between 1873 and 1882 provided 63 per cent of their new business.[58]

With the very large exception of industrial insurance (which is beyond the scope of this chapter), nearly all British life insurance agents in the nineteenth century sold policies alongside a separate trade or profession. Appointment patterns changed over time, as the proliferation of agencies forced companies to tap into new trades when supplies ran out in old ones; they also varied widely by region and by company. Published company histories provide some information on this topic for a few major firms prior to 1850: we know, for instance, that the Pelican (which specialized in life insurance) was twice as likely to appoint lawyers as the Guardian or Royal Exchange, which sold fire as well as life insurance. Casting a wider net – including other company records and trade directories – indicates many additional variations. In the late-1830s, for instance, more than two-thirds of all agents in Ayrshire were lawyers, compared with just 3 per cent in Kent, where most agents were merchants. Estate agents were popular choices in South Wales, shopkeepers in Herefordshire, and accountants in Glasgow.[59]

A database encompassing nearly seven thousand insurance agents, taken from trade directories for Scotland and five northern English counties in the 1870s, reveals appointment patterns at a time when branch networks were just getting off the ground. Among the Scottish life agents, 39 per cent were lawyers and/or bankers, and another 15 per cent were merchants or manufacturers. The third leading category behind bankers and lawyers, with 17 per cent of all agents, was shopkeepers. In the latter group, over a third were grocers (35 per cent), followed by drapers (26 per cent), booksellers (21 per cent), chemists (12 per cent), wine and spirits dealers (8 per cent), and ironmongers (6 per cent). The sample for northern England reveals the same proportion of shopkeepers, but far fewer bankers (5 per cent), 5 per cent fewer lawyers, and more merchants and estate agents. Scottish life insurance offices were much less likely than English firms to appoint merchants in Scotland, and more likely to appoint bankers in England. In both regions, bankers and lawyers more commonly represented companies that sold life insurance, while accountants and estate agents more commonly represented fire or accident insurance offices.[60]

The proliferation of insurance agencies by the end of the nineteenth century, and its impact on appointment patterns, is clear from an Atlas appointment book covering the years 1897 to 1907; this book also allows for a more thorough regional comparison of appointment patterns. In the quarter-century since the mid-1870s the Atlas went from employing just fourteen agents in Scotland to appointing 275; the increase for Yorkshire was from thirty-seven to 469. Although the Atlas appointed sixty-one Yorkshire lawyers at the turn of the century, nearly twice as many as it employed in 1878, this was only 13 per cent of its total appointments in that county – compared with 46 per cent in 1878. Among other regional variances, 20 per cent of the architects and 27 per cent of the bank clerks the Atlas appointed were Welsh, it appointed the highest proportion of merchants and shopkeepers in Ireland, and estate agents more often got the nod in London and Lancashire.[61]

One constant in nearly all these sources is that life insurance offices preferred to appoint 'a lawyer of standing' as their agent if they could find one. As Clive Trebilcock has noted, lawyers attracted an 'unending succession of clients who would inherit, worry about future income, wish to provide for their offspring, and eventually bequeath'; they also had experience remitting money, provided clients with well-regarded financial advice, and negotiated loans and marriage settlements that often required insurance as collateral. All these factors led English insurance offices to focus on lawyers when they first started appointing agents; this soon changed, however, with the emergence of 'legal' offices that expected their many affiliated lawyers to cut ties with the competition.[62] In Scotland, where legal offices had less traction, lawyers divided their services more evenly among all life offices. Scottish firms in 1878 employed more lawyers as agents in Scotland than any other occupation, with enough left over to comprise 21 per cent of the sales force of English firms doing business there. Excluding Edinburgh, where nearly a quarter of the country's lawyers worked, 59 per cent of all Scottish lawyers represented at least one life office in 1878 – not including many more 'country Solicitors' who sold insurance on a freelance basis.[63]

In Scotland the next most popular breed of life insurance salesman was the bank agent. Scottish banks started establishing regional branch networks in the 1770s, which were staffed by agents who earned commission on loans and who combined banking with other paid work. Such an agent was used to the idea of conducting a distant head office's financial transactions and was likely to have ample free time to do so. As one Scottish banker observed in 1889, insurance work was 'a great aid to an under-paid or not over-remunerated bank official,' and banks encouraged it as a means of attracting new customers.[64] This view was shared by few English banks, which employed salaried managers instead of agents once they started forming branch networks in the 1840s. A Scottish National committee reported after a canvassing trip 'a jealousy on the part of bank directors in England to allow their Agents and Clerks to hold such an appointment.' Even in Scotland, English life insurance offices appointed far fewer bankers than Scottish firms, although partly this was because most of their agents were in larger towns, where the ratio of available bank agents to insurance companies was much lower.[65]

Companies recruited agents from most other professions as well, each of which offered a different avenue into a potential demand for life insurance. Accountants were especially desirable in Scotland, where they often had family or business ties to life office managers or directors, and where they performed most of the professional work involving trust funds and other estates; but English accountants were also appointed in large numbers, in part because they had access to many of the same customers as off-limits bank managers. Less likely professional men sold insurance for 'class' offices that targeted their specific tribe. The Church of England Fire & Life, which mainly catered to Anglican ministers, hired many clergymen as agents (whom they dignified with the title of 'corresponding directors') and also relied heavily on schoolmasters to sell their policies. Even doctors, who almost never worked as insurance agents, received 20 per cent of the Clerical Medical's agency appointments in the mid-1860s.[66]

In many parts of Great Britain, and in many insurance companies, professions played second fiddle to merchants, manufacturers, and commission agents. Since the strategy was to find men with the widest and most valuable business contacts, life insurance offices followed the trail of local business where it led. In Bradford and Dundee, 40 per cent of the time it led to merchants or manufacturers (mainly relating to textiles), compared with just 35 per cent for professional men. In Hull, a shipping hub, 47 per cent of the insurance salesmen were merchants, ship brokers, or commission agents, compared with just 25 per cent from the various professions. In general, merchants and manufacturers were likelier to sell life insurance in larger cities: in the Yorkshire and Scottish directories, they comprised a quarter of the agents in cities with more than thirty thousand people, but only an eighth of them in smaller towns. Illustrative of the appeal of such men was the Cork flour factor John Carey, whose dealings with the town's 'most extensive & respectable millers' and whose location 'close to the Post Office, Commercial buildings & both banks' convinced the Scottish Amicable to appoint him as an agent in 1833.[67]

When the number of agents in force exceeded available stocks of professional men and merchants, life insurance offices inevitably resorted to lower-status occupations – in particular to shopkeepers of various sorts. By the 1830s many such men were central to civic life in small and medium-sized towns, and in many cases they were on friendlier terms with more townsfolk than were lawyers or bankers, who were more likely to be outsiders. Shopkeepers were also three times less likely than professional men to split their loyalties with a second or third life office. Despite these virtues, they were clearly the last resort for life offices that catered to a higher-class customer – although some firms split the difference, as when the Aberdeen Fire & Life hired an estate manager to sell 'insurances ... of a better class' and a retired grocer to sell 'smaller insurances ... in his own sphere.' Shopkeepers were more likely to be the first choice of firms like the Briton, United Kingdom Temperance, and Star, which targeted a lower middle-class clientele.[68]

The one last resort that practically no Victorian life insurance office appointed to be agents was women. Only two out of 865 Royal Farmers' agents hired between 1855 and 1873 were women, including a dead agent's sister and the postmistress of Mold; Jane Bland, the chemist Ann Whitwell, and the grocers Jane Ayre, Hannah Lance, Elizabeth Hawson, and Mary Dove were the only female agents in Yorkshire in 1875; and the Atlas appointed just twenty-three women between 1897 and 1907 –

including ten widows, six daughters, and a sister-in-law of deceased agents. Some insurance companies refused on principle to let widows of agents continue their husband's agency, and when the Positive Government's Manchester secretary proposed employing female agents he was told that he was 'at full liberty to appoint them, but the Board cannot offer them a stipend.' The only such plan that came close to getting off the ground was a 'Women's Life Assurance Agency' at the English & Scottish Law in 1891 (mainly staffed by Oxford and Cambridge graduates), which fizzled within a year. It was not until after 1918 that British women had any measure of success as insurance agents.[69]

Most lawyers, and to a lesser extent accountants and bankers, sold what was known in the trade as 'voluntary' insurance: life policies that accompanied another transaction with which agents assisted their clients. Most other agents needed to try a good deal harder to get people to insure their lives, especially after their circle of friends had dried up. To help them in this task, life insurance offices were full of advice, most of which revolved in an erratic orbit around the need to see things from the customer's perspective. All insurers assumed this was easiest to do with prior acquaintances, and hence they urged the agent to 'see *personally* your friends, and such individuals in your neighbourhood as may be accessible to you.' Friends made the best targets in part because an agent was likelier to know when they were likeliest to buy insurance (such as an 'approaching marriage') or whether they already had enough coverage.[70]

Whether canvassing friends or strangers, insurance agents were constantly reminded to exercise 'that undefinable something which we call tact.' This trait was variously defined as 'knowledge of human nature,' 'sympathy with men,' and 'getting into the right attitude with respect to the individual.' When advice manuals went into more specifics, they mainly provided a list of 'don'ts': the agent should take care 'not to *lecture* his friends and acquaintances to insure' and 'not to bore those he talks to.' More constructively, they urged agents to 'strike a sympathetic chord' by cultivating their 'own *heart-force*.' As one advice book put it: 'To make others feel, we must first feel *ourselves*. Deep conviction is contagious.' A more practical face of sympathy was the advice for an agent who had lost a sale to 'go home and write out all that you have said ... and then ask yourself whether you would have been convinced had you been the other fellow.' Although appeals to tact most often appeared in advice about canvassing strangers, it was also important among friends: the tactless agent, in such cases, was subject to 'a double loss of friends and business.'[71]

Regardless of who sold life insurance or how they went about selling it, the one thing that kept thousands of people doing it was the prospect of a commission at the outset and annual renewal commissions thereafter. As of 1825 most insurance agents apparently tolerated 5 per cent on the first year's premiums and either 2.5 per cent or 5 per cent on subsequent renewals.[72] By the 1850s most insurance offices had upped the ante in their push for new business: thirty-one of forty polled in 1856 paid 10 per cent on the first premium and 5 per cent on renewals, and some newer firms paid up to a third of the premiums in the first year. By 1887 most Scottish firms, and a handful of English ones, were paying 1 per cent of the sum assured for the first year plus a smaller (usually 2.5 per cent) commission on renewal premiums. This latter scale earned the agent between two and three times as much in the first year (depending on the customer's age and whether the policy was with-profit) and provided a continuing incentive to generate new business over the long haul.[73] Starting in the 1850s most Scottish and at least a few English insurance firms added to this incentive by offering sliding bonuses for new business, ranging from £1 to £3 on the first £1,000 up to £60 for £20,000.[74]

Being paid to sell life insurance was akin to receiving a small annuity, since the work that went into each sale created a future yearly income. Life insurance offices made sure their agents realized this: Nicholas Grut at the Palladium assured his Swansea agent in 1836 that 'at this rate you will soon raise an independence for yourself.' For practically all agents, such an 'independence' was decidedly small beer: based on the Crown sales figures cited above, the average English agent earned around £3 a year over his first ten years, increasing to £6 in twenty-five years. One of the Crown's most successful agents in the 1870s, A.T. Cross of Cambridge, earned (including bonuses for new business) around £7 in his first year, £26 in his second, £46 in his third, and £70 annually after five years. The fact that so many people signed on to sell insurance indicates that even these relatively small rewards were ample incentive. The case of the overstocked legal profession, in this context, is revealing: while their status and contacts made solicitors the most sought-after agents, their typical professional income – estimated at £200 per year in 1892 – made the prospect of an agency attractive from their perspective as well.[75]

To the small extent that it crossed their minds, most insurance customers did not seem to mind the fact that agents (who in many cases were friends or business associates) received part of their premiums; only occasionally did critics complain about the 'good round annuity' earned by insurance agents for little apparent work. Criticism grew louder, and stretched across the nineteenth century, when lawyers or bankers collected commissions on sales without openly representing a life insurance office. In the first third of the nineteenth century, when this practice was more common, most of the leading insurance authorities disparaged it as *'bribery and corruption'* that 'insidiously betrayed' policyholders.[76] Although life offices mostly stopped paying 'secret service money' during the middle of the century, it later resurfaced as a problem, and Parliament added life insurance to the list of 'illicit secret commissions' that were targeted in three anti-corruption laws promulgated between 1889 and 1916. Life offices ultimately emerged unscathed from such unwelcome scrutiny, but not before spending a nervous decade as their lawyers pointed out several potential conflicts of interest that 'might be held to be corrupt.'[77]

By the end of the nineteenth century several cracks were beginning to appear in the traditional system of selling life insurance through part-time agents. In the late-1860s a new breed of 'special' agents appeared, who did much of the paperwork previously left to the head office. With the rise of branches by 1900, secretaries predicted that 'dispensing with agents and doing all the work by ... paid officials' would soon become the norm, as was already starting to happen in the United States. And if structural changes within life insurance eroded the prominence of the part-time agent, an even bigger blow came from the neighbouring sector of marine insurance, which had always relied on independent brokers to generate business. When these brokers branched into life insurance after 1880, they increased the pressure on life offices to offer bonuses for procuring new business, introduced new business practices (including the offer of rebates to customers who bought large policies), and pressed for licensure as a means of weeding out amateur salesmen. Managers rightly worried that the rise of the insurance broker represented a shift in the balance of power between management and sales. As the Caledonian's general manager put it in 1906, 'the small agent, should he attempt to threaten, can be promptly and effectively dealt with, without that bugbear of a manager's life, the loss of a large slice of business at one fell swoop.' Brokers, in contrast, used their large volume of business 'to bully the Offices they represent.'[78]

Conclusion

'No outdoor official can have failed to observe,' noted the Liverpool secretary of the Scottish Widows' Fund in 1910, 'how various are the human specimens with whom he is called upon to deal.' In their line of work, insurance salesmen encountered some customers 'who apparently treat the matter as a huge joke' and others who filled in the form 'with a due appreciation of the seriousness of the business.' To be successful, it was necessary for the salesman 'to adapt himself perfectly ... to the innumerable and sometimes almost imperceptible gradations' between these two extremes. Another branch secretary similarly urged agents to 'know the main features of a hoped-for client's outlook on life,' and thereby learn 'why men yield.' What Sigmund Freud identified in 1918 as 'the narcissism of small differences' clearly had its part to play in life insurance.[79]

If an appreciation for variation in human nature helped agents do their jobs, it also came in handy for most other people in life insurance offices whenever they tried to get along with their fellow workers. The Queen's agency superintendent joked in 1884 that he 'would be loth [sic] to ask nine-tenths of our agents home to dinner' – and his company's directors, or the physician who screened its lives, or the solicitor who evaluated its securities, might well have said the same thing about him. To help bridge such gaps, life offices engaged in numerous rituals, many of which drew from common Victorian strategies for simulating social harmony. Actuaries and directors played cricket or golf with their clerks, and referred to employees as 'children' in 'a large and growing family.' 'Indoor men' modestly demurred that it was 'a much easier thing to sit snugly in a comfortable room calculating a rate than it is to fight the elements in getting at a probable proposer,' and they urged their clerks to 'remember ... the outside man' and 'help him in every possible way to meet the desires of his client.' Directors praised actuaries at shareholder meetings for their 'ability and ... power of organisation.'[80]

Social chasms in British life insurance during the nineteenth century were seldom as wide as they were, for instance, in the United States, where company presidents were plutocrats and insurance salesmen occupied 'the same category as the book-hawker.' One reason for this, ironically, was that class divisions in Britain were much wider, which made it possible for two varieties of life insurance to emerge – industrial and 'ordinary' – that came close to being mutually exclusive in their forms of organization. Industrial agents, who were accused of everything from plundering the poor to abetting infanticide, absorbed nearly all of the social opprobrium that was more evenly dispersed among American insurance salesmen. Even though their differences were smaller than was the case with their American cousins, however – or perhaps precisely because they were smaller, as Freud might have warned them – it was still vital for everyone involved to recognize and resolve conflicts when they arose. Without doing so, it would have been next to impossible to achieve what Freud called 'feelings of fellowship' while engaging in the complicated interactions that surrounded the selling of life insurance.[81]

4 Death and the Actuary

Man is now seen to be an enigma only as an individual; in the mass he is a mathematical problem.

– Robert Chambers, *Vestiges of the Natural History of Creation*, 1844[1]

Over the course of the nineteenth century, statistics in Great Britain went from being a superficial fashion – everywhere seen to be 'required to give to theory [a] modern colouring,' according to the *Contemporary Review* – to being an unseen foundation of modernity.[2] Life insurance companies were full participants in this transition. Early prospectuses trumpeted the impressive capacity of statistical thinking to create a profitable and secure industry out of nothing more than a few local death registries and painstakingly tried to teach prospective customers the basics of this science. Meanwhile, the Institute of Actuaries opened shop in 1848 as a specialized partner of more celebrated statistical societies that had formed in London and Manchester a decade earlier; one if its first orders of business was to collect, with Scottish colleagues in the Faculty of Actuaries, information about more than 150,000 insured lives. By the end of the nineteenth century this sort of data collection had become the undergirding of an industry that prided itself on its cautious management of the nation's savings. Instead of trying to teach people to understand how mortality laws worked, a new generation of insurers promised security without revealing its numerical underpinnings – and, as in other walks of life, most people trusted this promise most of the time.

Unlike other Victorian statisticians, who counted everything from church attendance to violent crimes, actuaries who worked for life insurance offices focused almost exclusively on one thing: the correlation of mortality with age. At the centre of these discussions was the life table, which charted the proportion of a selection of people who remained alive at every birthday.[3] As each new table appeared, at least a few firms embraced it as proof that other offices' premiums were too high or (more typically) that they subsidized one set of customers at the expense of another. Such debates disappeared after 1880, when nearly all insurance companies adopted tables that were based on vital statistics collected by the Institute of Actuaries and the Faculty of Actuaries. Premium levels, which were already reasonably uniform by the 1840s, were nearly identical by the turn of the century, when fewer than 10 per cent of firms charged more or less than 5 per cent of the mean.[4] Such uniformity pleased most of the people most of the time: specifically, the large majority of customers who qualified as 'healthy males' and therefore paid the same as everyone else in their own age cohort. Brushed to one side, both in terms of standardized premiums and statistical inquiry, was a residuum of policyholders – including women, customers with hazardous occupations, and customers travelling abroad – whose rates remained strikingly arbitrary into the twentieth century.

To non-specialists, including most insurance directors, the path leading up to the Institute of Actuaries' tables was neither very interesting nor all that obvious. Mortality statistics filled a black box, out of which emerged seemingly endless rows of columns linking different ages with different sums of money. Yet the process by which these columns evolved had significant consequences for both the image and the price structure of British life insurance. Actuaries celebrated their statistical achievements as proof that their profession had come of age. Salesmen shamelessly brandished alleged 'laws of mortality' as proof that nothing bad could happen to their customers' money – neglecting the many variables unrelated to mortality that could sink an office. Still, their professions of certainty did mean something, especially compared with other forms of insurance. Since life premiums were demonstrably more calculable than fire insurance rates, for instance, customers could more easily predict what they would pay for their policies over the course of their lives – and life offices could afford to allow customers to continue paying the same premium even after their actions or health had redefined them as higher risks.

Using Life Tables

Until 1837, when actuaries from seventeen British insurance companies commenced the world's first collective mortality investigation of insured lives, and when the General Registrar's Office began tabulating births and deaths throughout England and Wales, insurance offices relied on three different sorts of data for constructing premium tables and valuing policies: local burial and baptismal records, a survey of mortality among government annuitants, and claims from the Equitable. All these tables had adherents, but the successive front-runners were Richard Price's Northampton table, which the Equitable first used in 1780, and Joshua Milne's Carlisle table, which many companies started using from the 1820s. After 1837 actuaries continued to build on their initial foray into the statistics of insured lives, first producing tables from twenty contributing offices in 1869 and then forming the 'British Offices' tables from sixty firms in 1901.

The shift from using life tables based on uninsured populations to using company-generated tables was a major turning point in the calculation of insurance premiums and the valuation of policies. Insurance company records allowed actuaries to trace distinct cohorts of people whose age and health corresponded closely to that of customers in most life insurance offices. Actuaries also trusted the accuracy of these records more than they trusted data from eighteenth-century sources, or even from the General Registrar's Office, owing to the higher social class of their customers and the greater care taken in ascertaining their ages. In conjunction with new tables for the general population, company-generated tables also made it possible to specify the limits of medical selection in producing favourable mortality results for a life insurance office. This outcome infused a new element of caution into life insurance practice at a time when many new companies were throwing caution to the wind.

Insurers used life tables for two different purposes: to establish age-specific premiums for their customers and to determine the extent of their liabilities. In both cases, actuaries started with raw data charting the number of people alive at different ages and 'smoothed' these data into a continuous curve. Next, they added two other assumptions that affected their premiums or liabilities: the interest rate they thought their assets would earn over the duration of each policy and the amount of 'loading' that was necessary to add to cover expenses and unexpected contingencies. These latter two components often made a bigger difference to a company's finances than the specific life table it used. But these age-specific mortality data were the skeleton of insurance finance, and they were most responsible for the arrays of figures filling every prospectus. Both in setting prices and tracking liabilities, the fact that

life insurance offices charged dozens of different rates for the same service made it hard to coordinate the shifting variables of risk and reward. If they were first attracted to life tables as a basis for financial
security, they kept sending actuaries back to the drawing board in order
to achieve equity among their customers.

To the extent that insurance offices succeeded in this endeavour, it was
by focusing only on the large 'healthy male' subset of the lives they insured. Although insurance companies possessed information about female mortality and about risks associated with travel, occupation, and
poor health, they did not translate these data into premiums that were
uniform across the industry. Instead, a combination of entrepreneurship,
managerial discretion, and collusion determined such premiums: with
the result that customers in these risk groups might pay more or less
(usually more) than their risks merited at a given time or in a given insurance office. This section concludes with a discussion of these methods as
they applied to women, military officers, and publicans (the main hazardous occupations to attract the attention of life insurance offices), and
travellers. I return to this theme in chapter 10, when I discuss the complicated place of medical statistics in Victorian life insurance.

From Northampton to Carlisle

In the first half of the eighteenth century, life insurance societies charged
all customers the same premium, sometimes setting an age limit for
new entrants. In paying claims they either operated as 'mortuary tontines,' which dispensed the same sum of money each year to a varying
number of beneficiaries, or they sold only term insurance and paid
claims in proportion to the premiums they collected.[5] All these insurers
operated without reference to the fruits of 'political arithmetic' – including John Graunt's 1662 table based on London bills of mortality
and Edmund Halley's 1693 age-specific analysis of mortality in the
Silesian town of Breslau. Lorraine Daston has suggested that this was
because the 'gambling' side of life insurance predominated at this point,
delaying a search for mortality laws until a more prudent focus on financial security took its place. Geoffrey Clark has responded that at
least some early insurers were prudent enough to desire a firmer foot-
ing for their business, but demography (as it then existed) offered few
strong arguments in favour of age-specific tables.[6]

It was not until 1762 that mortality tables informed insurance premiums. The Equitable based its original set of rates on London's bills of

mortality, then in 1780 turned to Richard Price to reduce these without incurring too much risk. For this purpose Price turned from vice-ridden London to Northampton, whose residents he assumed to be healthier and hence more likely to correspond to those select customers who held Equitable policies. His data covered 4,689 deaths from 1735 to 1780 and included a census of the population in 1746; on the (erroneous) assumption of a stable population, Price compared registered deaths with age returns from the census to infer life expectancy at different ages.[7] After 1786, when Price convinced the Equitable to drop a 15 per cent surcharge on his rates, members paid £27 a year for a £1,000 policy if they entered at age thirty, £34 at age forty, and £45 at age fifty. All twelve London life insurance offices that subsequently formed through 1813 copied these premiums, as did the West of England. The Norwich Union charged 10 per cent less when it formed in 1808, justifying its lower rates on the ground that its customers would 'be chiefly ... residing in the country, where human existence is much less precarious than in the metropolis.'[8]

In 1812 Sun Life's actuary, Joshua Milne, began research that would result in a new table, based on death and age records that a local doctor had collected from the town of Carlisle between 1779 and 1787. Carlisle yielded much lower rates of mortality than Northampton, translating into unloaded premiums that were between 22 per cent and 28 per cent lower depending on age. Published in 1815, the table soon earned praise for its 'remarkable ... approach towards precision' and because its more recent statistics took into account alleged improvements in public health (see Tables 4.1 and 4.2).[9] Another justification for picking Carlisle over Northampton was that the latter discriminated against younger customers. Compared with the Carlisle table, the Northampton predicted life expectancies that were 24 per cent shorter at age twenty but only 13 per cent shorter at fifty-five. The result, in Augustus De Morgan's words, was that 'the young are made to work for the old,' which was especially unfair since 'the person who insures early in life' was 'the more prudent of the two.' Such appeals to younger policyholders were related to the fact that the average age of new insurance customers declined steadily in the decades after 1820, as family provision began to take the place of collateral for loans as the main reason to insure.[10]

The strongest argument in favour of the Carlisle table, though, was that it coincided very closely with the recorded experience of the Equitable, which its actuary had revealed in 1800 by giving ratios between the society's actual and expected claims. Working backward

Table 4.1
Life expectancy according to different mortality tables

Mortality Table	Age (years)								
	20	25	30	35	40	45	50	55	60
Northampton	33.4	30.9	28.3	25.7	23.1	20.5	18.0	15.6	13.2
Carlisle	41.5	37.9	34.3	31.0	27.6	24.5	21.1	17.6	14.3
Equitable	41.7	38.1	34.5	30.9	27.4	23.9	20.4	17.0	13.9
Finlaison (M)	38.4	35.9	33.2	30.2	27.0	23.8	20.3	17.2	14.4
Finlaison (F)	44.0	40.8	37.6	34.3	31.1	27.8	24.4	20.8	17.3
17 Offices	41.5	38.0	34.4	30.9	27.3	23.7	20.2	16.9	13.8
English no. 1 (M)	39.9	36.5	33.1	29.8	26.6	23.3	20.0	16.7	13.6
H^M	42.1	38.4	34.7	31.0	27.4	23.8	20.3	17.0	13.8
$H^{M(5)}$	40.2	37.1	33.9	30.4	27.0	23.4	20.0	16.8	13.7
O^M	43.2	39.1	35.1	31.2	27.4	23.7	20.1	16.7	13.6
$O^{M(5)}$	41.9	38.2	34.6	30.9	27.2	23.5	20.0	16.7	13.5

Sources: J. Jones 1843: Table VII; Walford V: 508; Institute of Actuaries 1872: 6, 114; Faculty of Actuaries 1902: 2–3, 106–7.
F = females; M = males; H^M = healthy males; $H^{M(5)}$ = healthy males excluding first 5 years; O^M = British Offices healthy males; $O^{M(5)}$ = British Offices healthy males excluding first 5 years.

from this report in 1823, Griffith Davies provided the Guardian with a table that achieved a close fit with the Equitable's mortality, and Charles Babbage and Benjamin Gompertz constructed similar tables in 1824. All these pointed to death rates that were nearly identical to those indicated by the Carlisle table.[11] Only a few companies actually used these 'Equitable Experience' tables, typically Davies's version.[12] Their real value lay in confirming companies in their decision to use the Carlisle over the Northampton table, and to embolden the Carlisle's advocates when the two were debated.

The proportion of life insurance offices using the Northampton table diminished from roughly half in 1826 to under 20 per cent fifteen years later. Some firms, like Sun Life in 1820, switched to the Carlisle table soon after it appeared, and many others adopted it upon forming. The Scottish National cited its 'ascertained accordance ... with the actual

Table 4.2
Unloaded premiums (in £) for £1,000 coverage, calculated by different mortality tables
and interest rates

Mortality Table	%	Age (years)								
		20	25	30	35	40	45	50	55	60
Northampton	3	21.79	24.04	26.67	29.91	33.96	38.96	45.29	53.33	63.67
Northampton	4	20.25	22.38	24.91	28.00	31.96	36.83	43.08	50.79	61.33
Carlisle	3	14.91	17.00	19.50	22.33	26.00	30.33	36.20	45.46	57.88
Carlisle	4	13.17	15.17	17.58	20.20	23.75	27.75	33.83	42.83	55.33
Equitable	3	14.75	16.88	19.25	22.04	25.38	29.83	35.50	42.29	50.63
Finlaison (M)	4	16.20	17.29	18.88	21.25	24.50	29.13	36.00	44.58	54.79
Finlaison (F)	4	12.50	13.83	15.46	17.46	19.83	23.00	27.50	34.04	43.08
17 Offices	4	12.96	14.70	16.96	19.88	23.67	28.83	35.75	45.00	57.54
English no. 1 (M)	4	14.20	16.20	18.54	21.41	25.00	29.70	36.17	45.70	58.63
H^M	3	14.27	16.25	18.80	21.93	25.89	31.14	38.00	47.25	59.87
$H^{M(5)}$	3	15.82	17.45	19.59	22.68	26.57	31.85	38.79	47.97	60.60
O^M	3	13.54	15.82	18.61	22.04	26.34	31.87	39.17	48.96	62.36
$O^{M(5)}$	3	14.63	16.67	19.20	22.46	26.66	32.15	39.42	49.18	62.53

Sources: Sturrock 1846: 16; Babbage 1826: 178; Institute of Actuaries 1872: 14, 122;
Faculty of Actuaries 1902: 56–7, 160–1.
F = females; M = males; H^M = healthy males; $H^{M(5)}$ = healthy males excluding first
5 years; O^M = British Offices healthy males; $O^{M(5)}$ = British Offices healthy males
excluding first 5 years.

Experience of Mortality in the principal existing Assurance Offices' to
justify its adoption when it formed in 1843.[13] Although the Carlisle table
was the most popular alternative to the Northampton, it did not have
the field to itself. Its leading competitor was a set of tables constructed
by John Finlaison for the National Debt Office, based on the lives of
more than twenty-two thousand people who had bought government
annuities. These predicted life expectancies that were shorter than the
Carlisle at older ages, longer at younger ages, and (unlike any prior
table) substantially longer for women than for men.[14] Companies using
other tables included the European, which based its premiums on

Swedish birth and death records, and the Bristol Union, which in 1818 based its rates on local burial records. A final set of firms kept Northampton-based rates, but tweaked them to take into account more recent information. The Clerical Medical did this after customers complained that 'the premium upon the younger lives is very high.'[15]

What companies did with their new tables depended on whether they wanted to pay the large bonuses that had become popular or reduce premiums. Many firms calculated their premiums using Milne's or Finlaison's table at 4 per cent interest (unlike the 3 per cent yield assumed in the Equitable's premiums), but added up to 40 per cent in loading. Even with that addition, the premiums were lower than the Equitable's at younger ages, but higher by the age of fifty (see Table 4.2). The heavy loading partly reflected the fact that these offices paid commission to salesmen, unlike the Equitable, but mainly allowed for reserves out of which the companies could pay future bonuses. They distinguished themselves from firms using the Northampton table by emphasizing their more equitable price distribution. When Sun Life introduced its new premiums in 1820, it bragged that they were 'proportional to the real Values of the Risks at the different Periods of Life.'[16]

Many newly formed life insurance offices, in contrast, used the new tables to justify reducing their premiums across the board. The European loaded its Swedish-based rates by only 10 per cent to offer with-profit premiums that were up to 27 per cent lower than the Equitable's. A few years later the Economic beat the European's rates up to the age of fifty, and two Aberdeen-based insurance offices created with-profit rates that were almost as low by adding 22 per cent to Finlaison's table. Finally, in 1837 the Scottish Provident introduced even lower with-profit rates by adding just 10 per cent to Finlaison's table. In other cases, existing companies turned to a new life table to catch up with what their closest competitors were charging. When the Caledonian discovered that its Scottish business was lagging because its premiums were 'higher in general than the other Scotch offices,' it traded in its adjusted Northampton rates for new ones 'calculated according to the Carlisle Bill' that were lower by around 3 per cent.[17]

Besides affecting premiums, the new life tables affected how companies valued their liabilities. Just as a table showing lower mortality could be used to justify lower prices, it could also be used to justify smaller reserves – since it predicted that customers would survive to pay more premiums before they died. As in the case of setting prices, many insurance companies did not use the new tables in this way, since they were committed to paying large bonuses to future generations. Hence, although many did switch to the Carlisle table for valuations, they compensated for this by reducing the assumed interest. The most typical decision, to use a Carlisle 3 per cent instead of a Northampton 4 per cent valuation, actually resulted in larger reserves. Although many companies doubtless gave in to the temptation to pair the Carlisle table with higher assumed yields, their record of doing so (and in many cases, one assumes, their business) did not survive.[18]

Against the growing trend in favour of the Carlisle and similar tables, William Morgan of the Equitable stubbornly defended the Northampton table in 1827 as 'the most correct ... for the mean duration of life in all private concerns.' He attributed his own society's lower apparent mortality to its large number of young, select lives, and warned that the effects of this selection would 'lessen ... in process of time.' Other older insurance offices, anxious to defend their higher rates, rushed to Morgan's aid. The Palladium, disparaging premiums that were based on 'some healthy situations in distant counties,' defended its rates as a security against the time when 'the true laws of mortality began to exert themselves.'[19] Arthur Morgan's publication in 1834 of an updated Equitable table made this line of reasoning easier to pursue. By excluding policies that had lapsed or matured prior to death, he reduced the younger members' life expectancy by two to three years; a table based on Amicable claims told the same story. In 1847 Samuel Brown, a clerk under Morgan, appealed to these data to conclude that no company-specific data should be used as a basis for premiums until that company had reached 'its maximum of mortality.' Since not even the Equitable had yet reached that point, he warned, 'it should be our lot to sober down the ardent imagination' of company promoters who were spinning 'aerial dreams' out of the new vital statistics.[20]

Seventeen Offices and the Registrar General

By the mid-1830s the relationship between vital statistics and life insurance had reached a crossroads. The waning authority of the Northampton table, combined with the proliferation of alternatives, led one critic to lament that 'the whole subject of premiums on life-assurance ... is still practically in a state of chaos.' Three different suggestions circulated in the late 1830s regarding the best way to remedy this situation. In June 1837 forty-two actuaries signed a petition calling on Parliament to pay for the publication of Finlaison's data, which they hoped would test the reliability of premiums based on them. Early in 1838 a committee of the Statistical Society of London, headed by Thomas Edmonds of the Legal & General, sent circulars requesting 'information from the Books of the Offices for forming Tables of the duration of Human Life.' And, later that year, Benjamin Gompertz revived an earlier proposal he had made for 'actuaries of the different societies' to 'collect for the common good of all ... that which they cannot gain from a less general observation.'[21] This latter appeal won the day, resulting in the appearance five years later of the so-called Seventeen Offices or Experience table.

Gompertz, Milne, and Davies joined a committee of ten actuaries to oversee the collection. Fifteen life insurance offices added their data to the existing Amicable and Equitable records, and an additional forty-one subscribed £46 each when the tables became available in 1842. All but two of the contributing offices (the Norwich Union and Scottish Widows' Fund) were based in London, and the total number of policies amounted to 62,537 – over a third of which came from the Equitable.[22] Although its compilers originally intended to limit circulation of the table to the subscribing firms, this hope evaporated in 1843 when Jenkin Jones, actuary at the National Mercantile, gained access to the data and from them published nineteen premium tables. His tables revealed life expectancies that were longer than in Finlaison's table through the age of thirty, shorter than the Carlisle past forty, and nearly identical with the Equitable at all ages.[23]

Many new life insurance offices took advantage of Jones's labours. Most prominent among these was the Experience Life Assurance Company, which (its prospectus claimed) combined the security of 'an approximation to the certain values of life' with 'equitably graduated' premiums.[24] Unlike the Carlisle table, which prompted many firms to reduce rates, the Seventeen Offices table did not dramatically affect premiums. Instead, insurance offices used it to engage (often irresponsibly) in what the Waterloo's promoter called the 'enlightened distribution of *realised profits*' – in other words, to pay out larger bonuses on the grounds that its predicted low mortality warranted this practice.[25] The table also made waves in the United States, inspiring an investigation of policyholder mortality that resulted, after some fits and starts, in the American Experience Table of 1868. Also, the Massachusetts Insurance Commission used the Seventeen Offices table to determine that a British firm doing business in the state was insolvent, rekindling a debate in Britain about the table's merits.[26]

In 1839, while plans were under way for the Seventeen Offices table, the first report appeared from the General Registrar's Office, which had been formed two years earlier as a central depot for English and Welsh birth and death records. The GRO's statistical superintendant, William Farr, appended to the report the first of more than forty letters that he would annually write on the potential of these data for determining 'the laws of vitality.' In 1843 Farr issued the first of three 'English tables' that he would construct (six more would appear between his death in 1882 and 1919). Based on the 1841 census and the registered deaths for that year, the table revealed expectancies of about a year less than the Carlisle table after the age of forty. Farr framed a premium table on its basis, as he did for his subsequent tables. Most famously, he invented the concept of a 'healthy district' which, with seventeen annual deaths per 1,000 living, occupied the tenth percentile on a list of England's most favourable places to live; he hoped this could be used to measure the progress of public health reforms in districts that failed to meet this 'natural' rate of mortality.[27]

Insurance companies greeted the General Registrar's Office with high hopes. The Norwich Union's actuary predicted that it would 'present us with materials of inappreciable value.' The Associated Scottish Life Offices urged its members to support it, and the Institute of Actuaries made Farr an honourary member.[28] Farr worked hard to influence the practice of life insurance. Calling his 1853 table 'the soundest and justest basis of life insurance business of the country,' he actively solicited its use. Many new firms that catered to lower-income customers answered his call, and Farr himself promoted several private and state-run insurance schemes.[29] Farr's life tables also played a crucial role in determining the extent to which selection improved the mortality rate among insured lives. In 1851 John Higham of the Royal Exchange compared life expectancy for people in the Seventeen Offices pool who had been insured for ten years with that for people at the same ages in Farr's table. When first insured, policyholders who were thirty had a four-month advantage over the general public, rising to eight months at age forty. Ten years later, the same cohorts had lost ground by seven months in the first case and by eight in the second. This proved, he concluded, that people who continued to enjoy good health let their policies lapse at a disproportionate rate. Although not everyone agreed with this explanation, few doubted that the problem of 'inferiority after a short period of assurance' henceforth needed to be taken into account when interpreting future life tables.[30]

This common ground between government statistics and commercial life insurance was more apparent than real. Although Farr ceaselessly championed life insurance, he criticized companies for relying on faulty life tables and for keeping their large store of vital statistics to themselves. Commercial actuaries, for their part, faulted Farr's tables for trusting too much in self-reported ages on census returns and doctor-reported ages on death certificates.[31] They also held radically different views about which people deserved to be counted. Farr developed his concept of the 'healthy district' in the mid-1850s to do something about the millions of lives that fell short of this standard of health. Fifteen years later commercial actuaries would construct a set of 'Healthy Males' tables that included only those men who passed their medical examinations. Far from warranting closer scrutiny, the rest of the population dropped out of sight for these actuaries: they were either excluded from insuring altogether or formed populations that were statistically insignificant from a business point of view.

Healthy Males and British Offices

Augustus De Morgan told a young Walter Bagehot in 1853 that 'an actuary's business nowadays consisted merely or mainly in pushing the office, that the mathematical work was done, that the tables were made, &c. &c.'[32] A year earlier Samuel Brown had charted a course for a new set of tables that would prove De Morgan wrong. The set of tables that resulted, in 1869, based on vital statistics from twenty offices, put the Institute and the Faculty of Actuaries on the map as productive scientific bodies, clarified the limits of medical selection, and forged a lasting consensus regarding the most applicable data on which to base premiums and valuations. This consensus grew even stronger at the end of the century, when the Institute and Faculty produced the British Offices tables. By the eve of the First World War, plans were in place for a continuous mortality investigation that would, from 1924, guide the industry through the twentieth century.

When in 1852 Brown urged that the 'vast quantity of scattered materials' possessed by life insurance offices 'be combined and published,' the Institute had already been corresponding with the Associated Scottish Life Offices about this topic for three years. Further progress would wait another decade, partly because it took Brown and other leaders of the Institute that long to convince insurance directors to stop treating their vital statistics as 'private capital.'[33] For a while, more progress occurred at the Actuaries' Club, where J.J. Downes hoped to update the Seventeen Offices data by using a card system that he had employed in publishing his own office's mortality experience. Although this collection was in 'a state of forwardness' in 1862, no further progress ensued. By the time Downes publicized his card system in a pamphlet that year, the Institute of Actuaries had revived its plans for a mortality survey. It decided to use his cards, which it started sending to participating London insurance offices in 1863. A joint ASLO-Faculty of Actuaries committee joined the survey in 1864, after adding various letters and stripes to the Institute's cards to allow for 'more exact returns.'[34]

Between 1865 and 1867 twenty life insurance offices contributed data relating to 160,426 lives to the Institute and the Faculty of Actuaries. Nine were Scottish, with over half of the lives, compared with just a single Scottish company in the Seventeen Offices table. The centrepiece of the collection was the Healthy Males (or H^M) table, which measured age-specific mortality among men who had not been charged extra for their insurance. Encompassing 81 per cent of the total lives, this table revealed shorter life expectancy than in the Carlisle table past the age of thirty-five and more favourable results than either the Seventeen Offices or Carlisle tables prior to the age of thirty. Since the average duration of policies in the H^M table was 7.5 years, just a year longer than in the Seventeen Offices table, it shared that table's problem of failing to predict the mortality of people for whom the effects of medical selection had worn off. Unlike the earlier compilers, who disavowed their table's relevance on that basis, the Institute and Faculty were ready with a plan to make their data useful despite this problem. This was the $H^{M(5)}$ table, which excluded the first five years of every policy from consideration and yielded expectancies that were shorter than the H^M table by nearly two years at age twenty and by five months at age forty (see Table 4.1). Besides the H^M and $H^{M(5)}$ tables, the Institute and the Faculty of Actuaries compiled tables for higher-risk men and healthy women, and the Faculty separately published data on whole life versus term policies, country of residence, and cause of death.[35]

The fact that the H^M table resulted in mortality that was 'too low at the young ages, and too high at the old ages,' as an actuary observed in 1900, did not stop many offices from using it to revise their rates after 1870. Its main impact on premiums concerned age distribution, since most insurance companies padded their prices to allow for bonuses; but a few firms turned the apparently superior vitality of the (younger) healthy males into lower rates.[36] By far the most important impact of the H^M and $H^{M(5)}$ tables, though, was on the valuation of liabilities. In

1870 more than half of all life insurance offices valued their policies with the Carlisle or Equitable tables. The H^M table made it next to impossible to persist in using either, once actuaries began insisting that they gave 'too favourable a mortality ... for policies of long standing,' and by 1890 nearly all offices had adopted the H^M table – either by itself or in combination with the even more stringent $H^{M(5)}$ table. Although results varied depending on a company's age profile, those that used the H^M table typically set aside more funds against future liabilities.[37]

When the Institute and the Faculty issued their tables in 1869, one of the only criticisms that emerged concerned their exclusion of the many newer, more 'pushing' insurance offices that had volunteered their records: this meant, claimed Cornelius Walford in 1874, that the tables failed to 'represent correctly the great bulk of insured life.'[38] The collection of the British Offices data, which took place from 1893 to 1896, put an end to this criticism, since it drew from the records of sixty insurance offices – including all the surviving firms from the Seventeen Offices collection and, for the first time, most of the major English firms that operated outside of London. What one actuary at the time called 'the greatest investigation into the mortality of assured lives that the world has ever seen' tabulated 1.75 million cards and yielded eight volumes of tables, which included results for annuitants and holders of endowment insurance as well as all the groups in the previous investigation. By and large, the tables confirmed earlier findings, with lower mortality up to the age of fifty (see Table 4.1).[39]

As in the earlier investigation, actuaries devoted most of their attention to the 'healthy males' table, which was designated O^M to distinguish it from the H^M table. This shared the spotlight with the $O^{M(5)}$ table, which was supplemented by a table that measured the effect of selection into the tenth year of each policy. The British Offices investigation also revealed that the mortality associated with endowment insurance, which was fast overtaking whole life insurance in popularity, was lower than for whole life policies – confirming the common assumption that attaching an annuity at the end of a term policy enticed healthy customers to keep their policies in force. Despite this new wrinkle, most actuaries would have agreed with their Yorkshire Fire & Life colleague who predicted that the tables would 'not make any great revolution in rates ... [or] materially affect the results of our valuations.' Interest rates had declined enough since 1870 to offset the improvements in mortality that the O^M table showed for younger ages, and at older ages the O^M and H^M tables were nearly identical.[40]

Although few actuaries doubted the usefulness or scientific merits of the British Offices tables, many after 1900 were starting to question the wisdom of staging such a huge operation every several decades. Calls for 'a continuous system according to which each year's experience of all the institutions may be added to the past experience' had circulated since the 1840s, and these resurfaced in 1912 in the context of a proposal put forward by the Associated Scottish Life Offices for a 'Permanent Bureau of Research' that would track the mortality of annuitants, healthy lives, and 'those who have ... certain points which are believed to be unfavourable.' These plans were in place by early 1914, but they were shelved owing to the Great War. The committee resumed its work after the war, and in 1924 commenced a 'continuous investigation into the mortality of assured lives.' Fifty-two insurance offices contributed to this project, a higher proportion of existing firms than the sixty that comprised the British Offices tables. Despite its original goal of including higher-risk lives, this part of the project fell by the wayside. In the end, the same focus on healthy men prevailed: contributors were asked to exclude from their returns 'cases accepted on special terms' and 'female lives if convenient.'[41]

Odd People Out

In the broader context of Victorian vital statistics, the work of British commercial actuaries was uniquely focused on the single variable of age. Their interest all but evaporated when the question concerned variations in mortality among men and women, different occupations, and British subjects living abroad – all topics that produced voluminous studies by other statisticians. Instead, life insurance offices typically treated women as if they were men (sometimes charging extra to cover the risk of childbirth), acted as though nearly all occupations posed the same risk, and only gradually paid attention to available data on insured lives abroad. (They treated a final set of risk groups, involving poor health, in a similarly cursory and arbitrary manner; this is the subject of chapter 10.) For sex and occupations, the result was to collapse individual lives into an aggregate in which everyone approximated an average man. The result for travel was to charge what the market would bear, which only occasionally approximated the actual risk.

Until 1826 sex made no difference to life insurance premiums. That year, John Finlaison's discovery of a 'very extraordinary' difference in mortality between female and male annuitants prompted the Eagle to frame a table under which women paid 13 per cent less than men in their thirties and 19 per cent less at fifty.[42] Four other insurance companies followed suit in the 1830s, with smaller discounts.[43] The main purchasers of these policies were husbands whose wives stood to inherit money, and they jumped at the chance to pay less for securing their access to that money. Nearly a third of Eagle proposals in the 1840s were on the lives of women, compared with only 10 per cent of policies in the Seventeen Offices survey.[44] On average, customers did very well financially by these schemes, which failed to take into account the adverse selection problem that expectant parents (carrying the risk of death in childbirth) signed up for them in disproportionate numbers. The Seventeen Offices table revealed that insured men in their twenties lived two years longer than women, and that women outlived men only after they stopped being able to bear children. Based on this information, Charles Jellicoe convinced the Eagle in 1848 to charge the same for men and women; he concluded that there was 'no room for any reduction in favour of the fairer portion of the community.'[45]

Once bitten, life insurance offices were twice shy about framing special premiums for women in the aggregate. Although the Institute and the Faculty of Actuaries did collect information in the 1860s on female customers, no company made any use of it. The newly standard Healthy Males table consigned women to statistical limbo, in which extra premiums were set more or less arbitrarily based on a combination of medical opinion, actuarial guesswork, and haggling. Depending on the company, women were subject to exclusion, a single extra charge at the outset, a smaller annual extra through their childbearing years, or equal treatment with men – which still meant paying more at older ages than their life expectancy warranted. Although maternal mortality in Britain actually increased between 1900 and 1935, before steadily declining thereafter, most insurance offices waived extra charges for women by 1910.[46]

If life insurance offices treated women and men as if they conformed to a single age-adjusted average, they applied similar thinking to occupational mortality. This was the situation Charles Ansell faced in 1862 when he took the unusual step of disaggregating the National Provident's mortality experience by occupation. His results were striking: a cluster of trades, including merchants, clergymen, and farmers, cost the office around 30 per cent less in claims than a cluster that included clerks, bakers, millers, and publicans. Ansell concluded that 'if persons embraced in the more favorable classes were to associate themselves

together in an Assurance fund,' they would have every bit as much reason to exclude the higher-risk occupations as 'a class of young men'
would have for refusing 'to associate themselves on equal terms with a
class of older men.' James Chatham of the Imperial reached similar conclusions in 1891, based on census data: by rights, clergymen should pay
15 per cent below the standard rates for their life insurance, doctors and
butchers should pay 20 per cent above the standard, and innkeepers
should pay twice that tax.[47]

By the time Chatham made this pronouncement, the General Registrar's
Office had been churning out data for long enough to convince anyone
that its figures were correct. Yet no British actuary (including Ansell himself) followed up the National Provident study with another survey of
company-specific occupational mortality, nor did anyone involved with
the Institute's and the Faculty of Actuaries' surveys ever suggest that it
might be a fruitful topic of study. One reason for this was that many occupations had, in fact, taken up Ansell's suggestion and formed lower-
risk insurance pools. One of the stated advantages of certain types of
'class' offices was the higher bonus that was assumed to follow from a
group's lower aggregate mortality. Along these lines, John Hodgson
tabulated the Clergy Mutual's (very low) death rate in 1864 and followed
this up with a pamphlet in which he appealed to those results as a reason
to pick that office. More generally, as one actuary concluded in 1907,
'most offices obtain the bulk of their business from the middle and commercial classes, and with one or two exceptions ... were not seriously
concerned with occupations that were distinctly hazardous.'[48]

Indeed, the two exceptions that this actuary noted – 'naval and military risks and those attaching to the liquor trade' – were the only cases
in which life insurance offices paid any sustained attention to occupational mortality.[49] They did so in very different ways, owing to the huge
difference in how death occurred among those who served their country and those who served their country drinks. The first group primarily died from residence in insalubrious climes and from waging war. To
cover the first risk, insurers typically added 10 per cent to their usual
travel surcharge, to guard against the fact that officers had less control
over where they were stationed. To cover the second (which was often
increased by exposure to tropical disease, since most Victorian battles
took place in Africa and India), insurers resorted to ad hoc charges that
could triple the price of a policy (see Figure 4.1).[50] Although these extras
were seldom sufficient to cover war-related claims, soldiers and journalists alike recoiled at the prospect of adding so much to the cost of

Figure 4.1
Lowest available premiums for civilians and military officers travelling to India, 1808–1908, for a £1,000 whole-life policy, age of entry 30.

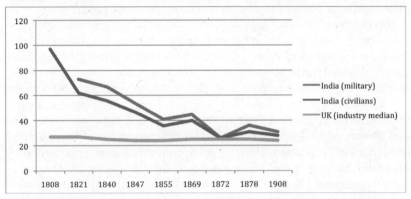

Sources: AtMB I (29 Sept. 1808); Tarn and Byles 1921: 51; Saint-Clair 1840: 61–2, 77–8; Eagle prospectus (1847); Tait 1855: 19–23; AMB VIII (3 Feb. 1869); *Statements* 1872, 1880; SLRV III (Sept. 1908); Pocock 1842: 166–74; *Life Assurance Premiums* 1910: 4–5.

fighting for one's country. Companies responded by offering peacetime licences that kept policies in force in the event of war – in effect folding the chance of war breaking out into their actuarial calculations. The Associated Scottish Life Offices set this charge at 10s per £100 in 1879, and by 1911 most other firms had followed the Scottish example.[51]

The risk of tending bar was less obvious than that of military service, and insurers paid relatively little attention to it up to 1860. New data from the General Registrar's Office, revealing death rates up to 70 per cent above the average, focused their attention on the problem, and a series of internal investigations confirmed Ansell's discovery that publicans were costing companies about 50 per cent more in claims than other customers.[52] Building on these studies, an Associated Scottish Life Offices survey in the 1890s revealed nearly double the expected mortality for publicans, which translated into a recommended extra of 25s per £100 coverage. Most Scottish firms followed these guidelines, but most English offices did not.[53] One reason that the Associated Scottish Life Offices results were less than definitive was that the primary risk associated with working in a pub was intemperance, and it was all too easy for a persuasive agent to insist that the candidate in question was unlikely

to imbibe. Another concerned the many shades of definition, and accompanying shades of risk, associated with the sale of alcohol: including Scottish licensed grocers, Irish 'spirit grocers,' and 'travellers in the
liquor trade,' all of whom died at markedly different rates.[54]

Travel abroad was a final category of risk that insurers devoted less
attention to than did many other statisticians. As with hazardous occupations, the main reason for this was that few enough British policyholders
travelled (less than 2 per cent, in the Healthy Males dataset) to pose a
major impact on their bottom line. On the other hand, almost no insurance companies lumped travellers in with the larger risk pool, as they did
with most occupations. In the 1840s they charged between 20 per cent
and 200 per cent higher than the standard premium, based (as one *Times*
correspondent complained) 'upon no scientific *data*, and ... governed by
no intelligible principles.' The main reason for this was probably the uni-
versally perceived association of foreign travel with risk: many people
about to travel were apparently willing to bite their tongues if the alternative was to die uninsured in the tropics. Already insured customers had
even less bargaining power, since they stood to lose several years' worth
of premiums if they failed to pay a travel extra and died abroad.[55]

Although travel surcharges steadily diminished over the course of the
nineteenth century, this decline followed a different pattern than was the
case for age-adjusted premiums. Instead of a cluster of insurance companies altering their rates in response to a published mortality investigation, a pioneering company would offer bold reductions in foreign premiums based on sketchy data and dare its competitors to follow suit. The
first such sea change came in 1845, when William Thomson framed new
rates for Standard Life and its sister company the Colonial, based on a
private store of 'information as to the duration of life in British North
America, West Indies, East Indies, Cape of Good Hope, Australia, and
other places.' Largely because Thomson's fellow actuaries trusted him
(the data were never published), this gambit led to an industry-wide reduction in travel surcharges in the late 1840s. A second shift occurred in
1870, when the Positive Government Security Life Assurance Company
took the radical step of eliminating all travel surcharges, based on an optimistic reading of a series of reports by the Royal Commission on the
Sanitary State of the Army in India. Although actuaries called its bluff and
forced it to revert to a higher scale, while its experiment persisted other
insurance companies' rates did decline significantly (see Figure 4.1).[56]

Thomson's private intelligence and the government-generated statistics that inspired the Positive Government Security summed up the

type of information on foreign mortality risk that was available for most of the nineteenth century. Companies doing business abroad relied heavily on data that actuaries collected while consulting for East India Company pension funds, as well as a series of government reports that tracked troop mortality in various British colonies.[57] For destinations further off the beaten path than India or North America, they relied on more qualitative information from foreign agencies or directors and customers with business ties overseas.[58] It was not until 1885 that the first published surveys of foreign insurance claims started to emerge, and these were few and far between – typically with sample sizes that bordered on useless.[59] To the extent that these statistics made any difference, they set a limit below which competition failed to drive prices. Above that limit, insurance offices charged what they could get away with, for as long as they could get away with it.

Manufacturing Actuarial Science

The tables that formed the basis of premiums and valuations in life insurance were the product of an extraordinary amount of work, only some of which was apparent even to the directors who paid for it. Actuaries moved from logarithms to life tables, generated columns of annuity values (which translated people's chances of living into monetary terms, compounded by yearly interest), and ended up with premiums or policy valuations. Along the way, life tables needed to be graduated to smooth out bumps in the mortality curve, and (for valuations) annuity values needed to be translated into distinctive policy values for each customer. Almost all of this work, up to (and sometimes including) the final set of premiums, would have been unintelligible to many of the people involved in selling life insurance, let alone the customers who bought it. On these tables, however, rested the financial stability, and in many regards the image, of the whole enterprise.

As much to further their nascent professional status as to enhance the reputation of their companies, Victorian actuaries loudly celebrated their conversion of raw mortality statistics into useable tables. In the first half of the nineteenth century, they were assisted in this by men of science, who recognized them as kindred spirits in the drive to make knowledge useful. Later in the century, as actuaries gained professional confidence, they honed their specialized knowledge in the more cloistered quarters of the Institute of Actuaries and the Faculty of Actuaries.

As actuarial science was evolving in this way, insurance salesmen paid attention to the claims to certainty (as opposed to mere probability) that this science produced. Early in the nineteenth century they marketed certainty by disseminating actuarial science as useful knowledge, mirroring the motives and style of the actuaries themselves. Later on, they dispensed with scientific instruction and jumped straight to (often overblown) claims regarding the actuaries' location in the pantheon of British scientific discovery.

Making Tables

As the historian John Eyler has observed, 'the construction of a life table in the nineteenth century was a laborious exercise in logarithmic computation.' The men who made such tables seldom hesitated to remind people of this, especially when they were hoping to be paid for their efforts. John Finlaison complained to a friend in 1824 that he spent eleven hours a day devoting his 'talents, time, and labour, like a galley slave ... on the calculations for the Life Annuities,' and Edward Sang told the Associated Scottish Life Offices in 1878 that his fifteen-place logarithm tables 'had cost him a prodigious amount of labour during many years.' Trade journals similarly commented on table makers' 'many weary hours of work unrelieved from the constant strain of mere mechanical effort' and referred to the result of such labour as 'monuments of industry.'[60]

In an era before the widespread availability of mechanical calculators, tables could not be made without a prior set of tables, the purpose of which was to save labour by converting complicated mathematical procedures into simpler ones. The most basic of these listed columns of reciprocals (allowing the calculator to convert long division into multiplication) and products.[61] The king of such tables listed logarithms, which rest on the equivalence of a number x and its corresponding function b^y. For instance, $\log_{10}$ of 3,000 is 3.466 ..., since $10^{3.466 \cdots} = 3,000$. Multiplication can be performed by adding two logs together, then matching the sum with its antilog (a log in reverse): 3,000 x 2,000 = the antilog of 6.767 ... (3.466 ... + 3.301 ...), or 6 million. Logarithms, which date back to the early seventeenth-century polymath John Napier, enabled actuaries to multiply numbers in succession without finding a separate product at each stage and to divide a series of numbers by subtracting successive logs. From there, they could perform the all-important task of calculating compound interest.

If £100 grows annually at 3 per cent, it is worth £103 at the end of the first year. Multiplying $\log_{10}103$ (2.013 ...) by 10 gives the value of £100 at the end of ten years: hence in that time the original £100 = the antilog of 20.128 ..., or £134.39.[62]

For logarithms to be useful, they needed to be accurately tabulated to several places, which meant that someone (typically an eccentric lover of mathematics with plenty of time on his or her hands) needed to calculate the squares of millions of irrational numbers. A wide variety of logarithm tables circulated during the nineteenth century, ranging from wallet-sized three-place cards to seven-place tomes with logs from 1 to 100,000 or more.[63] Two of Britain's leading logarithm producers were Herschel Filipowski, a Polish immigrant who performed odd jobs for various life insurance offices and briefly edited a Zionist magazine, and Edward Sang, who spent his long life working variously as a lawyer, a private mathematics tutor, a school and railway founder in Turkey, and a mechanics professor at Manchester New College.[64] Among numerous other tables, Filipowski produced a seven-place antilog table in 1849 that became the industry standard. From its initial publication in 1871 Sang's seven-place log table provided actuaries with 'a daily companion of great usefulness.'[65]

By the end of the nineteenth century, log tables and their ilk began to give way to mechanical aids to computation. The most basic of these, the common model of which reached British life insurance offices by the 1850s, was the slide rule, which multiplied or divided via ruled lines on two adjacent logarithmic scales. A more complicated device (and more expensive, at around £20) was the arithmometer, which was commercially available from the 1860s. This cylindrical machine multiplied or divided by turning a crank, which rotated attached dials. First introduced to British actuaries in 1871, the Alliance and Prudential soon used the arithmometer in valuations, and Ralph Price Hardy used one in constructing a Healthy Males table.[66] British actuaries were generally positive in assessing these 'uncanny instruments,' the 'self-checking' nature of which prevented the need for duplicate work.[67]

Armed with log tables or their mechanical equivalents, actuaries proceeded to the task of turning a compilation of mortality statistics into something that an insurance company could use. Once the data had been gathered (either by an industrious amateur, as in the case of the Northampton and Carlisle tables, or by a committee), they needed to be graduated – which was, as John Naylor told his directors at the Economic, 'the most laborious part of the process.' The point of graduation, Thomas

Bond Sprague wrote in 1875, was 'to deduce a satisfactory mortality table, that shall proceed without any abrupt changes and shall yet not deviate too far from the original facts.' This was also the occasion for Cambridge wranglers (like Sprague) to take their place among the actuarial rank and file, since it was the one problem in actuarial science that required 'the very highest mathematical attainments.'[68]

Into the 1880s actuaries assumed that mortality data needed to be smoothed because 'the intricate facts of nature' (in Farr's words) had been 'more or less imperfectly observed.' Assuming that mortality followed a naturally smooth curve was not the same thing, however, as presuming to know the law behind that curve. Neither Price nor Milne did, and even after Benjamin Gompertz announced such a law in 1824, it took time for actuaries to apply it to the smoothing of curves. Most eighteenth-century statisticians assumed that people died each year in an arithmetic progression. When Price published the Northampton table in 1783 he failed to observe a linear progression of death and, instead, converted the data directly into annuity values with only a few rough adjustments in cases where 'accidental and local causes' had obviously skewed the results.[69] Milne used similarly rough methods in 1815 to deal with the many anomalies that appeared in his Carlisle data, constructing 'death parallelograms' for each age (essentially a bar graph) and then drawing 'a line (as little curved as the other conditions will admit of)' along their tops.[70]

By the 1820s the growing interest in life insurance among skilled mathematicians produced several attempts to discover a 'law of mortality' that would more closely approximate a 'true' curve. The first such attempt was Gompertz's formula, which he developed in a pair of Royal Society papers presented in 1820 and 1825. Based on the assumption that some deaths were random and others were the result of 'an increased inability to withstand destruction,' Gompertz's formula exponentially related age with the random chance of dying (represented by the function q^x, where x = age and q = a constant) then multiplied that function by the initial 'power to avoid death'; the latter power was expressed as a constant, A, which (like q) needed to be determined with reference to the statistics that were being smoothed. In 1832 Thomas Rowe Edmonds published his own 'numerical law, regulating the existence of every human being,' which described three different curves that corresponded to the stages of infancy, manhood, and old age. Edmonds's formula was nearly identical to Gompertz's, initiating a priority dispute that persisted for several decades.[71]

Early Victorian actuaries used these formulas, but not extensively.[72] For the most part, they instead used increasingly elaborate methods of summation – a simple version of which, as deployed by Allan Curtis of the Gresham, entailed 'averaging for each age the sum of the figures against the two higher and the two lower ages added to its own.' Besides Curtis, who used summation to adjust his company's Austrian mortality, John Finlaison used it for his annuitant data, as did Charles Ansell for a table that he constructed on upper-class lives. The master of summation was W.S.B. Woolhouse, a Cambridge-trained consulting actuary, who used versions of this method (involving successively diminishing weighted averages) to graduate an Indian pensioners' table in 1839, the Seventeen Offices table in 1843, and finally the bulk of the Institute and Faculty tables in 1869.[73]

As actuaries started to make sense of the huge mass of data that the first Institute and Faculty investigation unearthed, they soon wearied of the 'old lengthy and complicated methods' that Woolhouse had perfected. In their place, they revived the search for 'an algebraic or analytic law among the numbers' that would circumvent 'cumbrous and extensive preliminary summations.'[74] The actuary who found such a law was William Makeham, who in 1867 added an extra constant to Gompertz's formula. In place of Aq^x, Makeham offered $Bq^x + \psi(x)$, with the extra function referring to 'certain partial forces, which we assume to be, in the aggregate, of equal amount at all ages.'[75] When Woolhouse graduated the Healthy Males table two years later, he worked from the adjusted data to determine Makeham's constants for British insured lives. With these in hand, it was easy enough to 'Makehamize' some of the British Offices data thirty years later.[76]

The British Offices tables provided Makeham's law with its first and last hurrah in relation to life insurance. After 1900 actuaries increasingly turned to integral calculus (which Woolhouse had applied to graduation as early as 1869) to improve on the 'cumbersome approximations' of earlier summation methods. Actuaries also turned increasingly to graphic methods of graduation, which had been almost unique to Milne through the 1870s. Sprague emerged as their leading champion, arguing in 1885 that drawing a graph to fit the raw data allowed 'the facts to speak for themselves and indicate their own law' – which neither Makeham's law nor Woolhouse's 'mechanical method of averages' allowed. For most tables, summation methods won out over graph-drawing after 1900, but either way the loser was what Sprague called the 'assumed law' of mortality. The *Insurance Record* greeted its passing with mixed feelings, noting that the new 'excellent and short formulas of approximate summation' meant that 'the search for a law of human mortality is now more or less officially abandoned ... relegated to the society of the philosopher's stone and the elixir of life.'[77]

Once a life table had been smoothed, it was safe to use it for pricing or valuing a policy. The first step in this process was to calculate the value of an annuity at a given age and interest rate. Using the Northampton table, for instance, the expectation of life at age forty-six is twenty years, so the value of a £1 annuity at that age is £20 minus the compound interest the annuitant collects on twenty annual payments: which at 3 per cent leaves £13.45. From 1825 the standard method for calculating annuity values was to construct 'commutation columns' labelled D and N, with D equal to the number living at age x multiplied by the fraction of £1 that is left after deducting compound interest from an annuity received for x years; and N equal to the sum of all the values for D from x to the age of the last survivor in the life table. Dividing N by D yields the value of the annuity – hence in the Northampton table, 3,270 of the original 11,650 people are living at age forty-six; £1 minus forty-six years' worth of 3 per cent compound interest is £0.249; D is 813.86; N (the remaining values of D through age 96) is 10,946.15; and N/D = £13.45.[78] First published in Britain in 1825, D and N columns greatly simplified the pricing and valuing of life insurance policies. Although some actuaries lamented that their 'powerful arrangement' deprived students of 'a knowledge of first principles,' the columns played an essential role in all subsequent premium tables and valuations in the nineteenth century.[79]

D and N columns formed the basis of David Jones's influential *On the Value of Annuities and Reversionary Payments*, published in 1843, which contained nearly fifty tables based on the Northampton, Carlisle, Equitable, and Amicable data. Jones's publication ushered in a golden era of readymade tables, most of which were the product of Scottish actuaries or clerks; an *Assurance Magazine* reviewer in 1853 wryly observed that 'the Carlisle Tables literally groan under [their] folio, quarto, and octavo labours.' Such tables indeed represented an immense amount of labour – in particular, the calculations of compound interest and the summations required for the N columns. The table-makers' labours lightened, but by no means eliminated, the subsequent hard work of fixing premiums and valuing liabilities. After 1870 the Institute of Actuaries and the Faculty of Actuaries took over most table-making work, the majority of which was done by assistant actuaries or clerks and paid for by life insurance offices.[80] These communal efforts stood in stark contrast to pre-Victorian table-making, which was more arduous, solitary, and private. When John Naylor created new premium tables for the Economic in 1828, he and two assistants performed thirty thousand calculations by hand; he came up with his own graduation formula when Gompertz's method did not meet his needs; and then the record of his labours remained buried in the company's minute books for the rest of the century.[81]

Selling Certainty

Natural laws, the philosopher Ian Hacking has observed, are at bottom nothing more than 'equations with some constant numbers in them.'[82] And, indeed, this is one way of describing the mortality laws that so many actuaries assumed to exist for much of the nineteenth century. Yet the concept of a mortality law encompassed more than merely a regular pattern among large numbers of deaths or a convenient formula for graduating the resulting curve. It captured the interest of many of the top mathematical minds in Britain during the nineteenth century and (along with the attraction of a regular salary) lured some of them to choose life insurance as their profession. Mortality laws also captured the imagination of company promoters, who associated their pursuit with the more general pursuit of useful knowledge. It is less clear whether insurance customers ever shared this interest in the scientific basis of what they were buying. Although life insurance offices certainly hoped they could be taught to do so, reports from agents and onlookers alike suggest that other factors – including the influence of friends and melodramatic appeals to death and destitution – carried more weight with customers.

Into the 1860s British actuaries repeatedly claimed that their life tables displayed 'the presence of a just order and law' or traced 'great *nature's* law ... within the narrowest limits.' Actuaries were encouraged in this way of thinking by many of Britain's most eminent men of science, whose advocacy of life insurance grew out of their campaign to reform the practice of British science, which they viewed as lacking in incentives for bright young men to pick as a career. Augustus De Morgan's *Essay on Probabilities* opened with the hope that life insurance would 'attract many from its commercial utility' and provide 'the gate through which some will find their way to ... other branches of science,' and natural philosophers tirelessly worked to accomplish this aim by explaining the basics of actuarial science in the *Penny Cyclopaedia* and in various treatises sponsored by the Society for the Diffusion of Useful Knowledge.[83]

This emphasis on useful knowledge spilled over into the marketing of life insurance. Several actuaries published treatises on the subject that doubled as promotional material for their own office. In his *Familiar Observations on Life Insurance* (1841), for instance, the Norwich Union's actuary provided 'a succinct account of ... the science of Life Assurance [in] its connection with many parts of philosophy and political economy' and praised the 'brilliant genius' of the men of science who had preceded him. When his secretary proposed to send a hundred copies of the book to a Liverpool agent, he insisted that 'education is all that is needed' for 'a greater number of lives being entrusted to us.'[84] Prospectuses distilled the substance of such treatises into five or six closely printed sheets, with the result that more abrupt truth claims prevailed: insurance premiums were 'settled on the infallible rules of mathematical truth,' and the average mortality in large populations had been 'reduced almost to a certainty.' Even these nutshells, however, trailed long lists of further reading, urging customers to tackle the more challenging validations of life insurance that writers like Babbage, De Morgan, and Milne had produced.[85]

By mid-century, when company speculation raged, promoters' claims regarding the scientific basis of life insurance verged on self-parody. William Bridges announced in 1854 that 'death and disease pursue their mission according to a law as rigid and mathematical ... as that of the planetary orbits,' the Briton Life's 1861 prospectus claimed that life insurance 'rests upon laws as certain in their operations as the movements of the Heavenly bodies,' and the Provincial's Robert Lewis declared in 1862 that mortality was 'subject to a law as immutable as the law of gravitation, or any other obvious law of nature.' The fact that the Mitre, which Bridges was promoting at the time, failed amid scandal within a decade, and that the Briton followed suit in 1886, underscores the wishful thinking that often went into these identifications between scientific and financial security. As De Morgan lamented to John Herschel in 1844, after reiterating his faith in the uniquely secure foundation of life insurance offices: 'That they do fail is evidence of something very wrong somewhere.'[86]

Owing in part to this obvious gap between claims to scientific truth and assurances of financial security, but also owing to a simple lack of interest in science, it was an open question whether customers paid much attention to the actuarial end of life insurance marketing. The Manchester surgeon Alfred Aspland, trying to explain the disrepute into which life insurance had fallen as of 1860, placed part of the blame on 'the technical formulae which overlay and obscure the whole subject' – concluding that customers found 'nothing very celestial in the science of algebra.' Closer to the action, Standard Life's English agency inspector complained in 1862: 'I cannot find that the public are able to understand these matters or indeed that they ever take the trouble.' Insurance salesmen were learning this lesson by the 1870s. One advice manual in 1874 urged agents to keep their minds 'well stored with apt and taking illustrations' as opposed to 'tedious figures and explanations,' since most prospective customers 'cannot appreciate the cost of the annual risk of death.' Another, writing in 1904, more succinctly urged: '*Don't* worry too much over actuarial figures.'[87]

Dispensing with 'scientific actuarial terms' in the marketing of life insurance (as one insurance handbook professed to do in 1876) was not the same as dispensing with science. Rather, it was an acknowledgment that more people were apt to trust in numbers than were interested in (or capable of) comprehending the numbers they were asked to trust. An *Economist* writer cut to the heart of this matter when he observed in 1865: 'There is no class of calculations of which people think so little or comprehend so little as insurance calculations. They pay their premiums; they receive their bonus. Even the best and most careful men of business do no more. They suppose some one understands how these figures are arrived at, and they know quite certainly that they themselves do not understand it. They accept what is allotted, but they do not comprehend the *rationale* of the gift.' One corollary to this proposition was that something more than science was needed to convince people to insure: perhaps the 'prejudices of a friend, or the flattering promises of an insurance agent,' as Aspland suspected, perhaps an appeal to domestic duty, or perhaps an appeal to life insurance as a savings mechanism. A second corollary was that public incomprehension heightened the ethical responsibility of those who did comprehend insurance calculations, namely, actuaries. This was the message Samuel Raleigh of the Scottish Widows' Fund hoped to convey in 1863 to Edinburgh's actuarial students. 'The fact that the true bearing of your investigations and calculations is but imperfectly understood by any portion of the public,' he cautioned, made it imperative that actuaries use 'the most scrupulous and conscientious care in regard to the principles on which you proceed.'[88]

Table 4.3
Mean annual premiums (in £) for £1,000 coverage, without profit

Year	Age (years)								
	20	25	30	35	40	45	50	55	60
1842 (52 offices)	17.73	19.91	22.52	25.74	29.84	35.06	42.02	51.30	63.70
1867 (96 offices)	17.03	19.23	21.90	25.05	29.10	34.24	41.26	50.98	64.22
1910 (57 offices)	15.83	17.65	20.06	23.22	27.32	32.63			

Standard deviation (% of mean), annual non-profit premiums

	20	25	30	35	40	45	50	55	60
1842	7.6	6.8	6.3	5.8	5.3	4.8	3.8	3.9	4.5
1867	4.0	3.5	3.2	3.3	3.3	3.6	3.4	3.5	4.2
1910	4.8	4.0	3.8	3.4	3.1	2.9			

Sources: Bridges 1842: 137–42; Dowdeswell 1846: 137–45; Hardy 1837: 245; Pocock 1842: 158–63; Walford 1867: 276–8; Life Assurance Premiums 1910: 6–7.

Disasters that Weren't: The Case of Epidemics

It would be easy to dismiss insurance salesmen's claims regarding the rigorous certainty of vital statistics as examples of Victorian scientific bravado. Indeed, Charles Dickens did exactly that in Hard Times when he had Gradgrind call the 'calculations of various life assurance and annuity offices' a case of 'figures which cannot go wrong,' as did Thomas Carlyle when he compared the compilers of the Northampton and Carlisle tables to 'some zealous scientific son of Adam' who 'had proved the deepening of the Ocean, by survey ... of two mud-plashes on the coast of the Isle of Dogs.'[89] But there was more than a grain of truth in what these salesmen said, and this is best seen in comparison with the status of underwriting in other forms of insurance, which lagged far behind life insurance both in data collection and (more crucially) in the calculability of their risks. Victorian actuaries routinely chided these insurers for failing to reduce fires and shipwrecks to the same statistical laws as crime, sickness, and fraud.[90]

It was certainly a fact that British life insurance premiums fluctuated far less than was the case with fire insurance. Throughout the nineteenth century, more than nine-tenths of Britain's life offices hovered

Table 4.4
Mean annual premiums (in £) for £1,000 coverage, with profits

Year	Age (years)								
	20	25	30	35	40	45	50	55	60
1842 (74 offices)	19.82	22.07	24.79	28.13	32.38	37.69	44.87	54.38	66.82
1867 (107 offices)	19.29	21.67	24.52	27.89	32.32	37.69	45.16	55.20	68.88
1910 (69 offices)	19.19	21.44	24.25	27.70	32.13	37.75			

Difference between with-profit and non-profit premiums (%)

	20	25	30	35	40	45	50	55	60
1842 (42 offices)	13.5	12.1	11.4	10.6	9.3	8.9	8.1	7.2	5.9
1867 (88 offices)	13.7	13.2	12.5	11.9	11.7	10.7	10.1	9.0	8.2
1910 (54 offices)	22.7	22.3	21.7	20.0	18.1	16.0			

Standard deviation (% of mean), annual with-profit premiums

	20	25	30	35	40	45	50	55	60
1842	7.4	6.5	5.8	5.2	4.8	4.2	3.6	4.6	6.3
1867	5.5	5.0	4.3	4.3	3.5	3.4	3.4	3.9	5.2
1910	5.5	4.8	4.3	4.2	3.9	3.6			

Sources: Bridges 1842: 137–42; Dowdeswell 1846: 137–45; Hardy 1837: 245; Pocock 1842: 166–74; Walford 1867: 272–5; Life Assurance Premiums 1910: 4–5.
Note: These averages and standard deviations do not include the London Life Association, which charged very high rates at the outset then offered substantial reductions in premium within ten years.

within 7 per cent of the industry's median premiums, a band that nar-rowed even more for older customers (see Tables 4.3 and 4.4). This stood in stark contrast to the fire offices' 'habitual price cutting,' which was especially prevalent prior to 1850, and which resulted both in wide disparities at any given time and major industry-wide swings over time. Much of this difference followed directly from insurers' relative ignorance of fire risks and consequent vulnerability to catastrophic fires, most notably London's Tooley Street fire in 1861. Major fires typ-ically resulted in a tariff agreement among several of the larger offices, which raised rates en masse – followed by customer dissatisfaction, a new round of lower rates by a few 'non-tariff' offices, and a gradual series of rate reductions.[91] From a customer's vantage point, the result was that it was much easier to anticipate the expense of insuring one's life over a period of many years than it was to guess how much it would cost to insure one's home or business.

Notwithstanding the clear shortcomings in fire underwriting during the Victorian period, it was also the case that mortality was simply more *calculable* than fires were.[92] As the American insurance commissioner Elizur Wright observed in 1859, fires were 'preventable on the one hand up to the limit of non-occurrence,' yet 'possible on the other up to the entire destruction of whatever is combustible'; in contrast, everyone died – it was just a question of when. Furthermore, fire risks were not always independent, since fires often spread from one insured building to the next. Specialist life insurance offices were keen to emphasize this as a point of safety, as when the Experience Life observed that offices with a fire insurance branch required 'a large and burdensome amount of capital' to guard against 'contingencies not admitting of the same certainty of calculation as those of Life Assurance.'[93]

Larger share capital was just one form of compensation for the lower calculability of fire insurance risks: others included the average clause, which paid only part of the claim if the loss was not total; imposition of rules regarding upkeep of property (installation of sprinkler systems, for instance); and above all, close cooperation among companies in adjusting rates to respond to new information.[94] And therein lay the most significant difference of all between fire and life insurance: since fire insurance policies could be cancelled by either party at the end of each year, it was possible for fire insurance offices to make money by reactively adjusting their premiums as they went along. This might render policyholders uninsurable if they suffered a fire, and might subject even fire-free customers to higher premiums if they owned a building that was reclassified as hazardous in the wake of someone else's disaster. In contrast, superior calculabilty meant that life insurance offices could afford to guarantee the same premium throughout the policyholder's life, regardless of new risks that might emerge owing to changes in that person's health or behaviour subsequent to buying the policy.[95]

Exactly how safe life insurance was is clear from the life offices' relative immunity from epidemic diseases, which were the closest imaginable equivalent to a major fire. Tracing the actuarial history of epidemics through the nineteenth century also indicates the life offices' growing confidence, over time, that they traded in a sure thing. At the outset of the century, several firms withheld their liability to pay claims in the event of such crises as 'the Plague or any contagious or epidemic disorder.'[96] When news reached Britain in 1831 that cholera was spreading in continental Europe, life insurance offices responded by rating up or refusing to accept new European proposals, although a later survey revealed that only forty-six of 150,000 insured lives had died in that epidemic. Insurance mortality from cholera in 1848–49 was higher, especially for offices with substantial Irish business, and opinions were split over its significance. The medical adviser for Standard Life worried that most victims had died 'at an age peculiarly unfavourable to assurance companies,' while the Scottish Amicable's medical adviser took heart from the fact that cholera mortality in life insurance offices had been 50 per cent less than among the general public.[97]

Since a third outbreak of cholera in 1853–54 was the last, at least in the British Isles, any further actuarial discussion of it was limited to the academic variety, and attention shifted to the still-prevalent threat of influenza, which was epidemic in Britain for most of the 1890s. On the one hand, influenza was a greater source of concern to life offices, since (as the Gresham's medical adviser urged in 1892) it 'attacked the well-nourished and the brain worker' who tended to insure, unlike cholera's alleged preference for 'the ill fed and destitute.' On the other hand, most people who died of influenza did so relatively late in life, so their deaths had little effect on profits. The average age of death from influenza was nearly seventy at the Rock, and 63 per cent of the £167,900 in claims that the Atlas paid on behalf of influenza victims in 1891 fell due when the policyholders were seventy or older. Comparable mortality ensued in the influenza pandemic of 1918, when it paled in comparison with war-related claims. By that time all actuaries would have agreed with George King's comment that 'even the most fatal plague ever known will hardly disturb the general average' of life insurance claims, in contrast with the impact of 'a terrible conflagration' on a fire insurance office.[98]

Conclusion

The development of the actuarial basis of life insurance during the nineteenth century epitomized the process that Max Weber famously identified as rationalization: the banishment of 'mysterious incalculable forces' and their replacement by 'the knowledge or belief ... that one can, in principle, master all things by calculation.' This was, after all, essentially the same lesson that a prospective policyholder could learn by reading T.C. Smithson's *Ten Minutes Advice to the Thoughtful and Prudent* (1852), in which life insurance taught 'the cheering fact, that ungovernable chance does not exist, and that what is commonly looked upon as uncertainty is governed by fixed laws of order.' This was also the lesson of an *Economist* article from 1882, which amended the magazine's earlier diagnosis of complacent incomprehension among policyholders. Recalling a time 'when, by the general public, the principles and practice of life insurance were regarded as mysteries which only the professional intellect could fathom,' the writer concluded that things had changed: 'The mathematical niceties of the business are, perhaps, as much as ever beyond the popular grasp. But the broad principles upon which the system is based are now pretty generally understood.'[99]

What had changed between the 1860s and the 1880s was that an unthinking trust in numbers had given way to a more 'thinking,' if not a more comprehending, trust. What brought this about was what Ted Porter has defined as a prerequisite for 'the uniformity of nature' to gain meaning in society: namely, sufficient levels of 'human organization – of regulation, education, manufacturing, and method.'[100] Most explicitly, regulation took the form of the Assurance Companies Act of 1870, which published annual statements of the bases on which life office accounts had been valued. Less explicitly, the well-regulated collection of vital statistics that resulted in the Healthy Males tables forged a consensus that ensured that these valuations, if not nature itself, were uniform. Education proceeded apace as well, but in a different manner than the 'useful knowledge' variety on display earlier in the nineteenth century. Instead of teaching customers 'mathematical niceties,' insurance guides taught customers how to recognize the impact of different valuation methods on the bottom line of premiums, bonus levels, and long-term financial security. Behind these visible faces of insurance science lay the labour-intensive manufacture of tables, which rested in turn on evolving methods for calculating and smoothing curves.

A second explanation for why life insurance customers came to trust in numbers by 1900 points to the many sorts of numbers that life offices did *not* compile. Well into the twentieth century, the bulk of their actuarial work remained focused on the same healthy males who provided the Institute of Actuaries and the Faculty of Actuaries with their signature life table in 1869. In stark contrast to most other Victorian regulatory projects that depended on vital statistics, life insurance companies refused to direct much attention to what Ian Hacking has called 'a governed class whose comportment is offensive.' With the exception of the handful of industrial offices like the Prudential, insurers neither collected statistics on these classes nor tried to 'change the laws of statistics' that such people obeyed.[101] Instead they stayed focused on the class of 'select' lives who obeyed laws that needed to be pruned around the edges, but never radically altered. As gatekeepers, they took an interest in all conceivable pathologies, ranging from intemperance to suicide to gout – but this interest disappeared once the insurance policy was in force, and only rarely reappeared after that, in the form of a disputed claim. The one pathology that truly interested them was pathological only in connection with the unattainable goal of immortality: it was, in the words of the actuary Edward Farren, 'the disease called time or age.'[102]

5 Death and the Salesman

Pray, don't forget, though healthy yet,
  You're subject to mortality;
The life of man we only can
  Foretell in the totality.
The first year's premium being paid,
  You may demise tomorrow, sir,
And then your widow will not need
  To either beg or borrow, sir.
  – from 'The Life Assurance Agent's Appeal,' 1860[1]

Selling life insurance hinges on convincing customers that death – their own or someone else's – makes a difference to them financially. Because of the enormous variety of financial implications that surrounded death in Victorian Britain, life insurance offices needed first to identify all the different customers who might be receptive to their sales pitch, then modulate their marketing to suit each type. Insured lives could be divided into two broad classes, each capable of further subdivision: breadwinners, whose premature death would interrupt the flow of income to their dependents, and debtors, whose premature death would impede the repayment of a loan. Within each of these groups, some needed life insurance more than others. At the top of the list, in either case, was the man 'who derives his income from any profession or trade,' as a Standard Life prospectus identified him in 1839.[2] A doctor, clergyman, merchant, or clerk typically had only his personal savings to pass along to his family, and often he could not save much if he died in the prime of life. For the same reason, such a man would also require a life insurance policy if he borrowed money, since he could offer nothing in its place as security for the loan. In contrast, many members of the aristocracy had sufficient property reserves to provide both financial security to their dependents and collateral to their creditors. This did not, however, preclude them from buying life insurance for either purpose. Life offices became adept at discovering the many cases in which an insurance policy was a more convenient method to provide for aristocratic families and at identifying spendthrifts whose need for credit outstripped their access to other forms of collateral.

Whether they were professing to protect the financial interests of dependents or creditors, life insurance offices presented themselves as future surrogates of the insured party. If the life in question belonged to a husband, the office held itself out as a breadwinner when his death interrupted the regular flow of income into the household. If the life belonged to a debtor, the office promised to pay what he owed when death snatched him from his creditor's clutches. The challenge of selling life insurance was different depending on whether a creditor or dependent stood to gain from the policy. Life offices assumed, apparently with reason, that it was harder to convince a husband to insure his life for the benefit of his wife and children than to get him to insure his life on behalf of his creditor. For one thing, they could sell policies directly to creditors, who would then pass along the cost of the policy as a surcharge on the loan. Issuing policies directly to wives or other dependents was impractical, and before 1870 it was also illegal for all but wealthy customers. Partly because of this, life insurance offices faced the difficult challenge of convincing husbands that since they might die at any moment, they had an obligation to start protecting their families as soon as possible. Consequently, whereas companies restricted their creditor-oriented marketing to brief descriptions of how a policy might add extra security, they targeted family men with melodramatic scenes of unanticipated death and tragic destitution.

The comparative ease with which companies could sell policies to debtors was convenient, since this form of insurance tended to attract negative publicity. Even insurance men had to admit that not all policies issued in connection with debts strengthened society's moral fabric. James Chisholm of the Imperial noted that some such policies did the good work of covering 'temporary indebtedness due to unexpected misfortune, which will make the struggle of life harder for a time,' but added that others 'afford security to enable a young spendthrift to squander his future inheritance.'[3] Such fine distinctions between deserving debtors and spendthrifts tended to vanish when this form of life insurance appeared in popular culture. Novelists in search of plot twists pounced on life insurance as a temptation for villainous usurers to speculate on the lives of others.

Partly to counter such negative stereotypes, life insurance marketing often shaded into imaginative realms. The same people who needed convincing to buy life insurance hungrily consumed evangelical sermons and melodramatic novels, each of which offered them comfort in a world beset by uncertainty. Like evangelists and novelists, life insurance salesmen brooded on death as a central fact in the drama of living, and they also offered continual reinforcements to the Victorian cult of domesticity. In contrast to these other cultural forms, which respectively suspended the hopes and dreams of their audiences in the afterlife and in fictions, life insurance offices needed to square their imaginative efforts with the hard financial realities that followed a breadwinner's death. Claimants discovered gaps between the implied promise of immediate payment and the weeks or months of delay that could accompany a claim; and often they learned that the coverage they had paid for was insufficient to meet the variety of costs associated with premature death. Life insurance offices worked to narrow these gaps between rhetoric and reality by liberalizing their contracts, by taking advantage of new laws that protected the property of widows, and (at the end of the century) by toning down their melodramatic marketing pitches.

Beneficiaries of Life Insurance

When Robert Southey became Poet Laureate in 1813, he used the accompanying pension of £90 per year to buy a £3,000 life insurance policy. He wrote to Walter Scott that 'this legacy to my wife and children' had filled him with 'the deepest feeling of thanksgiving.'[4] Twenty-five years later Charles Dickens wrote to his friend John Forster: 'I am going to insure my life this morning for Mrs D.' As it happened, he would have to wait six months to do so, since the first office he approached rejected him on the advice of its medical adviser – who, as chance would have it, was Southey's brother Henry.[5] What stands out in both of these cases, and in thousands like them throughout the nineteenth century, is that both men more or less accepted the sales pitch that life insurance offices invariably used when trying to sell policies to husbands: that life insurance was one of the best ways to provide for families dependent on middle-income men with minimal reserves of capital. Hence the 'chief utility' of life insurance, as *Chambers's Information for the People* noted in

1857, lay 'in securing a certain sum to helpless persons, in the event of the decease of those on whom they depend.'[6]

At the same time that life insurance offices were busy preaching the virtues of family provision, however, they were selling at least a third of their policies for the mostly distinct purpose of securing loans. Although the practice had been common enough since the previous century, the association of life insurance with loans – like so many other aspects of personal finance – spread during the 1840s and 1850s from the aristocracy deep into the middle classes. As with much else relating to credit, opinions about this development were decidedly mixed. Some insurance promoters called it an 'advance on the system of a person's assuring his own life,' which enabled lenders to 'grant facilities which they otherwise would withhold'; others condemned it as 'a *refuge* to escape the graspings of some modern Shylock.'[7] In fact, it was both: an inevitable by-product of the extension of credit to more people, prodded by aggressive marketing that came with the territory in the competitive mid-century life insurance market.

Protecting Dependents

The large majority of policyholders who bought life insurance to protect their dependents occupied what we would now recognize as the middle class. The best available index of this is a comparison by class of the proportion of 'own life' policies (paid for by the insured party) and third-party policies (usually taken out by a creditor to cover a loan). Among policies in force at the Legal & General in 1870, 81 per cent of those issued to professional men were 'own life,' as were 83 per cent of those issued to clerks, 75 per cent of those to merchants and manufacturers, and 74 per cent of the policies issued to shopkeepers. These proportions were much lower for military men (50 per cent), 'gentlemen' and nobility (59 per cent), and women (33 per cent).[8] Excepting those offices that specialized in insuring debtors, the proportion of 'own life' policies steadily rose over the course of the nineteenth century. At the Clerical Medical only 63 per cent of customers took out policies on their own lives between 1824 and 1850, compared with 91 per cent in 1871–95. By the end of the nineteenth century, the consensus was that in most life insurance offices 'family provision' as a motive for insurance prevailed against 'embarrassments and financial difficulties' by a margin of at least two to one.[9]

Even among middle-class customers, life insurance competed with other mechanisms for securing the support of dependents; the only

difference was that these other methods were both more firmly established among the aristocracy and more convenient for landowners to
carry out. The most common such mechanism was the marriage settlement, which reserved a fixed sum of money to be administered by
trustees while the husband was alive and which guaranteed the wife a
source of income during and after marriage. Legal fees for marriage
settlements started at £100, which made them impractical for sums
under £1,000 and were costly even for larger amounts. Most settlements were for £2,000 to £10,000, and typically they were invested in
low-yielding annuities. Middle-class property owners began to use
such arrangements more frequently after 1800, and they also had access to other forms of security, including urban real estate and goodwill in a trade or business, which could be realized upon death for the
benefit of their dependents.[10]

Compared with all these strategies, though, a life insurance policy
presented significant advantages, which extended to at least some aristocratic families as well. Life insurance offices urged the better-off merchant, who might hold enough property to provide for dependents if
he died prematurely, that a policy would protect 'his well-planned
schemes' from 'derangement' in that event. To less fortunate men, they
presented insurance as a simpler and lower-cost equivalent to a marriage settlement. A life policy, claimed one lecturer in 1857, was 'a valid
and legal settlement, and may be made to do the duty of a slender balance at the banker's.' In all these cases, the underlying assumption was
that the life of a middle-class man was 'a personal property,' giving his
dependents 'cause to fear' lest that property be withdrawn prematurely. Protection against this threat (whether through insurance or some
other means) was a special concern of middle-class men, who on average were several years older than their wives – increasing the chance
that they would die while their children were still in the home.[11]

The analogy between an insurance policy and a marriage settlement
took its sharpest form when a propertyless man desired to marry a
monied woman. Two days before Leonard Wolff married Virginia
Stephen, her guardian asked him to set aside 10 per cent of his income
(around £60) for a life insurance policy, in order to go part way towards supplementing her £9,000 in inherited wealth. Marriage to Lady
Emily Bulwer-Lytton in 1897 cost the architect Edward Lutyens even
more: an £11,000 insurance policy, which would have set him back
around £250 a year.[12] A less painful method of providing in this way
was to pay for a life insurance policy out of the interest that accrued on

a wife's settlement. Such arrangements were common enough to make it into contemporary fiction. When the vicar at the centre of Anthony Trollope's *Framley Parsonage* married a woman with 'a provision of some few thousand pounds,' he used the interest from her settlement to buy a 'heavy insurance on his life' – and had enough left over 'to furnish his parsonage in the very best style of clerical comfort, – and to start him on the road of life rejoicing.'[13]

Besides insuring his own life, a middle-class man who married into wealth often took out a policy on his wife, lest her premature death deprive him of his newfound fortune. When Lord Byron's mother-in-law died in 1821, he inherited property worth £2,500 a year, which at the time comprised nearly half his income. He immediately used a tenth of this income to buy a £10,000 insurance policy on Lady Byron's life, knowing that if she died this property would be diverted elsewhere. A Manchester timber merchant similarly took out an £8,000 Provident Clerks' policy on his wife in 1890 shortly after she inherited that amount from her father. Since the will stipulated that the trust fund would immediately pass to his grown children upon her death, he wanted to be secured against the chance that she died 'before a sufficient sum has accumulated out of the income to render insurance unnecessary.'[14]

Moving from men who married into the aristocracy to aristocrats themselves, there were often good reasons for such men to buy life insurance as a means of provision for the women and children who depended on them for income. Even when a landowner earned a large rental income, most of the property itself was typically pledged to his first-born son, leaving him in a very 'middle-class' position in relation to other family members. As long as he had inherited a debt-free estate, he could dip into this to set up trust funds for his wife and other children; but many such men had to mortgage their property to do so.[15] An alternative to this cycle of debt was to use part of the rental income to buy a life insurance policy. As the Rock urged in 1809, life insurance enabled a father possessing 'the largest landed property' to 'provide for all the younger branches of his family, without intrenching on the parent Stock.' Such provision was common enough, although typically relegated to a supplementary role. The £50,000 in insurance money that the Duke of Devonshire left in 1892 (half of which went to his only daughter) comprised nearly a third of his personal estate, but it was a pittance compared to the real estate, valued at £1.79 million, inherited by his only son.[16]

A second important sense in which life insurance protected the dependents of the very wealthy appeared abruptly in 1894, when Parliament imposed new duties ranging from 3 per cent to 12.5 per cent on inherited estates. Like death, taxation henceforth became a certain outcome with an uncertain appointed hour: and by taking out a life insurance policy, heirs could spread the cost and inconvenience associated with the new tax across many years and among fellow policyholders. It produced 'a large crop of special prospectuses,' most of which promised to pay the benefit directly to the government prior to the probate hearing. The effect was that a wealthy policyholder's executors would not need to sell off assets, possibly at a loss, in order to pay the tax.[17] Policies like these had a significant impact on the volume and quality of business done by many insurance companies. The Clerical Medical saw their new premium income increase by 27 per cent a year after the 1894 death duties came into effect; and industry trends away from larger insurances, whole life policies, and policies on older lives were slowed (if not reversed) by this new market.[18]

For the most part, however, these cases of aristocrats using life insurance to provide for dependents were exceptions that proved an increasingly reliable rule: Most life policies issued by most companies were purchased by middle- or lower-middle-class breadwinners. The Atlas at mid-century issued only 17 per cent of its policies on the lives of 'gentlemen' and military officers, with the rest covering merchants, manufacturers, and brewers (16 per cent); professional men (17 per cent); shopkeepers and clerks (17 per cent); other lower-middle-class tradesmen (13 per cent); women (13 per cent); and farmers (8 per cent). The Norwich Union and London Life yield similar proportions, with the only outlier being the Legal & General, which specialized in credit-related insurance. In the Atlas sample, the average sums insured by these groups reflect their wealth or income, and mark out with a kind of precision the second and third as 'middle class': £1,274 for officers and gentlemen; £987 for merchants, manufacturers, and brewers; £788 for professionals; and £367 for the rest (see Table 5.1).[19]

Protecting Creditors

Besides being used for family provision, life insurance also protected creditors against the contingency of a borrower's untimely demise. Such policies were typically issued directly to the lender (often another life insurance office), with the cost of the premium then passed along as a surcharge on the interest. Just as the proportion of 'own life' policies provides a rough indication of the relative proportion of

Table 5.1
Proportion of policyholders by occupation (%)

Company	Professions[c]	Merch/mfgr[d]	Lower m/c[e]	Gentry[f]	Other/n.a.
Norwich Union (1808–14)	19.5	12.5	9.2	6.9	51.9
Norwich Union (1815–17)	20.4	16.2	n.a.	12.9	51.5
Atlas (1845–52)[a]	16.5	15.8	16.5	17.2	34.0
Leg & Gen (own-life 1870)[b]	38.3	5.1	16.1	23.5	16.7
Leg & Gen (own-life 1871–90)[b]	31.2	5.1	12.7	34.6	16.1
London Life (1860–1918)	34.2	23.8	19.0	5.8	17.2

Sources: Ryan 1983: 1004; AtLD I–IV; LGLPR; LLRM.
[a] The Atlas sample does not include its Excise Department, which sold insurance at cheaper rates to excisemen.
[b] Legal & General policies are 'own-life' only: policies in force in 1870 and new policies issued 1871–90.
[c] Professions include bankers, clergy, attorneys, surveyors (all offices), and chemists (Norwich Union).
[d] Merchants and manufacturers include brokers, commission agents, and brewers.
[e] Lower middle class includes shopkeepers (including chemists, in London Life and Norwich Union), clerks, grocers, drapers, and other retail traders.
[f] Gentry includes peers, baronets, 'gentlemen,' and military officers.

life insurance policies that protected dependents, the volume of third-party policies offers a baseline for determining how many creditors resorted to life insurance. Hence (from the figures quoted above) only a third or so of the mostly middle-class policies issued by the industry at large performed that function – perhaps as low as 10 per cent in some offices. Such figures do not, however, reveal what happened to a policy after it was issued. At least some policies initially taken out to secure a debt ended up being kept up after the debt was discharged and used to provide for dependents. Many more that were originally issued as 'own life' policies subsequently migrated to creditors as collateral, where they often remained assigned until death. Roughly half of all the 'own life' policies issued by the Legal & General between 1836 and 1870 were assigned to third parties, and less than 7 per cent of these were ever reassigned back to the original policyholder.[20]

The fact that this market remained as vital as it did during the nineteenth century hinged on the unique exemption that creditors enjoyed under the 1774 Gambling Act, which banned all such policies where an insurable interest could not be proven to exist. Even so, it took several decades for their legal status to be settled. From the beginning everyone agreed that a policy was illegal if, at the outset, the claimant had no financial stake in the insured life. Far less clear was the case of a creditor who tried to collect on a policy after his debt had been repaid, since repayment apparently ended the insurable interest. Judges initially argued that life insurance offices were legally entitled to refuse such claims. Companies soon discovered that this privilege was double-edged, since it dissuaded creditors from taking out policies for fear that payment would be postponed until other means of securing the debt had been exhausted. As a result, starting in the 1820s they rarely denied claims on this basis. The Court of Common Pleas finally caught up with this practice in 1854, concluding that even if creditors who bought life insurance might often technically be gambling, they bought too much of it to allow a decades'-old statute to shake their confidence in receiving claims.[21]

Although the market for loan-related life insurance broadened after 1840, its original base and continuing anchor was the landed aristocracy. Reporting on mortality among insured landowners in 1861, the actuaries Arthur Bailey and Archibald Day attributed this market to 'the extent to which the practice of making settlements of property prevails in this country' – concluding on this basis that 'the practice of life assurance affords quite as much evidence of improvident as of provident habits.' Throughout the nineteenth century, the specialists in this market were the 'legal' offices, owing to their close ties to the attorneys who arranged loans for the aristocracy. Third parties purchased 52 per cent of new Legal & General policies covering 'gentlemen' or peers between 1871 and 1890, which (excluding policies issued on women) accounted for 44 per cent of the policies issued in that manner.[22]

Most aristocratic mortgages were adequately backed by rental income, which a creditor could almost always recover even if the original borrower died. Settlement trusts (and parallel Scottish laws of entail) invariably allowed a life tenant to borrow a specified amount on the security of his estate and guaranteed that his death would not endanger the credit that had been extended to him during his life.[23] Where life insurance entered the picture was in the many cases when a life tenant desired to borrow money for purposes not specified in the trust or in amounts that exceeded what his land was worth. In these cases, the money market appeared with a variety of loans secured by the rental income a tenant earned while he was alive (known as a life interest) or by the expectation of a future inheritance. Unlike a conventional mortgage, these loans were impossible to recover if the tenant died before they were repaid. Hence, at least from around 1815, they almost always came with a life insurance policy, the premiums on which could double the effective interest rate.

Even when accompanied by an insurance policy, lending money on the security of a life interest came with high interest rates. Although charging more than 5 per cent was illegal until 1854, life tenants got around this by selling life annuities to would-be lenders. In exchange for a lump sum, the debtor promised to pay an annual fee for the rest of his life – always supplemented by an insurance policy to protect creditors against his premature death. As their annuities piled up, landowners found themselves insured for enormous sums. Lord Chandos bought policies worth nearly £60,000 with a dozen companies to secure a loan from the Royal Exchange in 1827; by 1842 he was insured for £348,494 and was having trouble finding companies to increase his coverage. Although the mechanics of the loan were different after 1854, when life interests replaced annuities as collateral, the impact on insurance was identical. The Earl of Winchester, who borrowed £50,000 in 1865, paid £2,624 a year for a £55,000 life policy along with the £2,500 he paid in interest, which together comprised 28 per cent of his rental income.[24]

Another variety of loans, on so-called reversionary interests, catered to people whose prospects hinged on someone else dying before they did. To secure these, life insurance offices offered 'survivorship' policies, which guaranteed a fixed sum of money should a young heir-apparent die too soon to collect. Although some people bought them for family provision 'in the event of their survivorship *not* taking place,' as the Globe put it in 1857, they were more commonly used to convert prospective legacies into 'present negotiable securities.'[25] A similar type of policy that usually accompanied loans covered 'issue' risks – which guarded against such biologically implausible outcomes as 'Male issue from Husband and Wife aged respectively 65 and 56' and a seventy-five-year-old unmarried baronet producing a son. Compared with a standard whole life policy, such policies represented a fraction of the cost, since the risk was seldom likely to transpire.[26]

Middle-class debt, like its aristocratic counterpart, only occasionally needed to be secured by an insurance policy. Merchants and manufacturers, in particular, typically offered their merchandise or equipment as collateral, and all members of the middle class borrowed on their goodwill and on the personal trust of family or friends.[27] Still, to the extent that middle-class borrowers had shallower property reserves than the aristocracy, they patronized life insurance offices more frequently to shore up their loans. Life insurance in conjunction with middle-class debt flourished in the middle decades of the nineteenth century, both because of new forms of credit and because many companies pushed it. House purchase policies, offering diminishing term coverage in conjunction with annual mortgage payments, appeared from 1850 into the 1880s.[28] Other companies, including the Victoria and the West of England, lent money on customers' personal security (a very uncommon type of insurance investment) and backed each loan by a life insurance policy.[29]

With the exception of 'legal' offices, which quietly persisted in soliciting 'policies effected in connection with loans,' what had always been an ambivalent industry stance on that practice turned hostile after 1870 and remained that way until the turn of the century. In 1871, when the Edinburgh Life's London board urged a revival of such business, the head office roundly vetoed the plan, on the ground that they had 'turned out most unfortunate investments for the Company.' As competition heated up once again after 1900, though, new schemes revived links between life insurance and middle-class credit, as when the Scottish Temperance advertised in 1903 that 'a free home' had been 'at once provided for the wife and children' of a drowning victim who had included an insurance payment as part of his mortgage deed. To extend its traditional emphasis on aristocratic debt into the middle classes, the Legal & General offered a combined 'Building Society mortgage' and life policy from 1912, with eighty thousand of them issued by 1936.[30]

Although doing so could be lucrative, insuring debtors was the sort of business that gave life insurance offices a bad name. For one thing, creditors were more likely to sue a life office to recover a disputed claim, with the result that these often-sordid trials added to the public's impression that the typical policy was taken out by grasping usurers on the lives of dissolute spendthrifts. A case in point involved Richard Joddrell, who died prematurely in 1855 owing £21,000. When a life office disputed its share of the associated insurance claim on the ground that Joddrell had concealed intemperance from it, the creditor sued, and the whole story came out in the newspapers. Interspersed with tales of drinking binges and brawls were denouncements, by the life office's lawyer, of scoundrels who were 'ready to buy expectancies, and make such a bargain as often reduces young men to poverty for the remainder of their lives from the effect of the heavy charges they obtain on the estate.' This was not enough to turn the jury against Joddrell's creditor. When continually repeated by lawyers like him, though, it was more than enough to paint life offices as abettors of dissolution – and not, as their marketing efforts insisted, friends of the family.[31]

In fiction as well as in the courtroom, life insurance offices mainly appeared as encouragers of debt and enemies of domesticity. When the young hero of Edward Bulwer-Lytton's *My Novel* (1852) discovers that borrowing on a reversionary interest is his clearest path out of debt, his villainous rival adds insult to his injury by imagining 'nothing more likely to destroy natural feeling ... than to press the hand of a parent, and calculate when that hand may be dust – than to sit down with strangers and reduce his life to the measure of an insurance table – than to feel difficulties gathering round one, and mutter in fashionable slang, "But it will all be well if the governor would but die."' What William Thackeray called 'speculations in life and death' took centre-stage in the tragic final chapters of *Vanity Fair*, when Colonel Dobbin learns that Joseph Sedley (his wife's brother, who was smitten with Becky Sharpe) had 'effected a heavy insurance upon his life, whence it was probable that he had been raising money to discharge debts.' When confronted by Dobbin, Sedley insists his affairs are in order and says that the policy was intended as 'a little present' for his sister in case he died. When he does die three months later, with 'all his property ... muddled away in speculations,' it comes out that he had left half of the policy to Becky, and the company initially denies the claim on the suspicion that she had killed him for the policy money. Although she eventually collects, the Dobbins return their share of the claim and end all contact with Becky.[32]

Death and Dependence

Such depictions of life insurance made companies even more determined to drape themselves in images of domesticity, and even more likely to hide the loan side of their business from view. Fortunately for them, this latter form of business was usually handled with the requisite discretion by lawyers, and it did not require extensive publicity to find customers. Selling insurance to benefit the dependents of middle-class men, on the other hand, resulted in a torrent of prospectuses, pamphlets, and lectures designed to sanctify the life insurance policy as an inherent marital responsibility. These insurance stories followed rigid formulas, which both borrowed from and contributed to parallel accounts of death and domesticity that were available in evangelical religion and the Victorian novel. Death could strike at any moment; the uninsured would repent on his deathbed, but too late to help his wife and children; they would thereafter be plunged into destitution, after appeals to charity failed to suffice. The insured family, in stark contrast, acquired both strength and protection owing to the prudence of the husband and father.[33]

What emerges from this material is a deeper understanding of the resonance of female dependence in a culture that otherwise prided itself on independence. While the husband was alive, life insurance offices exaggerated his wife's dependence, in order to emphasize his duty to provide for her in the event of his premature death – as a Provident Life pamphlet put it as early as 1806, family provision was 'the great end of every honest man's solicitude.'[34] A necessary corollary of this was that widows would be incapable of fending for themselves without the benefit of a substantial inheritance. Yet at the same time, and in a departure from other Victorian archetypes of domesticity, life offices promised a form of *independence* for female beneficiaries, since they typically refused to interfere in how women spent their claims. Into the late nineteenth century, they presented themselves as surrogate breadwinners but not surrogate husbands. The extent to which these beneficiaries actually received enough money to achieve financial independence was a different matter, which will be explored in the final section of this chapter.

'The Shafts of Death'

Through the 1860s the most common method that life insurance offices used to instil in their customers a sense of domestic duty was to scare them with stories of unanticipated death. Insurance lectures and literature rang with ominous warnings regarding 'the sudden and uncertain tempest of the inscrutable To-morrow' and 'the proverbial and awful uncertainty of individual life'; depicted life as 'a fragile thread, which the slightest accident might break'; scoffed at 'the folly of anticipating a long life by mortals'; and chastised men 'for thinking their tenure of life so certain, while the shafts of death are every year flying in thousands around them.'[35] An especially rich illustration of this pervasive genre appeared in a Briton Life sales pamphlet in 1861, which peeked into the future of a man 'who to-day exhibits no sign of decay – who treads the earth ... in all the dignity of health, and sublimity of manhood.' Suddenly, this uninsured soul was 'cast upon a bed of sickness, and ... speedily called to his long account' – an account rendered longer still by relentless references to 'the unsparing hand of death,' 'the summons of the grim visitor,' and 'a visit from the King of Terrors.'[36]

As some of these examples suggest, life insurance offices diligently worked to put an end to what they depicted as an epidemic of bravado among potential customers: specifically, the belief that they would (literally) survive if they did not buy a policy immediately. An Era Life & Fire prospectus observed that most men 'thought of death ... merely as a vague and distant alarm, [to be] regarded without terror, and dismissed without reflection,' when in fact, it concluded, 'not one can say "I am safe."' A Star prospectus took this logic one step further, warning that an unexpected bout of sickness was just as fatal to one's best intentions to insure as premature death, since 'people can only insure when they are in the most perfect state of health,' and it concluded with a flourish: 'What anxiety must he who is waiting for the proper moment to insure, sustain at every incipient approach of illness? The spasm he feels may be the herald of cholera – the sudden ache in the temple the courier of death.'[37]

An equally macabre marketing message envisioned the actual deathbed of the uninsured breadwinner. A mid-century pamphlet asked its readers to 'behold your weeping, helpless dependents, gathered round your dying pillow'; and scenes of 'the Death-Bed of the Poet Burns,' stricken with remorse over failing to provide for his wife and children, embellished insurance literature well into the nineteenth century.[38] A related sales tactic was to conjure an insurance equivalent of Charles Dickens's Ghost of Christmas Future, and imagine the recently deceased husband looking over the tragedy that his failure to insure had bequeathed to his dependents. In place of 'the stone of the neglected grave' to which the ghost's finger directed Scrooge's gaze, life insurance pamphlets beckoned the customer to witness 'the miseries, which his widow and children would experience' should he die uninsured. Addressing an audience of Sheffield artisans in 1869, the Victoria Mutual's secretary appealed to the laws of mortality to claim that one in a hundred of them would be dead within the year, and concluded: 'If those who die could only rise from their graves and see how their good intentions had been frustrated – see their desolate wives and families – how bitter would be their disappointment.'[39]

To pressure indecisive customers into buying before it was too late, life insurance offices routinely broadcast examples of policies paid within a year of being taken out, with many retailing the same (possibly apocryphal) story about an army colonel who died on a life office's doorstep after paying his first premium on a £5,000 policy.[40] Examples of sudden deaths by explosions, epidemics, and accidents filled annual reports and rolled easily off of insurance salesmen's tongues. The Professional Life invited to a shareholder meeting several 'widows of policy-holders,' each mourning a husband who had died after paying a single premium. In this way costly claims provided insurance companies with the ample silver lining of increased sales. As the Scottish Equitable reported in 1887, after the Earl of Dalkeith died in a hunting accident within two years of taking out a £5,000 policy from them: 'Premature claims of this kind bring home to the public the uncertainty of human life; and if there were no premature claims, there would be very much less insurance.'[41]

Capitalizing on sensational tragedies was common to all forms of insurance, and life insurance was no exception. Hailstorms, railway collisions, cattle plagues, and a late Victorian London crime scare launched whole new categories of insurance companies, and major fires into the twentieth century 'frightened new clients into the market.'[42] For most insurers, disaster was a double-edged sword, since it posed major risks to their own survival as well as their customers' life or property. Life insurance offices, in contrast, could warn about calamity without overly fearing its effect on the bottom line – which at worst might be a failure to pay a bonus and most often had no noticeable effect at all. In this context, the most fearful (and hence profitable) Victorian calamity was cholera. Shirley Hibberd, in his pamphlet We Are Never Safe, observed that nearly half of the fatalities in the 1848–49 cholera epidemic had been 'hale, able-bodied – snatched ... from the freshest and hardiest blood of our land.' With or without such warnings, customers flocked to life insurance offices when cholera loomed. The Times reported in July 1831, when the disease was making its way towards Britain, that companies were 'so beset by applicants, to insure their lives, that the clerks in many offices have frequently been detained till 10 and 11 at night.'[43]

On first glance, the constant emphasis in insurance marketing on the uncertainty of life might appear to have been at cross-purposes with insurance companies' claims to be able to predict the mortality laws with scientific precision. Far from undermining their melodramatic claims, however, the collective certainty of mortality laws in fact enabled salesmen to heighten the individual uncertainty of death. One of the commonest quotes to appear in early Victorian insurance pamphlets was Charles Babbage's comment that 'nothing is more proverbially uncertain than the duration of human life, when the maxim is applied to an individual; yet there are few things less subject to fluctuation than the average duration of a multitude of individuals.' Other eminent popularizers of life insurance, including Augustus De Morgan and William Farr, echoed this assertion. Farr, for instance, pointing to a mortality table's prediction that 'of 882 persons aged 30 only 327 survive 42 years,' concluded that the rest 'drop off year by year; and at the beginning of the year no one can say, "I am not the man."'[44]

Dependence and Independence

At the heart of the life insurance offices' ceaseless focus on the death of the breadwinner and subsequent fate of his dependents lay specific assumptions about marriage. Insurance salesmen scoured newspapers for wedding announcements and otherwise kept 'a sharp look out on all newly-married people.' To men about to marry they presented a life insurance policy as 'a document which will prove that you have acted with prudence and forethought,' and they reminded parents of marriageable women that asking future sons-in-law to insure their lives would 'make your daughters' marriages less a lottery.'[45] Such rhetoric folded life insurance into a wider idealization of Victorian domesticity, whereby husbands were 'natural guardians and protectors' on whose continued health was 'suspended … the continued supply of the simplest and most necessary elements of support.' An insured husband, according to this formula, was 'a father to his children in the fullest sense.'[46] At least one life insurance office charged reduced premiums to its married customers, and many extolled the health benefits that allegedly followed from securing domestic happiness in this way.[47]

If insured men appeared in sales brochures as domestic heroes, their wives were portrayed more ambiguously. On the one hand, life insurance offices presented a view of female dependence within marriage that was exaggerated even by Victorian standards in order to emphasize the need for an insurance claim in the husband's absence: wives were 'help-less beings' who contributed 'little or nothing, ordinarily, to the product-ive power of the household.'[48] On the other hand, insurance companies were not immune from the sort of ambivalence that marked Victorian attitudes about women, whereby domesticity betokened power along-side helplessness. If a salesman's efforts to convince a husband to insure went nowhere, he turned to the wife, who possessed 'peculiar abilities' to sway 'the sterner but really weaker sex' with her 'gentle pressure and strong argument.' As 'the family purveyor ... and dispenser of all social requirements,' the wife could also be counted on to promote 'any economical action' of her husband. This portrait of the housewife as an insurance salesman's reliable ally, however, stood in tension with such countervailing stereotypes as 'delicacy of sentiment' and 'silly womanish prejudice' that were just as often presented as obstacles to selling insurance.[49]

The main focus on domesticity in life insurance marketing concerned its fate in the months after the breadwinner's death. Insurance sales-men presented a bleak outcome indeed for a woman, 'something worse than a widow,' whose lack of a claim subjected her to 'the rude waves of adversity, unprotected and unprovided for.' Act One of a typical insurance melodrama featured 'a steady, enterprising young chemist' who contracted fever, then spent days in 'an awful struggle between life and death' before his 'fitful gleams of consciousness ... faded into fevered madness.' Act Two inevitably ensued: 'He died; the business was sold, and shortly after the widow and children were applicants for parochial relief.'[50] Upon reaching this point in the story, the first thing a salesman faced was the possibility that the kindness of family or friends might alleviate the financial trauma associated with a bread-winner's death. To fend off this potential excuse not to insure, sales tracts bristled with references to the 'the forced charity of friends' and 'the cold and embittered assistance of more fortunate relations,' and appealed to adages like 'In prosperity friends are plenty, / But in ad-versity not one in twenty.'[51]

Putatively bereft of charity, the anticipated fate of an uninsured man's dependents was destitution, variously described in life insurance pamphlets as 'the despair of hopelessness,' 'the gnawing pangs of want,' and 'the rude shocks of poverty.'[52] One insurance salesman en-visioned a widow's fingers, once knowing 'no toil greater than that in-volved in the little offices of home,' now fated to 'blister and bleed over the roughest labour that is offered to unskilled and unsuited hands.'

Dependents of the uninsured fell swiftly from destitution to descent, which was grim for sons and worse for daughters. Poverty, warned one insurance writer in 1857, was 'the forerunner of crime, a gaol may be the destiny of your sons, and for your daughters a fate that makes your blood run cold even to think of.' A different author concluded that with even a £100 insurance policy, 'the home might have been preserved' to its mother.[53]

The obverse of the tragic tale of the uninsured breadwinner's premature demise was the hasty but remunerative departure of the recently insured. Although some writers conceded that the death of a husband and father occasioned 'pangs and sharpness' even for insured families, or recognized that there was no indemnification against the absence of a father's 'watchful eye [and] anxious care,' most rushed headlong to imagine scenes of unmitigated joy upon learning of the life insurance office's promise to pay. A pamphlet in 1843, for instance, boasted that 'the widow's and orphan's tears of love and gratitude would again and again gush forth, long after the heart that loved them had ceased to beat.'[54] It was at this point in the story that life insurance appeared most sharply as a surrogate breadwinner on behalf of the suddenly absent father. In its role as 'the protector of the fatherless and widows in their affliction,' claimed a Manchester branch secretary, the life office acted in lieu of the father as 'the benign guardian of the sacred tie of family life.' Others depicted the insurance claim as 'a substitute for [the husband's] personal aid,' which supplied 'the widow and the fatherless with bread.'[55]

Besides promising to be there with money when it was most needed, life insurance offices also claimed that this money would transform the widow's lot from dependence to independence. They could do so without departing from acceptable norms, since Victorian dependence often shifted rapidly from a virtue to a vice once it lacked a husband. Charity, one of the likeliest alternative means of support to an insurance claim, imposed on widows (according to one insurance writer) 'a deep sense of their altered and degraded condition.' In some cases, salesmen even extended this critique to remarriage, as when a British Equitable lecturer urged that life insurance would enable widows to 'exercise their own will' in that matter, instead of feeling 'compelled to marry again for the sake of a sheltering place, which might not be worthy of the name of a home.' The alternative to either charity or remarriage was for widows 'to live in peace and comfort in their own happy dwellings' – typically by using their claims to carry on the family business or to commence 'a genteel trade' on their own.[56]

Insurance, God, and the Novel

In their ceaseless ruminations on the chances and consequences of premature death, life insurance offices both drew from and helped to refigure pervasive Victorian sensibilities regarding death and dependence. Viviana Zelizer has described nineteenth-century American life insurance as 'a contemporary death ritual' that emerged alongside the commodification of funerals and the professionalization of estate planning. A similar trajectory unfolded in Great Britain, where Victorians celebrated death as an occasion for displaying their relative economic status, brooded over its implications for the transfer of property, and shuddered at its religious implications. Although many of these features of 'death culture' long predated the Victorian era, it was only in the nineteenth century that they became accessible, in some form, to most of the population.[57] Life insurance took full part in this transition, both by helping middle- and working-class celebrants of death to marshal the requisite financial resources and by nurturing attitudes towards death that resonated with broader cultural trends. To cite two prominent examples, few Victorians would have missed the substantial common ground that life insurance shared with evangelical Christianity and the novel. Although each of these quintessentially Victorian forms departed from the rhetoric of life insurance at crucial points, their many points of convergence helped to reinforce the sales pitch of the successful life insurance agent.

Life insurance and evangelicalism in Britain charted paths that were usually separate but closely parallel, and rarely in conflict. In addition to the large number of denominational insurers, the rise of temperance sections in many insurance firms after 1850 further solidified the institutional links between life insurance and evangelicalism. Clergymen often addressed customers at meetings, as when the Reverend John Anderson informed the Scottish Equitable that 'the refuge ... for the fatherless and the widow' embodied 'the spirit of the Gospel,' and the many ministers who held policies in offices like the Star set what one writer called 'an example to all to perform the Christian duty of providing for their wives and families.' Protestations against religious 'prejudices' against life insurance were common enough, but these mainly invoked straw men – as when a Dissenters' & General defender called such objections 'the mere drivelling of an unreflecting piety.'[58]

One clear point of overlap between life insurance and evangelical Christianity in the mid-Victorian period concerned their mutual obsession with death. The same 'shafts of death' that swirled through life insurance pamphlets filled the air in evangelical magazines.[59] Like the insurance company, these magazines reserved special consideration for tales of *sudden* death, which 'allowed no opportunity for spiritual preparation and repentance' in a theology bereft of the solace of purgatory. Pit disasters, shipwrecks, and other fatal accidents were common fare in evangelical magazines, which lingered on the tragedy of unrepentant sinners doomed to 'spiritual death.' Also like an insurance claim, evangelical salvation was available immediately and was only 'cashed in' at death. The only difference was that repentant sinners (as opposed to the unrepentant variety) rarely died in evangelical sermons, whereas death did not discriminate between the insured and the uninsured. A dead, recently repented sinner was of less use to the Salvation Army than a dead, recently insured policyholder was to an insurance salesman, because the saved soul was expected to lead a long life productive of good works.[60]

When life insurance offices moved from anxiously foretelling the breadwinner's death to pondering its financial implications, they departed further from evangelical discourse. For evangelicals, the married woman was the 'angel in the house,' burdened with the duties of converting her preternaturally sinful husband and of teaching her children to lead godly lives. Although uniquely empowering for women, this ideology introduced antagonism into the household and produced in men a painful tension between religiosity and masculinity, which they only partially remedied by such means as 'muscular Christianity.'[61] Life offices echoed this view of marriage, but only up to a point. Insurance salesmen pressured wives to preach to their husbands the virtues of insurance, which often qualified as a variant of the 'angel in the house' model. But it mattered, in this context, that wives were being enlisted to protect their own financial futures instead of their husbands' souls. In contrast to the soul-saving angel, who already had a sure ticket to heaven and faced the empowering challenge of passing that privilege along to others, the insurance angel desired to achieve financial independence after her husband's death. Whether she saved her husband's soul in the process was incidental to this fundamentally material objective.

A second vital cultural reference point that overlapped with life insurance was the narrative arc of the Victorian novel, which vied with life insurance in its devotion of energy to the themes of death and dependence. Even more than evangelical sermons, serialized novels often appeared side by side with insurance advertising in the same periodicals, aimed at precisely the same market. When the penultimate book in

George Eliot's *Daniel Deronda* unfolded in the *Fortnightly Review*, it concluded with Gwendolen 'crushed on the floor,' filled with grief that
'seemed natural in a poor lady whose husband had been drowned in
her presence.' Facing this passage was a back-wrapper advertisement
for the Scottish Widows' Fund.[62] In many cases such proximity might
have seemed too close for comfort, since those novels that directly discussed life insurance tended to focus on its sordid side. But this did not
negate their amply overlapping themes, and many insurance writers
took matters into their own hands by producing fiction themselves.
Hence the *Policy-holder* magazine ran a series of stories in the mid-1880s
with titles like 'Before the Wedding Ring,' and a collection of stories
published in 1869 bore the title *Kernels of Fact in Shells of Fiction*. An
earlier novella, *Dunston Magna: A Tale of Procrastination and Its Perils*,
told of an insurance agent who failed to sell a life policy to the local rector, then described the rector's tragic death from cholera while tending
sick parishioners.[63]

Like life insurance pamphlets, Victorian novels savoured death, with
depictions swerving between the coldly impersonal and the melodramatic. No novelist was more skilled in this art than Charles Dickens,
whose intermingling of Scrooge's fear of death and envy of domesticity
rendered *A Christmas Carol* one of the most popular books of the 1830s.
Death was virtually everywhere in *Bleak House*, where lawyers waltz
'equitably ... off to dusty death,' coroners witness death 'in its most
awful shapes,' and (most famously) the unfortunate Krook succumbs to
spontaneous combustion, 'of all the deaths that can be died.' Dickens
also found time in *Bleak House* for more conventionally melodramatic
treatments of death, as when the orphan Charley falls 'into heavy danger of death' before eventually 'growing into her old childish likeness
again.'[64] By constantly juxtaposing such sympathy-wrenching scenes
with impersonal reportage, Dickens and other novelists offered up the
same dual image of death that pervaded life insurance marketing. Both
used melodrama to convince people to take part in what Elaine Hadley
has called 'sympathetic exchange,' which humanized the 'literally non-
human institutions' of the market.[65] The only difference was that human-
ization was an end in itself for the novelist (albeit a painfully ambiguous
one), whereas the life insurance office hoped to use melodrama to en-
trench its customers more thoroughly into market relations.

Even more than death, domesticity was famously the domain of the
Victorian novel; and here, too, literary critics have uncovered striking ten-
sions between sense and sensibility that marked life insurance literature

as well. Nancy Armstrong, for instance, has identified a 'densely inter-woven fabric of common sense and sentimentality' in Victorian novels, which strove 'to individuate wherever there was a collective body.' In this reading, the female character is the key to unlocking the Victorian para-dox of the individual versus the social, since she was the one who inter-nalized the fears and desires wrought by the new market economy. Looking more closely at the regular rhythms of domestic life in the Victorian novel, Elizabeth Langland has noticed a more practical sort of agency enacted by female characters, who personified the wife's day-to-day challenge of squaring femininity with the supervision of household expenditure.[66] Armstrong's insights are very much in keeping with the domestic themes that emerged in life insurance writing, which only made sense if a woman (with her children as satellites) was present to personify the melodrama of loss in the context of financial interdependence. Langland's focus on women as managers similarly resonates with the insurance companies' ambivalent efforts to enroll women simultaneously both as potential passive victims and as domestic managers capable of convincing their husbands to insure themselves.

As with evangelicalism, it was in the resolution of the plot that life insurance departed most clearly from the novel. Here the departure was both more radical and less explicit than in the case of evangelical family values. Although people could die at almost any moment in a Victorian novel, novels more often than not reserved marriage for the final chap-ters, typically to invoke (however problematically) a final reconciliation of the contradictions that that moved the plot forward up to that point.[67] In life insurance fictions, marriage always took place at the outset, and the crucial choice was not whether to marry but whether to buy insur-ance. Death, not marriage, brought about the promise of reconciliation; instead of a husband emerging from the wings to shoulder his bread-winning duties, a wider social resolution followed the husband's inevit-able exit. For much of the nineteenth century, life insurance offices made little of this difference, choosing instead to identify their corporate per-sonalities as closely as possible with the Victorian family as depicted in the novel – even though, or perhaps because, novelists themselves usu-ally defined life insurance as an obstacle to domestic bliss.

Life after Death

If insurance companies were continually on the lookout to see how their sales efforts resonated with broader cultural attitudes about death and dependence, they also needed to be careful lest the gap grew too large between the depicted outcomes in their marketing literature and the real-life outcomes experienced by claimants. The immediacy of the financial reward, the relative financial autonomy of the widow and her children, and the sufficiency of the claim were all issues that could be called into question when a life insurance policy wended its way from the death of a breadwinner into the claimant's possession. Insurers moved slowly to address each of these issues over the course of the nineteenth century, in the process altering the way they did business. To the extent that any remaining gaps between the promise and reality of life insurance created dissatisfied customers, life insurance offices modulated their marketing in an effort to adjust.[68]

It literally went without saying in early Victorian sales tracts that most life insurance claimants would have to wait between three to six months after the policyholder's death before they could get their hands on the insurance money. Before 1825 the typical delay was six months after the policyholder's death, and most companies moved to a three-month waiting period by 1840.[69] The only justification they offered for these delays was that it took time to turn assets into cash, to conduct a title investigation, and to inquire into the policyholder's death. So things stood until the early 1880s, when a number of companies began to promise 'immediate' payment to go along with a wave of other liberal features that flooded the market at this time.[70] As with similar cases of liberalization, the majority of life offices had little choice but to follow suit once a critical mass started this trend, and the proportion of 'immediate' payers jumped from 12 per cent in 1882 to 73 per cent five years later.[71]

The type of claim that occasioned the lengthiest delays was also the type that was most commonly broadcast by salesmen – namely, that which fell due within weeks or months of its initial purchase. The Scottish Temperance's chairman referred, at its first annual meeting, to a £500 policy on the life of a Belfast man who died four days after it was issued, as a 'striking illustration of the uncertainty of life, and of the wisdom of even strong men making immediate provision for those who are in any way dependent on them.' In fact, his company had stoutly resisted this claim, arguing that he had never paid his premium, and only relented ten months after the man died when threatened with a lawsuit. A similar response greeted the sudden death of James Jolly in June 1880, eight months after he had taken out a £500 Edinburgh Life policy. After an initial investigation revealed that his 'certificates did not show very ascertained cause,' the company spent three months investigating the man's habits before deciding to return his first year's premium to his wife but deny the claim.[72]

Whenever a life insurance office imposed a delay in payment or disputed a claim, it subordinated its obligations as a surrogate breadwinner (caring for the widow after her husband had departed) to its fiduciary responsibility to the other members of the pool. This was seldom a popular move, since anything that appeared to redistribute income away from widows was ripe for criticism. This tension emerged most clearly in disputed claims, as when a sympathetic judge 'wrenched' a verdict from an indecisive jury so as to enable a cowkeeper's widow to collect £1000 from the Imperial Union. Companies that denied claims on the grounds of suicide were especially likely to risk backlash from jurors who bought all too fully into the widow's melodramatic plight. The *Insurance Record* reproached one such jury for setting 'their faces against ... law and fact' in a suicide case, acting instead 'from some bias of sympathy.'[73]

Despite delays and occasional refusals to pay, the fact remained that the large majority of legitimate claimants eventually did receive their money, which always provided valuable aid at a time of economic need. This was not always the same thing, however, as the financial independence that life insurance offices taught future widows to anticipate. At the most basic level, an insurance claim first passed through the hands of the executors of the will. Even when the widow was one of the executors, the claim's most typical transit from there, at least among higher-status families, was into a trust fund, where the widow often handed over power of investment to a set of trustees. Most wills appointed family members or close friends as trustees, on the basis of personal fidelity rather than any expertise at money management – which came with a clear opportunity cost, and sometimes resulted in financial disaster. Some wills restricted the widow's access to these funds in order to preserve them for the purpose of educating children or enabling a son to enter a profession. Especially when this was the case, the life office's role as surrogate breadwinner found its analogue in the trust manager, who continued after the husband's death to play the role of protector to the widow's role of dependent beneficiary and sometimes did so only until the widow remarried.[74]

When a widow did receive permission to spend her insurance claim, the outcome sometimes fulfilled the life office's promise of financial autonomy, although such cases were probably the exception to the rule.

When the Quaker bill broker William Alexander died at the age of fifty in 1819, a life insurance policy allowed his wife (once she had obtained his executors' permission) to keep the firm solvent; she also took the unprecedented step of taking over as head broker for five years until her son came of age and joined her as a partner. She steadily built the business, which had been tottering on the brink of insolvency in 1819, and left £14,000 when she died in 1861. Yet for every report of a widow who turned her insurance claim into a fortune, critics could point to a spendthrift claimant whose insurance money accelerated her descent. Exemplary was the case of Fanny Russell, whose husband fled to Australia to escape her 'irregularities and dissipation' and died shortly thereafter, leaving her with a £200 insurance claim. A few months later she appeared in criminal court; evidence at the trial revealed that she was spending her insurance money 'as fast as she could' and 'bringing her eldest daughter, a girl of 16, up to her own vicious habits.'[75]

Even if it was well invested and well spent, there was no guarantee that the coverage a policyholder could afford would enable his widow to maintain the lifestyle she had enjoyed when married. In his novels, Anthony Trollope was fond of countering the hopeful strains of the life insurance office prospectus with the harsher realities of just how little income even a relatively large policy generated. When a vicar in *The Bertrams* (1859) leaves a £600 insurance policy to his widow and five children, the eldest son has difficulty deciding 'whether their wants or their griefs were most heartrending' when he returns home from university. To avert 'such poverty as this,' he appeals to a marquis for a living far away from home, which separates him from both his family and from the woman he loves. More generally, the tragedy of the insufficient claim was a mainstay of Victorian melodrama. In Geraldine Jewsbury's novel *Agnes Lee* (1857), a £1,000 claim leaves the protagonist 'sitting sadly before the fire' with 'only herself to depend on.' A widow in another story from 1898 laughs that although her husband's £200 insurance policy would not generate 'enough to live on,' it might 'make enough to starve on.'[76]

Adding to the disparity between the promised independence and actual fate of beneficiaries was the fact that many life insurance policies, despite originally being purchased to benefit a man's dependents, were assigned to creditors by the time he died. On the other hand, since much middle-class credit was provided by family members or friends, a life insurance policy did at least mean that these people, if not the widow herself, were better off than otherwise would have been the case. And being able to repay a dead husband's creditors, of course, was better than nothing. The fact that the debt-ridden Sir Walter Scott maintained payments on insurance policies worth £22,000 went a long way towards enabling his executors to get his widow out of bankruptcy within a year. In contrast, because Bishop Samuel Horsley failed to renew his £5,000 policy shortly before his sudden death in 1806, his widow had to sell off all his property to get out of debt.[77]

R.J. Morris has shown that around the age of forty, the 'middle-class property cycle' turned breadwinners from being 'net payers' to 'net receivers' of interest. This suggests that chances were fairly good that a middle-class policyholder who died prematurely – precisely the envisioned context for so many melodramatic depictions of insurance-assisted independence – would still have 'many personal and business loans outstanding.' Revealing, in this context, is the story of Peter Ewart, a Standard Life secretary who died prematurely in 1854. Although he had taken out more than £5,000 in life insurance, its proceeds were insufficient to pay his debts, funeral expenses, education for his three children, and his widow's rent. In a failed effort to get the firm to chip in something extra, the London board recorded Ewart's 'deathbed ... hope as some consolation to his afflicted wife, that she and his children would be cared for when he was gone.' Although an older widow with few or no dependents could comfortably make ends meet on £200 a year, only around 5 per cent of all policies issued in the 1870s were large enough to yield even £50 a year – let alone £200.[78]

Such gaps between the promise of self-sufficiency and the reality of indebtedness led many life insurance offices to seek ways to place their claim money beyond the reach of creditors – extending to policyholders' dependents the same protection that marriage settlements routinely afforded. In this regard, British insurers lagged behind American and Australian legislatures. New York's Married Women's Act (1840) enabled widows to collect on a life insurance policy worth up to $300 in annual premiums free from creditors' claims. Massachusetts copied this law four years later, most other states followed suit within a decade, and by 1862 the Life Assurance Encouragement Act provided similar protection in New South Wales. Citing these precedents, the British insurance promoter Arthur Scratchley circulated a petition in 1863 for a law that would guarantee dependents a minimum amount of coverage regardless of the breadwinner's solvency at death. Commenting on the petition, the *Post Magazine* posed a dilemma that would resurface in later years: 'The plain English of this is, that assurer A, in order to provide for his children, ought to be legally privileged to deprive creditor B of the means of making like provision for *his* children.'[79]

Before any new British laws appeared, the Norwich Union produced a market solution in 1867 in the form of 'settlement policies,' which extended the mechanism of the marriage settlement to policyholders' dependents.[80] Although other life offices would not follow the Norwich Union's example until the 1890s, a new law in 1870 allowed them to protect their policies from creditors without having to set themselves up as trustees.[81] The Married Women's Property Act (first passed for England and Wales in 1870, then for Scotland in 1877) enabled a woman to effect a policy on the life of her husband or herself 'for her own separate use,' forming a trust not 'subject to the control of the husband or to his creditors'; roughly the same language appeared in a follow-up law in 1882, although this one revoked the trust if 'intent to defraud the creditors of the insured' could be shown. Life insurance offices responded with 'family policies' and 'marriage settlement policies' as soon as the first law was passed. The Scottish Provident promoted its new product as ideal 'for the benefit of wives and children without the risk of having them attacked by the husband's creditor'; the English & Scottish Law similarly advertised such policies as offering 'An Absolutely Secure Family Provision, *excluding the control of Creditors* and without a separate Trust-Deed.'[82]

The ability to shelter policies under the provisions of the Married Women's Property Act was a big advantage for life insurance offices, which had hitherto been guilty of promising widows an outcome that was contingent on the husband staying out of debt. On the other hand, policies issued under these acts brought into focus a different problem that insurers had long managed to keep out of view: namely, that policyholders often needed to borrow money to be able to keep up their premium payments. Prior to 1870 many insurance firms encouraged the practice by lending up to the surrender value of the policy. Policies issued under the Married Women's Property Act did not come with this luxury, with the result that lapse rates for such policies were much higher. Despite this problem, however, such policies were popular enough to lead many companies to alter the way they dealt with lapses in order to be able to keep offering them. In particular, some followed the American model (itself an adaptation to the statutory protection of family provision) of providing smaller paid-up policies in lieu of a surrender value for customers who could no longer afford to insure.[83]

Conclusion

By the 1880s, life insurance offices began to retreat from many of the core marketing strategies that had carried them through the previous fifty years. Partly this was an adjustment to gaps between promise and practice, but mainly this was a response to wider cultural shifts. Ceaselessly provoking anxiety about 'the heavy hand of death' was heavy going, even for a culture steeped in evangelical foreboding; and as atonement waned as a central Victorian tenet, so did the life insurance industry's effusive focus on their customers' demise. Around the same time, domesticity began to decline as a deeply held 'masculine' value, making the life office's status as a surrogate breadwinner less meaningful for its mostly male customers. Neither of these retreats was complete, however; and some of the deeper themes that underlay much Victorian insurance marketing not only persisted, but spread to other human activities.

When an insurance writer complained in 1884 about those who 'keep perpetually insinuating that you may be one of the unfortunate beings to be cut off in the prime of manhood and sent to an early grave,' it was a sign of the times. In a similar vein, a Scottish actuary expressed relief in 1900 that the more accurate term 'death insurance' was not used to describe his chosen trade, since talking 'perpetually upon the subject of death even in its relation to insurance would be a lugubrious vocation to engage in.'[84] Late Victorian life offices were not alone in this tendency to spend less time brooding about death. Around the same time, social reformers succeeded in toning down the tawdry and expensive trimmings that accompanied Victorian funerals, so that by 1910 the *Undertakers' Journal* lamented that 'there are many nowadays who, when the private bereavement comes, refuse to make themselves conspicuously sorry.' The anguished focus on the deathbed, long a middle-class staple, first took up new residence in working-class Salvation Army tracts, then quietly retreated as a quaint Victorianism.[85]

As death faded from the Victorian imagination, the ideal of domesticity likewise underwent major transformations that left it open to criticism on several sides. Men began to associate the domestic sphere with femininity, the evangelical decree to cherish home and hearth began to recede, and middle-class women either foreswore early marriage for the workplace or continued to work while married. In response, insurance companies fitfully began to market financial services directly to women and more generally started to downplay their old message that paying for a life insurance policy was a conjugal duty. In part, this transition was made easier by the fact that insurance was, indeed, as much a social as a domestic mechanism for maintaining financial security. This logic was apparent in a sales pitch one insurance manager recalled using in the early twentieth century, in which he expressed surprise that 'a man with your heavy family responsibility should be content to bear the whole burden of that responsibility upon your own back.' The manager concluded: 'If you will co-operate, others will share the risk with you, and your share would only be about 3 per cent. of the burden.'[86]

In no sense could these departures from the Victorian focus on death and dependence ever be complete, as long as the basic point of life insurance and the British embrace of the breadwinner wage continued to prevail. At least part of the challenge of life insurance marketing will always be the conversion of uniquely personal tragedies into indemnifiable risks, and the imaginative tools of melodrama have survived as an aid in that process. George Orwell could still plausibly have his insurance-salesman protagonist state in *Coming Up for Air* (1950) that a successful sales tactic was to 'scare' candidates 'in a subtle way with hints about what'll happen to their wives if they die uninsured.' And even a casual glance at latter-day advertising copy attests to the continued relevance of domesticity to life insurance marketing. The Phoenix targeted newlyweds in its new 'First Essential' policy in 1937, and one of the Eagle's most popular policies in the 1950s and 1960s was a 'Wife and Home' plan that urged customers to 'Keep it in the Family.'[87] Increasingly after 1900, however, these methods shared space with concurrent emphases on the value of insurance as an investment option, a tax shelter, or both.

If echoes of the melodramatic Victorian insurance story remained audible after 1900, its deeper messages persisted as well. This was most clearly the case with the simultaneous appeal to the uncertainty regarding one's individual fate and the secure scientific foundation that allegedly made buying insurance such a wise choice. Today, we all pass through life with a shady awareness of various risk factors associated with our diet, lifestyle, and environment. All these risks are identified through scientific research, and yet at the same time we filter them through a range of personal responses: from 'it will never happen to me' to 'I am at risk.'[88] The job of the insurance salesman in the nineteenth century, in this regard, is today the job of the primary care physician, the public health official, or the environmentalist: to generate a sufficient 'sympathetic exchange' with the relevant public in order to get them to take to heart personally what can scientifically only be defined as a collective risk. As risk-awareness becomes part of the solution to an expanding array of social and medical problems, it pays to remember that generating such awareness faces the same sort of complacent resistance that life insurance offices first confronted more than a century ago. To overcome that resistance, Victorian insurance promoters tried with endless creativity to convince customers that they were never safe; and in many more avenues of existence today, many people continue to try and convince us of exactly the same thing.

6 Consuming Interest

Throughout the scientific world of Life Assurance, there is ... a little tendency to find deep ways of adjusting very simple matters. I have met with perhaps a dozen ways of dividing profits.
    – Augustus De Morgan, memo to Alliance Fire & Life, 1867[1]

Even in the gloomiest corners of Victorian culture, life insurance was never exclusively about brooding over the untimely demise of breadwinners. From its earliest appearance, life insurance was also always about the accumulation of capital. This was a primary underpinning of the eighteenth-century association of life insurance with gambling, and it resurfaced after 1780 in the new guise of the bonus. Starting with the Equitable and subsequent mutual offices, and quickly copied by 'mixed' offices that split their surpluses between policyholders and shareholders, the life insurance bonus produced the potential of doubling or even tripling the face value of a policy by subjecting it to the reproductive power of compound interest. Customers registered their fondness for combining fund management with insurance in this way by almost exclusively buying whole life policies (which maximized their bonus-earning potential), and by paying 'participating' rates that could reach up to 35 per cent higher than was needed to cover the basic contingency of premature death.[2]

As Victorian life insurance offices used the bonus to communicate their investment potential to policyholders, they concurrently established themselves among Britain's biggest institutional investors. Although they spent less time cultivating this self-image than fashioning themselves as benefactors of widows and orphans, signs of their growing investment power were easy enough to spot by mid-century. In 1853 William Farr defined the life insurance office as 'a Company of Capitalists constantly looking out for long investments, and well organized, to deal profitably in securities at some greater risk than those returning 3 per cent. interest'; sixteen years later the *Economist* included life offices 'among the greatest capitalists in England.'[3] As more people insured their lives, life funds swelled in relation to those held by all other Victorian asset managers apart from banks. In 1880 British life offices boasted £150m in invested capital compared with £470m in bank deposits; by 1914 their assets stood at £530m, compared with £1,150m held by commercial banks, £256m by savings banks, £120m by building and friendly societies, and £90m by trust companies. In Scotland the gap between life offices and banks was narrower: £47m compared with £105.6m in 1886 and £118.2m compared with £167.8m in 1914.[4]

Although they attracted less than half as much capital as banks, life insurance offices were better than banks at focusing attention on investment as a social practice. Interest on a bank deposit was fixed, and it accrued in increments that were so small as to pass unnoticed by most customers. The money that life insurance offices added to their policyholders' claims, in contrast, was not fixed across time, nor did it accrue in small increments. Since life offices had to balance their bonus against the continued security of the life insurance fund, they periodically adjusted its level. And since the task of calculating a safe and fair bonus was hugely labour-intensive, most offices waited at least five years between declarations. These two factors turned the life insurance bonus into a significant event, to be first anticipated and then experienced with either gratification or disappointment. Although life offices did not originally intend this outcome, the bonus meeting would eventually become a potent marketing device, attracting customers' attention to a firm's underwriting efficiency and investment savvy.

Most economic historians have thoroughly appreciated the important contribution of life insurance to the Victorian capital market. Few, however, have heeded the more subtle sense in which life insurance offices, through their bonus declarations, publicized money's reproductive powers. This relative lack of curiosity about the companies' social role as fund managers dates back to Victorian times, when financial writers (if not the companies themselves) subordinated financial considerations to the quasi-sacred task of aiding widows and children. Sound portfolio management appeared in such accounts as playing a necessary but supporting role in the working of a life office, and it was seldom seen as the primary factor in the rising popularity of life insurance during the nineteenth century. Recent historians have noticed exceptions to this story without altering its main features. They have pointed to the rash of life offices that formed during the Napoleonic Wars as vehicles for shareholders to enrich themselves by pocketing the difference between fixed death benefits and inflation-leavened reserves. Yet, according to this version of events, the 'dissolute' behaviour of these early life insurance offices inexorably gave way to a more prudent wave of companies after 1825.[5]

These accounts minimize the debates that agitated British life insurance in the 1830s as offices formulated competing bonus schemes, and downplay the subsequent impact of bonuses on management and marketing. Most bonus schemes gave most British policyholders a tangible reason to pay close attention to both the administrative efficiency and investment yield of their life insurance office. And since most bonuses were not payable until after the policyholder's death, it was even possible for insurance companies to display a heartfelt interest in investment performance without relinquishing their reputation for thrift. Beyond drawing attention to the investment side of life insurance, bonuses brought the fair allotment of their assets to the fore as a marketing concern. As life insurance offices vied with each other to broadcast their 'peculiarly equitable' division methods (to quote the Edinburgh Life's 1885 prospectus), they taught Victorians a tangible form of distributive justice.[6] Such debates helped to revive and sustain a focus on mutualism among life insurance companies, even though that focus had shifted from its original altruistic aims.

Invest and Divide

Asset management has traditionally been a trade in which a special premium is placed on the possession of accurate information. The investor with the most current knowledge about the present and prospective position of the widest range of stocks will outperform the market to the greatest extent. It is hence ironic that life insurance offices, which from the late eighteenth century on prospered as institutional investors, owed so much of their initial prosperity to actuarial ignorance and failed foresight. Lack of accurate vital statistics led life insurance firms to set premiums that erred substantially on the safe side; this, together with an excusable failure to anticipate the inflationary windfall during the Napoleonic Wars that padded the value of their reserves, meant the price of a typical life insurance policy far exceeded what was needed to cover the risk. As offices watched their surpluses grow, they realized that part of this excess could be safely added to the value of policies, in the case of a mutual society, or to shareholder dividends, in the case of a 'proprietary' (or joint stock) society. As news of the Equitable's largesse to its policyholders surfaced, market pressures led many of the latter firms to share at least some of the windfall with policyholders as well. This new practice of paying a 'bonus' to customers would change the face of British life insurance by the mid-nineteenth century.

For bonuses to become popular, however, a more basic tenet of asset management needed to succeed: life insurance offices had to find outlets for their rapidly growing accumulations of capital. Clive Trebilcock has identified four such outlets favoured by 'enterprising' life insurance offices in the nineteenth century. The first relates to the war years of 1790 to 1815, when they lent money at high rates to an 'embattled Government.' The second runs from 1815 to 1835, when the most popular investments were loans secured by the estates and annuities of the 'fading landlord interest,' who were willing to pay to preserve their social status. The third covers the period 1835 to 1870, when 'proliferating towns and cities' generated a demand for municipal bonds and for loans on personal security. And after 1870, life insurance offices began to follow other institutional investors into a newly diversified stock market.[7] This basic story will be fleshed out in the next section, using new archival information and (for the period after 1870) a more detailed analysis of Board of Trade returns on the portfolios and yields of life offices. The subsequent section will discuss the large variety of ways in which life offices divided the resulting surplus among their customers, and the complementary role that non-participating policies came to play in the marketing and administration of bonuses.

Generating Interest

Which investments life insurance offices picked over the course of the nineteenth century depended on their availability, the presence of competing investors for the same type of stock or loan, and the unique demands and advantages that life insurance held as an institutional investor. On the latter point, the predictable nature of when their liabilities would fall due translated into much lower liquidity requirements than was the case for either fire insurance companies or banks.

Once life offices figured this out after 1820, they moved from government stock, which was very liquid but (for that reason) subject to large price fluctuations, into mortgages and debentures, which remained on the books for decades but yielded higher and more constant rates of return as a result. When other investors moved into this field after 1870 (resulting in lower yields), and when an agricultural downturn made lending on the security of land more risky, life insurance offices found their way back to a transformed stock market. Instead of a handful of stocks dominated by government issues, the market after 1870 featured a wide array of foreign and colonial bonds, and bonds and shares issued by railways and other companies. These fluctuated in price as much as had been the case earlier in the century, but their variety allowed life offices to turn a handicap into an advantage by diversifying their portfolios – cashing in high-priced stocks as claims fell due and holding the rest until their value had recovered.

Although early nineteenth-century life office portfolios did include some mortgages and company shares, the vast majority of their holdings between 1800 and 1820 lay in government stock – in particular the consolidated perpetual annuities (or Consols, so called since 1751) that nominally yielded between 3 per cent and 5 per cent depending on when they were issued. For life insurance offices that bought these before 1815, the yield was actually much higher, since they sold well below par for the duration of the war with France – their low price and correspondingly high yield resulting from new stock issues that exceeded the supply of available capital. In aggregate, Consols held by life insurance offices may have reached £20 million as of 1820. Although this was small beer in the context of an overall addition of £623 million to the national debt between 1793 and 1816, it was enough to generate upwards of £1 million in interest for life offices and thereby solidify their reputation as fund managers.[8]

With the end of the Napoleonic Wars came a steep rise in Consol prices, from £57 in 1815 to £93 in 1825. Life insurance offices that formed or grew in volume of business after 1815 sought new investment outlets from that point forward, since higher-priced Consols rarely paid much more than their face value of 3 per cent or 4 per cent, and since one of their advantages – liquidity – was seen to be less important now that the security of their premium tables had been well established.[9] Older offices, meanwhile, sold off most of their Consols over the next four decades, reaping the enormous capital gains afforded by the high sale prices. Government stock comprised just 16 per cent of aggregate life insurance funds in 1857 and less than 2 per cent by the turn of the century, and during that period they declined in absolute terms from more than £15 million to less than £4.8 million. One of the most popular early alternatives to Consols was to buy life annuities from people who had exhausted other avenues of credit.[10]

The other major alternative to Consols after 1820 was mortgages on property. Life insurance offices that began to move in this direction soon dominated a field they shared with unencumbered landlords and West-end banks. By mid-century many companies held 40 per cent or more of their assets on the security of real estate, yielding between 3.5 per cent and 5 per cent.[11] Especially before 1850 many of these loans came in huge chunks: two earls owed the Royal Exchange £268,000 in the mid-1860s, the Earl of Derby owed the Legal & General £100,000 in 1854, and the Duke of Buckingham owed the Norwich Union a whopping £446,000 (40 per cent of the firm's total assets) in 1848.[12] Historians have concluded that life insurance offices played a major role in encouraging sustained levels of aristocratic debt, at a heavy annual cost but rarely occasioning 'widespread financial embarrassment.' From the insurance companies' perspective, these mortgages formed part of a feedback mechanism: the insurance they sold to collateralize aristocratic loans reappeared as new mortgages, producing in their turn a demand for more insurance. What the landed aristocracy received in exchange for participating in this pyramid scheme was several additional generations of a viable estates system that secured their power and status.[13]

The Irish famine of 1845–47 and its aftermath cast a darker shade on the risks, rewards, and social consequences of lending on landed property. When rental income dried up during the famine, a wave of bankruptcies transferred huge tracts of mortgaged land to insurance companies, which evicted tenants by the hundreds to clear room for grazing. Although these firms claimed to be furthering 'the employment of the Irish people,' their actions often left them open to the charge, expressed by one tenant in 1862, that their 'sole object ... seemed to be to get as much as possible from the property and spend as little on it in return as they can.' If a few life insurance offices directly cleared land after the famine, many more lent money for that purpose. Between 1866 and 1880 the Scottish Widows' Fund alone lent more than £1.1 million in this way, and total life office loans on Irish land in 1885 approached £10 million.[14] Agitation for land reform and home rule in the 1880s quickly reversed this trend. Many insurance companies rejected all Irish applications for loans after 1881, and the lucky few without any Irish commitments advertised their good fortune. Reason number four in a leaflet entitled 'Twelve Reasons why I should Assure in the Sun Life Office' was 'Because none of its Funds are in Irish Mortgages, while many offices are thus heavily invested.'[15]

The problem of Irish mortgages after 1880 mirrored in amplified form that of a wider agricultural downturn that between 1875 and 1900 sent rental income in England down by 25 per cent. Since life insurance offices generally lent up to two-thirds of an estate's estimated rent, this wiped out much of their margin for repayment of old loans and greatly reduced the amount they were willing to pledge for new ones. Mortgages on property hence fell as a proportion of life office assets from 56 per cent in 1871 to 29 per cent in 1900.[16] Additionally, the nature of the property they did lend on changed, from large country estates to urban buildings. Only 45 per cent of Yorkshire Fire & Life mortgages in 1888, for instance, were on land, with the rest on shops, houses, warehouses, and factories. Attracted by interest rates of 5 per cent to 6 per cent, British life offices also lent aggressively on foreign and colonial land after 1880, with these assets reaching £12.6 million by 1895. Scottish firms led the way, contributing in no small measure to an Australian land boom in the 1880s and switching to North America and Argentina at the turn of the century after that boom had subsided.[17]

Compared with other insurance company investments, mortgages were the most onerous to administer. The work began with tracking down the property's title, which was one of the main tasks a life office's lawyer performed. This was especially hard work in England, where the absence of title registration could make for lengthy delays. Lending without a proper title could make it hard to take possession of foreclosed property (if the title could be shown to belong to someone else) or to sell off property once it was foreclosed.[18] Next came what the Prudential's actuary called 'going round to the properties to see that they are in good condition'; most firms relied on outside surveyors for this, although some had directors who were able and willing to act in that capacity.[19] Most labour-intensive of all was foreclosure, which (though rare) could agitate directors for years on end when it did occur. The Legal & General learned this when it foreclosed on a Birkenhead estate worth £40,000 in 1852, then spent the next three decades trying to sell it off at a profit.[20]

An increasingly popular alternative to private mortgages after 1840 was loans to local authorities for the construction of public works, poorhouses, schools, and cemeteries. Unlike mortgages on land, which could be repaid on short notice, municipalities repaid their loans in predictable instalments, usually on a thirty-year schedule; these loans were also more secure than private mortgages, since local taxpayers pledged their repayment. Life insurance offices typically waited until market rates were high to make municipal loans, since this let them freeze such rates (usually 4.5 per cent or 5 per cent) over a long period of time. Rates on municipal loans were also high through the 1870s because, like private mortgages, they were off-limits to trustees.[21] Especially for provincial life insurance offices, municipal loans also offered a means of signalling participation in the local community. The Scottish Amicable was the only life office to assist in financing Glasgow's new waterworks in the 1860s, the Yorkshire Fire & Life's only municipal loans in the 1840s and 1850s went to projects in or around York, and the West of England held 47 per cent of the debt owed by Devonshire's poor law unions in 1852.[22]

Besides exerting disproportionate influence locally, the cumulative impact of life insurance offices on municipal credit was enormous. In 1874 life offices were owed 62 per cent of total British poor law union loans, 78 per cent of Metropolitan Local Management Authority loans, 60 per cent of drainage and embankment loans, 40 per cent of sanitary authority loans, 32 per cent of burial board loans, and all but £430 of £252,530 owed by London school boards. Most of these loans were concentrated in a handful of firms: one hundred poor law unions owed four life offices £1.3 million, and six firms held 60 per cent of the debt that burial boards owed to life offices. This dominance only waned when local authorities began issuing bonds (which were more attractive to private investors) and when the Trust Investment Act of 1889 made it legal for trustees to lend on local rates. The resulting competition drove interest rates down to less than 3 per cent by the turn of the century, and municipal loans accordingly fell from 18 per cent of life office assets in 1871 to just 9 per cent in 1900. Although they rebounded in the following decade, nearly all this activity was overseas: only 43 per cent of loans on local rates in 1910 were in the United Kingdom, compared with 91 per cent in 1890.[23]

The towns that exchanged their mortgages for bonds after 1880 had discovered a method of raising money that railways had been avidly pursuing for forty years. Railway debentures, which were fixed-interest bonds issued on the security of a company's revenue and share capital, emerged as a popular instrument of railway finance after the stock market crash of 1847 created a slow share market. Several life insurance offices were quick to see the advantage in buying these bonds: eight of them held £4.2 million in debentures or debenture-backed mortgages in 1871. Most of these firms featured directors with special expertise or connections in railway finance: John Coles at the Clerical Medical was a stockbroker who specialized in debentures, and the Minerva, with close ties to the Great Western Railway, held 60 per cent of its assets in debentures when it was absorbed by Standard Life in 1864. A few insurance companies in the 1840s even took a chance on railway preference shares (which were less secure than debentures, but still paid higher dividends than 'ordinary' shares) – although the vast majority shared Griffith Davies's view that these were 'decidedly undesirable and incompatible' with a life office's 'high character.'[24]

This attitude started to shift in the 1870s, when company shares comprised 12 per cent of new life office investment. Most insurance firms waited longer to add debentures to their portfolios, since the failure of several debt-financed railways in the mid-1860s put a temporary hold on new issues of these bonds. When they did become available in the 1880s, 20 per cent of net new investment was in debentures and another 12 per cent in shares, and in the 1890s more than 60 per cent of net new investment occurred in these two areas. As with land and municipal loans after 1890, much of this activity took place overseas, especially in India (where local taxpayers guaranteed dividends on railway shares) and North America. Nor was the surge in stocks and bonds after 1890 limited to railways: foreign and colonial government bonds comprised an additional 15 per cent of net new investment in that decade, and at least a few life offices ventured into debentures issued by British breweries, retail chains, and trust companies.[25]

As this wide variety of investments implies (including overseas mortgages and municipal loans as well as bonds and shares of all sorts), diversification was the new watchword for most actuaries and directors by 1900. The days were long past when a company could afford to hold the large majority of its assets in a single type of investment; instead, as one insurance writer noticed as early as 1879, the new trend was to 'put out ... a thousand different sums in a thousand different directions.' To the increasing extent that actuaries informed fund management decisions after 1890, diversification was a logical extension of their 'usual cardinal rule of spreading risks' from lives to assets. After 1900, and especially after 1920, it was also a rational response to inflation, since holding fixed-rate mortgages went from being a wise to an unwise strategy in the context of rising as opposed to declining prices.

In that new context, liquidity gradually emerged as a priority – not to meet unexpected claims, but to stay abreast of price movements. Share prices, which held little interest for most life insurance offices for a century after 1830, became the new focal point of investment policy in the 1930s, when actuaries developed an equity index to help monitor them. Their Actuaries' Investment Index, first proposed in 1929, was published in the *Financial Times* from 1962 and was a direct forebear of today's FTSE .[26]

When diversification first emerged in the 1880s, it was primarily a response to an alarming erosion in yields, from an industry average of 4.45 per cent in 1874 to 3.75 per cent at the end of the century. This fall was part of a more general decline in interest rates, which resulted from Britain's surplus capital increasing at a faster pace than new investment outlets – and from the shrinkage of two very old outlets, as the British government and landed aristocracy reduced their respective debts. Owing partly to new investment strategies, and partly to improved financial markets, average yields rebounded after 1900 and crept back above 4 per cent by 1910. Worst hit during this cycle were those firms that expanded in the 1890s, when high returns on new investments were the hardest to find. The Star watched its yield drop from 4.3 per cent in 1890 to 3.5 per cent a decade later, as its net assets increased nearly 75 per cent from £2.8 million to £4.8 million. From a starting point of £3.6 million, the 'ordinary' branch of the Prudential generated a staggering £15.6 million in net new assets during the 1890s, on which it earned less than 3.3 per cent.[27]

Better-performing life insurance offices during the rocky decades after 1890 fell into four categories. At the top were American and colonial firms doing business in the United Kingdom, which had direct access to higher-yielding securities. The next best thing to having a head office abroad was to have well-established branches there: three of the ten British firms with the highest yields between 1895 and 1910 (the Gresham, Standard Life, and Norwich Union) were also leading exporters of life insurance.[28] A third category of top performers was the legal offices, which used their aristocratic connections to secure high-interest loans on property during an otherwise flat mortgage market. The Legal & General, which led all British insurers with an average yield of 4.25 per cent between 1890 and 1910, invested 67 per cent of its net new assets in mortgages, reversions, and life interests, compared with an industry average of just 11 per cent. Finally, the Legal & General and Norwich Union also picked the right time to expand, more than doubling their assets during the buoyant decade after 1900 – as did Sun Life, which built its life fund from £4.7 million to £10.3 million in that decade, and outperformed the average industry yield by nearly 8 per cent.[29]

Although the portfolios of nearly all life insurance offices were substantially more diverse in 1910 than they had been forty years earlier, firms diversified in different directions. In 1873 only 25 per cent of life offices held at least 10 per cent of their assets in more than two Board of Trade categories, and only four spread their assets to this extent in four categories. In 1910, 74 per cent of life offices held 10 per cent or more of their assets in at least three categories, and five firms held at least 10 per cent of their assets in five categories. Within this wider range of assets lurked a similarly wide range of different investment strategies. A recent analysis has revealed standard deviations of 7 per cent in preference shares, 10 per cent in municipal loans, 14 per cent in debentures and non-British government stock, and 18 per cent in private mortgages held by life offices in 1913 – variations that would remain constant or grow even wider as the twentieth century progressed.[30]

The Invention and Evolution of the Bonus

The first life insurance bonus, in the modern sense, was a cash distribution by the Equitable in 1776, fourteen years after it had been established. Its actuary, William Morgan, calculated an available surplus of £25,143, out of which he allocated £11,000 in cash among the society's members. Five more divisions followed between 1781 and 1795, which came as additions to the value of the policy and were payable, like the policy itself, upon the member's death. By 1809 a £1,000 Equitable policy taken out in 1770 had increased almost fourfold in value to £3,900.[31] From the individual policyholder's perspective, such impressive gains needed to be taken with a grain of salt, since they mainly compensated beneficiaries for forty years' worth of overcharges and for the reduced purchasing power that came with inflation. From the perspective of the Equitable as an institutional investor, however, the advantages of the reversionary bonus were less ambiguous. Since the transfer of funds was only on paper, the office could declare a substantial bonus without sacrificing its ability to make long-term investments.

By 1810 the Equitable's bonus policy was having two effects, neither of which Morgan savoured. The first was that the prospect of sharing in the Equitable's substantial wartime gains led to a dramatic increase in membership. To most life office managers this would have been gratifying enough – but Morgan was concerned that these new members 'would always be urging an improvident distribution of the Society's stock' by voting themselves extravagant surpluses. He first dealt with this threat in 1800 by stretching the interval between divisions to ten years, then again in 1816 by convincing a majority of members to restrict the bonus to the five thousand members who had been with the society the longest.[32] The first effect of the Equitable's financial success directly led to the second, which was that several life insurance offices formed in order to compete with its unique combination of life insurance and fund management. Some of these, like the Norwich Union, copied its purely mutual constitution; others retained the entire surplus for the benefit of their shareholders.

Initially, strictly 'proprietary' offices were content to let mutuals lure middle-brow customers with the prospect of profit-sharing, and they focused instead on the numerous upper-class customers who took out life insurance policies as security against personal debts. Under this system, policyholders got what they paid for (a licence to borrow), even though what they paid had been proven to be excessive. The obvious winners were the shareholders, who received in higher dividends what the fortunate five thousand policyholders in the Equitable were getting as bonuses. Offices that formed after 1800 pointed to the Equitable's track record and the continuing high rate of return on Consols to promise 'a handsome Dividend' on invested capital. This started to change after 1820, however, when a wave of new proprietary companies pressed against the built-in limits of the aristocratic market. The lament of the Globe's Chichester agent that 'owing to ... the Assured not participating in the profits he was able to do but little business,' had become common among such offices by the 1830s.[33]

An obvious strategy for joint stock insurers in search of new customers was to imitate the Equitable and return part of the surplus to their policyholders. Hence a new sort of 'profit-sharing' company emerged that periodically distributed bonuses to customers and shareholders alike. The Rock and the Provident pursued this strategy from their inception in 1806; others switched over once they recognized its potential for increasing market share, usually with immediate and dramatic effects.[34] By 1840 more than fifty of the seventy proprietary British life insurance offices were returning at least a third of their surplus reserves to policyholders, and the few remaining hold-outs relented one by one: the Royal Farmers and the Pelican in 1840, the Royal Exchange in 1842, the Albion in 1844, the Britannia in 1845, the Globe in 1852, and finally the Yorkshire in 1858.[35] Meanwhile the average proportion to be divided increased, from 65 per cent in 1839 to 81 per cent in 1867 (see Table 6.1).

Table 6.1
Life insurance office bonuses, 1842 and 1867

	1842	1867
Mutual offices (% of total)	22 (22.4)	25 (25.8)
Non-participating offices (% of total)	10 (10.2)	0
Other offices (average % divided to policyholders)	66 (66.1)	72 (80.6)
Interval between divisions (avg. in years)	5.11	4.68
Waiting period prior to participation (avg. in years)	4.32	2.50
Method of payment (% of total)		
Reversionary bonus only	3 (6.1)	3 (3.1)
Reduced premiums only	3 (6.1)	6 (6.3)
Reduced premiums or cash	0	2 (2.1)
Reversionary bonus or reduced premiums	32 (65.3)	24 (25.0)
Reversionary bonus, reduced premiums, or cash	11 (22.4)	54 (58.3)

Sources: Saint-Clair 1840: 56–60; Pocock 1842: 99–144; Post-Office Annual Directory 1841: lxxi; Rhind 1839: 13; Walford I: 585, and V: 222; AMB II (19 March 1834); Henham 2002: 17; Trebilcock I: 587; Hogg 1837: 389; Van Sandau 1856: 12; D. Jones 1843: 1096–1132; Companion to the Almanac (1846): 102–5; Assurance Gazette 1 (1847): 10; Walford 1867: 314–17.
Note: Average proportion divided excludes mutual offices and (for 1840) offices that paid no bonus.

As more life insurance offices began dividing their surplus, they evolved a wide array of division methods, each of which appealed to different classes of policyholders. At one extreme were the tontine offices, which reserved most of the bonus to those whose lives had been insured for the longest period of time. Some firms achieved this by restricting participation to the longest-standing members.[36] Others divided the surplus in proportion to aggregate premiums, which favoured those who had made the most annual payments, or they offered a compound bonus, which credited policyholders for previously accumulated bonuses in determining how much they received at each division.[37] The Scottish Provident, finally, only paid bonuses to people whose paid-in premiums equaled their coverage – which translated into only 26 per cent of its customers as of 1881.[38]

On the opposite end of the spectrum were life insurance offices that added an equal share of the surplus to all policies, based either on the premiums paid since the previous division or the original level of coverage. In 1870 a quarter of the life offices divided their surplus in this way. Around the same proportion began adding value to policies from the date of issue, although most required customers to survive a few years before becoming eligible to share in the surplus.[39] A few companies went to more complicated lengths to find a balance between policies of longer and shorter duration. The Edinburgh Life deducted from the accumulated paid-in premiums 'the sum which is found to be equivalent to the risk as increased by the advanced age of the party,' and Sun Life pioneered a similar 'contributive system' that balanced the cumulative premiums paid against the reserve needed to guard against an increasing risk of death.[40]

Several tontine offices, especially the Gresham, Scottish Provident, and Standard Life, enjoyed considerable success through the 1860s. Over time, however, most of them suffered from an actuarial Achilles' heel, which ultimately detracted from their popularity. As members of these life insurance offices collectively aged, the surplus was spread over an increasingly wide surface, which diminished average bonus levels in proportion to policy value. In response, many of them phased in 'equal' plans after 1870.[41] Tontines underwent a revival after 1890, when the introduction of 'deferred bonus' policies by American firms prompted many British imitators. Most of these companies learned from their forebears' experience and reserved more of the surplus to cover the likelihood of diminishing bonuses as their customers grew older. More generally, the revival of tontine policies and the continuing popularity of compound bonuses placed an additional premium on the maintenance of large reserves, at a time when declining yields and rising expenses made this especially challenging.[42]

A different source of variation among bonus schemes concerned the disposition of the surplus: as a reversionary addition to the sum insured (to be collected, with the original claim, at the policyholder's death), as a reduction in the premium, or as a cash payment. Nearly two-thirds of bonus offices in 1842 offered their customers a choice between a reversion and reduced premiums, with eleven more adding the choice of a cash rebate; by 1867 more than half of all life insurance offices offered all three choices. Available evidence suggests that most customers decided to add to their coverage when they had a choice, partly because most insurance offices made this the default option and partly because they typically pegged rebates at a lower rate to discourage that choice. Through the middle of the century, insurance companies preferred to add bonuses to future claims in order to take advantage of rising interest rates and also to hedge against the problem of healthier policyholders opting for rebates in disproportionate numbers.[43]

Regardless of how life insurance offices divided their surpluses, the fact that a surplus existed indicated that they were charging more than was necessary to meet the basic contingency of premature death. Realizing this, many life offices began offering, as an alternative to bonuses, lower premiums based on what they claimed to be more accurate vital statistics. Many others, starting with the United Kingdom Life in 1834, provided 'half credit' policies, which permitted customers to leave up to half of their premiums unpaid for the first five to seven years of the policy – after which point they could either pay the balance plus interest or allow the debt to remain until the claim was paid.[44] One sign that these low-premium offices were fighting an uphill battle in this regard is that they often borrowed the language of the bonus in their promotional literature. The Pelican called its reduced non-profit rates in 1842 'a fixed and immediate bonus,' and the Argus offered 'a Certain and Annual Bonus ... in lieu of the deferred and sometimes delusive prospect, of a periodical division of Profits.'[45]

Over time, competition between lower-priced offices and more expensive bonus offices developed into symbiosis, as life insurance firms folded the non-participating option into their set of offerings. The number of life offices without a non-profit option fell from twenty-nine in 1842 to just two in 1870, at which point every life office in Britain offered a bonus option.[46] When the Scottish Equitable introduced non-profit tables in 1863, its chairman defended this as meeting 'the wishes of the public, as well as the competition of other offices.' Beyond catering to consumer demand, life insurance offices discovered that aggressively marketing non-participating policies allowed them to use the resulting profits as a means of improving their bonus-paying power. Noting that 'non-profit insurers ... are producers only, and not consumers' of surplus, the Legal & General's actuary urged his directors to aim for 'a much larger share than it has yet done of this most profitable class of business.'[47]

Faced with a choice between paying higher with-profit rates and lower non-profit rates, policyholders generally picked the first option. Of Alliance policies in force in 1863, 81 per cent were with-profit, as were 88 per cent of the Economic's in 1859. In a sample of fifty life insurance offices' Board of Trade returns from 1869 to 1884, only six issued more than 40 per cent of their policies without participation in profits, and more than half shared profits with at least 80 per cent of their customers. Industry-wide, the proportion of with-profit life insurance policies peaked at 88 per cent in 1900 before declining slightly. The main exceptions to this trend were the legal offices, which issued between 27 per cent and 45 per cent of their policies on a non-participating scale in 1889; and the export-oriented Gresham, with 32 per cent of its policies on a non-profit scale in 1898, including more than 40 per cent in Austria, Hungary, and Italy.[48]

The Moral Economy of the Bonus

Among the defining traits of Victorian market culture were the contrary impulses of display, discipline, and fairness. The first tendency exhibited 'a rhetorical mode of amplification and excess' that framed much of Victorian life – and that has been identified as a salient aspect of commodification. The second attempted to moderate such representational excess by subjecting it to the discipline of transparent 'facts.' And the third harkened back to an earlier moral economy of just prices and negotiated resource allocation.[49] Although historians have taken up each of these facets of the Victorian economy, they have tended to do so in isolation from one another. Life insurance in the nineteenth century did not have that luxury, especially where the bonus was concerned. As in the case with other diverging aspects of modernity, insurers did their best to combine display, discipline, and fairness into a single business strategy. They did so, in large part, by folding them into a wider narrative about the sufficiency of institutions in a free market to communicate with, regulate, and adjudicate among the customers they served. This wider model bore a general resemblance to neoclassical economics, which offered consumer preference (mediated by mathematical models) as a substitute for moral philosophy and legislative art.[50]

Spectacle

In *The Commodity Culture of Victorian England*, Thomas Richards identifies six elements of 'a semiotics of commodity spectacle,' among them 'an autonomous iconography for the manufactured object; the use of commemoration to place objects in history; the invention of a democratic ideology for consumerism ... and the invention of the myth of the abundant society.' All of these apply to the life insurance bonus, which in its own way was as much a 'manufactured object' as any product of the industrial revolution. The bonus was autonomous in the sense that both the embodied clerical labour that went into each valuation and its dependence on arbitrarily chosen actuarial parameters were concealed, for the most part, from recipients; all they saw was the slip of paper announcing itself as so much new wealth. The commemorative side of the bonus was on display at their declarations, which provided actuaries and insurance company chairmen with opportunities to look back over the decades leading up to the present. Life insurance offices also applied a rich language of democratic ideology to their various methods of dividing surplus, allowing them to elevate the profane play of profit and loss into the more rarified sphere of political justice. Finally, by repeatedly associating bonuses with *'larger income* and *bigger Funds*,' as the Rock's centenary exulted, the life insurance office joined in what Richards has called 'the vanguard of permanent prosperity.'[51]

The complicated nature of most division schemes indirectly added to the spectacle surrounding the bonus declaration, since it meant that insurers could only afford to deploy the manpower needed for such calculations every several years. Hence what might have been a frequent, and relatively small, addition to policy values emerged as an anticipated event – with either positive or negative implications, depending on how closely the surplus lived up to expectations. Preparing for and staging a bonus declaration dramatically altered the rhythm of the Victorian life insurance office. A year before the declaration, insurance companies formed special committees to calculate the amount of surplus that could be safely divided. Directors worked with the actuary to determine the present value of the company's assets.[52] Then the actuary determined the proportion of actual to expected claims over the bonus period, to make sure that premium income was still sufficient to meet the claims that had yet to fall in, and considered whether to value using a new mortality table, either because a more reliable table had appeared since the last valuation or because of the changing age structure of the office.[53]

These activities were laborious enough, but they paled before the task of dividing the surplus among the policyholders. A surviving log of the Clerical Medical's 1905 valuation testifies to the Olympian drudgery that went into this ritual. Eight clerks spent all of August and September of that year calculating and checking the cash and reversionary bonuses, while others calculated prime cost arrears and surrender values, tracked down changes of address, identified yields, and called agency cards into books. From late October into November some clerks addressed envelopes and others continued to call and check bonus notices, while the actuary and his chief clerk prepared the bonus report and composed a 'circular letter to Agents.' Stuffing notices into envelopes occupied December, and clerks spent the week before Christmas sorting these into packets for the company's agents, who did the actual mailing. The actuary spent this time 'putting together some notes for [the] Chairman's speech' and converting the valuation results into the format required by the Board of Trade.[54]

Most insurance offices responded to these heavy labour demands by waiting several years between each bonus. At one extreme in this matter was the Equitable, which waited ten years between valuations, partly (in William Morgan's words) to enable 'a minute investigation of the real state of its affairs' and partly to equalize annual fluctuations in interest and mortality. Most life insurance offices settled on five or seven years, with similar justifications for the delay (see Table 6.1).[55] In the 1820s and 1830s influential critics urged that annual valuations would be both more equitable and could be done cost-effectively, prompting a handful of life offices to divide profits every year. Perhaps owing to valid concerns about labour costs, few offices followed their lead in the ensuing decades, although most switched from seven to five years at mid-century (Table 6.1).[56] What many did do was offer interim or 'prospective' bonuses to policyholders who died between valuations, usually prorated at two-thirds or three-fourths the level of the previous bonus they received.[57]

Although the initial impetus for long intervals between bonus declarations had more to do with manpower than with marketing, life insurance offices were quick to capitalize on the sense of anticipation that came to surround their periodical divisions. At annual meetings preceding the bonus, actuaries and directors hinted at the 'secrets of the prison-house' to be revealed at the upcoming division. Predictions tended to be coy in tone, to avoid raising expectations too high. The chair of the Scottish Equitable forswore any 'attempt to lift the veil of the future and give any opinion' regarding the upcoming 1902 bonus; it was, in the event, 10 per cent lower than in 1897.[58] In life offices where customers were immediately eligible for their bonus, managers ratcheted their sales pitch up a few notches in the final months of each valuation period. Typical was a National Mutual form letter noting that a test valuation had predicted a bonus that translated into 'an immediate *addition of £7.10.0* to a policy of £500' for customers who signed up by the last day of December.[59]

In the weeks leading up to the bonus, the final stage of the valuation was the actuary's report to the directors, which was read at a public meeting of policyholders (in the case of mutuals) or shareholders. Writing 'a good Report,' Thomas Bond Sprague told his fellow actuaries in 1883, was 'almost as important' as making accurate calculations. Bonus reports gave actuaries an opportunity to assess a company's strengths and to warn directors of risks ahead – a task most of them took very seriously, to the extent of producing 'ponderous' documents that were as painstaking to read as they were to prepare.[60] At the ensuing meeting (where the intended audience was as much the trade press as the shareholders or policyholders), directors offered commentary on these reports that tended to focus on their brighter sides. The Eagle used its healthy bonus in 1857 to justify a continued strategy of growth through mergers; for the Clerical Medical's chairman in 1882, the bonus report attested to his company's 'continued strength' and 'unexampled prosperity.'[61]

Self-congratulation at such meetings carried over into subsequent marketing efforts, with 'appetizing little paragraphs about big bonuses' inevitably appearing in their wake. In 1871 the Edinburgh Life initiated 'a wide system of advertising in connexion with the recent Bonus Declaration,' and the West of Scotland's secretary told his Belfast agent in 1833 that 'after the Bonus now declared we may assert with the greatest confidence that it is the *most beneficial* of any Company to the insured that has an Agency there.' In most cases, an improved bonus led to increased sales: after the Scottish Amicable increased its bonus by a sixth in 1900, new business increased by more than 50 per cent over the next five years.[62]

If a healthy bonus translated into a bump in sales, a lower-than-usual bonus had the opposite effect. The Reliance Mutual had to fend off a call for a committee of inquiry after adding just £51 to a member's policy that would be 'bearing £300 or £400' in other life insurance offices. Worse still was the declaration of no divisible surplus at all, as the consulting actuary Arthur Scratchley discovered at the Briton Medical & General's bonus meeting in 1874. Policyholders were outraged, not least because earlier that year the *Post Magazine* had reported Scratchley's promise that the bonus 'would be equal to if not in excess of that declared in 1867.' Scratchley denied the charge, offering 'a reward of £20 to anyone who would bring him the shorthand writer's notes containing those words in his speech,' but the damage had been done. By 1875 the BMG's new business declined 37 per cent, nearly landing it in Chancery.[63]

A non-declaration story with a happier ending concerned the Norwich Union, which passed bonuses in 1836 and again in 1866. The first time, angry policyholders vented their spleen into the following year, until order was finally restored when Daniel O'Connell – a Norwich Union member who had political ties with the firm's Irish sales staff – brokered a peace accord. In exchange for its members' continued business, the company agreed to open its board to six 'outside' directors and submitted to reforms suggested by outside actuaries.[64] Thirty years later – and fifteen years after assuring policyholders that 'their future Bonuses are not merely a probability, but morally a certainty' – the Norwich Union executive committee again came to the bonus meeting with no value to add to members' policies. This time, however, they legitimately claimed that the non-declaration, while a necessary caution, did not signify a deeper crisis.[65]

The real advantage in the Norwich Union's handling of its second non-declaration appeared in subsequent decades, when it successfully repackaged its apparent managerial lapse as the first stage of a long-term plan to put the society on a firm basis. In 1886, after declaring a good bonus, a director praised 'the Board of 1866' for having 'the courage of its convictions to do what was right.' Starting in 1887 a new actuary, J.J.W. Deuchar, built on this strength to turn the Norwich Union into one of England's largest life insurers. The chairman in 1901 celebrated its new stature at that year's declaration, then led the gathered throng across the street to where the mayor of Norwich laid the foundation stone for a new head office. At the subsequent dinner, Deuchar expressed 'his pride and satisfaction that they had that day completed the long struggle they had been making ... to place the Norwich Union Life Office in the very front rank of life insurance institutions.' He finished by toasting 'the policy holders,' who 'would experience great satisfaction in having received a really excellent bonus.'[66]

As yields declined and expenses rose at the end of the nineteenth century, such displays of prosperity increasingly shared the spotlight with awkward admissions of underperformance. The Gresham's high expense ratios after 1900 prompted agents to complain about its 'miserable' and 'wretched' bonuses. When Standard Life passed its bonus in 1906, owing to unduly low prior reserves and bad luck on the stock exchange, the grumblings could be heard as far away as British Columbia, where the company's agents 'appeared to have the idea that there is something radically unsound in [its] position.' Agents in Egypt and India registered similar complaints, and British customers sued the company (unsuccessfully) over its concurrent payment of a dividend to its shareholders. Citing the firm's 20 per cent expense ratio, one customer accused it of 'eating up the greater part of the extra premiums charged to "with-profit" policyholders, really their property,' and asked, 'How many brewery debentures ... does the Standard Life Office hold?'[67]

Accountability

If life insurance bonuses were commodities that were 'spectacularized' every five to seven years, they simultaneously performed a regulatory role in the Victorian money market, by transmitting information that, in theory, rendered companies more accountable to their customers and shareholders. These two functions were not fully complementary, any more than tabloid journalism is synonymous with government regulation. Still, in most cases some accountability was better than none at all, and the close attention paid to bonuses meant that these occasions (as with the Norwich Union) could prompt internal reforms. And significantly, when outside regulation did come to the industry with the Life Assurance Companies Act of 1870, its reporting provisions were closely modelled on the existing pattern of quinquennial valuations. The effect of the law was to strengthen policyholders' ability to discern the financial status of a life office, without substantially detracting from the recurring spectacle of the bonus.

As instruments of accountability, bonuses ranged from unwieldy to woefully ineffective. Their unwieldy side was apparent in the demise of the Albert, which went from declaring a large bonus in 1861 to declaring bankruptcy in 1869. Burdened by heavy expenses from misguided acquisitions, the Albert only avoided a non-declaration in 1864 by altering its interval between divisions from three to five years, and then it refused to offer any explanation for its lack of a bonus in 1866. The resulting anxiety led members of the recently acquired companies to demand an investigation into the company's affairs. A *Times* correspondent, signing himself 'Sixty-Six,' contrasted the fate of his Albert policy with his experience at his old insurance office, where 'each returning five years saw a distribution of bonuses among the insured, and all went merry as a marriage bell.' The Albert's spectacular crash paled before the even more disastrous failure of the European, which continued to declare bonuses right up to its bitter end in 1872.[68]

By the early 1870s it seemed clear, as Cornelius Walford urged, that 'bonus' was 'a word bearing in the eyes of most policy-holders ... the greatest signification of any word in the insurance vocabulary.' Exactly what any given bonus might signify, however, had been cast into serious doubt by the failures of the Albert and the European. One of the central tasks of the 1870 act was to stabilize the meaning of the bonus. The new law was far from perfect, but it did draw attention to the need to reserve a sufficient fund for long-term liabilities, and it forced insurance companies to divulge how much money they were spending on new business. It also held in check some features of accountability that lay dangerously (in many actuaries' minds) beyond their control. Actuaries successfully lobbied to exclude from the law a clause that would have empowered twenty or more customers to direct the Board of Trade to conduct 'an examination into the affairs of a company.' Revealingly, one scare story they used to secure its exclusion was that 'a diminution in the rate of bonus, disappointing sanguine Policyholders, might lead many from various motives to concur in an application to the Board of Trade' and thereby derail 'proceedings adopted by a Company with special regard to prudence and safety.'[69]

In the face of declining yields, life insurance offices that hoped to combine stable bonuses with growth had no choice but to strengthen their reserves. Subject to the publicity afforded by the 1870 statute, they soon discovered that the best way to do this was to value their assets using an interest rate that was well below their actual yields – which had the effect of concealing a presently divisible surplus from customers in order to spend it safely on convincing new customers to join them. In 1878, when yields averaged 4.4 per cent, half of all life insurance offices assumed 3 per cent. By the end of the century, when the anticipated 'diminishing future' came to pass, this proportion increased to 63 per cent, and ten years later a quarter of all life offices valued at less than 3 per cent. In 1889 the Atlas was the first to switch to 2.5 per cent, followed in 1892 by the Clergy Mutual and the Clerical Medical. These firms drew attention to their *almost unexampled strength*, whereby 'large profits in the future are practically assured.'[70]

Although the 1870 statute, combined with the threat of customer dissatisfaction, prompted most life insurance offices to save for future rainy days, this was not always enough to prevent lower-than-usual bonuses. Of the forty largest life offices at the turn of the century, twenty-two declared lower bonuses than they had twenty years earlier. Three of these – the Lancashire in 1899, the Gresham in 1900, and the Life Association of Scotland in 1901 – failed to declare a bonus altogether. Assurances of financial stewardship never fully took the sting out of a failure to add to previous bonuses, given how thoroughly bonuses had entered into the marketing and even the premium tables of life insurance. As the *Times* noted in 1913 (echoing the complaint by the Standard Life customer seven years earlier), such policyholders were justified in feeling let down: since 'premiums are deliberately loaded in order to produce certain rates of bonus,' they effectively got 'no return for that part of the premium' in such an event.[71]

Given such results, it comes as no surprise that life insurance men repeatedly spoke of the bonus system as a 'mischievous excrescence' and an 'incubus' starting in the 1880s.[72] Instead of abandoning the bonus, however (which would have spelled commercial suicide given its continuing popularity among customers), life insurance offices invariably opted to change their organizational structure to improve their ability to pay them. One institutional response to low bonuses was to introduce new forms of non-participating insurance, which could serve as a source of profits to leaven the bonus.[73] Another option was to mutualize, which diverted to with-profit customers surplus that shareholders previously absorbed. Standard Life's decision to do this in 1925 seemed to confirm Harry Nightingale's prediction a decade earlier, in a Royal Exchange memo, that life business in the future would only be offered by '"composite" companies transacting all classes of business' and by 'a few large mutual offices, who, by maintaining a high rate of bonus in the future, will be enabled to support a separate existence.'[74]

Perfect Fairness

When it came to distributing their mounting wealth, Victorians were fond of talking about fairness, if not always scrupulous in carrying it out. Robert Owen claimed that replacing gold with labour as a standard of value would dispense surplus produce with 'equity and justice, openness and fairness'; John Stuart Mill faintly praised capitalism's capacity to allocate wealth 'with some, though but a distant, approach to fairness.'[75] The life insurance bonus went at least some distance towards translating such conceptions of fairness into concrete terms. It also generated one of the only contemporary debates on distributive justice that focused on resource allocation across generations and not merely among different classes of people.[76] The diverging claims of participating and non-participating policyholders, and arguments on behalf of different with-profit division methods, generated ample heat as life insurance offices vied for customers. At the end of the day, however, most people involved with life insurance embraced the free market as the ultimate arbiter of fairness. As long as sufficient choice existed – between non-profit and with-profit scales of premium, or among division methods – life offices could indefinitely defer any resolution of the ethical issues arising out of their competing (and mutually inconsistent) claims to approach perfect fairness.

The first argument that life offices needed to confront when they started offering bonuses was that this new focus on investment unfairly diverted resources from families and creditors of policyholders who died prematurely. The Dundee banker John Sturrock called bonuses 'stumbling-blocks in the way of the provident and frugal' who wanted to insure their lives but could not afford an added contribution to a mutual fund. Charging extra to enable bonus payments, argued a writer for the *London Spectator*, was 'an evil if [the customer] lives, by depriving him of capital that might have been useful; and an unfairness if he dies early, because his money goes to swell the bonuses of other people.'[77] This argument worked even if, as was usually the case, the bonus generated a larger claim for the beneficiary as opposed to a cash refund for the policyholder. The extra cost associated with the bonus meant that beneficiaries whose needs were greatest – those whose breadwinners died prematurely – received less money than the dependents of people who had lived longer than expected.

Life insurance offices responded to this argument by calling the bonus a useful savings mechanism that was unavailable to policyholders who tried to invest money on their own, and by insisting that longer-living policyholders also deserved to be treated fairly. Far from depriving customers of useful capital, they claimed, the bonus gave them the opportunity to participate in the superior yields that derived from the life insurance office's unique advantages as an institutional investor.[78] Their second defence of the bonus, that it rewarded survivors, marked a clear, if cautious, departure from the altruism that is central to all forms of insurance. This was evident in the Gresham actuary's claim that it was 'quite just and right that those who live beyond the average time calculated should reap the advantage of the burden which they have had to bear in the payment of early claims.'[79]

If the question of whether or not to pay a bonus led life insurance offices to stake out different moral positions, the marketing of different division methods by bonus-paying offices created an explosion of appeals to distributive justice. At various points in the nineteenth century eight British life offices included 'Equitable' or 'Equity' in their names, and those that did not do so compensated by loudly proclaiming their equity in advertisements and prospectuses.[80] The Scottish Provident asserted its 'remarkably fair approach to uniformity of treatment of their members as a whole,' the Edinburgh Life's bonus came 'nearer to perfection than any that has yet been made known' by 'paying equal regard to the just rights of all classes of Insurers,' and the North British & Mercantile's bonus was 'as equitable a mode as any that could have been devised.' When American firms gained market share with their deferred bonus schemes, the British press draped all home-grown life insurance offices in a blanket assertion of equity: in Britain, argued the *Saturday Review* in 1902, 'policy-holders are treated fairly all round.'[81]

Although nearly every life insurance office claimed that its bonus was the fairest of them all, each division method unavoidably favoured one class of policyholders at the expense of another. This confusing profusion of potential winners and losers derived from the fact that customers paid different premiums based on their age of entry, then held onto their policies for different lengths of time. Older entrants, who paid higher premiums, gained when a company divided its surplus based on premiums received, while younger entrants gained when companies divided according to sums insured. The Scottish Widows' Fund defended the latter method by arguing that its profit margin on individual policies (i.e., higher-than-expected yield and lower-than-expected expenses and mortality) was the same regardless of entry age. When the Edinburgh Life divided its first surplus in 1835, its accountant condemned that plan as giving 'a great comparative advantage to young lives' and as 'cutting, not untying, the Gordian knot' by assuming (perhaps incorrectly) that the initial premiums were perfectly adjusted to the risks.[82]

The differential durations of policies occasioned another source of debate, with tontine offices claiming that 'parties who shall stand long assured with the office' deserved a greater share of the surplus. A second defence of the tontine, which applied to all members instead of singling out older ones, was that it attracted healthier lives to the office owing to the incentive to survive long enough to participate in the bonus: a Norwich Union bonus report emphasized the 'peculiar advantages [that] the young and healthy insurer' could expect to reap from its bonus. Critics assailed tontine offices for creating a 'privileged class' of policyholders and for offering all other customers what were in effect expensive non-profit policies. The latter argument was especially useful against the Scottish Provident, which charged very low with-profit rates but only divided its surplus with a fraction of its members. A *Bankers' Magazine* writer identified this catch, which competing life insurance offices had also started to notice by the 1870s: 'The proposer likes the good bargain ... and at the same time backs himself to be one of the good lives who will get the large bonuses, forgetting that to realize the one bargain he must die young, and to realize the other he must live to be old.'[83]

A final aspect of distributive justice that played out in life insurance offices concerned the respective claims of present and future generations of policyholders. This issue lay at the heart of the increased focus after 1870 on reserves, since the whole point of having large reserves was to be able to continue paying the same level of bonus several decades into the future. References to 'stringent' and 'rigorous' valuations were implied promises to entering customers that there would remain sufficient 'sources of future surplus' after each bonus declaration was made. In the rush to boast of large reserves, however, it was easy to neglect the claims of customers whose policies would not last long enough to take advantage of them. A *Post Magazine* letter signed 'Three-and-a-half Per Cent' urged that any lower rate benefited 'participants in the future at the expense of those who are receiving their bonuses now,' and the actuary Augustus Hendriks identified two types of customers as especially justified in complaining about lower assumed yields: holders of short-term endowment insurances and 'old men assured for the short remainder of their whole lives ... during which the higher rate of interest will continue to be earned.'[84]

When life insurance experts ascended from the world of the prospectus to the realm of abstract principles, they tended to fold the moral economy of the bonus into an amoral economy based on individual preference. Augustus De Morgan advised policyholders in 1838 to select a life insurance office with a division method that accorded with their own 'inclinations, views of fairness, or particular circumstances'; and a *Bankers' Magazine* columnist similarly urged that division methods 'must always be as numerous and as diverse as the desires of the public.' William Wood of Standard Life recommended a non-participating policy for 'a man who wants to secure a specific sum of money ... on the lowest terms,' a tontine policy for someone who 'looks forward to a long life,' and a scheme 'in which greater advantages are given to Policies of less duration' for someone who 'has no very great confidence in his length of life.'[85] This emphasis on choice was also apparent in the option that most policyholders had by the 1860s to take their bonus as a reversion, a reduction in future premiums, or a cash rebate.

It is difficult to reconstruct what the average policyholder made of all this talk of fairness and equity. It seems likely that if policyholders gave much thought at all to the way their bonus was divided, they did so after it was too late to do anything about it. A published exchange in the *Insurance Record* from 1878 is revealing in this regard. A middle-aged policyholder named Edwin Collard wrote that when he had complained to his life insurance office about the low level of his bonus, the company told him that 'their tables are so constructed as to be specially favourable to very old lives.' Although one correspondent supported Collard, urging that he had not received 'all the justice that science could have given,' an actuary blamed Collard for not asking about the office's bonus system before taking out his policy. The exchange ended with Collard insisting, in his defence, that 'young men of twenty-two must not be expected to be as much on the alert in such matters as a professional actuary.'[86]

If policyholders seldom complained that their bonus was unfair, it was the actuary's job to make sure this remained the case – and also to limit what the Guardian's actuary called 'inarticulate discontent' over unfair division methods. Such efforts were especially pronounced whenever a life insurance office moved to a new division method, which inevitably altered the allocation of surplus among different classes of customers. The Star, in adopting a new bonus scheme in 1884, chose one that gave 'an advantage to the older assured, at the same time making the transition from the former method as little abrupt as possible.' When the Clerical Medical decided in 1897 to revise a bonus scheme that 'was somewhat too generous ... to the younger members,' its actuary similarly accomplished this 'by steps so gradual that no Policyholder should ever be conscious of any sudden departure from old-established principles.' The Alliance's actuary, conversely, decided to make a similar revision all at once, 'rather than to do it gradually and have a continuing feeling of discontent among the policy holders.'[87] All these efforts indicate that actuarial artifice often played as important a role as free consumer choice in moderating the appearance of unfairness in the life insurance bonus.

Conclusion

Discussing the evolution of American life insurance in the nineteenth century, Viviana Zelizer identifies an 'enduring tension' between the 'contradictory demands of altruism and commercialism' – the first of which embodied 'trust, community solidarity, and community feeling,' and the second of which focused on 'efficiency, equity, and freedom.'[88] In Victorian Britain, few aspects of life insurance illustrated this tension more clearly than the bonus. On the one hand, it brandished commercialism in every transaction, by focusing customers' attention on the efficiency of a company's asset management and on the equitable division of its yield. On the other hand, precisely because life office funds were self-consciously mutual, it revived and sustained a focus on solidarity that had been present at the earliest origins of life insurance. And even though the result was not altruistic in the same way as an idealized insurance transaction (entailing a simple redistribution of wealth from more fortunate to less fortunate members of a community), most bonuses did accrue to contributors' dependents and not to themselves.

The most obvious sense in which the bonus revived an earlier focus on community was its creation of an incentive for life insurance offices to exclude customers who posed a risk to a steadily increasing surplus. Exclusions of this sort dated back to the early eighteenth century, when policyholders were 'disinclined to dilute their own financial interest through the admission of additional members, while the common moral purpose that brought them together also set them apart from society at large.'[89] Manifestations of 'common moral purpose' persisted in British life insurance throughout the nineteenth century, although these were unevenly distributed and often observed only in the breach. Life offices' frequent appeals to domesticity and thrift at least had the potential of imbuing policyholders with a sense of moral superiority. More tangibly, 'class' offices nearly always based their marketing strategy on appeals to social (if not always moral) solidarity – especially those catering to religious denominations and those associated with the temperance movement. The bonus dovetailed with this method for attracting business on the many occasions when life offices connected the lower mortality among their distinctively moral members to larger surpluses.[90]

A more persistent manifestation of community, and one that the bonus played a more central role in sustaining, lay in life offices' concern to protect the financial interest of their members by guarding against a membership that was too large or heterogeneous. The classic case of this was the Equitable's refusal to permit more than five thousand members to share in the bonus at any given time, and many life insurance managers continued to pursue this line of reasoning well into the nineteenth century – typically by way of defending a decline in new business. The Norwich Union's actuary argued, after new premium income fell by nearly 50 per cent from the previous year, that 'a small body of healthy insurers is far preferable to a great one carelessly admitted.' It is tempting to discount such statements as sour grapes, since life insurance offices just as routinely celebrated large new business figures without worrying much about their impact on the bonus. There is ample evidence, however, that concerns to maintain a large bonus for the existing community of customers reined in the extravagant pursuit of new business. Despite an explosion in branch formation, with the accompanying overhead costs this implied, expenses and commissions fell industry-wide between 1882 and 1902, from 14.1 per cent to 13.7 per cent.[91]

If the bonus did, in this way, keep attention focused on the communitarian side of life insurance, its impact on altruism was more complicated. Since most bonuses accrued to claimants after the death of the insured party, the most basic sense in which life insurance was altruistic remained intact. Indeed, it was possible to argue that the bonus diverted people's speculative impulses, which might otherwise have been exercised on the stock market or the racetrack, to altruistic ends. As the *Bankers' Magazine* quipped in 1893, the bonus exerted a 'gentle compulsion' on the policyholder when it charged 'rather more than it need, and increases his assurance' – concluding that if this was 'not a kindness to him, it is to his widow and children.'[92] This form of altruism, however, was narrowly restricted within a policyholder's immediate family. The bonus detracted from the more general sense in which life insurance was altruistic, by compensating those who survived long enough to pay more premiums than their policy was nominally worth.

The bonus also reinforced a more general limitation of the altruistic potential of commercial life insurance, by inhibiting its spread to a wider population. In this case it facilitated a convergence of the commercial and communitarian features of life insurance, since it created a profit motive for restricting the extension of business beyond a narrowly defined class of customers. The statistician William Newmarch, who managed the Globe in the 1850s, captured this point in 1875 when he observed that life insurance was 'not a philanthropic scheme,' but rather existed 'for the purpose of taking care of the money of the policyholder and turning it to the most profitable account.' When established life insurance offices ventured into the lower-income market, they quickly retreated once the impact on their bonus-paying ability became apparent. The National Life quickly abandoned a monthly payment scheme it had started in 1890 after its actuary predicted 'greatly reduced bonuses' owing to its cost; he recommended that they should only pursue that line of business 'where suitable opportunities may present themselves of conducting it at a profit.'[93]

The only companies that successfully departed from an exclusionary business strategy were the industrial offices, which spent more than twice as much as other offices aggressively selling life insurance to people who were all but ignored by the rest of the industry. The Prudential, which used up more than a third of its total premium income in 1891 on expenses and commissions, issued nearly sixty thousand policies in its ordinary branch that year covering an average of £102 per policy – less than a quarter of the industry average. At the same time, despite earning a meagre 3.4 per cent on its investments, it paid bonuses to these customers of 32s per £100 insured, more than most offices at the time were paying. Their directors pulled this off by subsidizing their 'ordinary' customers with profits earned from selling burial insurance to even lower-income 'industrial' customers.[94] Hence the bonus, which worked to limit the extension of business in most other companies, here acted as an incentive to expand the market by enabling lower-income customers to participate in a mutual fund. With the exception of offices with a fire insurance branch or a large non-participating business, which could use these sources of profit to prop up their bonus (and which, like the Prudential, featured less 'community solidarity' than other life offices), this model was not available to most of the Prudential's competitors.

The other secret to the Prudential's success was that 62 per cent of the policies it issued in 1892 were endowment assurances, compared with just 17.5 per cent of policies issued by other British insurance life offices that year.[95] These policies offered a further incentive for lower-income customers to insure their lives, since many of them faced the prospect of a declining income stream late in life. They also represented a further departure from altruism, in the sense that the insured party's own financial security now mattered as much as his family's. And unlike the

Prudential's primary business model of using burial insurance profits to expand its ordinary branch, this was a strategy that was available to all life insurance offices that wanted to expand their market without detracting from their bonus-paying power. Indeed, the rising popularity of endowment insurance among middle-class customers probably had as much as anything to do with the ability of life offices to reduce their expenses in the 1890s, since it required less pressure by salesmen to convince someone to save for his retirement. This and other related developments, which will be discussed in more detail in the next chapter, confirmed the basic tension in late Victorian Britain between the altruistic side of life insurance and the extension of life insurance to a wider audience.

7 Little Piles of Savings

It is well known how difficult it is to refrain from encroaching upon little piles of savings under all sorts of temptations, and with endless varieties of salves to conscience for broken resolves ... Considering what human nature is, even at its best, we think it is better not to wholly dissociate the investment and the assurance elements the one from the other.

– Archibald Hewat, *Bankers' Magazine*, 1892[1]

British life insurance spent most of the nineteenth century perched on a moral high ground, resting on the twin foundations of altruism and an advocacy of thrift that was uniquely disciplinary in its requirement of regular payments until the policyholder's death. These two aspects of the business were what, according to the mid-century company promoter Arthur Scratchley, elevated life insurance from being 'a mere matter of investment' to taking on a sense of 'moral urgency' – which, he concluded, afforded 'earnest reasons why the system should be more extensively adopted.'[2] Had they been strictly economic institutions, moral urgency might not have informed the efforts of life insurance offices to the extent that it did. Since life offices were also card-carrying participants in a culture that was steeped in self-help, however, moral urgency inevitably reared its scolding head. Because so many insurance promoters shared Scratchley's conviction that the best way to make money was by wringing it out of a suitably improved populace, they persisted in trying to do so – even after signs began to appear that such an emphasis on altruism and thrift might be more than their market could bear.

By the end of the nineteenth century life insurance companies were waking up to this possibility. Altruism – which in life insurance meant present sacrifice to secure the future well-being of someone else – receded with the rise of a new product, the endowment insurance policy, which combined term life insurance with an annuity. By that time, insurers had also introduced several changes to their contracts that modified their original disciplinary stance on saving. They more aggressively offered loans on the security of the policy, which could be used to cover premiums; created 'non-forfeiture' clauses that enabled customers to defer payment for a year or more; offered paid-up policies; collected premiums on policies in variable amounts depending on the customer's ability to pay (so-called deposit insurance); and increased the 'surrender value' they were willing to pay for a lapsed policy. Most of these initially appeared as part of newer companies' attempts to create a lower-income market, but by the 1870s they were starting to trickle up to higher-income customers as well.

All these changes chipped away at the altruistic side of life insurance. At nearly every turn, critics worried that these new plans were more 'selfish' than standard whole life insurance and less likely to provide ample coverage in the event of early death. They worried that letting a breadwinner borrow against the security of his policy would divert funds from his future widow and her children; that more liberal surrender values would tempt policyholders to abdicate saving for their dependents in order to gratify present desires; and that the higher premium scales required by endowment insurance (which were needed to accumulate enough funds to pay annuities as well as claims) reduced coverage for dependents. Although all of these concerns were valid up to a point, none of them made much of an impact for the simple reason that the new options were all popular among customers. Efforts to apply a purely altruistic ideal to the business of life insurance, which had started to recede with the advent of the bonus, became a rearguard battle by 1900.

The impact of these changes on life insurance as a savings mechanism was more complicated. Some changes, like liberal surrender values and deposit insurance, clearly moved life insurance closer to a banking model, whereby customers had easier access to their savings. In other cases, the goal was to bend but not break the requirement of regular financial contributions or to shorten the duration over which money needed to be laid aside, without altering the basic disciplinary logic of the transaction. Loans and non-forfeiture clauses enabled customers to keep their policies in force when times were tight, and paid-up policies and endowment insurance let them stop paying after retirement deprived them of a regular income. Like the bonus, these changes encouraged more people to save by buying life insurance: in the process converting their little piles of savings into enormous accumulations of capital – and accompanying profits – for the life insurance industry.

Refining Life Insurance as a Savings Mechanism

One of the most tangible ways that life insurance companies regulated their customers' lives was by threatening lapses in payment with the penalty of significant financial loss. This feature of life insurance was especially pronounced in the early decades of the nineteenth century, when grace periods were short and surrender values were small. In part, life insurance offices could afford to exert more stringent discipline on their customers' savings at this time because relatively few people would have felt sufficiently aggrieved at such treatment to take their business elsewhere. For most policyholders in the 1820s, annual premium payments did not represent a major proportion of their disposable income, and their income stream from year to year was reasonably constant.[3] Furthermore, the alternative of shifting their annual savings to a bank was less inviting than it would become a few decades later. English banks in the 1820s paid no interest on deposits, and Scottish banks paid just 2 to 3 per cent, whereas life insurance offices (assuming they offered a bonus) could promise compound interest at 4 per cent or more. Also, the relative stability and large share capital of most insurance companies contrasted sharply with the waves of bank failures (all involving small, undercapitalized partnerships) that shook England in 1815 and 1825.[4]

This set of circumstances largely disappeared when life insurance offices started to tap into a lower-income market in the 1830s. Whereas better-off customers could afford to meet their annual premiums with little or no effort, artisans and clerks faced recurrent bouts of unemployment and needed to make significant sacrifices to buy life insurance even when they were working. Also, whereas middle-class customers received little or no interest and doubtful financial security from their banks, lower-income customers could get much more for their smaller deposits in state-licensed savings banks. The turning point came between 1817 and 1823, when new legislation empowered registered banks to invest their funds with the National Debt Commission at 4.5 per cent interest and capped individual deposits at £200. Over the next two decades the number of savings bank depositors steadily rose and passed one million in 1844, by which time total deposits stood at £25 million. Nearly all of the banks that formed up to that point were on the trustee model, whereby middle-class volunteers (often local clergymen) acted as managers in a part-time capacity. When a series of mid-century embezzlement scandals shook depositors' trust in this system, the Post Office stepped in with a competing service that would attract nearly £38 million by 1870.[5]

Life insurance offices initially tried to lure customers away from savings banks by converting them to the moral duty of providing for their dependents, which a savings bank account might not be able to accomplish. Although this sales pitch worked with some people, especially when 'class' offices presented it to specific religious or occupational groups, its capacity for expanding the market for life insurance was limited. By the 1850s many newer companies sacrificed this moral high ground and instead altered the insurance contract to accommodate customers who were unwilling or unable to pay premiums on a consistent basis. Most of these schemes involved either lending money to policyholders to tide them over when a premium was due or adapting the payment schedule to the customers' income stream. Although few of the life insurance firms that pioneered these plans survived into the 1870s, older companies soon added them to a growing list of options in their effort to attract middle-class business. These innovations also overlapped in many ways with endowment insurance and relied on many of the same marketing appeals that accompanied the rise of that form of coverage after 1880.

Disciplining Policyholders

Among nineteenth-century savings mechanisms, life insurance was a uniquely disciplinary instrument, capable of compelling savings where others failed. The Commercial Life's 1840 prospectus warned that the life insurance contract 'permits no appetite or whim to interfere with the accumulation,' and a later Patriotic prospectus proclaimed that it forced the policyholder 'to regulate his expenditure ... and to persevere in the provident habits which are thus cherished.'[6] The disciplinary key to the insurance contract was the fact that the reward was not available until an unforeseen (but most likely distant) future and that a failure to pay even one annual premium towards that reward threatened one's dependents or creditors with the prospect of serious financial loss. Although life insurance companies were never in practice quite this

ruthless in punishing the improvident – they routinely offered surrender values for policies that had been in force more than a year or two –
neither did they ever wholly abandon the basic threat of forfeiture as a
method for maintaining a steady influx of premium income.

In addition to requiring customers to contribute regularly to a savings fund over much of their adult lives, life offices required these contributions to be paid in a timely manner. Most life offices that formed in
the early nineteenth century required payment within fifteen days of
the annual deadline, with the proviso that policyholders who could
present a clean bill of health could be readmitted within three months.
Firms that formed after 1820 typically offered thirty days of grace instead of fifteen, and by the 1850s most older companies had caught up
with this practice.[7] Insurers sent reminders to their customers shortly
before the premium was due and again near the end of the grace period
– although sometimes these notices went unnoticed, as one dilatory
policyholder lamented in 1839, among the 'many printed Circulars
[that] are continually left at peoples Houses.' For a valued customer, a
failure to meet even an extended deadline could be excused by special
order of the board, as when the City of Glasgow's secretary informed
the publisher John Blackwood that his directors had forgiven a late
payment on the understanding that he would 'endeavour in future to
let the amount be paid here not later than the 4th Aug. in each year.'[8]

Roughly a quarter of the mostly middle- and upper-middle-class
clientele of early nineteenth-century life insurance offices let their policies lapse, although the proportion varied widely from firm to firm. As
Augustus De Morgan pointed out in 1838, the aggregate percentage of
premiums that policyholders lost was much smaller than this, since
most people dropped their policies after just a few payments. When the
Duke of Buckingham, for instance, dropped a £3,000 Westminster &
General policy after two years, he had paid just £199 in premiums and
received a £43 surrender value.[9] Even though this case was typical, it did
not mean that customers were always pleased about having to forfeit
their insurance. The problem lay in pinning down where a policy's 'insurance' side ended and where its 'savings' side began. Customers who
thought of their policy primarily as a savings instrument (and many
more did so once bonuses became popular) were bound to be disappointed by their failure to get access to the money once their reason
for insuring, or ability to continue paying, had ceased. De Morgan re-
constructed this line of reasoning in order to debunk it: 'Since I did not
die, the office lost nothing by me ... why, then, should they not restore

me the premiums which I have paid?' The answer, he argued, was that they had paid for a risk (premature death) that had not transpired and hence were no more entitled to repayment than a fire insurance customer whose building had not burned down.[10]

Yet the problem was not quite so easily disposed of. Although it was true, as De Morgan insisted, that in a life office 'those who live pay for those who die,' it was also true that everyone in a life office eventually died. Hence it was fair for a customer to expect that at least some of his savings would be earmarked for his own creditors or dependents (or returned to him), instead of being paid to the beneficiaries of those who happened to die before his policy lapsed. The best proof of this were the many cases when customers who were unhappy with the surrender value offered for their policies found a higher price for them at a public auction. Buyers in these cases speculated that their purchase price, plus any future premiums due on the policy, would be amply offset by the claim that fell due upon the seller's eventual death – not to mention future bonuses that might accrue to it.[11] As will be discussed below, this factor as much as any other eventually pushed insurance companies to revisit the extent to which they were willing to refund premiums for discontinued policies.

Despite this obvious limit to the life insurance industry's disciplinary reach over its customers' savings, most companies persisted in arguing that people could not be trusted to save for future contingencies unless they were compelled to do so. Without a life insurance office obliging regular payment, urged a British Commercial sales booklet in 1848, even the best intentions might not guarantee that money would be 'perseveringly and regularly set apart, or, if it were, circumstances might occur leading, under the pressure of the moment, to its being used for other purposes.' Most insurance advocates did their best to turn this human frailty into a selling point, presenting the requirement of on-time payments as 'a regular item in the annual expenditure' that would protect a person's savings from 'the gratification of a passing whim of the day' or contrasting this healthy routine with the 'entirely optional' plan of the savings bank, which too often led people 'to squander needlessly.'[12]

If the threat of losing one's life savings was the stick that life insurance offices used to enforce thrift, the carrot was the higher yield those savings would earn when invested by them at compound interest. The Commercial Life's prospectus echoed numerous others when it claimed that life offices 'possessed ... much more ample opportunities of investing Capital advantageously and safely than usually occur to an individual,' and an extensive promotional literature contrasted the investment record of life insurance offices with the more sluggish performance of banks.[13] Number five on *Uncle Tom's Twenty Reasons why Life Assurance should be Universal*, for instance, was: 'you cannot invest a £5 Note every year at even 4 per cent. so well as you can by paying it to an Assurance Company.' The reason given for this varied depending on the target customer: a businessman would earn a higher yield with a life office in the form of the time he saved by letting someone else invest his money, while a lower-income customer with 'so small a sum' as £25 per year in available savings could not find the same investment outlets as a life insurance office with 'hundreds or thousands of pounds' to invest annually.[14]

A second form of compensation for submitting to the discipline of annual premium payments was that it allegedly lightened one's overall burden of saving. Once the contingency of premature death had been covered, there was no need to hoard every penny for a rainy day. To the Tory poet William Aytoun, the most appealing feature of life insurance was its help in combating the 'despicable' habit of miserliness. He contrasted 'Charley Skrimp,' who saved 'systematically for the mere sake of accumulation,' with a typical policyholder, whose premium payments of 10 to 15 per cent of his annual income left room for a 'liberal scale of expenditure,' which was a 'public blessing.' A similar argument held that life insurance enabled customers to avoid the Malthusian proscription against early marriage – a claim that followed logically from its status as a surrogate marriage settlement. As the American insurance reformer Elizur Wright put it in 1859, the life office told the young man: 'If Nature bids you marry, and only Poverty forbids, obey Nature, and we will take care of Poverty.' The savings bank, in contrast, told the same smitten fellow: 'No, my friend, the voice of Nature is premature and imprudent. You had better wait a few years – half a dozen at least.'[15]

Adjusting to the Lower-Income Customer

When directed at middle-income customers, life insurance offices' appeals to thrift seldom required too much sacrifice in practice and came with the advantage of reinforcing such people's tendency to congratulate themselves on their superior prudence. This message also resonated with several varieties of working-class self-help, including those on display in temperance and friendly societies. The 'voluntary obligation of self-denial' that Alexander Low of the Life Association of Scotland invited 'persons of smaller incomes' to undertake echoed the temperance pledge or the commitment to pay regular benefit club dues. Like insurance promoters, advocates of friendly societies frequently criticized the easy access of savings bank deposits, which made them 'entirely inefficient' as a protection against sickness, old age, or death.[16] Indeed, many of the life insurance offices that targeted lower-income customers, and that viewed themselves most explicitly as missionaries of thrift, registered under the Friendly Societies Act of 1830.

This strategy of preaching thrift was apparently enough to sustain a small number of life insurance firms, including the National Provident, Commercial Life, Provident Clerks', and Life Association of Scotland, all of which made solid inroads among lower-income customers in the 1840s. When a second generation of offices tried to expand that market further, they discovered that it was a good deal harder to preach to people who were not already converted. Instead of lecturing would-be customers on the evils of improvidence, these firms acknowledged the difficulties facing customers who could not or chose not to keep up premium payments. By amplifying several pre-existing methods for tiding policyholders over when they were unable to cover premium payments, these firms met savings banks halfway.

The most common approach for enabling cash-strapped policyholders to pay their premiums was to lend them money for the purpose, using the policy as collateral. One of the first life insurance companies to offer loans on policies as a distinctive marketing strategy was the National Loan Fund, which from 1837 enabled customers to borrow up to two-thirds of the premiums they had paid. Its prospectus urged the prospective policyholder that it was 'of equal importance to protect himself against the occurrence of *casualties and reverses while living*, as to provide for his family at death,' and presented its loan option as 'a door open to his savings, which will never be closed against his *wants or his use*.' The Western followed suit in 1842 by offering loans at 5 per cent interest to cover unpaid premiums, and the Provident Clerks' lent small sums to thousands of its customers throughout the 1840s for the same purpose.[17] A variation on policy-secured loans was the non-forfeiture clause, whereby the insurer promised to prevent lapses by lending against the anticipated claim to cover premiums once the grace period had expired. Several fly-by-night companies in the 1850s offered this plan, which they made available after three to five years' worth of premiums had accumulated.[18]

The logical extension of lending on the security of the policy was deposit insurance, which offered single-premium coverage with the option of adding premiums, or withdrawing all or part of them, at any time. Customers could find the services of a savings bank combined with life insurance at the United Deposit, the City of London, the City of Glasgow, and the United General (which all introduced this feature in 1845), the General Life Assurance & Investment Society (established in 1850), and the Deposit & General (established in 1852), or by taking advantage of new deposit branches that were formed by a number of other insurance offices. Even earlier, the British Empire simply added a savings bank to its services in 1843, in which funds could be left at interest; the company promised to use that interest to cover life insurance premiums for customers 'who may wish to release themselves from the trouble and anxiety of annual payments, and from the danger by neglect of lapsing.'[19]

Instead of presenting their customers with a clear choice between frugal saving for future needs and improvident spending on present desires, defenders of policy-secured loans and deposit insurance recognized a number of reasons why working-class policyholders should not always be condemned for failing to keep up their payments. As the City of Glasgow prospectus announced in 1846: 'Nothing is more easy than to imagine cases in which a party may, from various unforeseen causes or temporary embarrassments, be quite unable to provide for his premiums at the precise time they fall due.' These cases, as recounted in the promotional literature, included declining income with old age and loss of employment due to poor health, a commercial crisis, or new technology. If company promoters could easily sympathize with these obstacles to upholding the insurance contract, it was because they were also obstacles to a market for their products. Joseph Maitland of the United Deposit concluded that it was 'impossible to persuade the very large class whose incomes are fluctuating' to insure under conditions 'where they must, under penalties, continue to pay a specific sum on a certain day, annually, till they die, whether they have the means of doing so at the time or not.'[20]

Efforts to attract a lower-income market by altering the insurance contract did not pass without criticism. Defenders of savings banks were quick to condemn lending schemes as an expensive substitute for buying a low-priced life insurance policy and leaving the rest with a bank, which did not charge interest to withdraw it. Life insurance traditionalists claimed that these schemes went 'against the moral principles of assurance' and were 'entirely subversive of the object for which the policy was created.'[21] Although such qualms did little to slow down the liberalization of the life insurance contract, neither did many of the schemes unfold as their promoters hoped they would. After changing its name to the International, the National Loan Fund failed amid scandal in the mid-1860s, and the Western fell victim to an ill-fated merger with the Albert in 1865. Only one company that offered deposit insurance survived the 1850s – and that one, the City of Glasgow, dropped its deposit scheme within a few years of announcing it. None of this, however, meant that the schemes that these firms introduced, or their broader significance, disappeared when they went out of business. Instead, as with many other Victorian insurance innovations, changes in the contract that first appeared as an incentive to attract lower-income customers eventually trickled up to bigger spenders and were taken on board by more established firms.

Liberalizing the Middle-Class Contract

When established life insurance offices started to market non-forfeiture policies, flexible payment options, and more liberal surrender values after 1860, the object was less to tap into a new market than to preserve their share in an increasingly crowded middle-class market. Instead of justifying such schemes as necessary aides to help lower-income customers insure their lives, the rationale was to make it more convenient for inattentive customers to keep their policies in force – or, in the case of surrender values, to make it less costly to part with them. In 1864 the Atlas's actuary listed illiberal terms for lapsed policies as one of the selling points of 'younger offices, which had rid themselves of these obstacles.' As more insurance firms tried to keep up with the market leaders in this way, others felt more pressure to provide their policies with 'the latest Modern and Liberal Conditions,' as the Eagle called the guaranteed surrender value it adopted (along with many other new features) in 1889.[22]

Most of the older life insurance offices by the 1840s were willing to lend on the security of a customer's policy, although often with the rule that the policy be deposited at the head office.[23] On account of the expense involved in administering small loans, however, few firms actively promoted the practice, and some refused to lend less than £50. Even among insurance offices that were willing to lend smaller amounts, the average size of their loans (£129 at the Caledonian in 1859, for instance) suggests that they mainly did this as an extra financial service for their customers and not mainly to enable premium payments. By 1884 nearly 5 per cent of all life office assets were lent on the security of policies, and all but three life insurance firms had at least some loans of this variety on their books; by then, many firms had also lowered their interest rate for such loans from 5 per cent to 4.5 per cent. The leading lenders, however, continued to be those companies that catered to lower-income customers, indicating that the need to resort to such loans remained greatest among the people to whom they were originally marketed.[24]

A clearer example of a liberal feature moving from lower- to higher-income customers was the non-forfeiture clause. The first successful British life insurance firm to introduce non-forfeiture was the Scottish National, which from 1862 promised (on special application) to defray one year's worth of premiums out of every three years' premiums that were paid in. Nearly two decades passed before another company followed suit, when the Scottish Metropolitan included non-forfeiture as an automatic benefit in 1879, and by 1886 these firms were joined by at least eight more (four of them Scottish). Instead of presenting non-forfeiture as a boon for the customer who had hit temporary hard times, most of the marketing that surrounded these schemes envisioned neglect rather than penury as its primary reason for existing. The Caledonian, citing the 'penal regulations' imposed by other firms to secure 'the punctual payment of the premiums,' promised in 1883 that it would cover unpaid premiums in order to meet 'the very common case of a man who has accidentally omitted to pay.'[25]

From the mid-1880s paid-up policies (in various versions) emerged as an alternative to non-forfeiture for dealing with lapses. Instead of charging a debt against the policy to keep it in force, paid-up policies provided lapsing customers with reduced coverage, which would become available once the insured person died. The Life Offices Association reported in 1905 that 'automatic application of the surrender value for the maximum term is not so popular as was the case' and that several of its members had switched to paid-up schemes for this reason.[26] A variant on the paid-up policy was limited-payment whole life insurance, which anticipated a point in the customer's life when it would be inconvenient to keep a policy in force. By 1844 at least eight offices offered such plans, new versions of which continued to appear into the twentieth century. The number of limited-payment policies in force grew from 30,289 in 1890 to 82,743 in 1910 – still only 4 per cent of the market, but enough to lead the *Times* to remark: 'The days when the payment of premiums could be limited by no lesser event than death are passed for ever, and the wit of actuaries has been busy devising various schemes to meet varying contingencies.'[27]

A final variant of the paid-up policy was disability insurance, which paid the full claim on a whole life policy if disabilities prevented customers from keeping up their premiums. A handful of British life insurance companies offered something close to this prior to 1870, but most of these were abortive.[28] In 1892 the Law Life was the first to introduce the policy in the form that would become common in the twentieth century. Modelled on a German scheme, this plan covered premiums 'under circumstances involving temporary or permanent incapacity either by bodily or mental disorder,' and it was available to customers in non-hazardous occupations. To guard against taking on board the 'disability' of old age, the pricing structure was the same as a limited-payment plan that stopped at age sixty-five. Sun Life hatched a similar plan in 1898, and the Star followed in 1907. By that time such policies were starting to take off in North America, where they became more common than was ever the case in Great Britain. When the Gresham entered the Canadian market in 1910, it needed to offer disability rates in order to compete.[29]

Even deposit insurance, which appeared to be dead in the water by the 1880s, made a comeback after 1900 among established life insurance offices. The Norwich Union, which had long been among the most willing to lend on the security of their life policies, went further towards banking in 1904 with a 'current savings policy' that collected sums from £25 to £250 as a single premium 'payable at death or at a certain fixed age.' A year earlier, the Hand-in-Hand offered to collect deposits of £1,000 or more, available for withdrawal at six months' notice, on which it would pay 3.4 per cent fixed interest. The Commercial Union revived the scheme when it acquired the Hand-in-Hand two years later, apparently as a loss leader.[30]

Besides making it easier for customers to keep their policies in force, life insurance offices after 1860 took steps to clarify, and in some cases improve, the terms they would offer for a policy's surrender. Here, the driving force was less competition from newer firms than the growing realization that people who wanted to surrender their policies could often get a better deal from a private buyer than from their life office. From 1772, when the Equitable offered to buy customers' policies at 'reasonable and equitable' rates, surrender values were a standard feature of life insurance. By 1825, spurred by the prospect of receiving the Equitable's lucrative bonus, speculators were offering these same customers more than the society itself was willing to pay. Within a decade this pattern had spread to other firms, and the fact that life insurance policies were 'greed-ily purchased in the public market' led to a gradual rethinking among actuaries about what was reasonable for a company to offer.[31] Part of the margin between a policy's auction price and its surrender value lay in the fact that life insurance offices were unwilling to anticipate future bonus additions, and part of it was a simple case of buyers gambling – some-times based on inside knowledge about the seller's health or financial affairs – that the policy they purchased would result in an early claim.[32]

If life insurance managers could dismiss some auction prices as the result of rash speculation, they had a harder time ignoring competing prices offered by specialist 'reversionary interest' companies. Although the main purpose of these firms, five of which had formed by the mid-1850s, was to lend money on life interests, they also emerged as promin-ent buyers of auctioned life policies.[33] Besides turning what had been a sordid loophole to the Gambling Act into an accepted business practice, these companies had a clear effect on life office practice. In his 1883 presi-dential address to the Institute of Actuaries, Thomas Bond Sprague con-trasted the 'capricious conduct of private individuals' at policy auctions with 'the systematic purchases made by such buyers as Reversionary Interest Societies,' and urged his fellow actuaries to heed these trans-actions when calculating their 'official' surrender values.[34]

A key step in the direction of reaching a consensus on this issue was for life insurance companies to publish guaranteed surrender values, either in the prospectus or on the policies themselves. Although a few companies did this starting as early as 1823, the practice remained rare through the 1870s.[35] The tide turned after 1880, in part owing to a re-quirement to report sample surrender values under the Assurance Companies Act. Two surveys in 1892 revealed that two-thirds of all life offices offered guaranteed surrender values ranging from 30 per cent to 68.5 per cent of the premiums.[36] These variations reflected an unresolved debate among actuaries regarding the impact of surrendered policies on a company's profits. Many argued that higher surrender values created a moral hazard problem, since they tempted healthy policyholders to lapse at higher rates than those who were about to die. Others countered that people mainly surrendered their policies owing to financial troubles, which (as the *Economist* argued) mainly afflicted 'the dissipated, and those who are physically least able to fight the battle of life.'[37] In practice, life insurance companies resolved this debate by offering surrender val-ues that approached, though seldom matched, what customers could get for their policies on the open market.[38]

The changes to the insurance contract that became available to higher-income customers after 1870 generated less criticism than their lower-income precursors had. For their part, life insurance offices continued to discourage lapses even as they increased their surrender values. The Gresham's chairman reported in 1876 that it did 'everything it possibly can' to convince customers that insurance was a lifetime commitment, 'not one to be lightly given up from any caprice of the moment.' More generally, insurers never wholly abandoned their original disciplinary message, since doing so would have endangered their income stream: the Clergy Mutual's non-forfeiture scheme may have approached 'the utmost limit of liberality,' but its main purpose was to keep members paying into the life insurance fund. A good illustration of the largely rhetorical nature of many 'liberal' changes to the insurance contract was the National's decision, accompanying a new slate of liberal-sounding revisions, to 'make ... the "Conditions of Assurance" take the form of "Privileges granted" rather than that of "Rules to be enforced."'[39] Regulation by any other name was still regulation, even though customers might not notice. The continued financial success of life insurance, and its continued social utility, depended on this basic truth.

Saving for Retirement

For most of the nineteenth century British life insurance companies focused almost entirely on the contingency of premature death, as opposed to the financial risks attending old age. To the extent that they focused on this latter contingency at all, it tended to be in the form of annuities, which they sold to older customers who had already accumulated (or inherited) money and who wished to secure a livelihood that would last until they died. Only a few life insurance firms sold deferred annuities to younger customers to help prepare them financially for retirement. Endowments, which would eventually take centre-stage in combination with term life insurance, mainly referred before 1870 to schemes that enabled parents to store up money to help their children get a start in life. It was not until the 1860s, when some firms began offering lower-income customers the option of dipping into their anticipated claims after reaching old age, that the basic logic of endowment insurance began to take shape in more than a tiny segment of the market. And it was not until the 1890s, when the Prudential began aggressively selling endowment insurance to its huge lower-income customer base, and when most other life offices did likewise among higher-income customers, that this new form of thrift became established as the most popular in Britain.

Besides shifting customers' attention from death to retirement, the sale of endowment insurance and pensions moved British life insurance offices away from the other-directed nature of what they sold, which through the 1880s had mainly benefited dependents or creditors of the insured. In this, it marked a further step in the evolution away from altruism that had been initiated by loans on policies, deposit insurance, and liberal surrender values. On the other hand, endowment insurance did not depart as far as these other changes from the life policy's original disciplinary character. The only sense in which they did so was in the recognition that people were less likely to be able to continue paying premiums beyond the age of fifty-five or sixty. In other regards, they revived and reinforced earlier appeals to thrift, by adding a second incentive to save in a regular fashion (the need to pay for one's retirement) to the traditional incentive of providing for one's dependents.

Annuities, Deferred Annuities, and Endowments

For most of the nineteenth century the main way that life insurance companies assisted people who anticipated retirement was by selling them annuities, which converted a lump sum into annual payments over the final years of a person's life. In contrast to endowment insurance, which helped people prepare for retirement by getting them to start saving at an early age, most annuities commenced after people had already saved or inherited money. Life insurance offices were obvious candidates to undertake this business, since the same actuarial knowledge that enabled them to calculate profitable insurance premiums allowed them to offer safe rates for doling out people's savings until they died. There was a large market for such annuities, and they would have formed a much larger share of business for many firms had it not been for one thing: the British government, which had been mainly responsible for creating that market, took most of the century to give it up. As of 1714, of a national debt of £40.4 million 30 per cent was in the form of fixed-term annuities. Although annuitants converted much of this into company stock during the South Sea bubble of 1720, the British state soon went back to issuing annuities with renewed energy, this time for life instead of for fixed terms. Its annuity holdings stood at £564.4 million in 1802 (98.8 per cent of total public credit), increased to nearly £870 million in 1816, and still comprised £771.1 million in 1861.[40]

The looming presence of the National Debt Office was not enough to prevent a series of waves in the private annuity market between 1760 and 1840. Dozens of London firms appeared and rapidly disappeared in the 1760s, typically repaying only a fraction of their customers' savings before folding, and various professional organizations set up pension schemes on firmer bases around the same time.[41] The 'pernicious practice of raising money by the sale of life annuities' led to legislation in 1777, which in turn created an opening for life insurance offices between 1790 and 1805. These firms promised smaller annual payments than their forebears had done, but also survived long enough to pay to the end of their annuitants' lives.[42] Just when it seemed that annuities would play a major role in life insurance business, however, the British government issued a new set of rates in 1808 that paid more per year (at a huge loss to the National Debt Office) than most life insurance offices paid. This went on for twenty years, during which time British taxpayers effectively subsidized government annuitants, and private firms either stayed out of the annuity market or lost money trying to stay in. Although some life insurance companies went back to selling annuities when the government modified its rates in 1828, most had either given up by 1840 or only granted annuities as loss leaders.[43]

In contrast to annuities, which life insurance companies granted to customers who already had money to invest, a few early nineteenth-century companies offered deferred annuities as a savings mechanism for working-class or professional customers. In 1806 the Provident claimed that its deferred annuities offered 'the industrious and economical an opportunity .... by small savings during their years of vigour, to insure a comfortable support in their old age.' The Norwich Union, Scottish Widows' Fund, and British Commercial offered similar services prior to 1825, and in 1839 the Dissenters & General designed a policy that matured at age sixty 'to meet the case of superannuated ministers.'[44] From the 1830s many of the same companies that offered loans or deposit insurance to attract lower-income customers included deferred annuities among their options. These firms hoped that deferred annuities would lure such people away from friendly societies, which they accused (with some justification) of draining their pension funds through overly generous sick pay to younger members. The National Loan Fund identified 'the non-abstraction of a given sum for a separate benefit in sickness' as the main advantage of its deferred annuity plan.[45]

A variant on deferred annuities that many life insurance offices provided prior to 1850 was the family or educational endowment. These collected a few pounds per year from a child's infancy until he or she was a teenager, then paid out enough for the parents to cover tuition, apprenticeship, or a dowry. As such, they dovetailed with the emphasis in life insurance marketing on domesticity: the Commercial's prospectus, for instance, remarked: 'how essential it often is for the comfort of a family to command a sum of money to provide for the education of children, or on the occasion of settling a son in business, or a daughter in marriage.' By the 1850s over half of all companies included this feature.[46] A less successful version of this plan was Francis Corbaux's scheme 'for the endowment of unborn children,' which he sold to the newly formed Family Endowment Society. Basing his tables on French marriage and birth statistics, Corbaux failed to anticipate that childless couples would soon discontinue their policies, which meant the company lost money on the endowments they did pay out.[47]

Although it is easy enough to find references to deferred annuities and child endowments in Victorian insurance prospectuses, they never accounted for more than a tiny fraction of the business that all but a few companies transacted. In 1838 the Norwich Union earned just £1,098 from its deferred annuities, and ten Scottish life insurance offices issued only 193 endowments on children through 1863.[48] In contrast to annuities, these low proportions had nothing to do with competition from the National Debt Office, which had almost completely stopped granting deferred annuities by the mid-nineteenth century. Apparently, middle-class customers through the 1860s thought they had sufficient means to prepare for retirement – including savings, real estate, and interest from loans to relatives – to make contributing to a deferred annuity seem like a luxury they could do without.[49]

The Rise of Endowment Insurance

Although a few established life insurance companies offered endowment insurance from the 1840s, it did not become central to any firm's marketing strategies until the Briton introduced a modified endowment plan in 1861, and did not take off until the Prudential began aggressively selling it in its 'ordinary' branch in the late 1880s. This coincided with a resurgence of interest in old age pensions, prompted in part by a national political debate over the merits of implementing a pension scheme for the working classes. From there, a critical mass of life insurance offices began marketing endowment policies to higher-income customers, until it became a handicap not to feature them. In 1890 one-sixth of all life insurance policies issued were for endowment insurance, covering 8 per cent of sums insured. Twenty years later endowment policies accounted for three-fifths of total new policies and 34 per cent of new sums insured.[50] This transformation reflected both a shifting preference among middle-class customers and a surge in popularity among lower-income policyholders who were first-time buyers. Throughout the first half of the nineteenth century it had been possible for life insurance customers to buy a term life policy and a deferred annuity from the same company. What was new was the convenience of paying a single annual premium for these two services combined in one policy. At least five life insurance offices offered this combination starting around 1840, as did seven more between 1848 and 1856.[51] Like the deferred annuities that preceded them, these early schemes targeted less wealthy customers who might not be able to keep up payments into old age. A Palladium advertisement in 1841 urged that since endowment policies only required payment during a customer's 'years of health, strength, and active exertion,' they enabled 'every one, however limited his income may be ... to provide for the support of *himself* ... during his declining years.' Also like deferred annuities, endowment insurance comprised just a tiny fraction of the total life insurance market through the 1850s. A survey of companies contributing to the Institute of Actuaries mortality study revealed that only £1.66 million had been insured in that manner (1.5 per cent of the total) through 1863.[52]

In the 1860s a series of life insurance offices that expressly catered to lower-income customers began to offer what was, in effect, variable-term endowment insurance. The pioneer in this regard was the Briton, which introduced a bonus plan that first reduced, then eliminated, premiums payable after a period of time, after which point it started paying cash to the policyholder. Its inventor, Arthur Scratchley (who earlier had promoted policy-secured loans and deposit insurance), claimed that his new bonus scheme provided policyholders with 'a column of support when old age, and consequent inability to labour, shall render such support most needful.' Within a few years at least five other life offices, all of which attracted a large volume of lower-income business, had copied Scratchley's scheme.[53]

This market, like the lower-income market more generally, quickly migrated to the Prudential and other industrial offices in the 1880s. By 1887 the Prudential issued thirty-one thousand endowment policies through its ordinary branch, more than a quarter of all such policies issued in Britain; five years later, that figure had risen to 163,000. At the turn of the century the Prudential continued to lead the way as an issuer of endowment insurance, with 525,277 such policies in force (77 per cent of its 'ordinary' business), covering just over £100 per policy and accounting for 49 per cent of the total number of endowment policies issued by British life insurance offices. The Prudential's two leading industrial rivals, the Refuge and the Pearl, had more than ninety thousand endowment policies in force as of 1902 (covering £74 per policy), comprising 60 per cent of the business done in their ordinary branches. Other British offices lagged far behind these three industrial firms in their proportion of endowment insurance in force, with just 34 per cent of total policies and 20 per cent of total sums insured. By 1910 industrial offices held 1.08 million endowment policies (74 per cent of their policies and 64 per cent of the market), insuring £101.6 million (36 per cent of the market).[54]

This meteoric rise in the sale of endowment insurance to lower-income customers after 1885 can be attributed to at least three factors. Most basically, by 1900 more people were surviving into old age. The number of people over the age of sixty-five more than doubled between 1841 and 1901, from 700,000 to 1.5 million, and once people reached that age they survived an average of 10.8 years. At the same time, older workers increasingly found themselves shifted into marginal, lower-paying jobs or forced into retirement. Accompanying these trends, starting in the late-1870s social reformers waged a sustained campaign for state-subsidized old age pensions, which generated no political success until the 1908 Old Age Pensions Act but did keep the issue in people's minds during the intervening decades. Finally, the substantial marketing muscle of the Prudential and other industrial offices translated these contexts into sales opportunities. Together with friendly societies and the Charity Organization Society, which condemned state pensions as a threat to working-class thrift, industrial offices routinely presented themselves as a more virtuous alternative to relying on government handouts.[55]

While the Prudential was leaving its indelible mark on the sale of endowment insurance, other life insurance offices slowly began to create a demand for the product among a wealthier clientele: by 1910 endowment insurance comprised 49 per cent of all policies held by non-industrial firms and 28 per cent of sums insured. The main way that firms did this was to hitch endowment policies to the popularity of the bonus, which both made the insurance component more attractive than earlier plans and greatly enhanced the value of the annuity component for customers who lived that long. Standard Life first introduced with-profit endowment insurance in 1870, and Pelican Life did so in 1873 under the name of 'Survivors' Bonus Insurance'; others waited until the 1880s or later, sometimes because they needed to alter their deed to allow them to share profits on such policies. By 1895 only nine life insurance firms in a survey of sixty-eight paid no bonuses on their endowment policies, reversing what the usual industry practice had been twenty years earlier.[56]

Whereas industrial offices clearly used endowment insurance to attract new customers by the tens of thousands, most of the growth among non-industrial firms apparently reflected a shift in spending patterns among their usual customers rather than a new inroad into the lower-income market. Endowment policies issued by non-industrial offices in 1910 covered an average of £303, more than three times the average for those issued by their industrial counterparts. And even though this was only half the coverage of whole life policies issued by non-industrial offices (which stood at £601 in 1910), most of this disparity can be accounted for by the fact that endowment insurance was more expensive – between 33 per cent and 100 per cent costlier, depending on the term. A thirty-year-old customer who spent £15 a year for £600 in whole life coverage in 1910 would have paid a little more than that for a twenty-year endowment worth £300, and £12 for the same policy maturing in twenty-five years.[57] Hence although longer-term endowment policies were somewhat more affordable, for the most part it appears that the same customers that non-industrial firms had always catered to were moving part of their savings from family provision into retirement.

Partly because of its obvious attraction to lower-income policyholders, and partly because of its departure from earlier assumptions about the altruistic nature of life insurance, some insurance men took some time getting used to the idea of selling endowment insurance. A Scottish Equitable branch manager scoffed in 1891 that endowment insurance was 'a class of business ... not materially removed from that of an itinerant vendor of steel pens,' and the Clerical Medical's actuary worried that it cultivated 'the selfish instincts of mankind' as opposed to performing the 'proper work' of paying claims to widows.[58] As many life insurance officials, however, were happy enough to swallow their pride and rationalize the more 'selfish' nature of what they sold. The Scottish Equitable's assistant secretary joked in 1898 that critics of endowment insurance adopted 'the attitude of the pious bookseller, who regretted that he had sold more novels than Bibles.' As for the ethics of selling endowment insurance, most actuaries applied the same logic they used to defend the bonus and more liberal surrender values. As Thomas Bond Sprague put it in 1892, 'a very important part' of the business of a life insurance office, beyond the actual sale of insurance, 'consists in the investment of its funds'; hence it was 'a very legitimate development of the business ... that the Company should undertake to invest money for the assured to a limited extent.'[59]

Most of this relatively easy adjustment to the merits of selling endowment insurance was simply a response to a clear public demand for the product by people whose salaries depended on their employers turning a profit. But there were other reasons that endeared actuaries to endowment insurance, relating to its potential for diminishing losses from premature death. Actuaries inferred from the case of annuitants, who lived 'carefully and long' in order to get the most out of their savings as possible, that endowment customers would live longer than whole life policyholders; as one actuary said, when someone buys endowment insurance 'he "backs himself" to survive to a certain age.' Similarly, actuaries hoped that endowment insurance would reduce lapse rates, since the prospect of paying the final instalments on a twenty-year policy (to be followed immediately by a pension) was a stronger incentive than the prospect of a lifetime's worth of payment with no reward until an unpredictable date with death. This, in turn, stood to improve the life insurance office's revenue stream, which made it easier to frame a company's investment and marketing strategies.[60]

Life insurance offices learned to adjust their older marketing emphasis on providing for others to the more selfish motives that prompted 'the average middle-class individual' to buy endowment insurance. As early as 1860 the Westminster & General cited the 'gentleman in a profession' who desired 'an additional provision for the comfort of his old age,' while a Provident Life prospectus from the mid-1880s envisioned a man with 'no wife, no mother, no sister, and no poor relations to provide for' who should therefore 'provide for Number One.' An endowment policy, it concluded, would enable him to 'reap the benefit of his prudence long before his step became feeble or his hair turned grey.' An especially revealing line of thinking appeared in 1884 from a *Policyholder* correspondent, who urged that if a man was 'convinced that an endowment assurance is the best investment for his old age, *for himself*,' he would 'bear its cost with pleasure.' In contrast, the writer concluded, whole life premiums were 'invariably paid with a grudge, as a tax for the support of one's widow. Clothe it as you may, it is a necessary but most disagreeable duty.'[61]

Finally, endowment insurance meant that was that it was no longer necessary for salesmen to foreground the possibility of death, which emerged as a big advantage as Victorian 'death culture' began to wane at the end of the nineteenth century. As an early promoter of endowment insurance claimed: 'Death is the penalty to be paid for the receipt of the sum assured' in most life insurance offices, whereas his company's endowment scheme afforded 'protection to its holder when old age renders that protection necessary.' Although some insurance men continued to hold out for 'the old-fashioned death assurance,' many more jumped at the chance to balance the threat of premature death with the potential of living into old age. By the 1930s, when many life offices were moving aggressively into pensions as well as endowment policies, they had thoroughly shifted their marketing strategies to generate anxiety over old age as opposed to death. 'Killing the Dread of Old Age' was the headline T.A.E. Layburn from the Legal & General fed to his golfing partner who edited the *Sunday Express*.[62]

Conclusion

Although endowment insurance, liberal surrender values, and non-forfeiture blurred the boundary between life insurance and other forms of savings, they did not wholly erase it. Life insurance in 1900 still very much qualified as 'mandatory saving' which, as R.J. Morris has observed, had by that time transformed the way the British middle classes spent, borrowed, and accumulated money. In place of the dominant early Victorian middle-class property cycle that had favoured personal management of loans, often to and from family members, 'institutional intermediaries' – with life insurance offices front and centre – had emerged to 'spread the risk of investment' and thereby mask 'the process of acquiring and receiving rentier income.'[63] And the life insurance contract still counted as more mandatory than the competing opportunities to save that banks provided, since it placed limits on access to people's savings that banks seldom if ever did. This persisted even when, in the decades after the First World War, life offices took endowment insurance the next step and sold pension plans without a life insurance component.[64] Even in this case the basic logic of life insurance investment, that holding customers' savings for longer periods of time yielded higher interest than a bank could pay, still came with the corollary that customers could not expect access to that money to be as easy as in a bank.

The long distance that the life insurance contract travelled in the century after 1815, however, attests to the wide variety of meanings that 'mandatory saving' could carry at any given time, depending on customers' preferences and means. In life insurance offices that catered to traditionally middle- and upper-class policyholders, the change was primarily in terms of preference. Instead of embracing, or at least accepting, strict penalties for lapses and late payment, these customers increasingly preferred to buy life insurance from companies that paid more for their lapsed policies and took a more relaxed stance on tardiness. Instead of buying fully into the early Victorian identification of life insurance with family provision, they increasingly preferred to save for retirement as well as the contingency of premature death. To the extent that this saving came from the same disposable income that once paid for whole life policies, dependents of such customers had less to look forward to in the event of early death. Yet as with the bonus, which also diverted from the 'insurance' component of the contract, these new varieties of saving attracted more people to the market and arguably made up for their departure from more disciplinary forms of thrift by spreading the saving habit over a wider surface of people.

This was quite clearly the case for the millions of lower-income customers who could not afford to adopt life insurance as a form of saving unless the terms of the contract changed. It was for this reason that most of the newly liberal features of life insurance first appeared during the 1840s and 1850s, among the dozens of new companies that sought to attract such people away from savings banks and friendly societies. The incentive of tapping into this market led them to alter a set of disciplinary norms that proved to be unrealistic in application to people with uncertain income streams that were likely to dry up altogether in old age. Although most of these companies failed commercially, it was not for their lack of insight into how to design an insurance product that working-class people would buy. When the Prudential stepped in to fill the void created by these failed firms, it linked their novel technologies of thrift to its own unparalleled marketing might. In the process, it converted little piles of savings into enormous piles of profit for its shareholders.

8 Victorian Gatekeeping

It is pleasant now and then to meet in the body those whom we have only known by the description of themselves in their Proposals; for, like Baron Liebig with his process of making the extract of beef ... we also compress your noble selves into the small compass of the six sheets of paper which constitute the various forms required by the Office in a Life Assurance transaction.

– David Harris, Briton Medical & General Edinburgh branch
secretary, at a meeting of policyholders, 1867[1]

When insurance is bought and sold in the private sector, it typically attracts a disproportionate number of high-risk customers. This, in turn, creates an incentive for insurance companies to maximize profits by refusing to admit the highest risks – something that does not arise in social insurance (or, for that matter, many group insurance schemes), in which members cannot choose whether or not to belong to the risk pool. The technical term for this problem is *adverse selection*. Since it arises at the point of sale, adverse selection is a different (though related) problem from moral hazard, whereby 'insurance actually increases the occurrence of adverse events through its incentives to people who [already] have insurance.'[2] The most common response to adverse selection has historically been some form of gatekeeping, involving an interrogation of the property or person to be insured, although it is also possible to guard against adverse selection by restructuring the insurance contract. Responses to moral hazard are both more varied and longer lasting: instead of being limited to a one-off investigation conducted at the point of sale, insurers have an incentive to continue to guard against moral hazard throughout the duration of the policy.

Life insurance, especially as it was practised in nineteenth-century Britain, devoted far more resources to limit adverse selection than to limit moral hazard. Life insurance offices worried incessantly about detecting risk at the point of sale, whereas only in the cases of suicide and foreign travel did they try to prevent or penalize events that transpired after the policy was issued.[3] Even these exceptional cases diminished over time: by the end of the century, most companies paid suicide claims if the death took place more than a year or two after the policy was effected and issued 'free travel' riders to customers who held their policies for at least five years. The only other proscription against moral hazard in life insurance related to customers who held policies on other people's lives: to prevent the temptation to profit by cutting short the life of the insured, the Gambling Act of 1772 pinned coverage levels to insurable interest, and life insurance offices refused payment in the event of murder.[4]

Gatekeeping among British life insurers did not appear wholly formed at the beginning of the nineteenth century, nor did it remain unchanged in subsequent decades. Several early eighteenth-century responses to the threat of 'insuring upon old and infirm lives' bore a general similarity to later practices, including a personal interview at the head office, proxy certificates from provincial gentry, and probationary periods during which claims were refused. Selling tontine policies as a check against adverse selection was also alive and well before 1720.[5] Well into the Victorian era, life insurance offices refined these basic strategies without clarifying with any precision their effects or being able to show that adverse selection actually took place. After 1850, when actuaries started to ask these questions in earnest, a much clearer justification for gatekeeping emerged. This coincided with a time of heightened competition among insurers and succeeded in keeping firms focused on the need to guard against adverse selection, even when the drive for new business pulled them in the opposite direction.

These new justifications for life insurance gatekeeping in the 1850s coincided with a rethinking of older screening methods. Most firms in 1850 required customers to disavow any serious risks on a proposal form, to provide references from a friend and medical attendant, and to meet with the board of directors – and all three methods were starting to pose serious problems. The inadequacy of the proposal form was partly a matter of customers' dishonesty, but mainly a case of ignorance: applicants could not attest to a malady they were unaware of. Life insurance offices often screened such candidates on a post hoc basis, by denying premature claims on the ground that facts had been withheld, but by 1850 judges and the general public increasingly viewed this as unfair. Reference letters from friends were never the sort of thing life insurance offices trusted very much, and that trust diminished steadily over the course of the century. References from candidates' medical attendants continued to be valued as a source of information until the 1840s, but this quickly changed when the doctors started to demand fees for them. Once life insurance offices had to pay for this information, they started to look for ways to gather medical intelligence from sources that were less likely to be biased in favour of the candidate.

For all these reasons, the primary form of gatekeeping employed by most life insurance offices after 1850 ended up being the medical examination – typically combining a series of questions with a brief chest and head examination. From early on, many life insurance offices recognized a need to supplement the head office interview with such an exam, and they appointed specially qualified directors or hired medical advisers to do this. Then, as they began setting up provincial agencies, they appointed a further set of surrogates to perform this task. Head office medical advisers, who had once supplemented the directors' interview with a brief physical exam, took on the new responsibility of screening the dozens of examination forms that flowed in from country doctors. And disputed claims, which were already in decline, became rarer still, since it proved difficult for a life insurance office to counter the fact that their own medical adviser had certified the life in question.

This primary focus on adverse selection as opposed to moral hazard was unique among Victorian insurance providers. Although fire insurance offices, for instance, countered adverse selection by surveying property to classify fire risk and assess value, they focused much more on preventing moral hazard after the policy had been issued than on gatekeeping at the point of sale. [6] Examples of moral hazard in fire insurance included carelessness (a failure to exercise sufficient caution against fire) and arson (the fire insurance equivalent of murdering an insured life). To guard against carelessness, Victorian fire insurance offices insisted on a growing number of safety precautions as a prerequisite for coverage; and they regularly brought arson cases to trial – in which the goal was to prove that the fire was not an accident, and not (as in most life insurance trials) to accuse the policyholder of withholding from the gatekeeper a pre-existing risk. They also tried to remove the temptation to commit arson by promising only partial coverage of any property. Similar forms of moral hazard, and similar regulatory responses, emerged during the nineteenth century in companies that insured against personal injuries, boiler explosions, and embezzlement.[7]

This greater focus on moral hazard (and with that, governance strategies that more tightly restricted policyholders' actions) was partly the result of its greater incidence. Insurance-inspired murders and suicides trailed far behind the parallel occurrence of insurance-inspired arson, and their impact from a strictly actuarial standpoint was minimal.[8] Leaving aside these extreme examples, however, a huge grey area remained in which most other types of insurance companies paid far more attention to the behaviour of their customers than was the case in life insurance. As discussed in chapter 4, the main reason for this had to do with the greater calculability of life insurance risks. Especially once companies started to base their premiums and valuations on the mortality experience of insured lives, any moral hazard effects were automatically factored into these calculations. This was not an option for fire insurance, where a customer's careless behaviour might lead to a disastrous blaze, capable of bankrupting several companies.

In theory, of course, a life insurance office could increase its profits (or the bonus it paid to its customers) by extending surveillance over its customers beyond the point of sale. This was, in fact, the business model for the many late Victorian firms that set up abstinence sections, which penalized customers who fell off the wagon by denying their claims, raising their premiums, or (most commonly) shifting them into a risk pool that paid lower bonuses.[9] These, however, were the exceptions to what was otherwise a very popular rule, which promised an absence of most forms of regulation between the moment customers signed their policy and the moment they died. Indeed, the very popularity of this rule made it increasingly difficult for life insurance offices to defend medical exams at the point of sale as necessary for preventing premature claims. Such appeals to collective financial well-being looked different to individual candidates, who were often deeply ambivalent about subjecting themselves to surveillance as a prerequisite for buying insurance. When they acted on this ambivalence by refusing to insure, companies responded by liberalizing their rules in order to lure them back into the market. By the end of the nineteenth century, a few life insurance companies began to dispense with medical examinations in some cases, a policy that would gain in popularity over the course of the twentieth century.

Gatekeeping before 1870

From the 1830s into the 1860s, the Norwich Union required all applicants for life insurance to fill in and sign a document that ran as follows:

> I, _____ by profession or occupation _____ born in the parish of
> _____ on the _ day of __in the year ___ and now resident at _____ be-
> ing desirous of making an Insurance for the term of _____ on my own life,
> to the amount of £____ ... do declare that I have __ had the small-pox or
> cow-pox, have ___ had the measles, have ___ had the hooping-cough; that
> I have __ suffered a spitting of blood, am __ subject to asthma or other
> pulmonary complaints, have __ had the gout, am __ afflicted with fits,
> hernia, nor any other disease or any habit particularly tending to shorten
> the duration of life.

The bottom of the form left room for the names of two 'referees for the state of my health' and up to four previous medical attendants and reminded the candidate that his or her signature made the form a binding legal contract. After 1870, following a precedent that other firms had set several decades earlier, the company hived off the medical questions onto a separate, but still legally binding page; but in most regards the content of the proposal form remained the same into the next century.[10]

This proposal form, and others like it, reveals much about which types of disease and behaviour were thought to be most dangerous to life prior to 1850, and also about which sources of information were thought to be most trustworthy. Although they predated the availability of reliable medical statistics that linked mortality to specific causes of death, the appearance of such data after 1840 mainly confirmed life offices' suspicions. Other questions appeared on forms because they were relatively easy to confirm, either before issuing a policy or after a suspiciously premature death: these included queries regarding a candidate's habits, past residence, occupation, and prior insurance history. No proposal form was complete, finally, without a space for candidates to list their regular medical attendant and at least one friend, and these people were expected to provide supplementary information about health and habits; finally, all these filled-in papers needed to be vetted by a board of directors, usually in consultation with a salaried medical adviser, who would compare this 'paper' picture with a view of candidates in the flesh.

A Range of Risks: Early Victorian Proposal Forms

A sample of 110 medical forms from 1850 reveals the breadth and perceived significance of risks facing Victorian life insurers. The single most important concerned the state of candidates' lungs, as indicated by questions relating to 'spitting of blood,' 'habitual cough,' 'disease of the chest,' or 'symptoms of consumption.' All but six companies in the sample (95 per cent) asked about at least one of these conditions. Next in line were gout, hernia, and epilepsy, which featured on at least 90 per cent of these forms, followed by asthma (85 per cent) and insanity (76 per cent). Eighty-five per cent of all life insurance offices asked if candidates had previously had smallpox or had been vaccinated, and 65 per cent asked if their habits were sober, moderate, and/or temperate. Just over two-thirds of the sample (67 per cent) asked if the candidate's parents had died of a hereditary disease. Beyond this core set of questions, life insurance offices ranged the medical map far less systematically. Between 20 per cent and 35 per cent of companies asked about dropsy, liver disease, rheumatism, heart disease, and accidental injury; and between 10 per cent and 20 per cent asked about apoplexy, fainting, scrofula, gravel, and measles. At least four life insurance offices asked questions about bowel disease, cancer, dysentery, fistula, hemorrhoids, jaundice, kidney disease, piles, rheumatic fever, scarlet fever, stomach disease, stone, urinary disease, vertigo, and whooping cough.[11]

Consumption was at the top of this list with good reason. As the insurance director and public health expert William Guy pronounced in 1870, consumption was 'the chronic plague of the prime of life.' In the 1850s it killed 46 per cent of Englishmen who died between the ages of twenty and twenty-five, and 42 per cent of those who died between twenty-five and thirty-five. Life insurance offices fared somewhat better, but the figures were still alarming: according to a study of ten Scottish offices up to 1863, consumption killed 32 per cent of claimants who died in their twenties and 24 per cent who died in their thirties. Lung disease accounted for between 20 per cent and 29 per cent of claimants in mid-century surveys, and owing to the young age at which it killed its victims its cost was even greater than these numbers imply. The Scottish Equitable's physician discovered that claimants who died of consumption in his office only lived long enough on average to pay eight years' worth of premiums, and his company's experience was actually better than most.[12]

Although many life insurance offices asked their candidates outright if they had suffered consumption or 'disease of the lung,' even more asked if they had spat blood, an early warning sign that was more likely to be recognized by a layman. Hospital studies indicated that spitting of blood (or haemoptysis) preceded consumption around 70 per cent of the time, and insurance doctors' attitudes towards this condition ranged from cautious to severe. The Norwich Union charged extra for a Deptford clerk who had twice spat up 'half a teaspoonful' of blood six years earlier, and 'spitting of blood 2 yrs since' shot down the application of a Beverly draper.[13] Besides asking about physical symptoms, life insurance offices often asked candidates if any relatives had died of consumption. This danger sign took on increased weight in the decades following 1860, fuelled by statistical evidence from consumption hospitals.[14] Most life insurance offices took family history into account by the 1870s; they typically proscribed all candidates under thirty-five with two parents or more than one sibling who had died of consumption, and they urged extreme caution in cases where a sibling or grandparent had suffered from the disease.[15]

Questions about gout and hernia appeared on life insurance proposal forms nearly as regularly as questions about consumption. Offices worried about gout mainly because of its reputation as a special risk of aristocratic men, who before 1850 comprised the most important market for life insurance in Britain. One insurance doctor in 1862 referred to gout as 'a disease of those who can command all the comforts, and who indulge in the luxuries of life' – including a large insurance policy.[16] Although early surveys of claims indicated low mortality rates from gout, this did not shake insurance doctors' belief that the disease was 'a grave blot.' In 1853 James Begbie of the Scottish Widows' Fund linked gout to 'a long chain of apoplexies and palsies,' not to mention asthma, hydrothorax, dropsy, and liver and kidney disease. James Meikle's 1872 survey of ten Scottish offices, which tracked the mortality of candidates who had been charged extra for gout as opposed to dying of the disease, appeared to confirm this conclusion, and by that time most doctors recognized that gout was an equally serious disease among lower-born policyholders as well as those of 'good birth.' Forty years later, doctors had found new ways to articulate these older fears, now citing 'the slow but steady advance of arterio sclerosis' as the leading associated risk of gout.[17]

Hernia, in contrast, declined in significance as a perceived risk in the decades after 1850. Earlier, it was common for candidates to be rejected or charged heavy extras on account of hernia. By the 1850s physicians were advising that 'the Mortality from Hernia amongst assured lives is excessively small,' and Meikle confirmed this in 1872.[18] Life insurance offices had long known that wearing a truss removed most of the risk to hernia sufferers, and by the 1870s many were willing to accept hernia risks at no extra charge with a 'truss clause.' These clauses stood out among Victorian life insurance contracts because they extended the regulation of customers' health into the future. One such clause read, in part, that 'the life assured (who has hernia and has elected not to pay the usual extra) shall at all times except when in bed, wear a properly adjusted truss'; failure to do so empowered the insurance company to deny the claim.[19]

The frequent appearance of epilepsy and insanity on proposal forms had less to do with their effect on mortality than with their ease of detection. It was next to impossible for a candidate to conceal a past epileptic seizure or a stay in an asylum. Cutting against this was the substantial grey area between epilepsy and 'occasional fainting spells' or 'ordinary shivering fits,' and between insanity and eccentricity. A Glasgow surgeon informed the Aberdeen Fire & Life in 1844 that a female patient was 'subject to slight mental alienations,' but thought this was just the sign of 'a self-willed, hasty ... obstinate disposition.'[20] Doctors associated epilepsy with 'organic mischief in the brain' and apoplexy and linked insanity with 'paroxysmal intemperance,' consumption, 'moral depravity,' and above all suicide. By 1900 medical opinion firmly held that suicide was almost always the result of mental illness, leading companies to move it from the category of moral hazard to that of adverse selection – and to screen out potential victims before they insured rather than punish their families after they died.[21]

In contrast to epilepsy and insanity, doctors were hard-pressed to detect intemperance but most were convinced that it had a major impact on mortality. One medical officer suggested a connection between 'wine-madness' and epilepsy; another connected beer-drinking to urinary disease; and a third linked intemperance to 'cerebral disease' and 'diseases of the organs of digestion,' cholera, and accidental death.[22] Like epilepsy and insanity, drawing a line between intemperate and moderate drinking posed a problem. Although most doctors would have agreed with William Farr's definition of intemperance as 'habitual and excessive indulgence in spirits, wine, or fermented liquors,' that left 'excessive' in need of further clarification. Doctors frequently cited 'the physiological limit of 1 1/2 ounces ... of absolute alcohol per day,' which translated into a glass of wine or a pint of stout – and was only slightly in excess of the average daily consumption of Victorians who imbibed.[23]

As a gatekeeping device, the insurance proposal form's effectiveness hinged on the ability and inclination of applicants to answer its questions accurately. The primary means of enforcing this was the reminder, on the form itself, that it was a legally binding contract and the accompanying threat that anything short of full disclosure might result in the claim being denied. The Rock was typical, if sterner in language, when it required all candidates to agree that if their declaration 'be not true, all money paid to the Society by me, on account of the Assurance, shall be forfeited.'[24] This threat, in turn, hinged on life offices' success at defending denied claims in court, in the event that a claimant sued for recovery. Since that success was mixed at best, and since denying too many claims was bad for public relations, they resorted to a variety of methods to verify or clarify candidates' assertions: including an interview with the board of directors and/or a medical adviser, and references from candidates' friends and medical attendants.

Judging from Appearances

Into the 1840s a personal interview with the board of directors was in many life insurance offices one of the main screens standing between the initial proposal form and final acceptance. Every life office advertised a 'Board day' (really an office hour) when the directors assembled each week to interview candidates and determine their eligibility.[25] It did not take long for companies to figure out that a single office hour per week could not possibly be convenient for every customer, and from the 1830s several either agreed to arrange meetings by appointment or to schedule regular 'daily boards' with a rotating set of directors. In contrast to the proposal form's focus on medical and family history, what counted most to directors was a candidate's appearance – as is clear from a set of notes taken in 1834 and preserved by the Alliance. Of the lives they accepted, most displayed 'good colour' or were 'fresh looking,' were 'well made' and 'active,' and were tall rather than short. Among candidates whose proposals were deferred for further references were a 'Queer looking man,' one who was 'Very full & fat,' and one who was 'pallid'; and the lives they declined looked 'sickly,' 'full, fat ... [and] indifferent,' and 'very large indeed.'[26]

Although Richard Price twice urged the Equitable in the 1770s to appoint a doctor at a hundred guineas a year to assist in this screening process, the Equitable instead made sure that at least one or two of its directors had medical training. Several other early insurance companies took this route, including the Westminster, Globe, Atlas, and Pelican.[27] The company with the largest presence of medical men on its board was the Clerical Medical, which featured eight medical directors throughout the nineteenth century and included such eminent physicians and surgeons as Benjamin Brodie, Astley Cooper, J.H. Green, William Bowman, and James Paget. This plan had two overlapping rationales: the company's active effort to sell shares and insurance policies to medical men and its pursuit of the niche market of 'under-average' lives, which required a special breadth of medical expertise. The only other firm that mainly relied on medical directors through the end of the nineteenth century was the Norwich Union, where two board members with medical training went over all the proposals prior to each week's general board meeting.[28]

After 1820 many insurance directors started to pay consultants to advise them in medical manners. Nearly half of a sample of twenty firms did so in 1825, often with an 'official surgeon' as well as a physician. The men they appointed resembled the directors in all but their profession. When the Scottish Amicable's medical adviser died in 1837, its manager suggested that the new doctor 'should be a man of Gentlemanly and agreeable manners ... with whom they would feel pleasure in associating.' Life insurance offices expected their medical advisers to attend at the office at least once a week, normally to examine candidates and answer questions at the board meeting.[29] Many firms required office hours on other days or asked doctors to set aside times when they could be 'found at home' to examine candidates there, and some occasionally paid their advisers to make house calls.[30] For their efforts, medical advisers' pay ranged from twenty-five to 250 guineas a year before 1850 (averaging out to £87 a year). After 1850, a sample of twenty-six doctors earned £178, with Scottish offices occupying both the high and low ends of a broader spectrum: £50 at the Scottish Temperance and Scottish National and £400 at Standard Life.[31]

The two professional qualifications that insurance companies most valued in their medical advisers were hospital experience and expertise on diseases deemed to be risky to their profits. In London, almost two-thirds of a sample of 326 medical advisers held at least one hospital appointment, with higher-status teaching hospitals like St Thomas's and Guy's the best represented.[32] James Arnott, in his successful application to be the Westminster & General's physician, noted that his experience at the Middlesex Hospital had given him 'extensive opportunities of becoming acquainted with the influence of various diseases on the duration of life, with the best modes of discovering their presence when latent, and of detecting them when attempted to be concealed.' Hospital experience also provided doctors with the ability to examine candidates in a hurry. For a doctor whose only experience was in private practice, fifteen minutes to half an hour might have seemed like too little time to conduct a thorough examination; for someone like the St Bart's physician who once examined 120 hospital patients in under two hours, thirty minutes must have seemed like an eternity.[33]

Life offices also valued medical advisers with expertise in diseases that were likely to result in premature claims. Of 237 medical advisers who listed an area of expertise in a sample of doctors active from 1870 to 1910, over a quarter specialized in either consumption or heart disease. Other well-represented fields were nervous disorders, urology, obstetrics, alcoholism, and rheumatism – all sources of concern for a life insurance office owing to their tendency to strike at young or middle ages.[34] Several insurance doctors published important studies on the family history and age incidence of consumption; Dyce Duckworth, who advised the Law Life and Phoenix, was one of Britain's leading gout experts; the Scottish Provident's James Duncan published widely on obstetrics; the Guardian's William Gowers was a neurologist whose *Borderland of Epilepsy* was a landmark; and Thomas Bevill Peacock of the Mutual and National Provident published major studies of valvular disease and heart deformities.[35]

Friends and Medical Attendants

Besides expecting candidates to meet with them personally, insurance directors usually asked for testimony from at least one friend and one medical attendant. Early friends' reference forms asked searching questions about the candidate's health, often in nearly as much detail as on doctors' forms. A timber merchant's friend left his Norwich Union form blank in 1859, noting that he considered 'a Medical Gentleman the most proper person' to fill it in.[36] Very occasionally, a friend's report would reveal sufficient evidence to lead life insurance offices to reject a proposal. The Rock learned in 1812 that Matthew Howard's friends thought he was 'of delicate and various health'; and the friend of a retired army officer informed the Eagle in 1851 of 'one or two fainting fits,' a hernia, and 'a little operation *for piles*, which confined him for a few days.' Friends also occasionally let just enough slip regarding a candidate's habits to raise a red flag, as was the case with the mill owner whose friend reported that he 'may in his own house after dinner particularly if joined by a few friends indulge a little, as men of his grade in this country usually do.'[37]

Far more common, though, were euphemisms for disease and overstated assurances of perfect health. Approximating the standard was the character in a Dickens short story who told an insurance company that his friend was 'temperate in the last degree, and took a little too much exercise, if anything.' Dickens's own friend, John Forster, called him 'remarkably sober & temperate' in a form he sent to the Eagle in 1841; he did not mention a recent fistula operation by name, but only said that he had 'of late, for a short period ... been under the care of Mr Salmon, of Broad Street.' Both Forster and a second friend conceded that Dickens was 'sedentary,' but added that he was 'always active' and 'inclining to activity' in his ample leisure time.[38]

More valuable than a reference letter from a friend, although subject to many of the same problems, was a report from a candidate's medical attendant. Early on, such a report came in response to a simple request for a letter concerning the candidate's 'general, or present state of ... health.' By 1850 most life insurance offices had replaced such open-ended requests with a printed form containing anywhere from five to twenty-five questions.[39] Besides repeating most of the questions that appeared on the proposal form, life insurance offices asked medical attendants how long they had known the candidate and if their 'professional attendance' had been required for any serious maladies. The doctors who sent in these reports were quick to remind life offices that they possessed unique knowledge of risk factors that might otherwise go undetected; and well into the late nineteenth century, after life insurance offices had stopped relying on this source of information in most cases, they continued to recognize its potential value in revealing a candidate's past illnesses or accidents, family history, and habits. As Standard Life's medical adviser noted, medical attendants sometimes 'divulged some important defect not likely to be discovered ... during the usual examination of the company's referee.'[40]

Certainly the archives yield more examples of candid responses from this source than from friends' references. One doctor informed the Clerical Medical that a candidate was 'predisposed to inflammation, whenever any exciting cause was applied'; another cautioned that a Twickenham man was 'a very hazardous life' who had never fully recovered from a ruptured blood vessel; and a third recounted his patient's partial paralysis, swollen legs, conjunctivitis, and yellow skin.[41] Medical attendants could be especially helpful in reporting prior intemperance, which might otherwise be difficult to detect. The Aberdeen

Fire & Life rejected a £300 proposal entirely on the testimony of the man's doctor, who 'was quite decided as to [prior] attacks of delirium tremens'; and the Legal & General similarly discouraged a proposal when the man's doctor claimed he was '"not very" sober & temperate in his habits.'[42]

As with friends' references, however, life insurance offices read medical attendants' reports with a grain of salt. The central concern was that such doctors had a 'natural desire to please their patient,' which could lead to vague answers and the occasional 'suppressio veri.' Once doctors started to demand fees for their reports, this issue would be one of the main reasons that led life offices to stop requesting them; before that, insurance managers did their best to assure doctors that their responses would be held in strict confidence and hoped that they could rely on the 'integrity and probity' of the medical profession. A more concrete problem was that not everyone had a regular medical attendant whose name they could pass along to a life insurance office. Insurers typically dealt with this by confirming on the form that the doctor was in fact the candidate's 'regular' medical attendant, by asking if any other doctors had ever been consulted or (if not) asking for the name of a second private friend.[43]

Gatekeeping in Crisis

As the nineteenth century went on, the proposal form, attendance before a board of directors, and referee reports from friends and doctors all grew less effective as underwriting methods. The problem with proposal forms was twofold: life insurance offices stopped trusting proposers to be conscientious in filling them out (as indicated by a trend towards increasingly specific itemization), and the hope that even honest proposers would provide accurate reports proved time and again to be chimerical. The most public manifestation of this breakdown was a rise in disputed claims, often followed by a civil suit initiated by the dead policyholder's beneficiaries. The problem with candidates appearing before the board of directors grew in severity as the balance of business moved from the head office to provincial and foreign agencies, making board interviews more trouble than they were worth. The final foundation of early life insurance gatekeeping, reference letters from medical attendants and acquaintances, eroded in the 1840s once doctors began to demand payment for what had originally been a complementary service. Although most life insurance offices eventually agreed to pay for these reports, by the time they did so they had ceased to set much store by them.

Insurers responded to all three of these problems by relying increasingly on the physical examination of customers. Such an exam promised to identify more risks than a proposal form or an interview with the board of directors could accomplish, and extending it to the provinces also solved the problem of gatekeeping at a distance. Finally, a medical examiner with no connection to the insurance candidate was more likely to offer an opinion that was worth his fee – in contrast to the report of a medical attendant, who had a bias in favour of the candidate. The result was that some types of information became less accessible to life insurance offices while others took on greater significance. The director who did not like the look of a candidate, or the medical attendant who candidly volunteered an otherwise unknowable risk, gave way to the company's salaried medical adviser. For candidates who lived in the city where an insurance company was based, this doctor's personal assessment of risk directly affected their chance of getting insured. For candidates who lived farther away, this doctor framed the questions and evaluated the responses provided by his provincial surrogate.

Proposal Forms on Trial

A legal treatise in 1808, noting that the proportion of litigated claims in life insurance was 'extremely small' relative to fire insurance, attributed this difference to three causes: 'the great difficulty of practicing any fraud in such insurances,' the fact that 'the event insured against is always a fact of easy proof,' and 'the honour, integrity, and liberality of the several companies.'[44] The first two of these factors continued to serve life insurance offices well throughout the nineteenth century, and consequently the frequency of life insurance trials continued to be small compared with fire insurance trials. Although withholding information on proposal forms remained a problem for life offices through the nineteenth century, the number of times such cases went to trial paled in comparison with fire cases in which policyholders haggled with companies over the value of their lost property. During the decades between 1810 and 1860, what did change (at least from the perspective of many customers) was the life insurance offices' 'honour, integrity, and liberality.' What such customers were witnessing was a response to inadequate gatekeeping procedures: when the proposal form failed to screen a premature death, it tended to reappear in the courtroom as the basis for a company's refusal to pay.

Concealment of gout, consumption, pneumonia, dyspepsia, heart disease, epilepsy, and intemperance all routinely figured in life insurance trials during the first half of the nineteenth century. In all such trials the proposal form itself was often the star witness, since this was the contract that had allegedly been breached. Companies were most likely to win such cases if they could point to a specific disease that a customer had withheld on the form, especially if a doctor had treated the disease in question. The Alliance won a case in 1841 when a doctor testified that he had told a consumptive patient prior to buying insurance that 'he would follow his mother to an early grave,' and another company won after a doctor sued a woman's estate for her failure to pay medical bills that predated her insurance. Testimony of this sort did not always prevail, however. A York jury forced the European to pay a £4,000 claim on an allegedly gouty army officer, despite hearing from a surgeon who had found 'his foot and toe much swelled and very red.' Instead they believed the local magistrate who had 'often walked ... and shot with' the man and had 'never heard that he was afflicted with gout.'[45]

Into the 1840s the chance that an insurance company would win such cases gained from the fact that they usually only had to prove that a disease existed, not that a candidate had knowingly concealed it. In the leading case on this point, *Duckett* v. *Williams*, the Provident sued the Hope, which had refused to pay its share of a reinsured policy on the grounds that the insured party, who died of syphilis in 1830, had concealed the existence of fistula and 'eruptions' suffered in 1826. Although the Provident reasonably argued that it could not have been guilty of defrauding the Hope, since it had also insured the man's life, an Exchequer judge forced it to swallow the additional loss – claiming that 'non-communication of a material fact' was the equivalent of fraud.[46] As long as *Duckett* was the relevant precedent, life insurance offices were confident of their chances of winning enough civil trials to make litigation worth the risk. Winning even some cases gave insurance companies the ammunition they needed to settle many others out of court; and even getting a judge to allow an appeal could force claimants to settle in order to avoid additional legal fees.[47]

Whether in or out of court, however, the life offices' success at denying claims was double-edged, and hence ultimately an unsatisfactory response to the problem of inaccurate proposal forms. By the 1840s popular opinion had turned against the 'protracted litigations' and 'extorted compromises' surrounding disputed claims. The *Times* took insurance companies to task in 1846 for being too willing to 'accept proposals with carelessness, receive the premiums on the insurer's life so long as he happens to live, and resist payment at his death, on the chance of being able to show that he had some disease not specified in the declaration.' The *Duckett* precedent, meanwhile, receded after 1845, when a Scottish judge ruled that a customer could not be expected to declare 'any latent imperceptible disease, that could only be discovered by *post-mortem* examination.'[48]

Criticism of insurance company litigation also began to emerge within the industry, since nothing was easier than for start-up firms to claim that they would be less litigious than their older rivals. Typical was the London Indisputable's promise, in its 1848 prospectus, that 'all questions as to age, health, habits and other matters deserving of inquiry prior to the contract being entered into, are held as finally settled when the assured receives his policy.' This company's promoters took advantage of (and added to) rising anxiety among policyholders that they were, in one actuary's words, 'leaving to their families a lawsuit for a legacy.' At least twenty other new offices marketed 'indisputable' clauses as a special feature between 1848 and 1860, although few survived long enough to reap the fruits of their enterprise.[49] As with other new products in the 1850s, indisputability slowly entered the wider market when older firms adopted it in a modified form. This process began in 1851 with Standard Life's scheme of 'select Assurances,' which guaranteed complete freedom from litigation after what its actuary called a five-year 'statute of limitations.' Within a decade most Scottish and many English firms were following suit. Such policies probably did attract some business, and such talk was relatively cheap – since few firms bothered to dispute claims that fell due more than a year or two after a policy was issued.[50]

A more meaningful response to critiques of life insurance litigation was for companies to move from gatekeeping after the fact to improving their ability to detect risk prior to issuing policies. Anticipating this sea-change, the Scottish Widows' Fund promised in its 1842 prospectus to be 'most cautious and particular in their inquiries before admitting members,' instead of 'affording every facility to parties to join the Society, and afterwards throwing all manner of unnecessary obstacles in the way of settlement when the claim emerges.'[51] One manifestation of this new caution was a rise in the practice of comparing notes about customers. Whereas merchants had long traded such information in order to prevent bad debts, and fire insurers shared intelligence about suspected arsonists and other dishonest customers, life insurance offices waited until the 1840s to start doing this on a regular basis, and until the 1890s to formalize the practice.[52] The most ambitious scheme to this end was a 'Registry of Declined Lives' established by the Life Offices Association, which set up a card system for catching customers who concealed the fact that they had been rejected or rated up by another office.[53] From the companies' viewpoint, the best part of the registry was that it enabled them to guard against fraud without appearing to do so.

More generally, life insurance offices avoided going to trial after 1850 by paying more attention to candidates' family history and by appointing medical examiners rather than relying on often-biased medical attendants. The first line of inquiry enabled them to verify proposal forms with more discretion and at less cost, by consulting death certificates at the General Registrar's Office. One life insurance guide suggested that in all cases of a relative's premature death, directors should confirm the cause 'by searching the registers at Somerset House,' and another doctor observed that 'the ease with which the public records are inspected ... would sufficiently guarantee good faith' when candidates responded to such inquiries.[54] Meanwhile, the new reliance on medical screening reduced post mortem litigation by cutting down on the number of premature claims and also by diminishing the life insurance office's legal standing when customers did die prematurely. Going to trial in such a case invariably meant facing up to the fact that the life in question had been passed as 'first class' a short while before by a paid servant of the company.[55]

The one exception to what was otherwise a significant decline in life insurance litigation after 1850 concerned cases involving intemperance, which by one estimate accounted for more than half of all such trials at the end of the century. If post mortem investigation turned up enough evidence, companies at least stood a chance to win the ensuing trial, since intemperance clearly qualified under the post-1850 legal standard that only candidates who were aware of a proscribed pre-existing condition were guilty of fraud. And since medical screening at the point of sale had a poor track record at detecting intemperance, the older method of gatekeeping after the fact appeared to be the best alternative. On balance, though, the upshot of such trials was mixed at best. Their scandalous nature garnered extensive press coverage, and at least some of the mud that was dredged up stuck to life insurance offices. They were also difficult to win, owing to what one observer called 'much cross-swearing among the witnesses.' Claimants enlisted friends and family members to swear that the insured had been a moderate drinker, and life offices responded with an army of witnesses who swore the opposite. This latter testimony, though, typically came from servants, innkeepers, or fellow drinkers, whom many juries deemed to be less credible than claimants' higher-class witnesses.[56]

Gatekeeping at a Distance

During the same decades that the proposal form was losing its effectiveness as a gatekeeping method, inadequacies with the head office interview also became apparent. The companies' experience with disputed claims had already suggested that a mere interview by the board was not always enough to guard against undisclosed medical conditions, leading many insurers to lean more heavily on physical exams by their medical advisers. Even this option, however, was useless for the increasing number of customers who lived at a distance from the head office. Initially, directors simply imposed an extra charge for customers who failed to visit them, or tried to replicate the head office interview by appointing surrogates to conduct it. Neither option was ideal, and by the 1830s surrogate directors had given way to surrogate medical advisers, who conducted a physical examination that had been choreographed by the medical adviser back in the head office.

As the nineteenth century progressed, most life insurance companies dropped their required board interview and replaced it with a medical exam. Older life offices held out longest: the Amicable required interviews for all London candidates until it transferred its business in 1866, and five of the eight firms represented in the Actuaries' Club did so in 1876. By 1900 only customers in the Clerical Medical, with its eight medical directors, still appeared in at least some cases before the full board.[57] Several factors produced the decline of the board interview. The procession of candidates clogged meetings and board rooms and diverted time in the directors' busy schedules from other duties. Probably most significant was the fact that 'proposers hated it'; the ritual of being grilled by 'a board of sharp and experienced business men ... regarding one's private, and perhaps delicate, affairs' was an ordeal that customers tried to avoid if at all possible.[58]

Long before they stopped requiring local candidates to appear before the board, insurance companies came up with ways to accommodate people who lived too far away to visit the head office conveniently. One was to charge non-appearance fines, which ranged from 10 per cent to 50 per cent added to the first year's premium.[59] An early provincial life office, the Norwich Union, tapped into customer dissatisfaction with such fines by waiving them upon forming in 1808. Around the same time, some London companies started offering the option of a refund if the candidate could visit them and demonstrate 'unobjectionable' health within a year.[60] An alternative was the appointment of surrogates who could be trusted to offer an honest assessment of the life. The London Life used 'the Clergyman or Magistrate of the District,' the Legal & General delegated such interviews to country solicitors or 'two respectable housekeepers,' and the Atlas directed out-of-town candidates to see 'some public character ... such as the minister of the parish or a justice of the peace.'[61] Finding surrogates to interview candidates was much easier when companies already had local directors who oversaw business in large provincial centres. On the other hand, this sort of arrangement sometimes generated animosity when the local board and the head office disagreed about what constituted a hazardous life.[62]

An obvious, but obviously problematic, supplement to these strategies for gatekeeping at a distance was for salesmen to assist in the screening of lives. As early as 1725 the London Assurance required its agents to report on customers' 'state of health and manner of life,' and in 1808 the Atlas asked agents to 'make the most minute enquiries' regarding candidates' health and habits 'in cases when parties cannot attend at the Office.' By the 1820s most life insurance offices required their agents to fill in a questionnaire about the lives they proposed, and they continued to do so into the twentieth century. Pride of place on these forms went to queries about the candidates' references, the medical history of their family, their habits, and above all their appearance – both to replicate the directors' interview and to guard against impersonation.[63]

The problem with relying on agents to act as gatekeepers was that, as Augustus De Morgan observed, it was in their interest 'not to be *too particular* in the selection of lives.' This seems clear enough from filled-in Norwich Union agents' forms, which indicate a below-average ratio of below-average lives. Ninety-one per cent of the candidates were either 'middle-sized' or 'lusty' in girth and possessed necks that were 'in proportion' (as opposed to short or long), and 89 per cent were of 'middle' or 'tall' height. Only ten were 'thin,' just one was 'rather slight but wiry looking,' and none earned a check on the dash labelled 'bloated.' Only two candidates in the entire sample were returned as possessing narrow chests; the rest had 'middle-sized' or 'broad' chests. The only category with more than a handful of conceivably negative responses was 'complexion,' for which only 57 per cent of candidates were 'fresh-coloured'; the rest were brown, pale, sallow, or florid.[64]

Directors occasionally dressed down or even dismissed agents who failed in their gatekeeping capacity, as when the Atlas board expressed surprise that its Ledbury agent had 'been so much imposed on' by a Cheltenham victualler, or when the Mutual fired its Leeds secretary for failing to report a candidate's curvature of the spine. More often they tried to nip lax gatekeeping in the bud, by appealing to agents' 'discrimination and prudence' or by issuing variants on Samuel Bignold's pithy command to a Norwich Union agent in 1847: 'please don't send rubbish.'[65] Such injunctions persisted as the century progressed, but failure to heed them had less severe consequences once provincial medical examinations became the norm. With that shift, the primary gatekeeping role for agents became the purely administrative one of sending along proposal papers, either to the examiner or the head office. The only glimmer of their older screening functions appeared in pleas to exercise self-censorship in forwarding proposals that were likely to be rejected and warnings to avoid trying to 'warp the local medical examiner from the strict path of his duty.'[66]

A Controversy over Fees

The final foundation of early Victorian gatekeeping, reference letters from friends and medical attendants, also became harder to sustain after 1850. Friends' reports had always been of dubious value, and life insurance offices' trust in them waned further as their distance from the head office increased. Their relationship with medical attendants altered once these people started to ask for a guinea each time they reported on a patient's past medical history. Paradoxically, the act of setting a price on this information greatly diminished its value from the life offices' perspective. As long it had been freely offered and received, an insurer could ignore it if it was obviously partial, and challenge it in court if a premature death indicated that it had been misleading. The prospect of having to pay for it led insurance managers to think seriously, often for the first time, about alternative approaches – especially because many were convinced that such a payment would shatter their legal standing to subpoena medical attendants in the event of a trial.[67]

Hence although doctors were able to convince most life insurance offices to pay for medical attendants' reports by the mid-1850s, after 1860 life insurance offices increasingly stopped asking for these reports and chose instead to pay for a doctor they had appointed to certify candidates' health.

After 1860 nearly all references to the friend's report dismissed it as unnecessary, from a gatekeeping point of view, and embraced it mainly for its marketing potential. James Chisholm of the Imperial observed in 1901 that friends' reports were 'often of too good-natured a character to be relied on,' and the manager of the Scottish Temperance argued that in an age when people's friends were 'of at most a few years' standing only,' even honest respondents 'know very little of one's earlier habits and nothing at all of one's relatives.'[68] A handful of firms (starting with the National Mutual in 1911) began to dispense with the forms, and those that retained them apparently did so primarily as a means of drumming up business. Companies urged their agents to deliver forms personally to the parties named by the candidate, since this was 'a favourable opportunity for introducing the subject of Life Assurance to the Referees.' One agents' guide helpfully spelled this out in 1864: 'The first proposal should introduce the agent to two strangers ... If each of the two made out proposals, four more strangers would become known to the agent' and so on up to 2,047 people after 'the tenth course in this plan.'[69]

If the significance of friends' certificates receded with little commotion, the opposite was true for medical attendants' reports, which were at the heart of a sustained controversy over fees. Medical attendants fired the first shots in this struggle in 1837, when members of medical societies in Leeds and Canterbury boycotted life insurance offices that refused to pay. The turning point came a decade later, when Thomas Wakley at the *Lancet* moved from merely airing the doctors' complaints to actively supporting their cause. In November 1848 he began regularly printing lists of insurance offices that 'honourably pay the medical referee,' which prompted second wave of boycotts against holdouts.[70] Through these tactics, medical attendants soon prevailed in getting most life offices to agree to pay for their services: the number of paying offices increased from twenty-two in 1849 to eighty in 1853. The key to their success was the large number of new life insurance offices that formed after 1840, which recognized in the doctors' cause a relatively inexpensive way to present themselves as less hidebound than their older rivals.[71]

If pressure from new companies sealed the fate of 'non-paying' life insurance offices, the issues that emerged in the controversy ensured that life offices would dramatically curtail their reliance on this source of information after 1860. Foremost among doctors' justifications for fees was the claim that the facts at their disposal were uniquely valuable to life offices. They pointed to symptoms that were either intermittent (indicating epilepsy and haemoptysis) or only apparent over time (such as diabetes and gout), which life insurance offices had missed on the basis of a 'stranger's' exam.[72] By pressing this point, however, medical attendants painted themselves into a corner. To the extent that their knowledge was worth something to insurance companies, it would result in candidates being rejected or rated up. And since, as the *Lancet* astutely observed, 'the sick and the diseased' brought in the most medical income, doctors risked losing this income in exchange for their guinea fee. Under these circumstances, as one doctor concluded in 1846, it would be best 'to be rid altogether' of such forms, 'which most often involve a breach of professional confidence.'[73]

Increasingly, life insurance companies agreed with this position, much to the dismay of the doctors who thought they had won the debate over medical fees. When the Edinburgh Life began paying fees in 1850, it introduced a new proposal form that was 'intended to dispense with the Report of the Party's Medical Attendant, as a necessary part of the Documents.' In 1855, five years after it started paying fees for referee reports, the Norwich Union did without them more often than not, and by 1870 it did so more than 90 per cent of the time. Once medical attendants realized what was going on, they renewed their warnings that insurance companies would suffer as a result – but such protests fell on deaf ears. At the Liverpool & London & Globe's 1868 shareholder meeting, its manager brushed aside an investor representing 'the medical practitioners of Liverpool' by arguing that his company usually learned everything it needed from its 'confidential medical officers,' and added that medical attendants' reports 'were not of the character to render it essential they should in all cases be asked for.'[74]

The Rise and Decline of the Medical Examination

After 1860 all life offices continued to use proposal forms, most still referred to a candidate's medical attendant and friends at least some of the time, and a handful still insisted on an appearance before the board of the directors. These older procedures, however, were patently in decline. What replaced them was a new focus on physical examination, whereby intimate but unreliable information gave way to the signs yielded by a doctor's questioning, poking, and prodding. In the process, the role of medical advisers gained in significance. Instead of supplementing the directors' verdict, they became the primary screen for candidates who applied at the head office, and they also appointed and supervised a new army of provincial examiners. By the end of the nineteenth century the medical exam had become the most prominent aspect of life insurance gatekeeping, and as such will be discussed in more detail in the next chapter. Prominence, however, did not translate into permanence. The unpopularity of the exam with customers and agents, combined with its expense and the availability of new forms of insurance, prompted a few late Victorian companies to do without the exam in certain cases. As more insurance firms followed suit, some earlier gatekeeping methods (such as the medical attendant's report and the proposal form) made a comeback.

Appointing Provincial Medical Examiners

Although paid head office medical advisers were common enough among British life insurance offices by the 1820s, it took another decade before medical examination began to emerge as a standard practice in provincial branches and agencies. There were some exceptions, as when the Rock asked its Liverpool agent in 1808 to ask candidates 'to call upon, and be farther examined by, a Physician resident in the Town.' Several of the new provincial offices that formed shortly after the Rock required medical examinations for at least some policies and in some towns, as did the Alliance and Palladium upon forming in 1824. Most London and Scottish life insurance offices, though, waited at least until the 1830s before they started appointing medical examiners on a regular basis. The main reason many of them started to do so was to address the problems posed by relying solely on a medical attendant's reference letter. The West of Scotland, for instance, desired from 1833 to have 'a Medical Man *in our own interest*, to check any deficiencies of *their* Medical Man's report.'[75]

Wherever possible, life insurance offices appointed provincial examiners who resembled the head office adviser in status and qualifications: which meant, ideally, 'a Physician of high standing' with a large private practice and a hospital appointment. Some opted instead for family doctors, on the grounds that they were more likely to understand about hereditary disease and to possess the 'commonsense average broad view of the whole case, together with the knack of talking to a business man.' In practice, surgeons or general practitioners were at least as likely as physicians to be appointed – partly because there were not enough of the latter to go around, but mostly because agents found them to be more accessible and 'easy-going.'[76] A corollary to appointing more customer-friendly doctors was appointing doctors who could generate business. When the Scottish National named a new examiner in Dundee in 1847, the local board recommended a man who was 'likely ... to promote its business by his influence & connections.'[77]

From the provincial doctor's perspective, insurance work was a welcome source of supplementary income, joining a number of similar mid-Victorian opportunities including public vaccination, the examination of candidates for the Post Office and military, and poor law, friendly society, school, and public health work.[78] Into the 1840s the standard fee was half a guinea for all exams; later in the century most firms paid a guinea in some cases but held firm at 10s/6d for smaller policies.[79] As forms grew in length and required more time-consuming tests, and as the proportion of smaller policies increased, examiners began to echo the medical attendants' earlier complaints about fees. They resolved not to examine lives for under a guinea if the policy was worth at least £200 or if a urine test was required, and they complained about of the 'vicious system of brain-sweating which has become habitual in insurance circles.'[80] Some insurance companies responded by lightening requirements for smaller policies or paying more than a guinea for large ones, but most ignored them – which they could safely do owing to a large surplus of underemployed doctors who were willing to take what they could get.[81]

An insurance examination was sufficiently different from regular medical practice to require special guidance. Although proposals sometimes surfaced for special training in insurance medicine, either as a correspondence course or a medical school elective, medical examiners mainly learned how to do their job from how-to manuals and head office instructions.[82] William Brinton's guide, which he adapted from lectures he had given at King's College, remained the standard reference from 1856 until Edward Sieveking of the Briton Medical & General issued his *Medical Adviser in Life Assurance* in 1874. In 1889 the first guide appeared that was jointly written by a physician and an actuary, James Pollock and James Chisholm of the Imperial, and new guides appeared over the next thirty years. The extent to which provincial medical examiners consulted such books is a matter of guesswork, although requests for the name of 'a suitable book, at a reasonable price' did appear regularly in the *British Medical Journal*.[83]

Most medical examiners, however, would have received most of their guidance from the increasingly detailed forms that nearly every insurance company provided. These forms echoed what companies had long been asking medical attendants, with additional instructions for conducting the exam. Unlike the medical attendant, who could be assumed to know his patient's medical history without a fresh interview, the assumption was that medical examiners would relay each question about prior diseases to the candidate, who was often required to sign that part of the form. As for the physical exam, the instructions grew in number and specificity over the course of the century, forming by 1900 a detailed tour of the candidate's body. The Norwich Union supplemented an earlier query on the 'character of respiration' with 'Percussion notes' and 'Voice sounds,' and annotated 'character of the action of [the] heart' with questions about its rhythm, impulse and apex beat, alteration of size, and valvular murmur.[84]

By instructing or reminding doctors what to look for, medical examiners' forms also *routinized* the exam, with implications that medical advisers recognized from very early on. As one insurance handbook observed in 1856, a 'definite form' allowed a doctor to assure 'irritable' candidates that the procedure was not 'peculiar' to either the candidate or himself, but rather was 'a routine which you have no choice but to accede to; and that any question which he may be disposed to resent as impertinent is so pertinent, as to form a specific part of your printed instructions.' The author also implied that examiners' forms enhanced the doctor's authority over the candidate by providing 'a broad and common basis of diagnostic skill.'[85] To accomplish this, however, doctors needed to develop a consensus regarding what counted as 'diagnostic skill.' This was the primary impulse behind the formation in 1893 of the Life Assurance Medical Officers' Association, members of which regularly compared notes on diagnostic methods, medical statistics, and the association between symptoms and risks, and their published *Transactions* offered what one doctor called 'fixed points from which progressive movements should start.'[86]

Besides assisting in the routinization of medical practice in the provinces, head office medical advisers also saw their own jobs grow more bureaucratic as a result of the rise of the provincial exam. While continuing to examine candidates themselves, they also needed 'to criticise and compare all reports from the country.' This part of the job grew in proportion to the growth of provincial agencies and the accompanying rise in medical exams. At the Crown, the average annual number of new policies issued at the head office declined by 40 per cent between 1853 and 1874, while the number coming in from the rest of the country more than tripled. In practice, this meant that a typical office hour for its medical adviser might include only one or two medical examinations, but would usually entail sorting through a dozen or more sets of proposal papers. Although dull, the latter experience also qualified the medical adviser as 'a specialist in the subject' whose assessment of risk carried increasing weight with boards of directors.[87]

Dispensing with the Medical Exam

By 1900 the medical examination had emerged as the dominant screening mechanism used by British life offices. Although it solved many of the problems that had saddled earlier gatekeeping methods, however, it introduced new ones in their stead. Customers dreaded it, agents resented it, and directors lived with it as a necessary evil. Salesmen complained about examiners' incompetence or severity and criticized directors for having more faith in 'a set of papers' than in their own assurances. Insurance managers referred to candidates' 'irrational uneasiness' at 'being overhauled by a parcel of doctors.' These concerns were amplified by popular perceptions of the insurance exam that exaggerated its indignity: as when a magazine described an insurance doctor 'thumping [a candidate] suddenly in the lower region of his waistcoat; stamping on his toes,' and 'shouting suddenly in his ear.'[88] Over time, companies responded to these concerns by developing types of coverage that did not require a medical exam. Although customers and agents provided the main incentive for this trend, it was no accident that it coincided with medical examiners' demands for higher fees. Like medical attendants before them, they learned that it was possible to protest too much when dealing with insurance companies.[89]

William Sutton was one of the first actuaries to raise exam-free life insurance as a practical possibility, when he proposed selling deferred insurance policies in which the medical exam took 'a much less important and less formidable shape than it does.' Such a scheme, he suggested, would address the serious problem that insurance exams deterred 'thousands upon thousands of persons of quite as good health really as those who propose, from proposing at all.' Less than a year later Sun Life introduced a scheme that refused payment (apart from repayment of premiums plus interest) if candidates died within five years; although partly responsible for a temporary boost in business, it soon fizzled.[90] A different scheme, introduced in 1891 by the Caledonian, required a report from the candidate's medical attendant and (unlike Sun Life's plan) promised immediate payment. Its actuarial key was that it was a 'double endowment' policy – that is, it paid twice the pension that an ordinary endowment policy paid if the candidate lived a certain term of years. This added enough cost to the policy (since double the pension translated into nearly double the premium) to scare off sick people, and attracted candidates whose good health led them to think they were likely to collect that pension well into old age. The scheme contributed to a 48 per cent increase in business in 1891 and attracted nearly five hundred customers in its first three years.[91]

Insurance without medical examination began to gain momentum when life offices began more aggressively to pursue the lower-middle class market. Here the logic was primarily economic: smaller policies left a lower margin for expense, which made saving the doctor's fee more appealing. In 1900, coinciding with a new monthly payment scheme designed to attract working-class customers, Sun Life introduced an exam-free policy that paid partial claims for the first two years, full claims after that, and paid in all cases of accidental death. After receiving a 'considerable influx' of new business during the plan's first decade with no corresponding increase in its mortality rate, it began paying full claims on all such policies after six months, then eliminated any waiting period nine years later. Meanwhile, industrial insurers like the Prudential, which had never required medical exams for their small working-class burial policies, extended this exemption to larger policies as they began to seek lower-middle-class customers. By 1920 Prudential customers up to the age of fifty could buy a £100 policy on their own lives or could be insured by someone else for up to £50 without a medical exam.[92]

The other turn-of-the century opportunity for policyholders to avoid a medical exam was to join a group plan. Life offices that offered such plans were usually willing to waive an exam for one of two reasons: the employees who joined already had to pass a medical exam in order to get their jobs, or the plan was compulsory and hence prevented the threat of healthy employees opting out in higher numbers than unhealthy ones. The Eagle allowed 'some relaxation in regard to the Medical examination' for members of a National Union of Teachers group scheme who had 'been through a Training College,' the North British & Mercantile's civil service scheme waived exams for customers 'within five years of their medical examination for admission to the

Service,' and the Provident Mutual required each member of a group plan to certify that he had 'not been absent from his duties through serious illness since he has been in this employ.'[93]

Doctors responded with alarm to the concept of insurance without medical examination. A Lincolnshire physician predicted in 1901 that 'a Company without a doctor could not exist' and called schemes like Sun Life's 'a haven of rest for the sick, a home for the decrepit, and a sanctuary for the dying.' Another doctor worried that the North British & Mercantile's civil service plan would 'place insurance in the hazardous condition it occupied early in the century.' Conversely, claimed a Liverpool doctor, candidates who were 'diseased in imagination alone' paid more than they needed to under such plans, since a medical exam would have proven their fears to be groundless. Underlying such criticism was a more general suspicion that commercial motives were undercutting the legitimate policing function that the medical profession supplied to life insurance offices. Dyce Duckworth ascribed exam-free schemes to 'the same causes which so gravely affect the conduct of all business transactions of these days, to wit – hurry, pressure, and furious competition.'[94]

The doctors' sermons against competition had no effect, however, and their predictions of financial ruin proved to be groundless. Between 1908 and 1910 the Royal Exchange waived medical exams on 'thrift' policies, the Yorkshire introduced an exam-free double endowment plan, and the Star offered a special 'bachelor' plan with no medical exam. By 1934 thirty of seventy life insurance offices in a survey 'had a general non-medical scheme,' twenty-six had 'a special scheme,' and the other fourteen waived medical exams for participants in group schemes.[95] By the 1970s many companies were foregoing medical exams for more than half their customers, and they sent for doctors only to follow up suspicious proposal forms, for very large policies, and for old people. Some life insurance offices went further than that, waiving all medical inquiry for policies issued in connection with new home-owners, on the logic that few young people in poor health would borrow money to buy a home.[96]

With the waning dependence on the medical exam, older gatekeeping methods resurfaced. The proposal form took on new significance in 'non-medical' schemes, often including additional questions and always coming under enhanced scrutiny. Candidates' medical attendants played a more important role in exam-free policies, and insurance companies also placed greater faith in their reports owing to improved pay and training under the National Insurance Act. Actuaries, meanwhile, needed to monitor the impact of these shifting gatekeeping methods on the bottom line. Industry-wide mortality investigations into the 1960s revealed only 'slightly heavier' losses among 'non-medical' risks, which 'amply justified' them once the savings in doctors' fees had been factored in. This was not the case with the mortgage-linked non-medical policies that became popular in the 1970s. When a change in the tax code in 1983 led to flood in applications for this product, the mortality connected with these policies increased, and within a year companies reintroduced a medical form (if not an exam) in such cases.[97]

Conclusion

Nineteenth-century defenders of life insurance gatekeeping often urged its necessity by appealing to what was, for many of them, the reductio ad absurdam of a universal and compulsory state insurance scheme. Such a scheme would not need to screen lives, they admitted, because healthy lives could not refuse to pool their risks with unhealthy ones. In 1861 the actuary Morrice Black proposed the thought experiment of 'a Law which should compel every man, on attaining a certain age, to assure his life.' This law, he concluded, 'would be resented as flagrantly impolitic and unjust' and would be no less 'subversive of public morals' than 'the schemes of the Socialists for a re-distribution and universal equalization of property.' The political edge to this way of thinking grew sharper as some forms of compulsory national insurance became conceivable. Hence in 1911, coinciding with the passage of the National Health Insurance Act, one commentator urged that life offices were 'less – or shall we perhaps say more? – advanced' than 'democratic ... believers in political equality.'[98] Such scenarios identified a defining paradox of insurance when it is provided by the private sector: an equalitarian state will likely exercise less, not more, surveillance than a smaller enclave within the state that seeks to maximize returns for its members. This paradox haunted Victorian life insurance offices whenever they tried to draw a line between legitimate equalization of risk and an 'impolitic and injust' inclusion of high risks with healthy lives.

Insurers tended to avoid drawing this line whenever possible by allowing the market to decide who should be consigned to which risk group. They learned over time, however, that consigning the task of surveillance to market forces could have unpredictable consequences. On the one hand, underwriting ability rewarded companies with higher bonuses, and in this abstract sense the market reinforced a vigilant approach to gatekeeping. Descending from general principles to specific cases, however, competition often worked in the opposite direction, by pressuring managers to admit higher-risk lives in order to retain a customer's or agent's good will. By 1900, when the desire to attract business began to lead companies to dispense with the medical exam, insurers drew even closer to the 'socialism' that Black had warned against in 1861, with the potential for redistribution of income from healthier to unhealthier customers.

One generation's socialism was another's economy of scale, with very different political implications. Writing in 1976, the political scientist Richard Titmuss pointed to the decline of the life insurance medical exam as part of a more general subordination of 'considerations of individual equity' to 'considerations of economy of scale in market operations.' In such cases, he concluded, 'equity suffers in the conflict with bigness and those who suffer most are those who fail to fit neatly into predetermined large-scale classes.' The target of his criticism was not social insurance but rather American-style group health plans, which discriminated against 'older, displaced workers, the disabled and Negroes ... on ground of administrative costs and inadequate risk-rating.' Since the logic of exam-free life insurance pointed in the direction of group insurance, the proxy for underwriting ultimately became employability: which inevitably had less to do with actual risk of death than with issues of class, race, and economic climate.[99] What Titmuss observed more than three decades ago has come to dominate the debate over many types of insurance in the United States, and increasingly in Britain as well.

9 Detecting Deviance

The art of Diagnosis is carried to its highest perfection ... [by] putting together a number of small points of circumstantial evidence, unknown to the tyro, unremembered by the man of routine, but ever present to the mind and memory of the thoughtful and experienced; that marks the discriminating and specific difference between a Brodie and a bungler.
                                    – John Mann, British Empire Mutual medical adviser, 1865[1]

Working when annual medical checkups were far from the norm, Victorian doctors seldom had the chance to detect disease lurking in an apparently healthy patient. They consequently embraced the insurance examination as a rare opportunity to display their diagnostic skill. But to do this, they needed to change the way they interacted with their examinees, who were more interested in buying insurance at the lowest rate than in discovering what was wrong with them. This meant guarding against untruthful responses, which seldom came up when patients voluntarily visited a doctor with medical complaints; it also meant making candidates feel at ease, lest their anxiety at visiting the doctor make them appear less healthy than they actually were. Finally, they needed to do all this in a limited amount of time – owing both to the candidate's desire for the exam to be over quickly and to the company's unwillingness to pay for more than a half-hour of the doctor's services. To complete the exam in a hurry, insurance doctors privileged some skills – an ability to infer health from physiognomy, for instance – over others. To avoid relying too much on candidates' subjective testimony, they emphasized objective physical measures like girth, height, and weight, and (from the 1880s) diagnostic tests that took advantage of new medical technology.

All these considerations applied to exams performed by head office medical advisers as well as provincial medical examiners. Life offices placed different emphasis on them, however, depending on where and by whom the exam was performed. At the head office, medical advisers carried into their insurance work a preference for 'incommunicable knowledge' that they had developed in private practice in order to distance themselves from general practitioners. Such knowledge was all but useless coming from the dozens of doctors across the country who sent their reports to each company for a guinea or half-guinea fee. From these doctors, the head office preferred 'yes' or 'no' answers to a long series of questions, quantitative measurements, and the concrete results of diagnostic tests.

These criteria for detecting deviance rested on assumptions about what qualified as a normal life, and these assumptions changed as insurance exams migrated from the head office to the provinces. Head office physicians went into their jobs with a definition of 'perfect health' that exceeded what the market (and their directors) would bear as insurable at ordinary rates. It did not take long for them to arrive at more liberal criteria, which guarded against the highest risks of premature death without penalizing customers for every last imperfection. When asked to translate this normal-enough life into a form to be filled in by provincial medical examiners, medical advisers tried to quantify an acceptable range of shapes, sizes, and colours of body parts and to repeat this process for numerical measures of pulse, blood pressure, and urine. Distinguishing between normal and deviant lives did not, however, rest exclusively with the medical examination, even during its late Victorian heyday as the primary life insurance screening device. As chapter 10 will reveal, actuarial thinking and market forces also played important roles in defining insurability.

Asking Questions, Examining Bodies

Regardless of the purpose of a medical examination, doctors performing it typically processed two different sorts of information: that provided by a patient's verbal description of his or her condition and that provided by a patient's body. Victorian doctors respectively distinguished these varieties as 'subjective' and 'objective' symptoms. The latter, which doctors also referred to as 'physical signs,' comprised 'the indications of health and disease which are presented to the senses of the examiner' (according to one textbook in 1879), whereas the former were 'chiefly derived from the answers of the patient given to questions which have reference to the history of the disease and the sensations caused by the disease.' Most elite doctors were convinced that physical signs were 'least liable to mislead,' since they were 'independent of any misconception or exaggeration on the part of the patient.' On the other hand, even doctors who were wary of what patients told them were unwilling to discount wholly their testimony. In the words of one turn-of-the century clinical manual: 'The complaints of the patient form the text of the case, and should be referred to again and again during the examination.'[2]

To a large extent, this trade-off between objective and subjective symptoms replicated the trade-off between a life insurance medical examination as opposed to testimony from a medical attendant. One reason life offices were willing to rely more heavily on medical examiners after 1850 was the growing preference among elite doctors for 'physical signs.' Not least among the transformations engendered by the eighteenth-century 'birth of the clinic' was a clear shift in this direction. Emboldened by post mortem discoveries that linked damaged internal organs to detectable pathologies in living patients, doctors came to doubt the relative worth of the patient's own testimony. The subsequent appearance of new technologies, which enabled doctors to 'look inside' the body, further eroded their confidence in patients' accounts of their condition. As one medical historian has concluded, 'compared with data elicited through physical examination ... the long narratives of patients and their relatives had come to seem tedious and unprofitable' by the end of the nineteenth century.[3]

The objectives and constraints of the insurance exam dovetailed in many ways with this more general shift away from relying on subjective testimony, although they did so without fully following the accompanying 'progressive' trajectory of scientific medicine. Doctors' evolving suspicion of subjective testimony was exaggerated in the insurance exam, where examinees had a financial interest in concealing the truth about their condition. When patients visited their family doctor, in contrast, the whole point was to tell him what was wrong; even if some of these self-reported symptoms were untrustworthy, most at least provided a point of departure for diagnosis. For the Britannia's John Hutchinson, this was the signal difference between the two exams: 'In the consulting room, the patient is full of complaints, ready to acknowledge all the symptoms of disease which he may experience; but in the assurance office ... the applicant acknowledges no complaint.'[4] At the same time, insurance companies were cautious about fully exploiting

the potential of diagnostic technologies to supplement subjective testimony, since many of these risked offending the customer's dignity.
Conveniently for their employers, the medical advisers whom they
trusted thought the same way, as much out of concern for their own
social and professional status as for commercial reasons.

Besides the 'birth of the clinic,' the other central context for the insurance medical exam in the nineteenth century was the courtroom.
Insurance doctors regularly spoke of cross-examining, indicting, con-
demning, and sentencing candidates or their organs. Partly this grew
out of the mid-Victorian fondness for 'medical police' and their role in
preventive health. In this vein William Brinton called medical examiners 'the police of Life Assurance,' whose 'usefulness (like that of the
blue-coated guardians of our peace) must ... be judged of, not only by
what we detect, but by what we prevent'; and the medical adviser for
the Scottish Widows' Fund observed in 1875 that doctors 'acted as a
sort of "Insurance Police," whose duty it was to keep out bad subjects
from the membership of assurance offices.' References to insurance
exams as a form of litigation or prosecution persisted into the twentieth
century. One doctor in 1912 spoke of a candidate 'with a clean family
history sheet,' and a branch secretary urged agents in 1909 that they
served as 'a Court of First Instance' that determined 'whether the cases
go up for medical examination or not.'[5]

As with the promise of hospital technology, however, the association
of insurance exams with litigation collided with a countervailing fear of
driving away business. Even more than the doctors who examined
them, potential customers were all too prone to see the insurance exam
as a trial, in every sense of the word. For this reason, insurance doctors
could never fully live up to the ideal of 'medical police' evoked by
Brinton, especially as competition among companies intensified. Police
officers, medical or otherwise, derived power from the fact that they
operated outside the market economy: they did not owe their liveli-
hoods to the criminals they apprehended, but rather to the larger mass
of 'normal' citizens who funded a police force. The insurance examiner,
in contrast, was paid to interrogate everyone who expressed interest in
buying a policy, normal or otherwise. This made it harder for individual candidates for life insurance to remember that the point of the medical exam was to further their collective financial security, and not
merely to cause them unreasonable levels of annoyance. As a result, the
insurance doctor needed to be careful not to overplay his hand as a
white-coated guardian of the company's mortality rate.

Communicating with the Insurance Candidate

Ambivalence among doctors and directors about physical diagnosis meant that talking retained a central role in the Victorian insurance exam. Extracting useful information from taciturn insurance candidates, however, required special talents. Doctors constantly returned to the importance of 'a gracious bearing,' 'courteous language,' a 'quiet, easy, and assuring manner,' and avoiding any 'abruptness' or 'bullying.'[6] For the most part, this verbal part of the exam was a fishing expedition, in which doctors looked out for any incriminating statements a candidate might divulge. Unlike hospital doctors, who tried to keep the patient focused on the condition at hand, insurance doctors preferred 'to let the applicant talk freely if he will.' At this point in the exam the language of the courtroom made an appearance, in the form of 'mild cross-examination' to 'sift any doubtful assertion' – or, in the case of 'exceedingly vague' responses, 'very close cross-questioning to get at the truth.' Just as often, though, doctors took care to distance themselves from this way of thinking, cautioning their colleagues to avoid being viewed as 'hostile cross-examiner[s].'[7]

The open-ended nature of the insurance doctor's interview altered when the exam moved from the head office to the provinces. In the latter case, companies nearly always provided strict instructions for examiners to read questions from the printed forms they provided. As discussed in the last chapter, head office medical advisers defended this practice as the best way to get candidates to answer uncomfortable questions: in effect, it extended the authority of the head office to the country doctor by rendering the process as formal as possible. More concretely, however, these questionnaires existed because companies did not always trust country doctors to be sufficiently thorough. As one medical adviser stressed, the questions on the form were 'the result of a much wider experience than any one examiner perhaps possesses, and are framed to meet all possible cases which this large experience has suggested.' Such comments did not prevent medical examiners from recurrently complaining about 'the overloading of medical report forms by questions' or being reduced to parroting the company's proposal form.[8]

Whether in the head office or the provinces, insurance doctors typically embarked on their examination in an adversarial frame of mind. Throughout the nineteenth century they complained and compared notes regarding the various forms of 'involuntary deception or actual fraud' that went on during exams. They warned about candidates who used 'dyes, ... restorers, washes, tinctures, [and] balms' to preserve a youthful appearance, took 'digitalis to steady the heart' or calcium salts to conceal albuminuria, and provided urine samples from healthy friends.[9] Many doctors assumed that women were especially culpable in this regard, mainly because Victorian dictates of decency gave them more opportunity. As the Rock's medical adviser put it: 'We cannot very well ask the lady to strip herself in the same way as we can ask a man ... Women trade upon this fact, and will often make a difficulty about an examination.' Some doctors went further, impugning a less developed sense of commercial morality to women. A medical journal editor worried that women had 'a feebler sense of the obligations of truth in the ordinary business of life than men have' and warned that this led to greater losses on female lives.[10]

Conversely, insurance doctors needed to extract information without rendering candidates overly anxious. Urine 'passed in a fright' yielded abnormally low specific gravities, a nerve-stiffening glass of whiskey at lunch could blur the line between anxiety and intemperance, and 'insurance heart' became a well-documented phenomenon by the 1880s. Claud Muirhead of the Scottish Widows' Fund offered a typical description of the latter condition: 'owing to the ordeal through which the proposer is passing, the Heart gets out of control, and presents an extremely rapid and tumultuous action.'[11] It was not uncommon for such cases to appear in life office minute books – as when a Wrexham man's pulse of 100 was 'attributed to nervousness from examination' by the Norwich Union's board of directors or when the Scottish Amicable recorded that 'the heart's irregularity' in a proposer 'evidently arises from excitement.' In both cases the company paid for a new examination, which was in keeping with a later doctor's reasoning that a lower pulse might be detected at a later exam, 'when the novelty of a visit to a doctor has passed off.' Other remedies included taking the pulse at the beginning of the exam, before the chest examination had heightened the proposer's anxiety, telling 'a good story,' or engaging in a 'conversation about ... any indifferent subject.'[12]

Once deviance had been discovered, insurance doctors took a very different course of action than they would take in general practice. In the hospital, a medical attendant either proposed a cure (taking what Douglas Powell of the Clerical Medical called the 'relief and repair point of view') or, failing that, offered 'a hopefully expressed and confident opinion.' An insurance exam, in contrast, required a '£. s. d. point of view' that regarded 'the sum total of the viability of the individual' instead of just 'the immediate future.'[13] Nor was consolation always an option. Life insurance offices routinely turned down requests from customers to disclose the grounds for rejection or rating up and scolded medical examiners who told a candidate 'that "he will do" or that "he is all right."' The main reason for this was to protect the confidentiality of friends or medical attendants who had revealed flaws in a candidate's health or character and to make it easier to get customers to accept the prospect of paying extra for such flaws.[14]

Examining the Candidate's Body

In general practice, physical examination moved from the patient's revelation of symptoms, through diagnosis, to prognosis. Insurance exams were both less ambitious and more challenging than this. They were less ambitious because the point was merely to detect deviance per se, not to discover a cure or even a reason why an abnormal condition existed. They were more challenging partly because insurance candidates were less likely to tell the doctor what was wrong, but mainly because any symptoms were unlikely to have progressed far enough to be easily detected. The insurance doctor's diagnostic skills were 'taxed to the uttermost,' claimed the *Lancet*, because 'the frail and the abnormal' seldom applied for coverage. Instead of acute diabetes with 'well-marked symptoms,' a doctor might detect a small trace of sugar in a candidate's urine. Incipient consumption might be indicated by a 'short dry hacking cough,' which a candidate might assume to be 'a mere clearing of the throat'; it was the medical examiner's job to notice this and accordingly conduct 'a minuter examination of the lung.'[15]

Nor were technological magic bullets as readily available to resolve these issues in the late Victorian period as historians of medicine once assumed – for reasons having as much to do with doctors' social status as with the status of medical technology. Christopher Lawrence has identified a resilient backlash against new diagnostic techniques in the London teaching hospitals, where lecturers defined medical practice as 'an art which necessitated that its practitioners be the most cultured of men and the most experienced reflectors on the human condition.' Such men privileged 'the Practice of Medicine as a Fine Art,' and gently but firmly cast aspersions on the relevance of experimental science and pathology to healing. Moving from the elite hospital to the modest consulting room, many doctors could not afford to equip themselves with the latest diagnostic tools – the absence of which more often than not came as a relief to their patients. From the perspective of both doctor and patient, the 'traditional art of healing' typically counted for more than the diagnostic wonders afforded by technology.[16]

Against this grain, some historians have argued that because the insurance exam divorced diagnosis from therapeutics, and because it did so under unique constraints, it was uniquely positioned to take advantage of new technological innovations.[17] A case can certainly be made that many new diagnostic techniques had to wait several decades for doctors' therapeutic abilities to catch up with them, and that insurers hence had a clearer stake than most physicians in promoting innovation in this area. Yet although some constraints on the insurance exam encouraged life insurance offices to resort to new techniques, others tended in the opposite direction. Customers who had no incentive to discover what was wrong with them resisted invasive tests, and many doctors, especially in the provinces, had little or no experience applying them. Furthermore, the highest-status physicians in London and Edinburgh, who were most often appointed as medical advisers, were the least likely to defend the supercession of older diagnostic methods by new technologies. For all these reasons, most new forms of diagnoses waited almost as long to appear in British insurance medicine as in general practice.

A major impediment to the full-scale introduction of new medical devices into insurance medicine was the perception that they would scare away too many customers. Complaints about the invasive nature of medical technology were a common refrain in the insurance trade press. Following a *Post Magazine* announcement of a new 'health meter,' an agent anxiously asked: 'is it pushed down your throat like a stomach pump, or are you mounted between glass like objects for the microscope?' The same magazine earlier told of the candidate who had to have 'his pulse felt, his tongue scrutinized, the colour of his skin criticised, his ribs rapped, a trumpet looking instrument applied to his chest and, finally, another instrument presented to him for ascertaining the exact quantity of air his lungs will hold.' Medical advisers sympathized with such concerns. A candidate who was 'personally much disturbed' by a thorough chest exam, warned one doctor, 'may go to some other office where he may be less so.'[18]

Although medical advisers worried about the impact of medical technology on business, their suspicions ran deeper than that. Dyce Duckworth, who advised three life offices during his long career at St Barts, urged his colleagues to 'lift our eyes from the microscope, and away from the engrossing researches of the laboratories' in order to 'know more of the inwardness and due proportions of matters which relate to the life of the man.' Duckworth, who defined medicine as an art that was 'incommunicable by word or letter,' personified an ethic that was common to late Victorian elite physicians. Also deriving from this ethic was a concern that medical technology focused on specific organs at the expense of a general assessment of health. Byrom Bramwell, who advised the Scottish Union & National for more than two decades, warned his Edinburgh students in 1887 against viewing patients 'as so many cases of this or that disease ... rather than as separate individuals, each with his special tissue and constitutional peculiarities.'[19]

Despite these reservations about applying new technology to the insurance exam, insurance doctors clearly did think that physical symptoms offered a 'safer ground' for risk assessment (as the Sun's medical adviser claimed), for the simple reason that they were more suspicious of subjective symptoms than regular doctors were. For the most part, however, the physical signs that mattered most to them related to physiognomy, physical formation, respiration, and other symptoms that could be detected with the eye, hand, and ear – assisted only, in the latter case, by the stethoscope. Most insurance doctors would have agreed with the physician Mitchell Bruce, who claimed in 1900 that 'minor degrees of serious disease' were best discovered 'not by making use of novel methods of investigation, but by making better use of old-established ones.'[20] By and large, this dividing line favoured qualitative assessment over numerical measurement. As will be discussed in the next section, medical advisers only resorted to the latter variety of diagnosis when they exported the exam from the head office to the provinces, and even then they did so reluctantly and in the face of significant practical obstacles.

Of 'old-established' diagnostic methods, attention to physiognomy was among the oldest, and this appeared at the top of almost all insurance medical forms. Under the heading of 'general appearance,' companies asked doctors to describe candidates' countenance, muscular development, 'strumous symptoms,' or facial expression, and asked if the candidate looked 'older than is usual at his time of life.'[21] Doctors watched for 'full and distended' veins, 'red and ferrety' eyes, a blotchy face, and 'a characteristic bloated aspect' as signs of alcoholism.[22] Into the 1890s companies included 'temperament' on their forms, and textbooks taught insurance doctors to distinguish among the four temperaments (sanguine, lymphatic, bilious, and nervous). This emphasis on personal appearance was in part a carry-over from the days before the medical exam, when a boardroom interview determined acceptance or rejection: 'Looks were everything' in those days, the Royal Exchange's actuary later recalled.[23]

Physicians had valued physiognomy as a prognostic tool for centuries, and it continued to resonate in Victorian insurance medicine. John Mann of the British Empire Mutual, noting that candidates' facial signs were not so 'strongly marked' as in hospital cases, still insisted that an experienced medical examiner would be 'morally certain' if 'they mark some deviation from health.' What such doctors implied was that precisely because it was hard to translate physiognomy into numbers or words, trust needed to be based on 'experience,' not on replicable measurement.[24] Insurance doctors also valued physiognomy because recording this information entailed virtually no time or awkward interaction with the candidate: the 'looks' of a candidate could 'be gathered by a rapid glance,' as one medical adviser stated in 1861. This was detective work that could, if done properly, pass undetected by the person being observed. As such, it reinforced the medical adviser's self-fashioning as an artist: one doctor compared the insurance candidate to 'the immortal Pickwick in the Fleet ... sitting for his portrait,' and another cited the artist Joshua Reynolds as a guide to expert diagnosis.[25]

Thus performed, the 'intelligent looking' of the insurance examiner invited inevitable comparisons with Sherlock Holmes, once Conan Doyle's character became popular – and Doyle himself had experience as an insurance doctor, for the Gresham, in the 1880s. Standard Life's London medical examiner, in praising the observational skills that could 'only be gained by those who have, by long use, trained their special senses and their judgment,' concluded in 1897 that 'the medical examiner is probably none the worse of having a spice of Sherlock Holmes in him.' Although Holmes was a convenient persona to which insurance doctors could attach their vocational virtues, the character type dated back decades earlier. The hero of Charles Dickens's short story 'Hunted Down' (1860) was an insurance manager who prided himself on judging candidates 'from their faces alone, without being influenced by anything they said.' More generally, life insurance figured largely in the burgeoning Victorian genre of detective fiction, whereby an astute director, actuary, or 'private inquiry agent' got to the bottom of a fraudulent insurance claim.[26]

Besides honing their powers of visual observation, insurance doctors privileged their ability to hear deviant sounds. The Scottish Equitable's requirement that doctors examine 'the state of the Heart and Lungs by Auscultation and Percussion' was typical. Auscultation meant listening to heart palpitations and respiratory sounds, typically with the aid of a stethoscope; percussion recorded the resonance and pitch that resulted from striking the candidate's chest with a finger or hammer. Auscultation grew in popularity after 1816, when Rene Laennec invented an instrument that allowed doctors to hear the heart without placing the head next to the chest. By the 1830s stethoscopes came into use in Edinburgh hospitals; they migrated south to the London teaching hospitals by the 1840s, just when standard forms for insurance exams were emerging. At Standard Life, Robert Christison counted six cases between 1847 and 1852 where the stethoscope had 'revealed decided valvular disease of the heart, not indicated by any ordinary symptom.' Auscultation's power came from the one-to-one correspondence between transcribed sounds and specific diseases that could later be confirmed by autopsy. As Douglas Powell urged in 1878, comparing chest sounds in patients and cadavers enabled the diagnostician to 'gain at the bed-side ... an accurate picture of the lung or heart or pleura under examination as though the organ were exposed to his view.'[27]

John Hutchinson's catalogue of sounds that were audible through a stethoscope included the 'soft and silky' healthy chest, 'like a breeze among foliage'; the 'deficient or harsh' tubercular lung; and the 'large rough, dry or moist' sound that indicated either a chest cavity or bronchitis. The fact that these sounds 'revealed nothing except to the experienced auditor' made it the exception to elite physicians' general suspicion of medical instruments. Elite doctors were less well disposed towards the pleximeter, invented in 1826, which brought to percussion the same distance from patients as the stethoscope brought to auscultation. The standard pleximeter was a small ivory or metal plate, accompanied by a metal hammer. When talk turned to this instrument, insurance doctors reverted to their habit of privileging the human senses. Powell insisted that 'the sense of touch most importantly supplements that of hearing whilst percussing the chest,' adding that a doctor's touch enabled him to '*feel* qualities of dulness [sic] or hardness which the ear alone cannot detect.' Besides impeding diagnosis, noted Reginald Thompson, the pleximeter diminished patients' 'equanimity' in what was already 'a sufficiently trying ordeal.'[28]

If translating percussion and auscultation into useful diagnosis could be difficult in general practice, it was even more challenging in the insurance exam. The 'sartorial dominance' that most doctors could count on when ordering hospital patients to disrobe was more likely to be contested by a candidate for life insurance. As part of their efforts to be tactful, insurance doctors avoided 'unnecessary stripping' – especially when the candidate was a woman, in which case it was 'by no means required to uncover much of the chest at a time.' On the other hand, a thorough chest exam was by far the single most important feature of the entire procedure, since it was hard to diagnose consumption without it. Hence even while doctors insisted on the importance of tact, they were just as adamant that the chest be examined one way or another. Joseph Bell of the City of Glasgow urged examiners to 'coax [the candidate] gradually to get his shirt off or out of the way,' and most doctors insisted on the 'complete removal of all clothing' above the waist. [29]

Trust in Numbers?

For fairly obvious reasons, the same factors that privileged incommunicable knowledge in physical examinations performed by head office medical advisers made such knowledge problematic when the examination took place in the provinces. Although insurance company forms never ceased to require provincial doctors to transcribe their 'percussion notes' and candidates' facial features, the medical advisers who designed these forms doubted that they could get 'a perfect literary word-picture at the price' from doctors possessing doubtful skill and respectability.[30] Hence in the provinces, where the majority of life insurance customers lived after 1850, companies pursued a substantially different approach to the physical part of the medical exam. To their mostly qualitative tests of physiognomy and respiration they added numerical measurements of height, weight, chest capacity, and pulse; and at the turn of the century they called for further quantitative data regarding candidates' blood pressure and urine. Although they added these new features at the head office as well, a central motivation for introducing them was to compensate for the problem of transmitting incommunicable knowledge at a distance.

The very fact that such information was merely a transcription of quantities, however, meant that medical advisers never fully trusted its value in risk assessment. Even though they usually created the forms that were filled in by provincial examiners, the head office seldom set much stock in the responses, and nearly half of all forms as of 1886 reserved room at the bottom for the examiner's 'general opinion.' As one doctor worried, forms too often subordinated a 'general impression of the healthiness of the proposer' to 'definite data' regarding the heart, lungs and kidneys.[31] When the numbers they called for moved from mere measurement to

results of chemical or other diagnostic tests, the additional problem surfaced that relatively few provincial examiners were qualified to produce
reliable data. By the end of the nineteenth century, the status of the provincial medical examiner hovered somewhere between that of a skilled
diagnostician and a glorified stenographer.

Taking Measurements

Of all the standard measurements required by life insurance offices,
height and weight were the most durable. John Hutchinson, who in
1846 introduced one of the first height and weight charts to be used in
life insurance, called weight in relation to height 'our foundation upon
which we rest, and from thence reason upwards to the question, eligible or not eligible.' A century later, the author of *Risk Appraisal* called
a candidate's build 'the one phase of insurability where reliable and
positive information is obtained in 100 per cent of cases.'[32] In many regards, height and weight were perfect measurements from an insurance point of view. It could be assumed that candidates would never
perceive their measurement as overly invasive (in contrast, for instance,
to a urine test); they were simple enough for even the most ignorant
provincial doctor to take accurately; and (especially pleasing to actuaries) a normal range of heights and weights could be discerned from
aggregate data.

Hutchinson's chart encompassed 2,650 'healthy males,' including
'sailors, firemen, policemen, Grenadier guards, watermen, cricketers,
gentlemen, Oxford and Cambridge rowers, and the like.' A later chart,
introduced by the Montreal actuary Thomas Macaulay in 1881, took the
average of 2,000 'healthy English-speaking lives.' These two charts remained in use until 1912, when the Actuarial Society of America issued
a new table that had the singular advantage of being comprised entirely of insured lives.[33] From such charts, insurance doctors carved a
variety of normal ratios of height and weight. William Brinton allowed
five pounds per inch, give or take 20 per cent, above and below an ideal
weight of ten stone (140 lb.) for a man 5'6" tall; Macaulay employed the
formula $W = h^3/2{,}000$ and thought a divergence of 15 per cent or more
from his 'standard of ideal perfection' was cause for concern. He later
came around to the position that taller men tended to be thinner and
added that men weighed more as they got older; other doctors allowed
for variations for insurance candidates living in foreign countries.[34]

Besides defining normal ratios of height and weight, medical advisers identified specific health risks that accompanied candidates who fell outside these boundaries. Into the late-nineteenth century, doctors viewed the underweight body with more foreboding than the overweight body. The main reason they gave for this was that thin people were 'not able to withstand much wear and tear'; after 1880 they attached the more specific risk of consumption to 'the long, lanky and weedy looking individual.'[35] By the end of the century more insurance doctors were starting to worry about overweight candidates, although as early as 1850 they associated obesity with 'heart disease, apoplexy, and congestion.' Besides continuing to cite the risk of heart disease later in the century, they worried both that overweight people did not get enough exercise and that when they did exert themselves they might die from a ruptured blood vessel or from syncope (lack of blood to the brain). Insurance doctors also agreed that not all thin or fat people should be treated equally: 'heavy men with immense bone and muscular development' were safer risks, as were underweight people 'coming from a thin but wiry and tough family.'[36]

Nearly as common as the measurement of height and weight in an insurance exam was the measurement of chest capacity. The European had its medical examiners in 1859 measure this by stretching 'a common tape measure round the chest over the region of the nipples,' requesting the candidate 'to inspire or fill his chest as much as possible,' then recording the circumference before and after; the London Life similarly asked medical examiners to take the 'measure of chest at nipple line on full inspiration and expiration.' According to one insurance manual published in 1908, the chest of an 'ordinary healthy man' expanded from two to three inches while inhaling, compared with an inch or less for someone suffering from consumption or emphysema. Chest circumference and breathing capacity were crucial determinants of insurability. The Norwich Union rated up a Birmingham man in 1879 because his chest measured only thirty inches in diameter, despite the fact that it expanded more than three inches when inhaling. His 'small chest measurement,' together with a winter cough, counted for more than the fact of his 'healthy' appearance and absence of 'signs of tubercular deposit.'[37]

Although many life insurance offices were satisfied to determine breathing capacity by applying a tape measure before and after inhalation, some medical advisers favoured fancier devices. Hutchinson at the Britannia was a strong advocate of the spirometer, which received air through a tube, then elevated water in an outer tube to enable the number of cubic inches to be recorded. By applying 'the definite language of numbers' to respiration, Hutchinson claimed to have discovered a reliable indicator of deviance: anything beyond a 'healthy' range (which was 230 cubic inches for a man who was 5'8" tall) signified trouble, even though one might 'never find the cause.' This line of reasoning should have made sense to insurance doctors, who were interested in deviance per se rather than etiology, and some did endorse the spirometer when it first appeared. Most, however, regarded it as 'a pretty toy' that was too difficult to use properly.[38] Simpler chest-measuring devices had a longer shelf life, including the cyrtometer (a jointed whalebone connected by rubber tubing, which girdled the chest) and the stethometer (which compared the mobility of two different parts of the chest by means of a silk cord attached to a dial).[39]

A further measurable element in the Victorian insurance exam concerned the circulation of blood, as indicated by pulse and blood pressure. For the most part, life insurance offices were satisfied with a qualitative assessment of the pulse, despite the availability of numerical standards from the early nineteenth century. A typical question on an exam form asked if 'the arterial pulsations' were 'natural in rhythm, volume, and force,' and even forms that asked for the number of beats per minute added a query regarding its 'character.' Along these lines, an 'intermittent' pulse was grounds for rejection as often as a pulse that was too low or high.[40] On the other hand, most doctors could be trusted to record the number of beats per minute even if not specifically asked to do so. Handbooks for medical examiners did indicate a 'normal' pulse (64 to 86, according to one doctor) in these terms, although some medical advisers admitted that they had no firm evidence regarding 'the point at which a slow pulse becomes abnormal.'[41]

Although technology was in place for measuring blood pressure by the 1880s, few British life insurance offices used it until after 1900. An Austrian physician introduced one of the first working blood pressure meters (usually called at the time a sphygmomanometer) in 1876, consisting of a rubber bulb that expanded with water and was pressed against a patient's arm. By the 1880s air replaced water in the bulb, and by 1905 meters existed for measuring systolic as well as diastolic pressure. Although many North American insurers were using these machines by 1900, British firms took longer: perhaps indicative of the suspicion, expressed by an elite London doctor in 1905, that their use threatened to 'pauperize our senses and weaken clinical acuity.' A

Standard Life doctor noted in 1922 that the importance of blood pressure was 'becoming more and more recognised' in connection with life insurance, but added that the 'considerable care and skill' that was necessary to get 'reliable results' with the sphygmomanometer had limited its use.[42]

In 1883 the humorist Hargrave Jennings offered a description of insurance doctors with their 'finger and thumb delicately placed ... upon the pulse of the newly-caught "Assured,"' busily 'prying into Fate's secrets.' The 'secrets' that doctors hoped to discover from measuring the pulse or blood pressure included diseases of the kidney and liver as well as the heart. Byrom Bramwell associated an abnormal pulse with 'earlier stages of chronic Bright's disease' and cirrhosis; a weak pulse, warned another doctor in 1912, was a sign of 'fatty degeneration of the heart'; and high systolic blood pressure (defined as anything over 140 at age twenty, with an addition of 5 mg for every five years) indicated gout, syphilis, intemperance, and kidney disease. An abnormal pulse could also signify a number of less dangerous conditions, which argued for retesting rather than rejection. Besides 'insurance heart,' doctors often associated a rapid or irregular pulse with tobacco smoking or 'tea intoxication,' which they tended to view benignly. Salesmen were always ready to provide an optimistic spin, as when a Norwich Union agent attributed a law clerk's 'rapid action of heart' to the fact that he had been 'very busy & running about Court a good deal today.'[43]

Suspicious Secretions

The final measurable quantities to appear in most Victorian life insurance exams were the albumin (or egg protein) and sugar found in candidates' urine. Ever since Richard Bright had first linked albumin to kidney disease in 1827, doctors had been on the lookout for it, although detection remained unreliable for several decades. Bright's disease was commonly associated with dropsy, which accounted for 7 per cent of deaths in early company surveys of mortality and was directly assigned as the cause of 5 per cent of deaths in later surveys. Sweet urine (glycosuria) signified diabetes, which steadily increased as a matter of concern for life insurance offices during the nineteenth century. Between the 1850s and the 1890s the mortality rate from diabetes nearly tripled, and the fact that it mainly affected people 'in the upper and middle strata of society' (as one doctor noted in 1900) made it 'of special moment to the insurance world.'[44] On the other hand, neither disease killed people as early in life as consumption, and by 1900 Bright's disease was deemed by most doctors to be curable. At least to some extent, one is left with the impression that offices tested for these conditions as much because tests existed as because of their impact on mortality.

Into the 1880s most life insurance offices only tested urine to confirm prior suspicion of kidney disease or diabetes. When in 1852 George Johnson, a kidney expert, urged the Equitable to test all candidates, the directors refused on the grounds that 'this would cause annoyance and give offence.' One of the first life offices to require urine tests in all cases was the Caledonian, which in 1882 joined the North British & Mercantile as the only Scottish firm to do so – although this proved to be easier said than done. The North British, it turned out, had experienced 'considerable difficulty, chiefly in cases where the fee allowed is only 10s/6d, in getting their requirements carried out,' and in fact only half of the proposals considered at a recent board meeting included urine results. To avoid these problems, the Caledonian paired its new testing policy with a new fee scale, reducing the minimum policy size for which a full guinea would be allowed and asked branch secretaries to 'revise the lists of Country Medical Examiners' to include only doctors who knew how to test for urine.[45]

With the new testing policy came a new question on the examiner's form. The query, as framed by the Caledonian's medical officer, read: 'What is the condition of the urine as ascertained by examination? If not normal, state its specific gravity, and whether albumin or sugar is present; and should there be any deposit, state the nature of such.' To answer this, a doctor would need to know how to perform at least two different chemical tests. The most common albumin test involved adding nitric acid and boiling the solution. The main sugar (or glycose) test used Fehling's solution, a mixture of copper sulphate, potassium tartrate, and sodium hydroxide, which was added to urine that had been boiled and filtered to remove any albumin.[46] Most forms that asked for a urine test included a reference to specific gravity, which compared the urine's mass (ranging from 1,005 to 1,050) with that of distilled water (forming the base of the scale at 1,000): higher than 1,025 was a sign of sugar, and lower than 1,015 was a sign of albumin. Smell and colour were final potential indicators of diabetes. Normal urine was 'a pale, straw-coloured and transparent fluid' and 'slightly aromatic,' whereas a diabetic's urine was reddish or brown and smelled like 'new-mown hay.'[47]

During the 1880s an increasing number of life insurance offices began requiring urine tests in all cases, and medical advisers grew more vocal in advocating this.[48] A handbook informed medical advisers in 1889 to send back exam results that did not include urine tests, adding that it was 'notorious that a man may have glycosuria or albuminuria, and yet neither know it himself nor carry in his personal appearance any evidence of the disorder.' This ability to detect the unseen dovetailed with the insurance doctors' increasingly urgent raison d' être, which was that they alone had the skill to identify certain risks. One doctor fended off the notion of granting insurance without medical examination by appealing to a patient of his whose 'excellent physique' was belied by 'urine nearly solid with albumen.' Measurable signs of albumin or sugar also had a way of convincing a life office's directors when a mere hunch on the part of the examiner failed to suffice. The Law Union's medical adviser noted that detection of albuminuria 'might decide the matter' when 'candidates impressed the examiner unfavourably without it being possible to find adequate reasons for rejection.'[49]

Once a critical mass of life insurance offices began testing all comers' urine, however, problems arose almost immediately. The new testing regime coincided with an emerging belief among doctors that albumin and sugar in urine could often be consistent with perfect health. In a watershed paper, the Scottish physician Grainger Stewart reported in 1887 that 'albuminuria is much more common among presumably healthy people than was formerly supposed.' Subsequent doctors reported that albumin levels were increased by 'cold sea bathing,' scarlet fever, excitement, prolonged exertion, eating cheese, and masturbation, few of which conditions were grounds for rejecting an insurance proposal.[50] After 1900 doctors similarly listed various causes of 'temporary' glycosuria, including breastfeeding, anxiety, gout, and the ingestion of ginger beer or certain drugs prior to the exam – although others worried that it could also signify a precursor of full-blown diabetes. Inexperienced doctors could also send in false positives, especially when testing for sugar.[51]

All of this meant that doctors needed to learn how to 'discriminate the different meanings which may attach to ... abnormal constituents of the urine' once they had discovered something amiss. To this end, medical advisers recommended fermenting and retesting the urine or requiring a subsequent exam after a 'test meal,' if Fehling's test had indicated diabetes, and referring to the candidate's *personal* elements' or running a lab test for blood casts, in the event of suspected albuminuria. Many of these suggestions, however, were either costly to the life office or inconvenient for the candidate. One doctor noted that 'we cannot ask the proposer ... to come again and again for the purpose of proving that the condition was only temporary,' and another observed that asking for a test meal was only likely to work 'where the proposer is not a man who has been pestered into making a proposal by an agent.'[52]

Even when all signs in a urine test pointed to a 'structural' defect, its nature and associated level of risk were often far from clear. Doctors representing eight reinsurance partners on a Dublin merchant's £20,000 proposal spent several weeks in 1880 debating the significance of traces of blood and albumin that had been discovered in the merchant's urine: one discerned the 'beginning of Brights Disease,' another diagnosed 'slowly contracting kidney – a form of chronic Bright's disease,' and a third suggested 'a small stone in the kidney, which caused once the bleeding, & always the albuminuria.' The only thing they could agree on was the need for an additional premium to cover the risk, which added 40 per cent to the cost of the policy. More generally, even if Bright's disease was clearly behind the albuminuria, some insurance doctors questioned its danger to life. Theodore Williams of the English & Scottish Law noted that 'though we talk a great deal about Bright's disease, it does not seem to kill any great proportion of people who insure,' and George Johnson thought it was 'essentially ... curable.'[53]

A final problem with testing urine was that it substantially added to the annoyance of the medical exam. Asking candidates to urinate (typically in the same room as the doctor, to prevent fraud) was even more awkward than asking them to bare their chests, especially where women were concerned.[54] If asking candidates to urinate caused annoyance, so did rejecting them on the basis of the test result – precisely because such a result was likely to reveal a condition the candidate had been unaware of. Especially once they were convinced of the prevalence of false positives and of non-pathological albuminuria or glycosuria, many actuaries and insurance doctors singled out these cases to be well adapted for endowment insurance as an alternative to rejection or rating up. Besides making it easier to sell life insurance policies to such people, this solution relieved the company of the need to pay in the years when the associated disease was likeliest to be fatal. Other doctors recommended retesting a year or two after the policy was issued and removing the extra premiums if the albumin or sugar could no longer be detected.[55]

Conclusion

In one way or another, nearly all of the practices that went into the life insurance medical exam implicitly defined what counted as normal from an insurance perspective. It did not take doctors long to realize that this perspective drew a very different boundary between the normal and the pathological than they were accustomed to drawing in general practice. As one medical adviser concluded in 1861, after providing a long list of prerequisites for a 'model life' (including an absence of scars and hoarseness, a 'capacious and symmetrical chest,' an 'equable' pulse, and 'a considerable warmth of skin'): since 'not one in a hundred' met these criteria, the insurance examiner had to allow for 'very liberal ... deviations from the strict standard of health' to arrive in the end at 'a *good assurable life*.' Such doctors did their best to preach this message to provincial medical examiners, especially recent college graduates who wrote 'elaborate reports, showing why you should reject this case on rather trivial grounds.' Vivian Poore of the Law Union & Crown told younger examiners that they should not be 'too finikin' lest they 'keep away profitable lives.'[56]

If their diagnostic skill tempted doctors to reject candidates that insurers might be happy to accept, their therapeutic impulse pushed them in the opposite direction. Here, the logic was that a present-day pathology would not necessarily shorten life if a cure was around the corner – a view that few life insurance offices embraced. This tension first emerged among provincial medical examiners, who sometimes practised forms of medicine that were farther ahead of the therapeutic curve and who often were inclined to act as advocates on behalf of the candidates in their neighbourhood. A focal point was tuberculosis, which a growing number of provincial doctors (especially those who ran sanatoria) identified as curable – and also as infectious, with little reason to be considered in light of a candidate's family history. One Leeds doctor called tuberculosis 'a disease one may hope to see exterminated,' while another from Birmingham faulted life insurance offices for focusing on 'the hereditariness of the disease to the total disregard of its infectivity.'[57] From a different angle, advances in surgery led to what the Rock's medical adviser called 'some perplexing questions in life assurance' by diminishing the risk to an unforeseeable extent of such conditions as piles, tumours, and hernia.[58]

As prospects for treatment of disease improved towards the end of the nineteenth century, the physician's propensity to good cheer increasingly came into conflict with the goals of the life insurance office. Edward Symes-Thompson discovered this in 1885 after giving a lecture to medical students on heart disease and life insurance. In reporting his lecture, the *Post Magazine* took him to task for concluding that most heart diseases were 'amenable to remedies' as long as a patient 'would subject himself to the necessary treatment'; this, the writer argued, would make it harder for life offices to justify rejecting or rating up a candidate diagnosed with a heart problem. Symes-Thompson's response underscored the widening gap between life insurance offices and doctors who were newly confident in their healing powers. While insisting that he took seriously the 'very grave symptoms' of heart disease, he excused his remarks on the grounds that his lectures were 'attended by many sufferers from Heart Disease, and in such cases it is incumbent upon a lecturer to speak as cheerfully and as hopefully as possible.'[59]

The key to this tension lay in the fact that few turn-of-the-century therapies worked very well without the patient's cooperation, whereas life insurance companies (with few exceptions) stayed out of their customers' lives once they had passed the medical exam. With the exception of truss clauses for hernia sufferers, there was nothing in any insurance contract to void the claim if a policyholder failed to follow his or her doctor's orders. This was, in effect, Theodore Williams's justification for rejecting anyone with a personal history of tuberculosis: 'I never take a case of phthisis if I can possibly help it ... The reason is that you can never be certain of their future. Everything may look well, and you may think you know the limit of the disease, but something happens, the man gets under depressing circumstances, he has a terrible domestic loss, or loses his money, or over works, or contracts some other disease ... and the case is no longer insurable.'[60] Hence, at the end of the day, most doctors who worked for insurance companies found themselves repeating the actuaries' mantra that the future could be predicted only for aggregate populations and never for individuals. No amount of therapeutic optimism in their professional practice outside the life insurance office would alter that basic truth, at least as long as the life office refused to extend its regulation of people's health beyond the preliminary medical examination.

10 Dealing with Deviance

The practice of charging extra premiums is not only vexatious to an intending assurer, but it would appear to be governed more by individual caprice or rule of thumb than by principle ... Offices generally make an addition of three years in cases wherein hernia or gout exists, yet with some little pressure upon the part of the agent, the office will eventually waive the extra in order to get the business.

– Letter to *Post Magazine*, 1890[1]

The increasing prominence of the medical examination after 1850 accompanied a related shift towards 'rating up' risky lives by charging them as if they were several years older than their actual age. Originally spurred by the formation of two 'under-average' offices in the mid-1820s, this practice developed without the aid of any reliable statistics. Partly this was because actuaries doubted that they could extend the precision that seemed to hold for age-specific mortality to deviations from health, and partly it was because doctors were ambivalent about slotting individual customers into pre-set categories based on clinical or statistical research. Although some actuaries and doctors did incorporate this sort of information into risk assessment, especially regarding the age-incidence and relative mortality associated with specific diseases, the sort of collective effort that had resulted in the Healthy Males table never materialized for medical statistics. The result was an acceptance of blatantly arbitrary extras, on the grounds that these were sufficient to protect the companies' profit margins even if they might not be fair to every policyholder.

Since it was perceived to be so arbitrary, the verdict of the medical examiner or board of directors regarding surcharges was often merely the opening round of a drawn-out negotiation, which further eroded life insurance offices' claims to be equitable to all parties. From the 1860s insurers began to seek alternatives to rating up that would both redress some of that system's inequity and appease customers who bristled at having years added to their lives. The most popular of these was the contingent debt, which deducted from the claim if customers failed to survive the full term of their normal life expectancy. Then, when endowment insurance became more popular after 1880, life offices added this as an alternative to paying extra for whole life policies. At least for those risks that were more likely to strike after a person reached middle age, this allowed companies to shift the financial burden onto policyholders (since death would more often result in a smaller pension rather than an early claim) without losing customers who assumed they would live longer than the medical examiner predicted. Neither of these alternatives, however, would replace rating up as the general practice for nearly all British companies into the twentieth century.

The way British life insurance offices dealt with deviance in the nineteenth century stood out from the pattern in North America and the rest of Europe. When the British doctor Glover Lyon returned from an American fact-finding mission in 1895, he reported that 'additions to premiums are almost unknown' there and that 'endowment policies for variable periods take their place.' He was correct – it was not until 1896 that a major insurance company (the New York Life) started surcharging policies on a regular basis.[2] When British medical advisers turned from North America to the European continent, they discovered a different and equally distinct approach to under-average lives. The *Lancet* reported in 1887 that 'the custom of French offices appears to be this: a case is accepted or declined, but no hint is given of meeting an increased risk by loading the premium.' A later observer confirmed that this was the case 'all over the Continent,' noting that 'we English people are peculiar' for not adopting the 'take it or leave it' method.[3]

Specialized Offices and the Development of Rating Up

With the exception of a handful of risk groups, most British life insurance offices prior to 1850 either accepted candidates at ordinary rates or rejected them. Of 94,749 lives tabulated by the Faculty of Actuaries through 1863, only 3,551 (3.7 per cent) were rated up on account of poor health.[4] Apart from travel and occupation, companies reserved the vast majority of extra charges for the relatively minor afflictions of gout and hernia, with average surcharges of around 10 per cent on top of the regular premium.[5] This practice of charging a fixed percentage to the premium would become the exception for health risks after 1850, when life offices instead added years to the customer's age; it was also different from the typical mode of handling occupational and travel extras, which was to add a fixed percentage of the sum insured. It did make a difference which of these three methods a company used, especially when moving from younger to older lives. The most important features of these early surcharges, though, were that they were not very high (the same companies that added 10 per cent for gout charged well over twice their basic premiums for a trip to India) and that companies typically rejected a candidate rather than charge more than 10 per cent extra for a physical infirmity.[6]

'Under-average' and Invalid Life Insurance Offices

This general rule against accepting any life with more than a minor health risk would become a leading foil for two companies that formed in 1824. With significant differences in approach, the Asylum and Clerical Medical both claimed that it was possible to determine extra premiums for these risks that were both safe for the company and fair to hitherto-uninsurable customers. The Asylum's promise of safe and equitable surcharges rested on alleged vital statistics that its founder, George Farren, claimed to have collected; the Clerical Medical's rested on the list of eminent physicians and surgeons who made up half of its board of directors. Although there was more to each company's business plan than the insurance of under-average lives – the Asylum also catered to travellers and military men, and the Clerical Medical sold itself as a 'class' office to doctors and clergy – that feature was a source of pride for both offices.

The Asylum Foreign and Domestic Life Assurance Company targeted customers who were 'slightly afflicted with such maladies as would subject them to ... an uncertain rate of Premium or rejection at other Offices.' It was the brainchild of Farren, a bombastic company promoter prone to both polemic and self-aggrandizement. In 1826 he claimed that he had 'ascertained, by great care and research, the true law of mortality for various climates and diseases,' and later referred to 'materials of the most perfect character' regarding such risks – but most of this apparently never existed. The next thirty years were marked by profligacy at all levels of management, and when the bubble finally burst its business was absorbed by the London Assurance in 1857. That company's actuary discovered no trace of any disease-specific statistics in the Asylum's records and concluded that 'no law beyond mere guesswork seemed to have been acted upon in fixing the premiums.' Another actuary who had clerked under Farren confirmed that 'the data about which so much was made were mere moonshine.'[7]

A less disastrous, but still rocky, trajectory lay in store for the Clerical Medical's claim that it could fix premiums 'in a just ratio with the amount of hazard' for such conditions as intemperance, haemoptysis, and urinary disorders in addition to the more standard risks of hernia and gout. Founded by a doctor, the Clerical Medical featured a more respectable directorate than the Asylum's and did not base its extra charges on allegedly 'perfect' statistics. Instead, it presented as its *distinguishing safeguard* the fact that extra premiums were 'calculated upon a minute investigation of each individual case' by a board filled with medical luminaries.[8] A second important contrast with the Asylum was that the Clerical Medical was willing to learn from its mistakes. Upon discovering in 1834 that the company's 650 rated-up lives had died at twice the rate of those who had paid regular rates, while paying only 30 per cent more in extra premiums, its directors determined 'to exercise much greater caution than heretofore in accepting unhealthy lives' – resulting in more favourable mortality results in a follow-up study a decade later. Although continuing to insure more rated-up lives than other life insurance offices, the Clerical Medical's ratio of such proposals declined steadily after 1833, and its average surcharge increased.[9]

Although most established life insurance offices greeted the Asylum and Clerical Medical with scorn, a few responded with special 'under-average' rates of their own.[10] The real turning point, however, came in the three decades after 1840, when at least fifty of the 335 offices that formed included 'declined lives' as a special feature. Like most in their larger cohort, few of these firms survived more than a few years, and the only one that made it past 1900, the Gresham, abandoned this feature by 1870. Besides charging extra premiums for customers whose proposals had been spurned by other offices, the Gresham also sequestered that class in a separate section for the purposes of receiving a bonus, which it only allowed in the form of reduced premiums: a plan that was both safer than the Asylum's and more equitable than the Clerical Medical's. It rated up nearly half of its policies in its first year, and continued to pool declined lives into the 1860s, but by that point it had shifted its sights to the European market.[11]

If most of the newer 'declined lives' offices helped turn rating up into a standard practice without profiting from it themselves, a handful of new companies took the idea of insuring high-risk lives even further, by accepting people who were actually sick when they applied for a policy. The two main entrants in this field were the Medical Invalid (est. 1841) and the Athenaeum (est. 1851). Both were inspired by new data generated by William Farr at the General Registrar's Office on chronic diseases in British towns, which suggested both that their specific mortality rates could be accurately predicted and that people suffering from them comprised a huge, hitherto uninsurable market. As the *Post Magazine* quipped in 1854, it was the principle, if not the practice, of these firms 'to take every life that presents itself, even if the bearer of that life comes with an undertaker at his side with a piece of black tape in his hand ready to take a measure for the length of his coffin.'[12]

To embark on such business with any hope of commercial success required surcharges even higher than those levied by the Clerical Medical. Although the Medical Invalid did not publish the premium tables it used for its 'diseased' cases, an internal report indicates that it charged double for candidates with consumption and epilepsy, triple for sufferers of hernia, heart disease, and gout, and four times the standard rate for intemperance. Although its overall mortality only slightly exceeded what its premiums anticipated, most of its 'diseased' customers were consumptives and alcoholics (both of which groups lost the company money); the rest of that potential market was apparently unwilling to pay such high rates.[13] Whatever the reason, the Medical Invalid stopped pursuing invalid lives in the early 1850s and the Athenaeum wound up in 1856 – after which time life insurance ceased to be an option in England for people with actual, as opposed to merely potential, disease.

In Scotland, meanwhile, insurers found a way to turn a profit on diseased lives by establishing a reinsurance pool. Formed in 1852, the Under Average Association spread risks on these lives with the express intent of preventing 'such risks being carried away to the English Cos. which advertise to take rejected Proposals.' Most Scottish offices annually referred lives to the pool. Besides spreading the risks on these, the pool paid for medical reports and, in 1889, an actuarial investigation. By that point, member firms were rating up substantially more lives than they sent to the pool, with the result that it was shut down in

1893.[14] Its principles would lay dormant in Britain for more than fifty years, before resurfacing in the form of pools for certain otherwise uninsurable risks. Between 1949 and 1957 the Mercantile & General, a specialist reinsurance company that had formed in the 1920s, created 'declined pools' for customers with diabetes, hypertension, and heart disease. Like the original Scottish pool, one goal was to collect data on high-risk insured lives that would enable individual life insurance offices to bear the full risk on them in the future.[15]

Rating Up after 1850

By the end of the nineteenth century, the practice of rating up risky lives, like many other insurance innovations, had turned from being a niche market to being a standard practice for all life insurance offices. Archival evidence and contemporary commentary point to a four-fold increase in rating up during the four decades after 1850. Offices like the University and the Legal & General, which rarely if ever rated up before 1850, did so close to a tenth of the time by the 1880s; other offices between 1856 and 1890 rated up from 12 per cent to 21 per cent of their proposals. An Eagle study in 1872 suggested that life offices after 1850 also expanded the range of risks they were willing to accept with a surcharge. Of 3,147 rated-up lives in this study, only 29 per cent suffered from hernia or gout, which had been the only maladies the Eagle had surcharged prior to 1824. The top risk group was family history (18 per cent), with substantial representation as well from respiratory disease (9 per cent), intemperance (4 per cent), and heart disease (3 per cent). Instead of rejecting far more lives than they rated up, as the Atlas did in 1831, life offices after mid-century surcharged up to four times as many customers as they rejected (see Table 10.1).[16]

The many life insurance offices that rated up lives to a greater extent after 1850 needed to charge extra premiums that were actuarially safe but still low enough to attract business. For the most part, they did so by asking medical examiners to place candidates into a series of classes, then asking their actuaries and medical advisers to convert that judgment into a number of additional years. In James Chisholm's survey of eighty-four life offices, thirty provided doctors with a list of three or four classes into which to place each candidate, always including 'unexceptionable' or 'first-class' for completely healthy proposers and 'inferior' for rejected cases. In between these two extremes, some companies distinguished between 'Average' and 'Doubtful' lives, bumping

Table 10.1
Rated-up and declined proposals in proportion to total proposals
and to completed policies

Life office	Years	Proposals			Proportion of policies (%)		
		Rated-up	Declined	Total	Rated-up	Completed	Declined
British Empire	1857–8	409	118	2,081	19.7	(18.0)	5.7
Eagle Life	1856–60	364	261	3,192	11.4	(9.7)	8.2
Eagle Life	1860	105		840	12.5	9.9	
Edinburgh Life	1867–9	266	92	2,281	11.7	(10.3)	4.0
Star Life	1875	348	75	2,092	16.6	(14.8)	3.6
Legal & General	1871–89	381		3,806	10.0	(8.4)	
Crown Life	1873–90	1,673	974	13,986	12.0	10.7	7.0
Eagle Life	1874–8	355	131	1,689	21.0	(19.7)	7.8
Scottish Un. & Nat.	1878–88	2,119	737	12,976	16.3	(14.9)	5.7
University	1881–90	65	36	735	8.8	7.9	4.9
Caledonian	1883–90	1,136	299	8,058	14.1	(12.5)	3.7
Eagle Life	1885	52	19	260	20.0		7.3
Eagle Life (whole life)	1905	37	18	325	11.4		5.7

Sources: BEMMB; CMB VIII–XI; CAB I–II; EMB; EdMB XII–XIII; LGPR III–VII; SMB; SUNMB; UMB.
Note: Percentages for completed policies in parentheses are estimates, based on the assumption of 10 per cent uncompleted 'healthy' and 25 per cent uncompleted rated-up policies.

candidates from the first to the second class if directors discovered a non-medical problem.[17] Most offices offered minimal guidance regarding the criteria medical examiners should use in slotting candidates into these classes – in contrast to fire insurance offices, which precisely specified different categories of risk and fixed uniform extras to buildings occupying each class.[18]

By the 1860s nearly all life insurance offices had settled on adding years to a candidate's life as the most common method of charging extra for health risks, in contrast to the earlier practice of adding a fixed percentage to the premium. The Edinburgh Life made this move late in that decade, adding years only a quarter of the time in 1867–68, over half the time in 1869, and 82 per cent of the time in 1883–84; archival evidence from six other companies indicates that they switched around the same time, if not earlier (see Table 10.2). The Yorkshire appended to its form an abbreviated mortality table so doctors could see how long 'a Healthy Male Life' might be expected to live, but most let medical examiners 'assess the risk broadly.' One actuary concluded that although adding years to a proposer's life was 'far from perfect' it was 'a convenient *modus operandi*,' and others argued that this method was the best that could be hoped for given doctors' imperfect understanding of the relationship between medical risk and expectation of life.[19]

Most actuaries and medical advisers agreed that it was not worth the trouble to rate people up any less than five years, and most companies added an average of six to eight – translating into 16 per cent to 30 per cent of the premium depending on age. This did vary depending on the risk: in the 1872 Eagle study, the average extras for hernia and gout were relatively small (three and four years, respectively), compared with seven years for circulatory or respiratory problems. Industry-wide conventions emerged in the 1870s that favoured extras of five, seven, or ten years in the majority of cases, exposing the unscientific nature of the procedure. A more general problem with adding years to riskier lives was that this translated into a higher tax (by around 5 per cent) on older candidates, since 'healthy' premiums were higher at advanced ages. On the other hand, data from the Eagle study suggest that life insurance offices corrected for this by adding fewer years to older candidates: an average of eight years for proposers in their twenties, six in their thirties, five in their forties, and four beyond that (see Table 10.2).[20]

Negotiating Deviance

Despite the emergence of standard conventions governing the rating up of risky lives, the practice generated criticism from policyholders, doctors, and actuaries throughout the second half of the nineteenth century. Policyholders, who almost never complained about being charged different rates based on their actual age, were much more likely to appeal for exceptional treatment if they were informed that a health risk required an addition to that age. Agents took the side of customers in these disputes, with the result that extra premiums were often dropped or reduced after protracted negotiation. Medical diagnosis and statistical inquiry framed one side of this negotiating process, but not the only side. This result was inequitable, since it favoured customers

Table 10.2
Mean and median number of years added to rated-up lives; mean proportion of premium added to with-profit premium (%), age 30 and age 40; and cases in which 5, 7, or 10 years were added (%)

| Life office | Years | Years added (n) | | Premium added (%) | | % Rated |
		Mean	Median	At age 30	At age 40	5, 7, 10
Star	1856	5.76	5	15.3	19.6	
Eagle	1856–60	6.04	5	16.1	21.7	
British Empire	1857–8	4.79	5	14.1	16.8	34.4
Edinburgh	1866–9	6.46	6	20.0	24.2	68.7
Legal & General	1861–70	6.23	5	16.8	21.4	37.5
Clerical Medical	1868–77	10.27	10	34.4	38.2	43.3
Legal & General	1871–80	7.41	5	21.2	26.4	44.8
Eagle	1874–8	7.30	6	20.2	27.4	
Star	1875	4.87		14.4	15.6	
Crown	1879–84	6.83		21.0	26.9	
Legal & General	1881–9	8.15	7	23.7	29.6	64.6
University	1881–90	6.76		17.5	22.0	
Edinburgh	1883–4	6.40	5	19.8	24.0	85.5
Caledonian	1883–90	6.61	5	19.8	22.5	69.8
Eagle	1885	8.69	8	24.8	33.7	
Crown	1885–90	7.07		21.9	28.1	
Caledonian	1893–4	7.70	7	23.8	27.2	78.6
Eagle (whole life)	1905	4.93	5	14.2	17.1	

Sources: BEMMB; CMB VIII–XII; CMRL 1868–77; CAB I–II; EMB; EdMB XII–XIV, XIX; LGPR I–VII. Legal & General 1861–70: policies in force.

who were willing to complain and who bought their insurance from more influential salesmen, but it was a result most British life insurance offices were willing to live with. This result also eroded customers' confidence in the authority of the doctors who examined them, since it sent the message that a medical opinion was not the last word in gatekeeping.

Many doctors responded to this situation by asking their companies to sponsor statistical investigations that would create precision where guesswork had so far prevailed. They felt ill-equipped to translate their judgment of a customer's health into so many extra years and sought to improve their authority within the life office by recourse to better data. Some actuaries worked closely with medical advisers in an effort to achieve that, and together they did generate some useful data. They also appealed, in recurring waves, for industry-wide statistics to be compiled on the mortality experienced by rated-up lives and for uniform rates to be forged from the results of such an investigation. For the most part, however, better statistics and uniform extras remained mostly talk, accompanied by little action, well into the twentieth century. One reason for this limited success was that some doctors, and most actuaries, doubted the need for uniform extras. As long as policyholders were free to compare rates among different companies, they assumed, the least-insurable lives would pay higher premiums and those who could convince at least one office that they posed no special risk would pay less.

There was nothing inevitable about this preference for the market over statistical knowledge as a sorting method. For most of the nineteenth century, British fire insurance offices fixed uniform extras for a wide range of hazards, and after 1900 most American life insurance offices did the same. What set British life offices apart was a distinctive understanding of the individual's place in a risk pool and a different choice regarding where to draw the line between competition and collusion. When they did consider ways to render the coverage of higher-risk lives more equitable, they spurned uniform extras and instead applied actuarial fixes ('contingent debt' schemes and endowment insurance), which allowed customers to wager against the company that they would survive. These fixes were popular with policyholders, in large part because they reinforced the suspicion that insurance doctors did not always know what they were doing when they assigned candidates to risk groups.

Bargaining with the Gatekeepers

John Mann of the British Empire Mutual noted in 1865 that rating up 'frequently gives rise to grievous discontent on the part of the proposer, apparently more grievous than prompt and absolute rejection.' This was certainly the case for the overweight London merchant who told his Norwich Union agent that he 'did not at all like the idea of adding

"5 years to his age,"' or the Glasgow man who considered his extra premium to be 'oppressive' and refused to insure unless the Scottish Provincial reduced it from seven years to two.[21] Ironically, however, such expressions of unpopularity entrenched the practice of rating up, by giving salesmen access to a new currency in which bargains could be negotiated. Such bargains had been much less common in the days when the only choice was between acceptance and rejection and when most candidates could only appeal by writing to the head office. It was only with the arrival of the provincial agent (and later, the branch manager) that rejected or rated-up candidates found an advocate with a real chance to convince a board to alter its original verdict. Adding ten years to such a life might be too much to snare the sale, if the office down the street was offering five. Make it seven, and the customer might be willing to accept.

If pressure from salesmen was a leading factor behind the popularity of rating up, it was also a primary obstacle to companies settling on uniform extra premiums for specific risks. As James Chisholm lamented in 1886, life insurance offices commonly allowed 'lives that might very well be called upon to pay an extra ... to pass muster at the ordinary rate, in order that the general growth of the business may not be checked, or a particular agent be discouraged.' Managers and medical advisers were always ready with reasons why bending to such pressures was neither fair nor necessarily good for business, as when one secretary worried that 'first-class' customers would feel 'justly dissatisfied with the whole affair' if they realized that a 'weakling' paid the same rate.[22] Such sentiments carried less weight in the boardroom, where directors were more likely to pay attention to agents' appeals. In 1899 David Drimmie, the English & Scottish Law's Irish agent, argued that the company's extras, 'though justified' for the individuals who had been rated up, 'were more than counterbalanced by the loss of good business which would, but for the surcharge, have been obtained through the Agent introducing the proposal.' The board agreed forthwith to give 'due weight ... to any representations which Messrs Drimmie may make, with a view to waiver or reduction of the surcharge on general business grounds.'[23]

This general exchange was repeated countless times in correspondence between salesmen and directors from the 1860s on, as a brief tour through the Norwich Union's minute books makes abundantly clear. A forty-year-old Norwich clergyman, rated up five years in

1864, successfully negotiated 'a medium Rate between 40 & 45.' In 1880 a London clothier, rated up five years for blood in his urine, found a medical friend who undertook 'to guarantee his acceptance at the ordinary rate by a number of sound life offices'; the Norwich Union took him without an extra three weeks later. The same year, the board rated up a Manchester man by five years, but agreed to 'accept 4 years extra rather than lose the policy.' In 1881 the board agreed by a 5–4 vote to waive a gout extra for a Liverpool proposer; refused to waive it a second time when he applied for an additional £500 coverage two weeks later; then caved in when his agent appealed. The following April, a Norwich man with suspicious urine got his extra reduced from five years, although the board refused to 'accept the life of a man who has twice passed Calculi without some extra charge.' When a Wakefield man protested an addition of five years in 1885, the board replied that '5 years is a small addition on a life which has had 3 attacks of Rheumatic Fever'; after a second letter from the agent, they came down to three. Two letters from the society's London agent and one from its medical examiner was enough to reduce another proposal by the same amount.[24]

In protesting on behalf of their customers, agents commonly appealed to extenuating circumstances, often accompanied by the argument that 'the life should be taken at the ordinary rate, because other proposals would follow if it passed as first-class.'[25] Two cases from the Norwich Union archives must suffice by way of illustration. The first involved a Liverpool cotton broker named John Lightbound, who applied in 1880 to add £1,250 to a policy he had taken out three years earlier, and was rated up five years on the grounds that two of his sisters had died of consumption since the original policy had been issued. The agent, W.H. Andersson, first claimed that the sisters' deaths should not count as evidence of poor family history since they 'were *nuns* (the family being very strict Catholics) & had to undergo very hard privations – the male side of the family all being good.' When that failed, he added that he saw 'most of this family daily all of whom I consider good insurable lives & ... very steady & regular' and implied that, since 'we have the *whole* of the family' insured, losing this policy would hurt that connection. All this was enough to reduce the extra to three years, and even then Lightbound only assented because Andersson agreed to cover it out of his commission. Five years later, Lightbound was still complaining 'most bitterly at the Extra 3 Years charged him,' and Andersson again reminded the head office that 'we have all the family in our Books.' The board agreed, in this case, to re-examine the man, and eliminate the extra if nothing showed up.[26]

The second case involved John Cook, a Hull solicitor who was already insured with two other companies with an extra premium when he applied for a Norwich Union policy in 1880. Although their medical examiner cleared him as first class, the board added five years on the ground that the other two companies had found him to be at risk of rheumatism. Their agent in Hull, William Mabb, wrote to Charles Naismith, his Manchester supervisor, to say that Cook found these terms unacceptable and chimed in that they were 'most unfair' since he had passed 'the very severe exam^n of our medical referee.' He added that because of the extra, he had already 'lost the proposal of his partner which under liberal treatment in Mr Cook's case I should have had *today*.' Naismith sent this letter along to Norwich, adding: 'As Mr Mabb is indefatigable in his efforts to advance our interests & much deserving of encouragement I sincerely trust that an appeal to the Board to dispense with the proposed extra will not be made in vain.' Apparently the board held firm in this case, because a week later Naismith wrote back with the news that Mabb had talked the man into accepting an extra of four years, to which the board quickly assented.[27]

In such cases agents took advantage of the patently arbitrary quality of rating up lives in order to hammer out a premium that both the customer and the company could accept. Insurance companies, on the other hand, took advantage of the new practice of rating up to provide a middle ground occupying the once-stark choice between accepting a life at normal rates and rejecting it outright. Negotiations over the number of years added to an 'under-average' life sometimes did identify cases that really merited exemption from an extra premium, owing to personal or physical circumstances the medical examiner had missed. But many other decisive factors had little if any relevance to underwriting per se. It helped, for instance, if the agent who sold someone a policy was in the directors' good graces. In 1861 the Norwich Union's Chippenham agent got the head office to reduce a hernia extra and drop a gout extra; a year later, when the same agent was in hot water with the company for accounting improprieties, his appeals on behalf of a rejected housewife went nowhere. It also helped if the life in question resided at a distance from the head office and hence could negotiate through an agent instead of directly with the board of directors – as is apparent from the fact that the Crown rejected customers who applied to its head office 11.3 per cent of the time, compared with only 6.7 per cent of the time when proposals were sent in from the provinces.[28]

All of this suggests that market forces did not invariably lead to the 'rationalised assessment' of insured lives, as some have claimed.[29] Still, these apparent lapses in rationality (however defined) did not make the system of rating up lives any less bureaucratic. The anthropologist Michael Herzfeld has observed that the 'taxonomic devices' employed in bureaucracies 'have the capacity, like the trappings of hospitality, to benefit and to demean,' depending on whether or not clients are able 'to persuade their bureaucratic interrogators to accept what makes their case "different" as belonging to the bureaucrats' "own" social world.'[30] When the 'taxonomic device' in question was the 'second-class' status requiring an extra insurance premium, the challenge of the customer (working through his agent) was to persuade the life insurance office that he was the exception that proved the rule. Rather than challenging the premise of rating up, successful negotiators merely rejected that the principle applied to their individual client.

A Quixotic Quest for Precision, 1850–1900

What seemed fair to a successful negotiator, of course, seemed unfair to a customer whose appeal for leniency went unheeded. As a result, complaints regarding the 'purely arbitrary' nature of rating up continued to bedevil British life insurance into the twentieth century. Doctors responded to this situation by calling on their employers to make collective use of their stores of information to pin down a more precise scale of extra rates. The Mutual's medical adviser, Glover Lyon, pled this case before the Institute of Actuaries in 1892. 'The actuaries, knowing the doctors could not swim, pushed them into deep water,' he claimed. 'They have laughed long enough at their clumsy aquatic struggles – it is time they came to the rescue.' Forty years earlier, the Gresham's medical adviser made essentially the same plea. If actuaries could provide doctors with 'the rate of mortality for each state of the human frame,' Alfred Smee argued, medical examiners could solve 'arithmetically' problems that they presently solved 'mentally.'[31]

When Smee issued this call, published data for such an inquiry were nearly non-existent.[32] Faced with this relative paucity, doctors at eleven different companies (with the blessing of their directors) took matters into their own hands in the quarter century after 1850, issuing extensive inquiries linking mortality claims with various causes of death.[33] An important inspiration for this newfound focus on insurance claims was William Farr's compilation of cause-of-death statistics for England and Wales, which he annually appended to his General Registrar's Office reports. James Begbie used Farr's nosology to classify the Scottish Widows' Fund deaths, as did John Fleming at the Scottish Amicable.[34] More tangibly, insurance doctors benefited from the death certificates that the GRO produced. Although most insurance companies required beneficiaries to provide them with an independent certificate, they often turned to the GRO as a last resort, and in any event gained from the fact that most doctors soon learned how to classify deaths 'in the best way the present state of medical science ... will admit.' In his 1868 report Begbie praised the increase in returns of 'morbid conditions' like cancer and heart disease and the decline in vaguer causes like atrophy, dropsy, and old age.[35]

The main end to which medical advisers put their data on causes of death was to measure their performance at selecting lives – in effect, to justify their existence. Instead of simply identifying which diseases accounted for the highest proportion of deaths, Robert Christison of Standard Life calculated the 'ratio of survivance after assurance' for different disease categories. When Begbie applied this method in a report on the Scottish Widows' Fund, he determined that people who died from nervous disorders survived their expected mortality by an average of more than sixteen years – and took comfort in the fact that deaths in this category had increased between 1853 and 1860.[36] Survivancy data also allowed medical advisers to compare 'high quality' lives (with no blemishes discovered by medical examiners) with 'low quality' lives (either rated up or otherwise). Much to Christison's relief, the former turned out to live more than ten years longer at Standard Life. A final test of the value of medical selection involved a comparison of a life insurance office's disease-specific mortality figures with Farr's tally of deaths among unselected lives.[37]

Insurance doctors hoped that company-generated medical data, besides indicating prognostic performance, would enable a closer fit between extra premiums and actual risk. The Scottish Widows' Fund reduced its extra for hernias after Begbie's data revealed only five deaths from that cause in fifty years, and Standard Life did likewise in 1856 after learning that only six of 161 hernia sufferers on its books had died since 1825.[38] Most common of all was the confirmation, in study after study, that consumption took a major toll on profits. At the British Empire Mutual, John Mann reported that consumption, though accounting for just 26 per cent of deaths, amounted to 77 per cent 'of the total losses of ... annual premiums.' This focus on consumption accompanied a widespread interest among insurance doctors in establishing the statistical parameters of family history as a risk factor for that disease. Many medical advisers worked in consumption hospitals, and they appealed to those hospitals' records (supplemented by data from private practice) to conclude that the disease was inherited up to two-thirds of the time. Begbie and Mann both mapped these findings onto their life insurance office data with partial success, and when Lyon issued his call for actuarial aid in 1892 this was the question he was hoping to settle.[39]

In at least some cases, actuaries were pleased to encourage their medical advisers to conduct such inquiries. Doctors from five life insurance offices either jointly published with actuaries or acknowledged assistance from actuaries and their clerks.[40] Despite these strides, however, the medical statistics of British life insurance remained almost wholly limited to a dozen or so company-specific studies. Actuaries' Club proposals in 1856 and 1876 to tabulate disease-specific death rates went nowhere, and although the Institute of Actuaries included rated-up lives in its mortality survey in the 1860s it did not disaggregate this data into risk groups. The only exception was the Faculty of Actuaries, which made room in its mortality investigation to identify lives that had been accepted despite suffering from gout, hernia, other personal health problems, or poor family history. The results confirmed Begbie's finding that hernia mortality was lower than most offices had assumed and indicated for the first time that gouty lives were much more serious risks than had previously been thought.[41]

Attempts to generate comprehensive medical statistics went hand in hand with efforts to achieve uniformity in rating up from office to office. These goals reinforced one another, since most actuaries assumed that better statistics would be pointless without a commitment to uniform surcharges. As James Chisholm argued in 1886, actuaries knew enough about the risks of tubercular family history by that time to be confident that adding five years in all cases would be sufficient – but this would only work 'if the whole class will only keep together and continue the assurances to the end of life in every case.' In practice, he pointed out, all the candidates who felt superior in 'present health, age attained, build, and occupation' would 'move off to some other office which discriminates between the individual lives of a class, and which will accept them at the ordinary rate' – leaving the first office with the worst risks.[42] Archival records indicate that concerns about adverse selection by rated-up customers were justified. Nearly a quarter of rated-up lives at the Eagle in 1860 failed to complete their policies, compared with 2.6 per cent for those accepted at normal rates; at the Crown between 1873 and 1890, the non-completion rate was 28 per cent for rated-up lives and 11 per cent for 'healthy' candidates.[43]

At least a partial solution to this dilemma was for life insurance offices to agree to charge uniform extras for specific risks. Actuaries urged that uniformity in this regard would provide customers with 'something like certainty as to the modes in which their proposals would be treated' and would allow for a reduction of premiums for healthy lives. At present, Chisholm worried, rated-up customers viewed their premiums as 'altogether a matter of bargaining' and doubted 'the existence of any principle at all on which rates are fixed.' Despite these best intentions, however, British actuaries could not convince their directors to settle on uniform extra rates. When Gilbert Finlay tried to get the Associated Scottish Life Offices to include health risks along with climate and military service in a package of standard rates they were about to impose on member companies, his resolution was vetoed on the grounds that 'it was so dependent on the Age and circumstances of the party that each individual case must stand on its own merits.'[44]

Although calls for better statistics and uniform extras would continue to appear regularly, progress remained piecemeal at best into the 1920s. The 1872 study by the Faculty of Actuaries would prove to be the last collective investigation for many decades into disease-specific mortality among insured British lives. Begbie's successor, Claud Muirhead, did muster a follow-up study of the Scottish Widows' Fund that covered nearly 10,000 claims over a twenty-one-year period, and the Prudential mounted a massive survey between 1903 and 1913, covering over 140,000 claims that had fallen due since 1893. These investigations were major undertakings, relying on close collaboration among several medical and actuarial officials. More typical, however, was Frederick de Havilland Hall's survey of 3,066 Rock claims from 1847 to 1893, which he compiled in his spare time, and Charles Hoar's classification of 394 Kent Life policies over the decade preceding 1897.[45]

The main reason interest in better medical statistics remained sporadic throughout this period was that many insurance doctors and actuaries remained ambivalent regarding their relevance to gatekeeping. Although some doctors were eager to learn from statistics, others preferred to rely on 'the clinical plan of grouping experience about single well marked cases,' which had always served them well in general practice. Even those who valued statistics always returned to the idea that their job was to judge the insurability of individual candidates, not to arrange them into risk groups: Muirhead, for instance, urged 'the necessity of attention to individual cases as well as to average.'[46] Actuaries, for their part, sent what must have been frustratingly mixed signals to doctors who sought such data. The Edinburgh Life's actuary insisted that 'there can be no such thing as estimating an individual risk *per se*,' since 'the whole business of selection consists in referring each case to its appropriate group.' Yet many others viewed medical diagnosis as an essentially subjective enterprise that could not be easily translated into statistical categories: Benjamin Newbatt of the Clerical Medical cited the fact 'that judgment necessarily differed with regard to difficult cases' as an obstacle to collective medical data. The upshot was that 'a sort of rough justice' (in James Macfadyen's words) was all that most actuaries hoped for well into the twentieth century.[47]

In reaching these different conclusions, all actuaries appealed to an abstract law of large numbers – they just drew different lines around what was large enough to matter. They occupied what William Palin Elderton of the Equitable identified in 1913 as 'two distinct camps in the profession': 'the one that felt it was their business to pursue their investigations as far as possible, and the other which felt that they had got on successfully in the past, that the data would be small in quantity, and that it was not worth the trouble and expense of carrying out any further investigations.' Macfadyen sympathized with the first camp when he conceded that 'the rougher the classification, the less likely was the individual case to have its mortality closely defined by it.' Along with a critical mass of British actuaries, though, he did not let this concern count for much. In first-class cases as well, he concluded, risks were 'taken every day ... that the premium does not exactly represent; for it can not be supposed that all lives taken at the ordinary rates are of the same vitality.'[48]

Alternatives to Rating Up

The fact that British actuaries turned their backs on refining medical statistics did not mean they were oblivious to perceptions that the existing method of dealing with deviance was inequitable. Their most common response, however, spurned uniform extras in favour of restructuring the insurance contract. Two such alternatives that emerged were the contingent debt and endowment insurance.[49] The first deducted a percentage from the claim, which it restored once the customer reached a pre-specified age; the second exchanged a term life policy for an annuity once the policyholder had survived a set number of years. Over time, actuaries came to realize that contingent debts were especially suited to risks that were likely to arise within a few years, and that endowment insurance was better adapted to risks that waited until late middle age. Statistics remained relevant, since they helped to clarify the age-incidence of different causes of death. But this regulatory role of statistics, which was all too obvious when a customer was rated up, was far less prominent in these alternatives. A salesman could play down the fact that the insurance company was hedging the bet in its favour and play up the fact that customers could 'back their own life' by taking the chance that they would survive long enough disprove a mistaken diagnosis. Not for the first time, life insurance offices used the grey area between statistical thinking and gambling to their advantage in finding a way out of a marketing dilemma.

One of the earliest alternatives to rating up to appear in Britain was to charge a debt against the policy, which would be redeemed if the policyholder survived 'his expectancy of life.' A number of new companies offered this in the 1860s, and it became a standard option by the end of the nineteenth century. In a typical plan, a thirty-one-year-old man who would normally be rated up ten years (paying £34 instead of £25 a year for a £1,000 policy) would pay £25 a year but receive only £706 if he died before the age of fifty-five. If he survived that age, he would receive his full benefit.[50] When contingent debt schemes first appeared, their primary justification was the alleged incapacity of insurance doctors to rate up lives with anything approaching precision. The London & Yorkshire's chairman presented it as a corrective to the 'despotic power which our good friends the doctors have always manifested' – joking that these 'fallible' physicians 'poke your ribs and liver ... and then pronounce you to be five or ten years' worse than your neighbours.' More constructively, since such plans put the onus on customers to prove the medical adviser wrong, they would be more likely to lead 'careful *sober lives*' in order to collect their full claim.[51]

Actuaries initially greeted contingent debt schemes with derision, accusing them of a 'fundamental error of principle' since they made payment 'depend on the issue of the event.' Doubtless because it was their prognosis being called into question, doctors also criticized such schemes through the end of the century. Douglas Powell of the Clerical Medical compared them to a game of 'heads I win, tails you lose' and worried that customers bought them without fully understanding how they worked. Frederick de Havilland Hall of the Rock made the salient point that such a policy would be useless as a security against a debt, since the creditor would have to pay extra in any event to make sure that the full claim was paid from the outset. He assumed that the main reason they had found favour was pressure from agents, who 'sometimes are very desirous of not losing a particularly useful man who will help them in their canvassing.'[52]

Such protests started to recede at the turn of the century, as more life insurance offices adopted contingent debts as an alternative to rating up: by 1907 more than half of thirty-five British offices surveyed offered a contingent debt 'in suitable cases.' Popular in Britain, it was even more common in the colonies, where the Sun of Canada and the National Mutual of Australasia made contingent debts a leading marketing feature.[53] One actuary admitted that it went against the principles of life insurance, but shrugged that 'the public at large' did not see it that way: 'They back their own lives against the opinion of the medical officer.' At the end of the day, this was what mattered. Life offices had discovered a means of 'soothing [the] wounded feelings' of a rated-up candidate, as another actuary put it, and they were not about to let go of it. Insurance doctors warmed up to contingent debts only to the extent of endorsing them in cases where the risk was greatest in the early years of a policy – including consumption and insanity.[54]

A second alternative to rating up was endowment insurance, which became the most popular form of life insurance sold in Britain by the 1880s. As these policies grew in popularity, actuaries gradually discovered that they came with an unintended benefit in application to customers who were exposed to what Thomas Lister of the Royal Exchange called 'explosive extra risks' and other doctors called 'late risks' or 'increasing risks.' Death in middle age, which carried a dead loss for a whole life policy, stood a chance to make money for the insurer in a policy that converted to an annuity after twenty or thirty years. North American life insurance offices, which popularized endowment policies two decades before they caught on in Britain, had applied this lesson to higher-risk customers since the 1870s.[55] British life offices more cautiously followed suit a decade or so later. The Norwich Union started offering endowment policies in 1887 to customers who complained about being rated up, and from the mid-1890s the University routinely offered a choice between rating up (or rejection) and an endowment insurance.

British insurance doctors, who largely remained committed to the ideal of refining their tools for rating up lives rather than seeking alternative approaches, were at first deeply suspicious of this American innovation. Glover Lyon of the Mutual scoffed in 1895 that in the United States, 'competition was so great that it was useless for an office to rate up an applicant; he would be sure to be offered an endowment policy at ordinary rates at some other office.' As with contingent debt policies, however, medical advisers recognized the potential for endowment policies to provide a closer approximation to the incidence of risk in certain cases. By 'cutting the end of a man's life off' from an insurance company's perspective, they appeared to be well adapted to risks like gout, slight albuminuria, or a family history of cancer, which increased over time. More generally, doctors and actuaries after 1880 commonly spoke of an 'early *"breaking-down age,"*' or 'premature age,' as indicated by relatives who died in their fifties or early sixties.[56]

Numerical Rating: A Path Not Taken

At the turn of the twentieth century, just when British life insurance offices were starting to imitate the Americans by offering modified insurance contracts as an alternative to rating up, American insurers were taking the first steps towards a system of standardized extras that promised more numerical precision than anything the British had come close to achieving. The first step in this direction was the 'specialized Mortality Experience' tables compiled by the American Society of Actuaries between 1900 and 1902. These contained ninety-eight different risk groups, including personal medical history, family history, height, weight, and occupation. A year later, drawing on these data, the New York Life instituted a new method of calculating extra premiums that it called 'numerical rating.' This system allocated nine different risk factors for each life, then asked the medical examiner to rate up or down from a standard of 100 for each factor. If the average of the nine factors exceeded 125, an extra premium was charged. Borderline cases were referred to the chief medical officer for further inquiry, and the rest (according to company spokesmen) were 'passed through the hands of trained clerks without [being] brought to the attention of medical experts at all.' The goal was two-fold: to save time and money in processing proposals and to ensure that 'the judgment of the individual medical selector' was 'steadied and restrained by the use of standards.'[57]

Oscar Rogers, the New York Life doctor who developed numerical rating, was alive to the need to pair such a method with uniform standards throughout the industry. Within two decades, he had succeeded in spreading the gospel of standardization, with much help from a continuing wave of collective investigations into risk-specific mortality. The American Society of Actuaries, together with the Association of Life Insurance Medical Directors, published an updated 'Medico-Actuarial' survey in 1913, then issued three further 'Medical Impairment' studies between 1929 and 1951. A detailed ratings manual accompanied the 1929 study, which pushed North American insurers closer to what one medical adviser called the 'millennium' of 'uniformity in action.' American underwriting had become so uniform by the 1950s, in fact, that concerns about anti-trust prosecution prevented such an industry-wide manual from appearing after the 1951 investigation. Instead, large companies and reinsurance firms published their own manuals (all based on the same body of information), which they distributed to their agents and clients.[58]

Although the initial ASA study revived calls in Britain for improved statistics on rated-up lives, in the end these made little more headway than earlier efforts had done. The London medical adviser for the Mutual of New York, S.W. Carruthers, presented a paper in 1905 at the Institute of Actuaries on 'a system by which every office would be enabled to "pigeon-hole" ... lives with similar impairments,' and in 1912 the New York Life's actuary provided the Faculty of Actuaries in Scotland with 'very full information' regarding the scope and cost of the nearly completed 'Medico-Actuarial' survey. From there, Faculty members asked the Institute of Actuaries to join them in tabulating data on customers who had been rated up over the preceding thirty years for consumption, albuminuria, syphilis, heart disease, and obesity. The Institute first scaled this back to the previous ten years, then agreed only to cooperate in a 'Permanent Bureau' that would collect such data from the present time forward. The First World War interrupted plans for such a bureau, and what emerged after the war was the Continuous Mortality Investigation, which transformed the way British actuaries kept track of vital statistics – but included no medical component whatsoever.[59]

As with earlier efforts to improve the statistical basis for rating up British lives, the consensus among English (if not Scottish) actuaries was that such an investigation was not worth the effort. Samuel Warner of the Law Union & Crown spoke for most of his colleagues when he cautioned Carruthers in 1905 that 'it was almost hopeless ... that actuaries should be able, scientifically, to estimate the mortality of each class of impaired lives.' He concluded that the 'very rough and ready' system presently used by British insurers was, after all, adequate for their purposes, since 'the backbone of life assurance companies' business did not consist of impaired lives, but of lives which were considered to be in average health.' The most telling critique of this mode of thinking came not from a fellow actuary, but from the eugenist Karl Pearson, writing in 1930. From the standpoint of eugenics, if not commerce, the insurers' approach struck him as the height of unfairness. It was 'not just to the insured,' he fumed, when a company merely guessed at the premium because it was 'too ignorant, or too inert, to obtain the knowledge requisite to insure ... at a reasonably approximate rate.' The problem, as Pearson accurately identified it, was that life offices had no commercial incentive to split hairs any more finely than they were doing at present: enough 'first-class lives' were willing to subsidize the rest 'to pay ample dividends on their invested capital.'[60]

Such hopes for a closer integration of medical and statistical methods would in the end not materialize in Britain until well after the Second World War. In 1952 discussants of an Institute of Actuaries' paper on 'the treatment of sub-standard lives in practice' variously referred to the 'British tradition' of doing things as 'subjective selection,' 'intuitive underwriting,' and 'educated guesswork.' In 1956 the Scottish actuary Andrew Davidson voiced a lament that doctors and actuaries had by then been repeating for nearly a century: that the 'whims and idiosyncrasies' that marked rating up in Britain needed to be 'restrained by the stern influence of statistics.' A decade later, the actuary Arthur Steeds (paraphrasing G.K. Chesterton) was still wondering if such information would ever be available: 'It is not the case that an investigation into the mortality of impaired lives has been tried and found wanting; it has been found hard and not tried.'[61] As for numerical rating, it remained marginal in British life insurance into the 1960s. Rating manuals, which had been common in North America since the 1920s, were not used in Britain until 1965, and the first to appear mainly relied on American and European medical statistics. Even in the 1970s, when British insurers started to consult rating manuals on a regular basis, they mainly left their compilation up to specialist reinsurance companies (like Steeds's firm, the Mercantile & General) and devoted relatively few of their own resources to the problem of extra risk.[62]

Conclusion

The outcome of this evolution of underwriting in Britain, if not necessarily the intent, was to make life insurance more affordable for all but the most unhealthy lives. Karl Pearson was right to suspect that as long as ample dividends accrued to their shareholders and ample bonuses kept policyholders happy, British life insurance offices had little incentive to prevent customers who complained about being rated up from trying to get a better deal. Revealingly, Steeds ascribed the more rigorous approach taken in North America after 1900 to two factors, the 'limitation of equity investment' and 'strong competition,' that had increased the pressure to cut losses on the underwriting side of the ledger.[63] The fact that neither of these factors was as severe in Britain doubtless played a role in the more easy-going approach there, as did the declining incidence in mortality over the first half of the twentieth century. That decline, combined with continuous growth in investment performance, meant that British life insurance offices felt little pressure to tighten underwriting standards in order to keep premiums down or bonuses up.

As Davidson put it, British insurers had 'been on a good wicket' since the late-nineteenth century in that regard, and he worried that 'the steady and still-continuing improvement in the vitality of the people' had 'obscured the effect of defects ... in their methods of selection.' Steeds made this point in a different way, by listing a wide range of debilities (including gout, ulcer, primary syphilis, and 'psychoneurosis') that 'would previously have been held to justify ratings' but no longer did in 1965. Part of this was owing to the intervening development of cures or treatments of many common Victorian risks – in particular tuberculosis, the decline of which contributed in no small measure to the British life offices' 'good wicket.' Much of it, though, was owing to the fact that 'the standard of acceptance had ... been broadened.' Leaving aside the widespread growth in group schemes and other forms of 'non-medical' underwriting, which (as Steeds noted) had resulted in only 'slightly heavier' mortality, there remained the perception that charging an extra for a borderline risk was 'bad for public relations, and irritates the agent.'[64]

Declining mortality enabled British life insurance offices to keep both premiums and bonus levels more or less constant while liberalizing their underwriting standards, and the entrenched popularity of the bonus meant that even slightly higher premiums were not necessarily bad for business. Such was the case in 1874, when the Crown's actuary reported to his board that despite the 'strict justice' afforded by its high extra premiums, they had 'always caused much dissatisfaction both to the applicants and to the agents,' and had 'tended in a considerable degree to cause the public to form the opinion that the Crown is over particular in the admission of members.' His proposed solution was to increase the regular premiums slightly (no more than 4 per cent at any age), which would enable the company to shift some previously rated-up lives into that class without affecting the company's profits.[65] This was just a more precise version of what happened every day when an agent succeeded in getting his company to waive an extra. To the extent that the doctors were right and such customers did pose a higher risk, the healthier customers paid for that decision with lower bonuses. To the extent that the company could compensate with lower overall mortality or a better investment strategy, its directors could rest assured that the healthier customers would probably not notice.

Conclusion

At the City Liberal Club there is what most of you have seen, a self-print-ing telegraph, where long slips of paper issue from the machine momen-tarily, with the incidents of the day printed upon them. History is writing itself every moment, and perhaps some day the brightest lines in the hist-ory of the latter part of the nineteenth century will be the history of the growth and progress of life assurance.
> – W. Sutton Gover, British Equitable managing director,
> at its 1883 annual meeting[1]

In theory, the geographer David Harvey has argued, modernization (and its cultural partner, modernism) was 'about the pursuit of bet-ter futures,' whereas postmodernism 'strips away that possibility by concentrating upon the schizophrenic circumstances induced by fragmentation.' In practice, and upon even cursory scrutiny, mod-ernity's bright light has always refracted into numerous rays, which cross each other's paths but fail to converge on a single point. This fragmentary nature of modernity is not a problem for the post-modernist, whose gaze (to paraphrase Frederic Jameson) rests on a series of pure and unrelated pasts. Hence, we find, for instance, Foucauldian genealogies of criminality, of insanity, of poverty, and of numerous corners of modern bureaucracy, with few claims to link these together into a single project.[2] Theorists of modernization con-front the possibility of multiple modernities in a different way, by folding as many stray fragments as possible into a single grand nar-rative. When the subject is economic modernization, for instance, the most common response to this problem is to fit all foldable evidence into a Marxist or neoclassical template and jettison the rest as 'super-structure' or 'externalities.'

Throughout history, anyone who has interacted with or within actual economic institutions has lacked the luxury of ignoring whatever does not fit a master plot. Such people have more likely spent most of their time behaving like postmodernists, attending to their own 'unrelated pasts' with little regard to surrounding fragments. For institutions to work, however (which is to say, for them to adjust to changing circum-stances), it is vital for individual actors to engage in some minimal rec-ognition of those fragments. The division of labour can only go so far to shield people from what their co-workers are doing before becoming dysfunctional, just as commodification can only go so far to shield con-sumers from what goes into the product they buy. In Mary Douglas's words, although institutions create 'distinctive types ... of classificatory process' that fit people into niches, 'people are tempted out of their niches by new possibilities of exercising or evading control. Then they make new types of institutions, and the institutions make new labels, and the labels make new kinds of people.'[3]

Few institutions in the nineteenth century were as adept at juggling multiple modernities as life insurance companies were. As they ex-panded their market, life insurance companies drew from and con-tributed to new narrative genres that penetrated to the mental interior of their fictional characters, new statistical thinking that first invented and then proliferated risk groups, and new medical thinking that de-fined boundaries between normal and pathological bodies. Above all, life insurance companies dwelt in an abundant commodity culture that attached a money value to every thing and person that it touched, then found ways to get consumers to remake themselves by buying into this new process.[4] A full assessment of the development of life insurance over the course of the nineteenth century is not possible without taking into account these intersecting modernities. Such an assessment, in turn, has the potential of producing a much fuller nar-rative about modernity, without falling prey to postmodernist ahis-toricism. In what follows I offer two different strategies for assessing these intersections, by way of summarizing this book's conclusions: a consideration of life insurance as a site of interdisciplinarity and a consideration of the sense in which Victorian life insurance created and contained risk.

Forging Interdisciplinarity

Life insurance is a useful case study of interdisciplinarity in large part because of its relative lack of interest in the pathological. As long as doctors or statisticians focused on pathologies, they were free to divide themselves into the proliferating range of specializations that marked the late Victorian human sciences. Each of these disciplines focused on a variant of what Georges Canguilhem has called the 'enormous ... problem of pathological structures and behaviors in man' in order to perform the normalizing task of curing diseases, reforming criminals, or preventing epidemics.[5] Even many projects that were avowedly interdisciplinary tended to reduce collections of pathologies to a single cause: for instance, nature (for eugenicists) or nurture (for social hygienists). Because these projects identified a perfectionist norm and sought to alter society so as to attain it, they expanded their view of the pathological to include everything that did not accord with that norm.

Victorian life insurance offices challenged disciplinarity in two ways. First, by inviting doctors and statisticians to work together towards a single aim, they prompted these professions to depart from the territorialism that otherwise motivated them and to focus, instead, on forging links with other disciplines as a means of enhancing their status and power.[6] Second, they facilitated these links by diverting the attention of their expert employees from specific pathologies to a common-enough conception of what counted as 'normal' or 'natural' in a field of knowledge. As a result, the interdisciplinary aims of life insurance did not replicate the normalizing agendas of eugenics or social hygiene. Instead, they took the normal as they found it, because it was easier to make money that way than to try and convince people to aspire to a norm that did not yet exist. Doctors and actuaries could choose whether or not to bend their disciplinary commitments to this end, and enough did so to provide companies with ample levels of expertise. As subjects of a history of interdisciplinarity, these actors remind us that the disciplines that shaped their knowledge – with their tendency to focus on pathological behaviours in order to regulate and reform the human or social body – did not necessarily signify the last word on the shaping of late Victorian society.

Normal Bodies

To be useful to their employers, insurance doctors needed to alter their assumptions about where to draw the line between normal and pathological bodies. Their inclination in this regard was on display in the second chapter of Edward Sieveking's *The Medical Adviser in Life Assurance*, entitled 'The Normal Man.' In it, Sieveking claimed that for an insurance candidate to qualify as being in 'good health,' it was necessary that he 'possesses no hereditary taint, and that his organs and functions are in a condition to enable him to bear the wear and tear of life without unnecessary detriment' – that he should, in short, 'approach as nearly as possible the ideal or typical man.' Such notions of health emerged alongside Victorian doctors' expansive definitions of disease, which encompassed 'the systematic destruction of bodies, physically, socially, [and] spiritually.' For those who formed the customer base for insurance companies, warding off disease required regimens of diet and exercise that included 'how to govern one's passions, choose a career, or raise children.' More generally, health for Victorians resulted in bodies that were 'purposively functional,' that is, 'not just working but working usefully.'[7]

This way of defining health had little place in insurance work, which required doctors to walk a line between excluding high-risk lives and turning away customers that another company would gladly insure. Head office medical advisers like Sieveking, who typically combined a busy hospital practice with a wealth of high-paying aristocratic patients, were secure enough in their professional status to subordinate their perfectionist tendencies to the insurance office's demands. When these doctors recognized the need to descend from the 'normal' life (as defined by the clinician or health inspector) to the insurable life, they indicated their awareness that life insurance as a business hinged on accepting 'fair risks,' not on eliminating risk altogether. Medical advisers noted the need 'in practice to make certain recognised exceptions ... to the necessary standard' and deemed lives with 'some slight departure from the normal in the physical condition' as 'a fair business risk.'[8]

It was one thing for doctors to shift their assumptions from 'normal' to 'normal enough' in order to accommodate insurance companies' conceptions of acceptable risk. It was another thing for them to embrace the classificatory thinking that deeply informed the actuaries who managed these companies. A central basis of life insurance was the law of large numbers, which asserted a great deal of confidence about predictions concerning people en masse but remained staunchly agnostic about predicting outcomes at the level of the individual. In one sense, insurers made a major exception to this rule when they invited doctors to examine individual lives and predict whether or not each candidate qualified as a good or bad risk. But, as doctors soon discovered, they could not opt out of classifying people just because they examined lives one candidate at a time. It was in this sense that their tendency to focus on singularity (whether defined as a pathological condition that was not exactly like any other or a 'normal' standard of health that no human being precisely achieved) was ill-suited to their insurance work.

This was less of a problem before 1850, when most insurers either accepted lives at standard rates or rejected them. After that time, owing to competition from firms that specialized in insuring higher-risk lives, most companies increased the proportion of candidates who qualified as 'under-average' but still insurable at higher premiums. Once this occurred, many life insurance offices began requiring doctors to group candidates into classes ranging from 'unexceptionable' to 'inferior.' Although doctors complied with these new instructions, they did so reluctantly. The Equity & Law's medical adviser argued that 'we cannot classify': it was 'in the estimation we form of the individual before us that we can best do our work.' Another insurance doctor complained that 'in most cases of defect there is such a variety of influences at work, and so interwoven, that it would be practically impossible even for Actuaries to make any sort of classification that would be at all satisfactory.'[9] Nor were actuaries inclined to provide doctors with data that might have helped them classify more precisely, since they assumed the medical profession to be incapable of using (or generating) such data effectively. The result was to blunt the doctors' urge to normalize lives at the individual level without enabling them to normalize those same lives through a process of rigorous classification.

Normal Curves

If insurance doctors only grudgingly classified, actuaries classified as a matter of course. The philosopher Henry Mansel, writing in 1860, stated what had by that time become a staple of life insurance marketing: 'The actuary of an insurance company, if he were to predict the duration of life of any one individual on the books of his office, would in all probability guess wrong ... But if the same experiment is tried on a sufficiently large scale, opposite errors will counteract each other, and the general approximate result attains almost to a moral certainty.'[10] This formulation was central to insurance marketing because it combined a reason why people should desire to insure their lives (no individual, not even an actuary, could be certain when he or she would die) with a reason why they should trust insurance companies to pay when that uncertain hour arrived (premiums were based on the law of large numbers). For the large majority of customers who passed their medical examination as 'first class' or 'average' lives, finding a price to cover the risk of premature death was a simple matter of looking up their age on premium tables, which actuaries refined by compiling new data sets throughout the nineteenth century. The fact that actuaries spent much less time generating relevant statistics for doubtful and inferior lives set them apart from most other Victorians who made a career out of appealing to statistical laws.

The large majority of the time and money that life insurers spent gathering vital statistics concerned the class of people whom they deemed to be insurable at standard rates. To find a price that would cover the risk this group posed, actuaries sought data on the mortality of a healthy subset of humanity. Initially, they collected this from towns that they deemed to be healthier than most: first Northampton, which (in one actuary's words) was 'a small central and healthy borough town, which in itself combines many of the advantages of both town and country,' then, from the 1820s, Carlisle, which yielded mortality data that Augustus De Morgan deemed to be 'the most correct representative of healthy life in England which exists.'[11] By the 1850s actuaries turned from using healthy towns as proxies for their medically certified customers to mining their own policy registers for mortality data. In 1869 twenty firms combined to produce the 'Healthy Males' (or H^M) table, charting the mortality of more than 130,000 men whom doctors had deemed to be sufficiently average to pay standard premiums. This was followed in 1901 by the O^M table, which was also limited to healthy male customers but this time encompassed nearly a million lives from sixty companies.

When actuaries began processing the data they had collected on insured lives, they looked for regular distributions and interpreted these as naturally occurring statistical laws. The main practical use of such laws, which (according to one actuary in 1867) approached 'Newton's discovery of the law of gravitation' in their claims to certainty, was to help actuaries smooth their raw data into curves and thereby map them onto premiums that increased with age in even increments. In their Newtonian pretensions, these mortality curves were similar to the 'normal curves' that contemporary statisticians were starting to generate – most famously the curve that gave birth to Adolphe Quetelet's 'average man.' Life insurance companies directly applied variants of Quetelet's approach in assessing risk, starting with his favourite example of the normal distribution of height among a random selection of men and extending to mean values for insurance candidates' pulse and for the specific gravity of their urine.[12]

What Quetelet actually said about the average man, however – that his 'qualities were developed in due proportion, in perfect harmony, alike removed from excess or defect of every kind' – was much closer to doctors' conceptions of 'normal health' than to actuaries' working definitions of 'healthy enough.' The crucial difference was that while Quetelet valorized the mean, insurance companies worked outward in both directions from the mean until (in the direction of poor health) they finally reached a class of lives that they deemed to be uninsurable. A similar gap separated what counted as normal for insurance companies from later adaptations of Quetelet's average man, which appeared in the realms of both social hygiene and eugenics. As Ian Hacking has observed, these late Victorian exercises in 'taming chance' avoided the statistical fatalism that was inherent in Quetelet's conception in one of two ways. In the first case, statisticians identified pathological classes in society and tried to alter the statistical laws they obeyed by changing their living conditions and behaviour. In the second, statisticians focused on people who occupied the 'tails of the distribution' and sought, by manipulating their relative success at breeding, to shift the mean towards the tail that approached perfection.[13]

Each of these projects viewed the life insurance industry as a potential ally in their respective efforts to apply statistics to the improvement of mankind. The social hygienist A.J. Hume, for instance, called on insurance companies to 'have a voice in county, municipal, and legislative councils in so far as health is concerned,' and G.W. Hambleton, the president of the Polytechnic Physical Development Society, urged them to 'become powerful agents in the promotion of national physique and public health.'[14] The eugenics pioneer Francis Galton, for his part, asked insurers in 1887 'to combine in order to obtain a collection of completed cases for at least two generations' to help determine the effect of heredity on disease. When the actuary William Palin Elderton suggested in 1902 that such an effort was feasible, Galton drew up a circular citing 'a serious actuarial need, namely of better data than are now available for computing the influence of family and personal antecedents on the longevity and health of individuals.' Such a study, he hoped, 'would be especially serviceable for my own inquiries into what the University of London has now recognised under the title of "National Eugenics."'[15]

Besides coveting insurance companies' resources (whether financial or statistical), social hygienists and eugenicists hoped to tap into their potential to regulate their customers' lives. The Manchester physician G.H. Darwin proposed that insurers could give all their customers 'a small pamphlet' containing rules regarding 'the upkeep of the body' and 'sanitary regulations of a simple character, according to which the home should be managed.' Hume similarly hoped that insurance companies would issue 'a short Code of Rules by means of which longevity is to be attained ... to every accepted life along with the policy' and would exact 'some pledge for future conduct' upon admission. Defenders of eugenics also hoped to enlist life insurers as allies, this time by amending their system of classifying lives to reward those who exceeded the merely average. James Barr, a Liverpool physician and Eugenics Society vice president, called for special treatment of 'unexceptionable lives' who were 'muscular and proportionally developed' and of 'long-lived stock.'[16]

It is possible to find some fellow travellers in the insurance industry who recognized its potential to assist in the goals of either social hygiene or eugenics. Henry Porter, an assistant actuary at the Alliance, urged insurers to 'take their share' in 'the work of sanitary, political, and moral improvement' that was under way in the 1850s. Two generations later, the Eagle Star and British Dominions Insurance Company issued a *Guide to Health* as part of a 'Household Series' of pamphlets, which taught (among other things) that although 'disease germs are always floating about in the atmosphere,' it was 'possible, by means of disinfectants, to destroy them while they are still outside the body.'[17] Eugenic ideas, at least in the most general sense of favouring hereditary over environmental aspects of disease, had a wide currency among most actuaries, who were convinced that family history was an important indicator of risk. A few actuaries went further than this, and personally took part in the eugenics movement. Besides Elderton, whose sister Ethel worked at Galton's Eugenics Record Office, the Scottish Life secretary Lewis Orr spoke to the Eugenics Society in 1913 regarding the 'identity of interest between Eugenic and Actuarial Science.'[18]

Yet such support among life insurance actuaries for social hygiene and eugenics had narrow limits. In the case of social hygiene, this was because the target population of most public health reforms was a class of people that insurance companies already excluded and hence had little interest in improving. The Scottish Amicable's manager argued that sanitary reform only meant 'prolonging weakly lives a short time longer, and in the process of nursing them deteriorating the lives of the mothers.' As for eugenics, even Orr admitted that the actuary was 'at once a cold critic and a warm friend' to that movement, since he 'looks upon human life ... with a more restricted range of vision.'[19] In both these cases, the more basic issue separating life insurance from social hygiene or eugenics was that it was a profitable business seeking to insure normal lives, as opposed to a (usually unprofitable) project seeking to normalize pathological lives. Any hoped-for alliance between eugenics and insurance died on the vine, and only industrial insurance companies, which had a direct financial stake in improving the health of their working-class customers, gave any support to social hygiene projects. Even these firms ran afoul of reformers in other ways, by enabling working people to pay for costly funerals instead of siding with reformers in advocating the reallocation of their scarce resources into more nutritious meals or new shoes for their children.[20]

Life Insurance, Risk, and Gambling

As François Ewald reminds us, insurance literally invented risk, at least in an etymological sense: he traces the term to 'the Italian word *risco* which meant "that which cuts," hence "reef" and consequently "risk to cargo on the high seas."' Ewald goes on to argue that the insurer 'produces risks' by convincing people to reconceive all events as accidents instead of feeling 'obliged to submit resignedly to the blows of fortune.' The creation of risk where none was previously perceived to exist had major economic and social consequences. From a strictly economic perspective, it created a huge potential demand for the risk-spreading technologies of insurance: if everything was subject to accidents, everything could be insured. From a social perspective, it created an ongoing symbiotic relationship linking insurance, risk, and gambling: a heady brew that perpetually invented new forms of anxiety and pleasure as insurers continually discovered how to attach money values to newly defined risks. Although all these risks were calculable (to at least some extent), and hence 'radically distinct from a bet or a lottery,' policyholders did not always appreciate this distinction – nor was it always in the insurer's interest to emphasize it.[21]

In his account of the rise of life insurance in early eighteenth-century London, Geoffrey Clark has depicted the risk-induced anxiety and gambling-induced pleasure that it generated as part of a common 'consciousness about the possibilities of establishing civic virtue in a commercial society.' He associates this with a 'pre-actuarial phase' that gave way after 1750 to a regime in which policyholders were 'reduced from being equal and self-governing proprietors of their societies to being corporate customers.' Both the rise of new governance structures (joint-stock insurance companies and mutuals with tighter executive controls) and the passage of the Gambling Act in 1774 (which required all policyholders to prove insurable interest) assisted in this transition. Clark claims that this transition did not entail a complete victory of the 'prudential' over the 'speculative' side of life insurance, but rather a 'thoroughgoing attempt to sunder activities that had previously been carried out side by side within a common domain and to consign them to different legal and moral spheres.'[22]

To the extent that such attempts succeeded in the nineteenth century, the segregation of prudence and speculation had the effect of strengthening the power of each in its own sphere. Insurance companies pinned prudence to the principle of 'safety in numbers,' both in the communitarian sense mentioned above and in the alleged certainty of the laws of mortality. Together, these were deemed sufficient to enable the Victorian breadwinner to trade his dependents' uncertain future for one in which the life office would care for them in his absence. Once prudence had been thus disposed of, speculation was free to perform its good work of enticing people into the market with promises of large bonuses and retaining recalcitrant customers by offering them opportunities to back their own lives against the experts who had set the odds. Like doctors and statisticians, who found ways to work together in life insurance offices by rethinking what qualified as normal, the prudential and speculative sides of life insurance combined in the nineteenth century to create new ways of thinking about life and death.

The willingness and ability of life insurance offices to combine prudence and speculation in the same institution signified another partial departure from the perfectionist aims of other Victorian instruments of governmentality. If social hygienists and eugenicists felt frustrated about the failure of insurance to further their normalizing aims, Victorian advocates of social or moral improvement were similarly disappointed whenever they took a close look at how insurers actually went about their business. Victorian novelists registered this disappointment by depicting life insurance offices as bubble companies or abettors of spendthrift debtors, and by continually identifying life insurance with the most sordid sorts of gambling.[23] After the Victorians, these resonances of life insurance persisted, although the accompanying moral condemnation was either

muted or absent. The title character of H.G. Wells's *History of Mr Polly*, for
instance, first defrauds a fire insurance office to escape a hapless marriage, then defrauds a life insurance office to provide financial support for
his supposed widow.[24]

Domesticating Risk

As an emblem of Victorian domesticity, life insurance took its place at
the middle-class hearthside next to the dog-eared Dickens novel and the
purring Persian cat. In the process, it enabled Victorians (in Elaine
Freedgood's words) to 'imagine that danger could be banished from the
domestic scene and relocated in the world outside.' The risk-filled
'world outside,' however, often appeared very close to home in the case
of life insurance, since (if salesmen were to be believed) all that was
necessary to experience danger was to avoid buying insurance. Indeed,
the very fact that insured and uninsured people freely commingled was
a wonderful sales opportunity, since it allowed the insurance agent to
contrast the known financial fates of respective members of these groups
who died prematurely. Since images of safety always coexisted in such
close proximity with images of imminent death, perhaps a more appropriate feline companion for Victorian life insurance than the domestic
cat was the tiger in the Regent's Park Zoo: caged, presently harmless to
the viewer, but formerly capable of striking a deadly blow.[25]

The claim to provide a 'consoling promise of safe and uncomplicated
places ... in a dangerous world' – which Freedgood has identified as a
'Victorian moment of modernity' – was brandished in the very names
of many nineteenth-century life offices: Absolute Security, Aegis (which
meant, in the 1830s, a 'protection, or impregnable defense'), Anchor,
Argus, Ark, Asylum, Defender, Guardian, Palladium (the image of
Pallas, a goddess who guaranteed the safety of Troy), Preserver,
Protector, Refuge, and Safety.[26] Such offices based their assurances of
security on the twin pillars of voluntary association and scientific certainty. According to one mid-century tract, life insurance worked by
joining 'a combination of means and a brotherly participation of risks'
to the proven 'regularity in the ratio of mortality.' In tandem, these two
elements allegedly enabled policyholders to obtain what the Mutual
Life's founders called 'that great desideratum in Life Assurance, a full
and fair return, in proportion to the premiums paid, with the utmost
safety to the assured.'[27]

Insurance promoters who promised utmost safety as a reward for the
regular payment of premiums predicted the opposite for breadwinners

who failed to insure their lives. As discussed in chapter 5, prospectuses and pamphlets routinely recited litanies of misfortunes likely to befall the uninsured, including cholera, typhus, influenza, railway accidents, mining explosions, and shipwrecks – which were matched in pathos only by the harrowing destitution awaiting their dependents. Although such warnings had at least some effect in enhancing the anxiety of a culture already prone to seek out safe places, it is also likely that they fell on deaf ears more often than not. Someone who listened to a salesman's account of potential death and destitution without acting on it hardly counted as a consumer of insurance as a risk-domestication device. A more tangible sense in which life insurance offices created or reinforced perceptions of risk concerned the many people who actually wanted to insure their lives but were turned away. It was with this in mind that insurance doctors strategized about how to console candidates who had assumed they were insurable, only to be informed of a previously undetected malady.

A different juxtaposition of safety and risk occurred when an insured party decided to travel abroad. In these cases, the 'world outside' was not merely a rhetorical device that salesmen could use to attract business: it was literally the outside world, with risks to life and limb that actuaries only gradually and incompletely tamed over the course of the nineteenth century by means of better statistics and longer underwriting experience. Foreign travel was one of the only activities that carried a surcharge on Victorian insurance policies after they had been issued, without which payment the policy was void. (As critics of travel extras liked to point out, someone could go to great lengths to endanger his life without endangering his policy, but only if he did so without leaving home.) Life insurance offices singled out travel partly because it was easy to prove that someone had died abroad and partly to avoid the moral hazard of people insuring their lives in anticipation of a dangerous journey. From the insured's point of view, they could either pay the surcharge as a tangible reminder of the white man's burden, or they could avoid informing the company of their travel plans and take the risk of being discovered dead in Cairo or Calcutta.

As these examples make clear, safety and risk existed in close symbiosis in life insurance marketing and practice throughout the nineteenth century: one was impossible to conceive without the other. Salesmen occasionally paired the spread of life insurance with a decline in destitution, as with one prediction of 'fewer beggars in the world, fewer foundlings, fewer criminals, more contented industry, and greatly increased solaridity [sic] between class and class.' Such pronouncements inevitably appeared in the future tense, however, since a full eradication of risk would have made it all but impossible to sell insurance. More generally, insurance marketing relied on the inevitably incomplete regulation of life, since the survival of untamed chance created the imaginary space in which accidents were always possible. As the *Policy-holder* concluded in 1884, 'until the duration of human life can be regulated, life insurance will still retain the power of benefiting mankind.'[28]

Life Insurance as Gambling

British life insurance straddled what Viviana Zelizer has identified as a division in the moral economy of risk-taking between 'rational speculation that dealt with already existent risks' and 'pure gambling which created artificial risk.' It mainly occupied the latter side of this divide for much of the eighteenth century, infamously fuelling the morbid aristocratic pastime of wagering on the demise of at-risk strangers, until the Gambling Act of 1774 intervened by requiring all beneficiaries to have a legitimate financial interest (either as a dependant or creditor) in the life insured. Even in the formal sense defined by this statute, many insurance transactions continued to occupy a legal grey area into the 1850s, since it was common practice for creditors to insure a debtor's life and receive complete or partial repayment without giving up the policy. Similarly, policyholders who could no longer keep up their payments routinely sold their policies at auction, where third parties openly speculated on the chance that the claim would exceed their bid plus the future premiums they would have to pay. Although the legal landscape cleared somewhat when a judge ruled in favour of the first practice in 1854, and when life offices liberalized their surrender values sufficiently to reduce the frequency of auctioned policies, this did not stop people from identifying life insurance as a species of gambling in less strictly legal senses of the word.[29]

The fact that people continued to debate this issue into the twentieth century is clear from a series of letters published in the *Times* in 1907. The exchange originated in an editorial comparing limerick contests in the tabloid press, gambling at Monte Carlo, and 'gambling on the Stock Exchange.' To this list a correspondent added life insurance, since (he claimed) paying £25 for a £1,000 policy was 'nothing but a bet by the insurance company of 39 to 1 that the insured will live for 12 months.' Another writer compared life insurance to 'a "hedging" bet,' akin to placing a smaller bet on one horse in order to defray the potential loss from a larger bet on a different horse – in 'the same spirit,' he concluded, 'I have insured my life, and wish to lose the bet at fairly long odds which I shall still win if I die within the next few days.' This line of reasoning was guilty of comparing apples and oranges, insisted a final correspondent, who anticipated Zelizer's distinction between pre-existing and artificial risks. In life insurance, he argued, 'the original bet is not under our control; nature insists on our staking heavily on continuance of life.'[30]

A different sort of Victorian argument that opposed life insurance to 'pure gambling' pointed to the winners and losers in the two transactions. One insurance promoter in 1842 contrasted 'the immense prizes which [a man] may by bare possibility obtain from a lottery' with 'the steadiness and certainty' of an insurance policy's returns, and concluded that this was what removed it 'from the character of a ruinous gambling scheme.' William Farr made the same point when he called life insurance 'a Lottery in reverse, as for unequal sums it sells equal prizes.' Central to this argument was a carefully scripted history of probability theory, the 'earliest aliment' of which (according to Augustus De Morgan) had been 'cards and dice,' but which had since become 'generally recognised in all the more delicate branches of experimental science.' The very fact that life insurance took advantage of this more refined doctrine of chances, which rested in calculable laws of large numbers, placed it at the vanguard of 'the increase of education and occupation' before which an earlier 'universal rage for games of chance' had subsided.[31]

For people who insisted that life insurance was the opposite of gambling, it made sense to fold gamblers into the same at-risk category they reserved for the uninsured. Hence the chairman of the British Equitable urged in 1880 that since the uninsured 'leaves the fate of his dear ones to chance,' he resembled 'the gambler who trusts his fortune to the turn of the dice, or luck of cards.' The problem with this way of thinking was that it preached to the converted, who were likely to provide for their dependents without needing to hear such arguments. In the real world of life insurance marketing, salesmen were willing and able to descend from their moral high ground if it would get unrepentant gamblers to buy their product. James Barr, whose eugenic ambitions for life insurance apparently did not get in the way of his appreciation of human nature, had this to say about the life agent's 'noble work': 'You interest men in their own lives and in the lives of their families ... It is, however, the great uncertainties of the life of the individual which often enables you to induce him to take a hand in the game; because man is essentially a gambler, and it is this feeling that he may score off the insurance companies ... that induces him to insure.'[32]

Salesmen who wanted to associate life insurance with gambling found all the arguments they needed in the bonus, which by raising the issue of investment enabled them to embark down the slippery slope that started with 'rational speculation.' When soliciting customers who were 'fond of excitement,' urged a broker in 1904, the 'very uncertainty' of bonuses added 'a zest to life compared to which Kaffir Ketchup is insipid.'[33] The bonus, in this scenario, provided the spice that made the sacrifice of providing for one's dependents (or providing collateral for one's creditor) easier to digest. Although some of the speculative appeal of the bonus mirrored the parallel speculation that transpired on the stock market, by far the larger portion of it went back to the basic wager embedded in the insurance contract itself. As discussed in chapter 6, virtually no life insurance office carelessly invested its customers' premiums, since to do so would have departed too radically from their claim to act as responsible breadwinners in the insured's afterlife. Instead, life insurance offices found numerous ways to encourage customers to back their own lives against the field of their fellow policyholders.

The most obvious way to do this was with deferred or compound bonuses, which rewarded policyholders who lived longer with larger accumulations of surplus capital. When the Caledonian announced a scheme in 1891 that deferred the bonus on term policies until the insured had survived two-thirds of the term, the *Bankers' Magazine* attributed its popularity to 'the element in human nature which disposes every individual to regard his own chances of life favourably.' Critics were always ready with the response that such policies were 'not Life Insurances in the highest sense, but partake more of the nature of speculative lotteries,' as one broker scoffed in 1883, but this did not prevent 'tontine'-style insurance from continuing to be a popular option throughout the nineteenth century.[34] Actuaries were typically willing to devise this sort of policy, at least in part because it offered one of the best solutions to the problem of healthier lives lapsing at a higher rate than unhealthy ones – since 'backing one's life' required the continued payment of premiums. The same reasoning applied to endowment insurance, which invited policyholders to hedge the bet that they would die within a pre-specified term with a second gamble that they would live long enough to collect an annuity long after that term ended.

Confronted with these many associations between life insurance and gambling, most Victorians were quite content to have it both ways. The Law Union's medical officer urged that his line of work was 'a very moral thing, and is very charitable; but there is no doubt it is a form of gambling ... and we all go to the office, and back lives instead of horses.' This sort of admission was possible because of the inevitable lack of information that came with every life insurance transaction, which kept people sufficiently in the dark about their chances of living or dying to gamble on those prospects – much in the same way that an inevitable lack of regulation made the world sufficiently uncertain to attract people to the life office. And as *Chambers's Edinburgh Journal* concluded in 1852, getting people to insure was the important thing: 'If a man chooses to regard life-insurance as a wager made by the insurers concerning who shall live longest, and if he finds excitement under the idea that it is betting or gambling, there certainly are the elements of such ... We cannot eradicate men's tendencies, but we can sometimes bend them.'[35]

It was with this sort of thing in mind that Gregory, the death-obsessed insurance clerk in Julian Barnes's novel *Staring at the Sun*, observes that 'life insurance ... had its aptness.' It had the power to evoke 'greed and calculation' among customers, he discovered, when they learned of 'all this money they would get in exchange for such a simple thing as being dead': 'Of course there was much euphemism involved, much disguise of a policy as a pension; but when it came down to it, what people were trying to do was get the best deal they could out of being dead ... Even those who admitted that they themselves would not actually get the money could still be entranced by the transaction. Death may come and steal me away, but oh boy, what a daft move it is on his part, because it leaves the wife rolling in money. If only Death had realized *that*, he wouldn't have been so greedy.' Gregory concludes by musing that people who 'didn't seem at all surprised to be alive in the first place ... made the best of it; and when departing, they struck the best deal they could. How strange. How admirable, he supposed, but how strange.'[36]

Put this way, of course, neither death nor life was such a simple thing. As life insurance emerged in the nineteenth century, at least part of its strangeness derived from the fact that it brought so many strands of modern life together into one place, yet created a product that defied any easily articulable definition of the modern condition. When prospective policyholders met with insurance salesmen they heard horrific stories about death and destitution, only to be assured that perfect safety awaited them if they filled in a proposal form and paid a visit to the doctor. On these forms and at the doctor's office they encountered daunting lists of potential pathologies, only to be assured by the actuary (in four out of five cases) that they were normal enough to qualify for insurance at standard rates. Finally, in deciding whether or not to pay extra for a bonus, they faced a choice between the pleasure of speculation, the security of a sure bet, or a combination of the two. None of these experiences taken on its own, and all of them taken together, signified life insurance for the average Victorian policyholder. To a large extent they signified modernity as well.

APPENDIX 1

Life insurance offices with a head office in Great Britain, 1800–1914 (minimum fifteen years in existence). Constitution type: M (mutual) or P (proprietary, i.e. with shareholders).

Office	Type	Location	Opened*	Closed (acquired by)
Aberdeen Fire & Life[1]	P	Aberdeen	1825	1889 (North Brit. & Merc.)
Aberdeen Mutual	M	Aberdeen	1831	1853
Albion	P	London	1805	1858 (Eagle)
Alfred	P	London	1839	1858 (Eagle)
Alliance	P	London	1824	1960 (Sun)
Amicable	M	London	1706	1866 (Norwich Union Life)
Anchor Life	P	London	1842	1857 (Bank of London)
Argus	P	London	1833	1888 (Imperial)
Asylum	P	London	1824	1857 (London Assurance)
Atlas	P	London	1808	1959 (Royal Exchange)
Birmingham Life	P	Birmingham	1810	1826 (Provident)
Blue Ribbon[2]	M	Birmingham	1883	
Bristol Union	P	Bristol	1818	1844 (Imperial)
Britannia	P	London	1837	1865 (Briton Medical)
Britannic	P	London	1866	
British Commercial	P	London	1820	1860 (British Nation)
British Empire	P	London	1820	1845 (Licensed Victuallers)
British Empire Mutual	M	London	1847	1902 (Pelican)
British Equitable	P	London	1854	1924 (Royal Exchange)
British Legal	P	Glasgow	1863	1922 (Britannic)
British Life	P	Glasgow	1896	1958 (Reliance Mutual)

Office	Type	Location	Opened*	Closed (acquired by)
British Mutual	M	London	1844	1868 (Prudential)
Briton Life[3]	P	London	1853	1892 (Sun Life)
Caledonian	P	Edinburgh	1833	1957 (Guardian)
Century	P	London	1885	1917 (Friends' Provident)
Church of England[4]	P	London	1840	1893 (Imperial)
City of Glasgow	P	Glasgow	1838	1913 (Scot. Union & Nat.)
Clergy Mutual	M	London	1829	1918 (London Life)
Clerical Medical & General	P	London	1824	2001 (HBOS)
Colonial	P	Edinburgh	1846	1866 (Standard)
Commercial (Ireland)	P	Dublin	1799	1826 (Guardian)
Commercial Union[5]	P	London	1862	
Consolidated	P	London	1846	1865 (Prudential)
Co-operative	M	Manchester	1867	
Crown	P	London	1825	1892 (Law Union)
Dublin Widows' Fund	M	Dublin	1837	1881
Eagle	P	London	1807	1917 (British Dominions)
Economic	P[6]	London	1823	1911 (Alliance)
Edinburgh & Glasgow[7]	P	Edinburgh	1838	1968 (Nat.-Niederlanden)
Edinburgh Life	P	Edinburgh	1823	1918 (Commercial Union)
Emperor	P	London	1852	1885 (Whittington)
English & Scottish Law	P	London	1839	1918 (Eagle Star Brit. Dom.)
Equitable	M	London	1762	

Office	Type	Location	Opened*	Closed (acquired by)
Equity & Law	P	London	1844	
European	P	London	1819	1858 (People's Provident)
Family Endowment	P	London	1835	1861 (Albert)
Farmers & General[8]	P	London	1840	1888 (Alliance)
Freemasons & General[9]	P	London	1838	1869
Friends' Provident	M	Bradford	1832	
General Benefit	P	London	1820	1854
Globe	P	London	1803	1864 (Liverpool & London)
Great Britain Mutual	M	London	1844	1882 (National of Ireland)
Gresham	P	London	1848	
Guardian	P	London	1821	
Hand in Hand	M	London	1836	1905 (Commercial Union)
Hibernian	P	Dublin	1808	1838
Hope	P	London	1807	1844 (Imperial)
Imperial	P	London	1820	1902 (Alliance)
Imperial Union	P	London	1866	1881
Industrial of Great Britain	P	London	1866	1890 (Lond. Edin. & Glasg.)
Lancashire	P	Manchester	1852	1901 (Royal)
Law Life	P	London	1823	1910 (Phoenix)
Law Property & Life	P	London	1850	1898
Law Union[10]	P	London	1854	1919 (London & Lancs.)
Leeds & Yorkshire	P	Leeds	1824	1864 (Liverpool & London)

Office	Type	Location	Opened*	Closed (acquired by)
Legal & Commercial	P	London	1834	1857 (Victoria)
Legal & General	P	London	1835	
Licensed Victuallers[11]	P	London	1835	1857 (Liverpool & London)
Liverpool[12]	P	Liverpool	1836	1919 (Royal)
Liverpool Victoria Legal	M[13]	Liverpool	1843	1913 (Commercial Union)
London Assurance	P	London	1809	1965 (Sun Alliance)
London & Edinburgh & Glasgow	P	London	1881	1910 (Pearl)
London & Lancashire Life[14]	P	London	1862	1961 (Royal)
London & Provincial Law	P	London	1845	1883 (Guardian)
London & Scottish	P	London	1862	1923 (Northern)
London & Southwark	P	London	1864	1879 (London & Lancs.)
London Equitable	M	London	1784	1863 (British Nation)
London Life	M	London	1806	
Manchester Life	P	Manchester	1824	1846 (Pelican)
Marine & General	M	London	1852	
Masonic & General	P	London	1868	1886
Medical Invalid & General	P	London	1841	1860 (Albert)
Metropolitan	P	London	1835	1928 (London Life)
Midland Counties	P	Lincoln	1853	1892 (Royal)
Minerva	P	London	1836	1864 (Standard)
Mitre	P	London	1846	1869
Mutual Life	M	London	1834	1896 (National Life)
National Assurance & Investment	P	London	1844	1861 (Waterloo)

Office	Type	Location	Opened*	Closed (acquired by)
National Endowment[15]	P	London	1837	1866 (Eagle)
National Guardian	P	London	1865	1902 (National Union)
National Industrial	P	London	1854	1880
National (Ireland)	P	Dublin	1822	1904 (Yorkshire)
National Life[16]	M	London	1830	
National Loan Fund[17]	P	London	1837	1868 (Hercules)
National Provident	M	London	1835	
North British[18]	P	Edinburgh	1823	1959 (Commercial Union)
North of England	P	Sheffield	1844	1858 (Liverpool & London)
North of Scotland[19]	P	Aberdeen	1836	1968 (Commercial Union)
Norwich Union Life	M	Norwich	1808	(see note 5)
Nottingham & Derby	P	Nottingham	1832	1869 (Norwich Union Life)
Palladium	P	London	1824	1856 (Eagle)
Patriotic	P	Dublin	1824	1906 (Sun Life)
Pelican[20]	P	London	1797	1910 (Phoenix)
People's Provident[21]	P	London	1854	1872
Pioneer	P	London	1891	1971 (Slater Walker)
Positive Government Security	P	London	1870	1896 (British Empire Mut.)
Preserver	P	London	1844	1870
Progressive	P	London	1891	1909 (Lond. Edin. & Glasg.)
Promoter	P	London	1826	1862 (Guardian)
Protestant Dissenters & General[22]	P	London	1839	1924 (General Accident)
Provident	P	London	1806	1906 (Alliance)
Provident Clerks'[23]	M	London	1840	

Office	Type	Location	Opened*	Closed (acquired by)
Provincial	P	Wrexham	1852	1889 (Alliance)
Prudential	P	London	1848	
Queen	P	Liverpool	1857	1891 (Royal)
Refuge	P	Manchester	1864	
Reliance Mutual	M	London	1840	1893 (Norwich Union Life)
Rock	P	London	1806	1909 (Law Union)
Royal	P	Liverpool	1845	
Royal Exchange	P	London	1721	1968 (Guardian)
Royal Exchange (Ireland)	P	Dublin	1799	1822 (National of Ireland)
Royal London	M	London	1835	
Royal Naval & Military	P	London	1837	1866 (European)
Salvation Army	M	London	1867	1972 (Wesleyan & General)
Sceptre	P	London	1864	1917 (Eagle & Brit. Dom.)
Scottish Amicable	M	Glasgow	1826	1998 (Prudential)
Scottish Commercial	P	Glasgow	1865	1880 (Lancashire)
Scottish Equitable	M	Edinburgh	1831	
Scottish Imperial	P	Glasgow	1865	1906 (Norwich Union Life)
Scottish Legal	M	Glasgow	1852	2007 (Scottish Friendly)
Scottish Life	P	Edinburgh	1881	2001 (Royal London)
Scottish Metropolitan	P	Edinburgh	1874	1912 (London & Lancashire)
Scottish National	P	Edinburgh	1845	1879 (Scottish Union)

Office	Type	Location	Opened*	Closed (acquired by)
Scottish Provident	M	Edinburgh	1837	
Scottish Temperance[24]	P	Glasgow	1883	
Scottish Union[25]	P	Edinburgh	1824	1959 (Norwich Union Life)
Scottish Widows' Fund	M	Edinburgh	1815	
Solicitors & General	P	London	1846	1866 (Eagle)
Sovereign	P	London	1845	1890 (Sun Life)
Standard Life	P	Edinburgh	1824	
Star	P	London	1843	1917 (Eagle & Brit. Dom.)
Suffolk & General County	P	Ipswich	1834	1850 (Alliance)
Sun Life	P	London	1810	
United Kent	M	Maidstone	1824	1901 (Royal)
United Kingdom Life	P	London	1834	1862 (North British)
United Kingdom Life & Guarantee	P	London	1866	1889 (Lond. Edin. & Glasg.)
United Kingdom Total Abstinence[26]	M		1840	
Union	P	London	1813	1907 (Commercial Union)
Universal	P	London	1834	1901 (North Brit. & Merc.)
University	P	London	1825	1919 (Equitable)
Victoria Life[27]	P	London	1838	1865 (Standard)
Victoria Mutual[28]	M	London	1860	1909 (Norwich Union Life)
Wesleyan & General	P	Birmingham	1841	

Office	Type	Location	Opened*	Closed (acquired by)
West of England	P	Exeter	1807	1894 (Commercial Union)
Western Counties	M	Plymouth	1861	1889 (British Empire Mut.)
Western Life	P	London	1841	1865 (Albert)
Westminster & General	P	London	1835	1906 (Guardian)
Westminster Life	P	London	1792	1863 (Guardian)
Whittington	P	London	1855	1891 (National Life)
Yorkshire Fire & Life	P	York	1824	1967 (General Accident)
Yorkshire Provident	P	Burnley	1870	1906 (United Provident)

* For fire and life offices, refers to the year in which the life branch opened.
Sources: Insurance Directory and Yearbook (1987): 199–221; Return 1845; Abstract Return 1856 and 1863; Return of Names 1864–97; Walford I–VI passim; CWP passim; Post Magazine 46 (1885): 38, 50, 62–3, 74, 86; Hutchison 1846: 75–80; Bridges 1842: 23; Drew 1928: 52–4.

[1] Changed name to Scottish Provincial, 1852.
[2] Changed name to Abstainers' & General, 1890, and to Beacon, 1933.
[3] Changed name to Briton Medical & General, 1863.
[4] Changed name to England, 1892.
[5] Changed name to CGNU, 1999; changed name to Aviva, 2002.
[6] Converted to mutual office, 1844.
[7] Changed name to Life Association of Scotland, 1841.
[8] Changed name to Royal Farmers, 1843.
[9] Changed name to Albert, 1849.
[10] Changed name to Law Union & Crown, 1892, and to Law Union & Rock, 1909.
[11] Changed name to Monarch, 1857.
[12] Changed name to Liverpool & London, 1847, and to Liverpool & London & Globe, 1864.
[13] Converted to joint stock company, 1907.
[14] Changed name to London & Scottish, 1919.
[15] Changed name to National Mercantile, 1842.
[16] Changed name to National Mutual, 1896.
[17] Changed name to International, 1855.
[18] Changed name to North British & Mercantile, 1862.
[19] Changed name to Northern, 1848.
[20] Changed name to Pelican & British Empire Life Office (PABELO), 1902.
[21] Changed name to European, 1859.
[22] Changed name to General, 1847.

[23] Changed name to Provident Mutual, 1917.
[24] Changed name to Scottish Mutual, 1952.
[25] Changed name to Scottish Union & National, 1879.
[26] Changed name to United Kingdom Temperance & General, 1847.
[27] Changed name to Victoria & Legal & Commercial, 1858.
[28] Changed name to Victoria Assurance 1881.

APPENDIX 2.1

Agents' occupation by head office location (%) (Life/fire & life only)

	Occupation						
Scotland, 1878	A	B	E	L	M	O	S
London (1,082)	4.8	9.2	3.7	20.4	16.7	4.0	19.2
Provincial/U.S. (637)	8.5	16.6	4.1	23.7	18.6	3.0	16.9
Scottish (2,349)	5.6	26.8	3.0	28.2	12.5	5.0	15.2
Total (3,634)	5.5	19.6	3.7	24.1	14.8	4.6	17.4
North of England, 1875–77	A	B	E	L	M	O	S
London (1,245)	7.8	4.7	6.8	20.9	20.2	3.8	17.0
Provincial (730)	4.4	5.1	7.8	23.2	19.2	5.5	22.1
Scottish (740)	8.0	8.5	5.9	19.2	21.6	4.1	13.4
Total (2,510)	6.6	5.3	6.8	19.3	20.6	4.3	17.8

Note: since some agents worked for life insurance offices from more than one region, the numbers listed in parentheses exceed the total number of agents.
Sources: Slater's 1878; Slater's 1875; Slater's 1877.
A = accountant, bank accountant, cashier; B = banker; E: auctioneer, estate agent, factor, house agent, house factor; L: advocate, solicitor, writer; M = agent, bleacher, builder, brewer, cabinet maker, commission agent, dealer, dyer, hatter, manufacturer, merchant, miller, rope maker, ship owner, spinner, stockbroker; O = poor inspector, postmaster, registrar, revenue clerk, sheriff, stamp distributor; S = bookseller, chemist, draper, grocer, ironmonger, tailor, wine merchant.

APPENDIX 2.2

Insurance offices (including non-life) and life insurance offices per agent, by selected occupations, Scotland and North of England, 1875–8 (%)

Occupation of agent	Insurance offices per agent					Life insurance offices per agent			
	1	2	>2	Average	n	1	2	>2	Average
Bankers (886)	51.3	33.5	15.1	1.68	(836)	66.9	27.6	5.5	1.39
Lawyers (1,420)	58.9	28.4	12.7	1.59	(1,344)	71.9	21.9	6.3	1.36
Accountants (410)	60.2	23.7	16.1	1.63	(366)	77.9	18.1	4.1	1.28
Merchants/ mfrs (1,196)	77.7	15.6	5.8	1.32	(1,039)	87.8	10.1	2.1	1.15
Shopkeepers (1,204)	81.5	15.5	3.1	1.24	(1,069)	90.0	9.2	0.7	1.11
All agents (6,886)	69.0	22.3	3.8	1.28	(6,144)	80.3	16.3	3.4	1.23

Sources: as in Appendix 2.1.

APPENDIX 2.3

Scottish agents employed by selected companies, 1878

| | Occupation | | | | | | |
Company	A	B	L	M	S	Total	Towns*
Briton	3.7	1.5	10.4	13.4	26.1	134	61
Caledonian	6.3	32.4	34.8	6.8	11.1	207	126
Imperial	4.0	16.1	22.6	21.8	6.5	124	53
Life Association of Scotland	6.8	32.6	30.3	9.5	14.9	221	157
Liverpool & London & Globe	8.8	22.5	29.4	23.5	17.7	102	67
North British & Mercantile	6.4	34.2	35.9	10.4	7.4	298	152
Northern	6.8	28.1	22.3	12.0	10.6	292	153
Queen	10.6	11.5	21.2	23.0	15.0	113	52
Royal	7.1	17.0	21.4	19.2	19.2	182	129
Standard Life	2.4	37.0	35.6	12.0	8.7	208	131
Total	5.5	19.6	24.1	14.8	17.4	3,634	263

Note: Abbreviations and sources as in Appendix 2.1.
*Number of Scottish towns with agents.

APPENDIX 2.4

Northern English agents employed by selected companies, 1878

Company	A	B	E	L	M	S	Total	Towns*
				Occupation				
Alliance	10.2	3.0	10.8	22.9	30.7	6.0	166	36
Atlas	5.3	10.5	38.6	12.3	17.5	20.7	57	46
Briton	6.9	0.0	9.2	5.3	6.9	10.3	87	58
Imperial	11.7	8.5	3.2	20.2	21.3	18.1	94	61
Liverpool & London & Globe	3.4	5.4	8.8	25.5	19.6	18.6	204	100
North British & Mercantile	11.7	10.4	9.1	23.4	15.6	15.6	77	42
Royal	3.2	3.8	9.0	14.7	25.6	18.6	156	98
Standard Life	7.9	12.7	0.0	22.2	12.7	15.9	63	41
Star	2.4	4.8	3.6	1.2	18.1	27.7	83	46
Yorkshire	6.4	10.1	5.5	33.0	10.1	22.0	109	86
All Scottish offices	8.0	8.5	5.9	19.2	21.6	13.4	740	117
All English offices	6.7	4.4	6.7	19.0	18.6	18.3	1,995	168
Total	6.6	5.3	6.8	19.3	20.6	17.8	2,510	168

Note: Abbreviations and sources as in Appendix 2.1.

APPENDIX 2.5

Insurance agents' occupation, selected regions and life offices (no. of agents in parentheses)

Regions, years (n agents)	Occupation					
	A	B	E	L	M	S
West Riding 1823 (78)	4.8	0.0	3.7	34.6	23.1	25.3
Gloucestershire 1830 (62)	6.5	6.5	8.1	32.3	4.8	21.0
Ayrshire 1837 (35)	0.0	8.6	0.0	68.6	5.7	10.4
Kent 1840 (72)	1.4	1.4	5.6	2.8	22..2	34.7
Glasgow 1842 (75)	29.3	1.3	0.0	33.3	24.0	2.7
Cork 1856 (68)	4.4	1.5	0.0	36.8	25.0	8.8
South Wales 1859 (124)	4.8	4.0	12.9	17.7	16.1	28.2
East Cornwall 1873 (81)	2.5	4.9	6.2	6.2	23.5	18.5
Yorkshire 1875 (1,591)	6.7	4.3	7.8	18.8	21.1	18.3
Cumberland 1877 (197)	5.6	7.1	5.1	25.9	19.8	18.3
Durham 1877 (444)	7.7	6.1	6.1	16.7	16.4	13.5
Northumberland 1877 (430)	6.3	5.6	4.4	14.7	24.0	17.5
Westmoreland 1877 (63)	3.2	3.2	6.3	20.6	17.5	17.5
Ayrshire 1878 (219)	5.3	25.9	7.0	28.5	15.1	18.9
Berwickshire 1878 (82)	1.2	15.9	6.0	22.0	11.0	35.4
Edinburghshire 1878 (264)	8.7	11.4	3.8	21.2	15.9	10.2
Lanarkshire 1878 (564)	12.1	15.1	6.4	17.2	14.5	9.6
Cardiff 1880 (99)	12.1	5.1	20.2	30.3	13.1	3.0

Life offices, years (n agents)	A	B	C	E	L	M	S
Guardian 1821–30 (254)	na	na	11.1	2.8	17.5	20.5	26.8
Royal Exchange 1848 (555)	na	4.5	na	4.9	17.1	20.2	31.0
Pelican 1850 (281)	na	7.1	na	7.1	33.8	22.4	24.9
Edinburgh Life 1854–65 (433)	5.1	6.9	7.4	8.3	19.2	15.0	20.8
Royal Farmers 1856–73 (865)	4.2	3.2	7.5	13.3	5.7	16.0	19.2
Clerical Medical 1864–5 (123)	4.0	4.0	13.0	7.9	7.1	4.8	20.6
Edinburgh Life 1868 (292)	3.4	1.0	11.3	7.2	7.2	28.1	15.8
Clerical Medical 1876–78 (123)	5.7	10.6	20.3	5.7	17.9	8.1	12.2
Atlas 1897–1907 (5,051)	7.6	5.5	16.8	12.0	10.7	21.1	7.1

Sources: *Baines's Directory for 1823* (West Riding; accessed at http://www.genuki.org.uk/big/eng/YKS); *Pigot's Directory for 1830* (Gloucestershire; accessed at http://www.genuki.org.uk/big/eng/GLS); *Pigot's Ayrshire Directory for 1837* (accessed at http://www.maybole.org/history/Archives/1837directory/Ayr.htm); *Pigot's 1840 Directory* (Kent; accessed at http://freepages.genealogy.rootsweb.com/~shebra); *Post-Office Glasgow Annual Directory* (1842); *Slater's Commercial Directory, 1859* (South Wales) and *Slater's Commercial Directory, 1880* (Cardiff: accessed at http://www.genuki.org.uk/big/wal/GLA); *Slater's 1856 Directory Of Cork* (accessed at http://homepage.tinet.ie/~ridgway); *Kelly's 1873 Directory* (East Cornwall; accessed at http://chrisuphill.tripod.com/kel9.htm); Pearson 2004: 278 (Guardian); Supple 1970: 154 (Royal Exchange); Trebilcock I: 548 (Pelican); EdR, EdMB XIII (Edinburgh Life); RFMB XV–XVIII (Royal Farmers); CMBM XIX, XXIII (Clerical Medical); AtAAB (Atlas).
Note: C = Clerks, other abbreviations as in Appendix 2.1. Agents for Scotland and north of England, 1875–8, as in Appendix 2.2.

APPENDIX 2.6

Agents appointed by the Atlas Assurance Company, 1897–1907, by region and occupation

Region (n agents)	Occupation						
	A	B	C	E	L	M	S
London (1,091)	4.5	6.8	14.9	14.8	4.5	14.9	14.8
Lancashire (703)	11.2	3.7	14.9	13.8	11.2	14.9	13.8
Yorkshire (469)	12.4	3.6	16.2	7.2	12.4	16.2	7.2
Wales (445)	5.8	8.1	23.1	7.9	5.8	23.1	7.9
Scotland (275)	11.6	6.9	17.5	8.7	11.6	17.5	8.7
Ireland (133)	3.8	4.5	12.0	5.3	7.5	30.1	14.3
Other (1,935)	6.9	5.2	14.1	12.7	9.0	18.8	9.7
Total (5,051)	7.6	5.5	15.5	12.0	10.7	21.1	7.1

Source: AtAAB.
Note: Abbreviations as in Appendix 2.1.

APPENDIX 3.1

Approximate annual net new life insurance investments, 1871–1910 (% of total assets)

This table follows Scott (2002), who provides a similar table for 1923–37. These results were reached by subtracting the previous year's asset levels in each class from those listed in Board of Trade returns for each year. This yields net new investment ('purchases minus sale and amortization') with the main distortion being, in Scott's words, 'changes in book values which do not represent capital expenditure or amortization' (2002: 84). (For a critique of this measurement approach see Baker and Collins 2005: 147–8.) All figures are for 'ordinary' (i.e., non-industrial) life offices and branches only. Colonial and foreign securities are national and state or provincial bonds only. Average yield is on total assets, not net new investments; the latter were estimated to yield 0.5% less than the former during most of this period. Yields were typically calculated after deduction of income tax.

Year	Mortgages	Personal loans	British govt	Colonial securities	Foreign securities	Debentures	Company shares	House/ ground rent	Municipal loans	Reversions/ life interests	Other assets	Total (£m)	Avg yield (%)
1882	8.3	-3.2	3.2	27.6	-2.1	16.5	18.4	23.7	-2.3	3.3	6.6	4.39	4.36
1883	31.2	3.6	-5.5	11.4	-0.7	4.3	22.4	2.0	37.3	2.2	-6.4	4.75	4.30
1884	42.0	5.2	-2.7	14.6	-5.6	18.1	3.1	12.1	2.1	-0.4	11.5	3.92	4.34
1885	15.6	2.6	4.4	31.5	-4.0	5.0	9.5	11.8	5.4	7.0	11.1	4.19	4.29
1886	15.7	4.7	4.4	15.6	4.4	8.7	25.4	10.1	6.5	1.5	-2.1	3.90	4.13
1887	39.9	2.7	3.3	6.7	-0.7	18.7	-2.4	15.7	3.0	2.2	12.6	4.06	4.15
1888	10.4	5.7	3.9	4.3	-7.6	28.3	15.7	16.6	5.3	-2.2	7.8	4.77	4.17
1889	7.7	2.7	3.5	13.8	-1.6	36.2	8.0	11.6	-4.6	0.2	24.6	5.37	4.18
1890	12.1	2.4	2.9	3.8	-0.8	35.2	8.2	4.3	-5.1	4.4	31.4	6.03	4.07
1891	59.4	5.5	3.1	-0.9	-0.1	43.4	-0.5	11.2	-29.6	-0.8	10.1	6.73	3.93
1892	15.2	8.7	-12.0	15.0	3.9	20.5	11.8	7.7	-0.4	5.0	24.6	5.15	4.12

Year	Mortgages	Personal loans	British govt	Colonial securities	Foreign securities	Debentures	Company shares	House/ ground rent	Municipal loans	Reversions/ life interests	Other assets	Total (£m)	Avg yield (%)
1893	17.1	5.4	-6.8	15.7	2.5	36.6	1.2	14.4	19.5	6.6	-12.7	5.07	4.07
1894	3.7	8.0	-1.2	19.6	4.3	31.6	11.5	11.3	14.8	1.1	0.8	7.10	3.93
1895	-4.9	3.7	0.7	16.4	5.9	26.5	24.1	9.4	14.7	8.7	-4.6	7.53	4.00
1896	-16.3	1.3	-1.5	-1.4	9.3	45.5	42.9	10.5	-2.2	4.9	6.9	9.86	3.88
1897	-18.1	2.8	1.0	3.0	11.8	51.0	42.4	10.8	4.8	1.6	-11.1	11.01	3.81
1898	-1.1	3.1	-1.0	6.6	6.5	38.5	31.3	9.6	1.3	4.0	3.0	11.52	3.86
1899	13.5	5.6	0.6	3.0	10.2	22.9	33.7	14.8	-7.8	5.8	-4.2	10.17	3.75
1900	-16.6	3.7	0.4	2.8	15.6	33.0	21.6	11.1	19.0	7.3	2.1	9.88	3.76
1901	26.2	7.2	10.7	6.1	3.3	8.8	8.3	15.9	11.7	2.5	-0.7	8.87	3.79
1902	16.9	11.4	14.9	2.0	-1.5	24.8	8.8	10.0	7.4	7.8	-2.5	8.42	3.82
1903	15.1	7.4	4.8	1.6	0.9	28.1	16.7	5.9	10.2	2.0	7.1	13.31	3.83
1904	19.7	10.9	-1.3	-1.1	-2.5	37.0	9.2	10.3	15.4	4.5	-2.2	13.10	3.85
1905	30.0	11.9	-2.1	0.3	-0.4	16.0	2.0	9.8	23.4	3.5	5.6	11.70	3.86
1906	4.2	8.1	-1.1	-0.1	7.4	40.2	8.7	7.5	12.5	3.9	9.3	14.82	3.92
1907	25.5	13.1	-16.1	-5.2	6.8	54.7	2.9	13.0	6.8	3.6	-9.5	8.35	3.94
1908	14.8	9.8	1.6	-1.5	7.2	42.8	2.1	8.8	8.3	2.4	5.5	15.06	3.97
1909	3.1	12.0	-1.1	-10.5	9.1	46.2	12.5	10.5	14.4	-3.6	7.2	13.29	4.00
1910	-5.1	9.2	-3.1	-0.4	12.7	52.8	3.3	1.4	21.2	0.7	7.2	27.08	4.10

Year	Mortgages	Personal loans	British govt	Colonial securities	Foreign securities	Debentures	Company shares	House/ ground rent	Municipal loans	Reversions/ life interests	Other assets	Total (£m)
1872–81	20.6	4.3	-7.6	4.1	7.3	0.4	11.9	5.9	-0.1	2.3	6.8	43.87
1882–90	19.4	2.9	2.0	13.8	-2.1	20.2	12.1	11.6	4.9	2.0	11.7	41.39
1891–1900	1.9	4.4	-1.0	6.7	7.9	35.9	25.4	11.1	3.2	4.4	0.6	84.02
1901–10	11.9	9.9	0.1	-1.0	5.5	37.9	7.1	8.1	14.3	2.3	4.1	134.0
Total assets												
1871 (£m)	61.77	7.08	8.21	5.26	1.23	10.41	2.73	4.69	19.40	1.69	7.55	109.61
1871 (%)	56.3	6.4	7.5	4.8	1.1	9.5	2.5	4.3	17.7	1.5	6.9	
Total assets												
1910 (£m)	96.26	27.10	5.05	17.10	17.46	99.86	43.80	32.28	43.19	10.35	20.44	412.89
1910 (%)	23.3	6.6	1.2	4.1	4.2	24.2	10.6	7.8	10.5	2.5	5.0	

Sources: *Journal of the Institute of Actuaries* 17 (1873): 296; *Statements 1882–1911*; Hewat 1896: 796; Watson 1900: 22; Supple 1970: 331.

APPENDIX 3.2

Annual yield above or below industry average, selected life insurance offices, 1895–1910 (% of total assets)

Life office	1895	1896	1897	1898	1899	1900	1901	1902	1903	1904	1905	1906	1907	1908	1909	1910
Legal & General	.13	.31	.28	.27	.38	.36	.28	.40	.45	.46	.54	.38	.39	.43	.34	.15
Sun Life	.07	.26	.40	.30	.45	.43	.36	.27	.40	.28	.35	.32	.24	.16	.13	.32
National Mutual	–	.14	.27	.19	.53	.29	.29	.42	.47	.16	.16	.18	.20	.16	.39	.41
Law Life	0	.23	.29	.07	.35	.27	.38	.36	.19	.45	.15	.38	.29	.25	.41	.22
Law Union & Crown	.02	.19	.22	.14	.23	.15	.03	.16	.25	.29	.26	.44	.45	.45	.42	.45
Commercial Union	.05	.22	.23	.27	.36	.26	.26	.22	.27	.35	.39	.34	.24	.10	.20	.11
Standard Life	.17	.15	.10	.08	.14	.21	.27	.23	.30	.33	.27	.31	.32	.31	.29	.18
Economic	.01	.15	.21	.21	.16	.21	.20	.19	.25	.26	.29	.30	.29	.32	.34	.25
Norwich Union	-.07	.16	.20	.23	.34	.32	.30	.20	.26	.25	.41	.34	.23	.26	.10	-.01
Gresham	-.10	.03	.17	.17	.34	.35	.29	.22	.26	.25	.22	.28	.32	.17	.19	.04
Life Assoc. of Scotland	-.02	-.03	-.14	-.25	-.10	-.09	-.25	-.14	-.14	-.07	-.05	-.05	-.05	-.02	-.03	-.08
Guardian	-.10	-.01	.04	-.06	-.02	-.04	-.17	-.21	-.17	-.17	-.15	-.14	-.17	-.21	na	.15
City of Glasgow	-.19	-.18	-.18	-.20	-.11	-.16	-.23	-.16	-.11	-.10	.01	-.05	-.06	-.12	na	na
U.K. Temperance & General	-.30	-.13	-.01	-.12	-.12	-.16	-.18	-.22	-.20	-.17	-.19	-.10	-.09	-.11	-.14	-.16
Star Life	-.26	0	0	-.14	-.22	-.29	-.33	-.24	-.21	-.20	-.14	-.12	-.19	-.13	-.20	-.15
Liverp. & London & Globe	-.15	-.07	-.08	-.16	.04	-.09	-.18	-.13	-.16	-.36	-.38	-.37	-.40	-.32	-.13	-.17
Northern	*	*	*	*	*	*	-.14	-.16	-.14	-.12	-.22	-.20	-.24	-.26	-.25	-.40

Life office	1895	1896	1897	1898	1899	1900	1901	1902	1903	1904	1905	1906	1907	1908	1909	1910
Equitable Life	-.36	-.32	-.31	-.38	-.45	-.51	-.53	-.48	-.29	-.09	-.18	-.14	-.14	-.07		na
Prudential	-.75	-.59	-.46	-.56	-.38	-.48	-.59	-.57	-.55	-.51	-.47	-.51	-.46	-.46	-.47	-.30
Refuge	-1.13	-1.00	-.40	-.57	-.36	-.58	-.50	-.70	-.43	-.42	-.44	-.32	-.29	-.28	-.39	na
Industry average	4.00	3.88	3.81	3.86	3.75	3.76	3.79	3.82	3.83	3.85	3.86	3.92	3.94	3.97	4.00	4.10

* Life fund supplemented by shareholders to pay 4% interest.

APPENDIX 3.3

Annual yield above industry average, selected foreign and colonial offices doing business in the United Kingdom, 1895–1910 (% of total assets)

Life office	1895	1896	1897	1898	1899	1900	1901	1902	1903	1904	1905	1906	1907	1908	1909	1910
Australian Mutual Provident	–	1.14	1.04	.88	.84	.72	.69	.64	.61	.60	.63	.56	.56	.50	.49	.38
National Mutual of Australia	–	1.24	.96	1.01	.99	1.05	1.06	.93	.95	.95	1.04	.92	.83	.80	.83	.75
Sun of Canada	1.70	1.65	1.41	.77	.99	.82	.93	1.03	1.02	.83	1.38	1.28	1.56	1.55	1.37	1.19
Equitable (U.S.)	.27	.52	.72	.49	.55	.86	.39	.36	.24	.35	.22	.50	.72	.68	.65	.55
Mutual of New York	.69	.70	.62	.57	.73	.49	.32	.33	.53	.51	.48	.66	.90	.90	.73	.65
New York Life	.46	.64	.80	.86	.44	.33	.24	.25	.46	.33	.37	.35	.61	.56	.45	.40

Source: Statements 1882–1911.

Notes

Introduction

1 Young 1896: 708.
2 'Hedging against Fate' (1863): 584.
3 Clark 1999.
4 Supple 1970: 111–12. See Appendix 1 for list of major life insurers with a British head office in the nineteenth century, including date of formation and location of head office.
5 Jones 1847: v–vi; CMC (Rev. James Macdonald to John Pinckard, 6 July 1824).
6 *Post Magazine* 48 (1887): 58; ILOAMB III (18 March 1910).
7 *Post Magazine* 56 (1895): 195; *Report ... on Children's Life Insurance* 1890: 140, 182.
8 Foucault 1979. Among many other works that have applied this idea to present-day insurance, see Heimer 2003; Ericson, Doyle, and Barry 2003; Simon 1988; Defert 1991.
9 Vernon 2005: 696.
10 Jalland 1996; Richardson 1989.
11 Poovey 1998: 120–38; Foucault 1975.
12 Brewer and Staves 1996; Holcombe 1983.
13 'Assurance and Insurance' 1839: 139; *Insurance Record* 16 (1876): 309.
14 Walford I: 390 (British Standard prospectus); Standard Life prospectus (1839); A.A. Fry, *Pocket Diary*, repr. in Saint-Clair 1840: back matter (National Endowment prospectus).
15 Brown 2001: 36–7; Stern 2007.
16 Edmonds 1832: title page.
17 Brinton 1856: 4–5.

18 Stevenson 1899: 31 (letter to Mrs Fleeming Jenkin, 15 or 16 April 1886); *Chambers's Journal* 2 (1899): 816.
19 Saint-Clair 1840: back matter (Agricultural & General prospectus).
20 Kinnear 1910: 102.
21 Supple 1970; Ryan 1983; Trebilcock 1985 and 1999.
22 Among the best histories of British life insurance companies published by non–academic presses, see Moss 2000; Dennett 1998; Conder 1979; Lindsay 1987; Ogborn 1962; Liveing 1961.
23 See Alborn 2001: 657–59.
24 In British economic and social history see Baker and Collins 2005; Scott 2002; Pearson 1990; Supple 1977. For history of science and medicine, see Porter 1995; Dupree 1997; Jureidini and White 2000. For labour history see Dohrn 1988.
25 Keller 1963; Zelizer 1983; Murphy 2005.
26 See Yates 1989 and 2005; Kwolek-Folland 1994, esp. chapters 4–6; Zunz 1990, esp. 90–100, 113–22.
27 Robin Pearson's claim that 'life insurers innovated in investment rather than underwriting' in the nineteenth century is representative: Pearson 1997: 246.
28 For discussions on the impact of World War One on British life insurance see Butt 1984: 155–7; Supple 1970: 417–18; Warner 1927.
29 Two remarks are also in order regarding terminology. Following Geoffrey Clark, I have chosen to use the (mainly North American) term 'life insurance' instead of 'life assurance' throughout the book. Although the latter was more common in nineteenth–century Britain, and is still widely in use there, many Victorians (especially doctors) did use it. I also frequently use the term 'life office' to refer to an office that sold life insurance as one of its products. This term was in wide circulation during the nineteenth century.

1 Insuring Britain

1 *Post Magazine* (19 Oct. 1850).
2 Supple 1970: 111–12, 220; Woods 1995: 10.
3 Lightfoot 1825; *Return of ... Stamps for Policies* 1873: 365–6. The value of money, which had increased between 1826 and 1830, decreased in a somewhat lesser degree in the 1850s; hence in real terms the proportion of policies under £500 was even less in 1869–72.
4 Ryan 1985: 166–7; *Statements* 1892: 394; Woods 1995: 10.
5 Clark 1999: 73, 78, 100–1; Supple 1970: 62.

6 Clark 1999: 52–4, 57, 78, 105, 187, 203–6; and 1997: 28–35.

7 Ogborn 1962: 109–12, 117; Raynes 1948: 134; Supple 1970: 64–6. On Price's Northampton table, see chapter 4 below; on bonuses see chapter 6 below.

8 Simpson 1936: 145; AMB I (12 March 1824); Trebilcock I: 34; Palladium prospectus (1827); Appendix 1.

9 Liveing 1961; McAfee 1948; Dennett 1998. See chapter 2 for a discussion of failed companies.

10 Saint-Clair 1840: 56–60; Dowdeswell 1846: 129–32; *Hand Book* 1856: 108–41; Dennett 1998: 93–6; *Insurance Record* 6 (1868): 269; EMB XV (Nov.–Dec. 1863 *passim*).

11 *Norwich Union Magazine* 7 (1897): 21–4; Hazell 1935: 36–40; *Post Magazine* 51 (1890): 597.

12 Walford I: 303, 368, 409; Cockerell and Green 1994: 146; Raynes 1948: 236–7; Pearson 2004: 236–7, 200–1.

13 Pearson 2004.

14 *Insurance Record* 16 (1878): 296; *Economist* 42 (1884): 747; Walford IV: 153; CWP (Queen Life & Fire); *Insurance Record* 13 (1875): 176–7. On Liverpool's dominance in the fire insurance market see Livesay 1884: 10–17; Supple 1970: 214.

15 Bignold 1948: 66; Francis 1962: 18–24.

16 *Economist* 42 (1884): 747; Dalgleish 1883: 21; *Bankers' Magazine* 60 (1895): 107; *Post Magazine* 40 (1879): 289. On the Associated Scottish Life Offices see chapter 2.

17 Dow 1975; Scottish Widows' Fund prospectus (1842): 21; Ogborn 1962: 198; *Scottish Equitable* 1835.

18 See sources cited in Figure 1.1; Moss 2000: 32–3. The North British formed as a fire office in 1809 but added a life branch in 1823.

19 Harrison 1992: 22, 37–40; *Post Magazine* 43 (1882): 428; Stewart 1825: 208.

20 Walford III: 91.

21 AtMB I (29 Dec. 1809); Pearson 2002: 22, 27; Ryan 1983: 314–17; Supple 1970: 177; CMB III (27 Jan. and 10 Feb. 1841).

22 AtMB VI (8 May 1838); Trebilcock I: 567–8; Pearson 2002: 23–6.

23 CMB III (27 Jan. and 10 Feb. 1841); AtMB VI (4 May 1841).

24 Steuart 1937: 18; McAfee 1948: 16.

25 Harrison 1992: 32, 52; *Economist* 46 (1888): 140; CAB I–II; Walford II: 151; CWP (b/s Manly); Moss 2000: 38, 61, 68–69, 87–88; ESLMB VIII (10 March 1865, 5 March 1869).

26 GVS; Moss 2000: 150; SMB XXIII; Ryan 1983: 1112–13. Overall premium income from non-U.K. sources among British life offices in 1910 was 10.7%: *Statements* 1911: 812.

27 Trebilcock I: 554; Walford V: 289, and II: 32; Campbell-Kelly 1994: 12.

28 See, e.g., CEMB V (14 Dec. 1866, 29 March 1867); CWP (Lion Life).
29 *Once a Week* 1 (1880): 94; McAfee 1948: 32, 39; GAH; GVS; GSBE; GMTS. Three other life offices with success in Europe, all after 1890, were the Star, Standard Life, and Norwich Union: see Blake 1958: 69, Moss 2000: 135–6; SMB XX (1 Feb. 1899).
30 Stalson 1942: 343, 787, 839; Ransom and Sutch 1987; Murphy 2005: 305–15.
31 Malcolm and Hamilton 1875: 392; *Insurance Record* 14 (1876): 407, 414; Watson 1884: 13.
32 Moss 2000: 57, 93; Norman 1950: 23; Walford I: 611.
33 Walford I: 431, 435, 614, and II: 465; Norman 1950: 103; *Insurance Record* 14 (1876): 158–9, 16 (1878): 162; Steuart 1937: 26, 28; Moss 2000: 89; EdMB XVII (memo by D. Maclagan, 1878); CWP (Life Association of Scotland).
34 Stalson 1942: 833; *Times* (16 Dec. 1913); *Post Magazine Almanack* (1907): 50.
35 Bailey 1869: 91; Gray 1977: 10–23.
36 CoMB I (25 Aug. 1863); *Post Magazine* 40 (1879): 491, 47 (1886): 206; Cooksey 1981: 14; *Post Magazine* 59 (1898): 74, 356; *Times* (12 Aug. 1901); Gray 1977: 24–67, 101–28.
37 Norman 1950: 225–7; Van Selm 1945: 1–3, 29–31; Tarn 1899: 519; Ryan 1983: 405, 599; *Review* (14 Jan. 1921).
38 Walford I: 613; Scottish Amicable, Jamaican prospectus (1876): 11; Karch 1997: 10–14, 30; Beckles 1990: 133.
39 Walford III: 158–9, 164–5, and I: 49; *Times* (17 Jan. 1860); Tait 1874: 21.
40 Slater 1893: 10–13; Moss 2000: 134; GIB; GVS; *Short History* 1924: 29.
41 Walford V: 304, and IV: 278; Best 1989: 160–2; *Post Magazine* 56 (1895): 862; EMB XXV (13 Nov. 1901); ESLMB XV (25 July 1901); Buley 1967: 732–3; SMB XXIII (13 May 1908); Norman 1950: 116; EdMB XVII (memo by D. Maclagan, 1878); Liveing 1961: 40.
42 Stalson 1942: 297–99; Walford V: 284, 294; *Saturday Review* 100 (1905): 333; Equitable 1873: 1, 8–9, 27–8; *Post Magazine* 56 (1895): 861, and 42 (1881): 441; Stout 1886: 399.
43 AMB X (22 Nov. 1876); GAH; SACR; LURSA; ESLMB XI.
44 *Insurance Record* 14 (1876): 35; Curtis 1876: 238–40; GAH.
45 Pritchard 1898: 34; SLRV III (Blount, report on South Africa, 31 Jan. 1913); *Post Magazine* 41 (1880): 52.
46 Trebilcock I: 168, and 1986: 156–63; Supple 1977: 74–5; Raynes 1948: 271, 274–5; Dickson, *Sun Fire*, 1960: 221.
47 *Insurance Record* 12 (1874): 28–9; Trebilcock I: 267–74, and II: 139, 238, 241–4.
48 *Post Magazine* 50 (1889): 551–2.
49 See Alborn, 'Senses,' 2001, for a discussion of parallel differences between friendly societies and industrial insurance offices.

50 *Insurance Record* 16 (1878): 299; Clark 1999: 54–7; Raynes 1948: 119–21.
51 Deuchar 1874: 324; Parshall 2006: 85.
52 *Insurance Record* 7 (1869): 42; Walford III: 25; LGBM I (18–25 June 1836).
53 *Post Magazine* 43 (1882): 50, 123; LGRGM (report by Ernest Colquhoun); English & Scottish Law prospectus (1839): 32–3.
54 LGLPR; Pearson 1990: 248.
55 Cannadine 1994: 24; Digby 1994; Corfield 1995: 189–94.
56 CWP (University Life); Campbell 1975: 9; Walford I: 577; Royal Naval prospectus (1840).
57 Walford I: 9, 44, 181, 212, 246, 364, 369, 371, 403, 545, 554, 559, 563; II: 242, 505; III: 35, 171; V: 545; and CWP (United Mercantile & Travellers and United Mutual Mining); Syed 1997: 56; *Post Magazine* 46 (1885): 111, 158.
58 Pocock 1842: 115; Walford II: 286.
59 Tregoning and Cockerell 1982; Champness 1937; Walford I: 544–5; Star Life 1907; Topliss 1976.
60 Walford V: 224; Star Life 1907: 66; *Post Magazine* 51 (1890): 755; Star prospectus (1910): 10; *Post Magazine* 41 (1880): 78; CEIMB X.
61 Cited in Champness 1937: 26.
62 See, e.g., *Post Magazine* 43 (1882): 133, and 42 (1881): 182; LGRA (report by Ernest Colquhoun, 1891); *Equity and Law* 1994: 8.
63 CMRL; Walford I: 577; *Insurance Record* 43 (1903): 349; UMB XII (30 April 1884).
64 *Star Life Assurance Society* 1900: 13; Tregoning and Cockerell 1982: 36.
65 Sales figures from *Post Magazine, Assurance Magazine, Times, Assurance Register, Insurance Register*, Walford I: 380, 391, 579, 613; II: 443, 451,and V: 140, 209, 544, 571; Sprigge 1897: 455–7; Dickson, *Sun Life*, 1960: 18; WMB I–III.
66 NULMB XXI (30 April 1886); Scottish Widows' Fund prospectus (1842): 47; Medical Clerical & General prospectus (1824); *Insurance Record* 4 (1866): 5; Alliance 1896: 25; Pocock 1842: 132 (Promoter).
67 Saint-Clair 1840: 35; GMTS.
68 Walford I: 302; Gosden 1973: 210–216; Cordery 2003: 85–97.
69 *Farmers'Magazine* 25 (1824): 400; *Times* (10 Nov. 1854); Supple 1974: 229, 234–8, 250; Hazell 1935: 3, 22–3, 28; ASLOMB I (25 April 1849, 2 Feb. 1852); *Report ... on Friendly Societies* 1852: 19, 27, 38.
70 For lectures and meetings see Hazell 1935: 17–20; Sherriff 1940: 66; *Post Magazine* 15 (1854): 141. For almanacs and diaries see Erith 1854; *Post Magazine* 43 (1882): 52. For novellas see chapter 5. New products are discussed in chapter 7.
71 *Post Magazine; Times;* Downes 1859: 25; EMB *passim;* CAB I; Docherty 1974: 61; Dickson, *Sun Life,* 1960: 18; WMB I–III; Sprigge 1897: 455–7; *Return of*

Names 1864–69. Available data range from one year for 21 companies to ten or more years for 15.

72 PCSB 1 (clipping from *Morning Herald*, 29 Aug. 1840; first annual meeting, 7 Feb. 1842); *Times* (4 Feb. 1864, 3 Feb. 1865, 8 Feb. 1867, 6 Feb. 1868); Sherriff 1940: 53, 85–6; Humpherson 1952: 9–15, 19–22.

73 Withers 1951: 84–90; *Post Magazine* 44 (1883): 276; Burns 1873: 59–61.

74 Friend in Need 1864: 7; Walford II: 491; Syed 1997: 72; *Insurance Record* 6 (1868): 347, and 13 (1875): 322; Cockerell and Green 1994: 124; *Times* (7 Aug. 1952 and 7 Jan. 1969).

75 *Insurance Register* (1869): 28; Walford I: 387, 392; Supple 1970: 114.

76 Dennett 1998: 107; Prudential 1868; *Insurance Record* 40 (1902): 95, 107, 400; *Assurance Agents' Review* 19 (1906): 57; Ryan 1983: 249; *Industrial Life Offices' Association* 1951: 41.

77 Gibson 1893: 6; ILOAMB (21 Sept. 1909); Rodger 1913–14: 37; Herriot 1924: 38.

78 Minnitt 1985: 44–6; *Post Magazine* 51 (1890): 842; NLAR (31 Oct. 1892).

79 NLAR (9 May 1891).

80 *Report ... into the Condition and Management of Lights* 1861: 161; EdMB V (22 and 25 Jan. 1839); *Policy-holder* 1 (1883): 62; AtMB VII (28 Oct. and 29 Nov. 1842, 9 Jan. 1844); AtLD I–IV (1844–51 *passim*).

81 CWP (Post Office Widows and Orphans Fund); Hill and Hill II: 304–7; *Post Magazine* 15 (1854): 257–8; ASLOMB I (25 Feb. 1854); Alliance 1860, and 1874: 19–20; Scudamore 1861: 8; Daunton 1985: 108.

82 *Post Magazine* 51 (1890): 713–14, 53; (1892): 319; *Times* (21 April 1892); ESLMB XII (21 July 1892), XIII (5 March 1896); EMB XXII (29 Feb. 1891, 3 Aug. 1892); *Economist* 53 (1895): 316, 418.

83 McCormack 1919: 331; Butt 1984: 166; Hannah 1988: 35–6. On bank schemes prior to 1900 see CMSB I (16 Jan. 1884); *Policy-holder* 1 (1883): 62; ESLMB XI (31 Oct. 1890); *Post Magazine* 51 (1890): 891.

84 Even more than composite insurance, industrial insurance was mainly an English (as opposed to Scottish) innovation.

85 See sources cited in Figures 1.2 and 1.3.

86 Blake 1958: 63–6; Ryan 1983: 407–9; Alborn 2008: 40.

87 'Indisputable' policies and liberalized travel conditions are discussed in chapters 8 and 4 below respectively.

88 *Insurance Record* 3 (1865): 146.

89 CMB XII (12 Sept. 1893); *Post Magazine* 48 (1887): 154; *Times* (13 March 1911); NLAR (2 July 1900, 26 March 1902); *Economist* 56 (1898): 232; Blake 1958: 67.

90 Rodger 1900: 26; Cockburn 1905: 3; Penman 1909: 19.

91 NLAR (20 Feb. 1905).

92 De Morgan 1837: 342; LGBM XIX (7 Nov. 1865); Walford II: 434, and V: 570; *Economist* 14 (1888): 1474.

93 Appendix 1 and sources cited therein.

94 *Statements* 1894: 378–82; Ryan 1983; *Post Magazine* 9 March 1850; *Hand Book* 1856: 132; *Return of Names* 1864.

95 Schooling 1924: 3, 101; Walford III: 42; Baylis 1852: 12.

96 Ryan 1983: 958; Trebilcock I: 746; *Slater's* 1878.

97 Sources cited for Figure 1.4.

98 Liveing 1961: 260–3; Walford IV: 153; *Insurance Record* 13 (1875): 176–7; Moss 2000: 16–33; Worland and Paterson 1976: 20–1.

99 *Post Magazine* 80 (1919): 140; Supple 1970: 299.

100 *Post Magazine* 47 (1886): 514; Biddle 1997: 226; Walford I: 329; Supple 1970: 228–9, 268; Cockerell and Green 1994: 123–88.

101 Walford III: 282–9; Westall 1993: 195, 197, 207; Supple 1970: 205, Cockerell and Green 1994: 9–10. Guarantee (or guaranty) insurance is also known as fidelity insurance in the United States.

102 Raynes 1948: 373, 388; Times (11 July 1907).

103 Trebilcock II: 360; Supple 1970: 262–8, 284–94; Liveing 1961: 157; Raynes 1948: 387.

104 Westall 1997: 1–8.

105 Supple 1970: 441, 451; Trebilcock II: 299; 323; Schooling 1924: 53; Post Magazine 80 (1919): 140–1; Moss 2000: 191–3; Rodger 1913–14: 39.

106 Besso 1887: 431–5; Post Magazine 26 (1885): 459; Trebilcock II: 539.

107 Supple 1970: 275; Rodger 1900: 24; Mills 1904: 201; Post Magazine 58 (1897): 5; *Times* (22 Jan. 1912).

2 Regulated Insurance Offices

1 Macfadyen 1874: 339.

2 The sole exception was the Albion, a sham company that included provisions in its deed rendering policyholders liable for its outstanding debts to outside creditors: *Post Magazine* 40 (1879): 288.

3 Of 306 English life offices that formed between 1800 and 1870, 50 failed and 116 were acquired by a company that failed. See sources cited in Appendix 1.

4 Harris 2000: 107–9, 125, 139–41, 207–10; Ogborn 1962: 33–7; Raynes 1948: 138; Trebilcock I: 456; Dickson, *Sun Fire,* 1960: 96. On the original 1720 charters see Supple 1970: 15–48.

5 Ogborn 1962: 44; Raynes 1948: 139; Harris 2000: 239, 158; Pearson 2002: 854.

6 Besant 1924: 31–7; Champness 1937: 15. Between 1807 and 1891 80 life offices went to Parliament 128 times to amend their deeds: *Index to Statutes* 1860: 635–54; *Return of Number of Private Bills* 1847–1891.

7 *Morning Chronicle* (12 Jan. 1808); Pearson 2002: 857–8; Ryan 1983: 184; Blake 1958: 37–38.

8 *Times* (7 Sept. 1838); see also *Times* (15 Nov. 1839); De Morgan 1840: 49–59.

9 Examples of these include Clark 1818; Farren 1823; Morgan 1841; Beaumont 1842.

10 See, e.g., Babbage 1826; Baily 1810; De Morgan 1838; D. Jones 1843. A reviewer of Babbage concluded that 'in conducting worldly affairs, mere abstract mathematicians are not among the wisest of mankind': Barrow 1827: 4.

11 *First Report* 1844: 3–6; Francis 1853: 225–30.

12 *First Report* 1844: iii, vii; Robb 1992: 16–18; Taylor 2006: 137–41. Besides the Independent & West Middlesex, the committee examined the recent failures of six other insurance companies and three mining companies.

13 Taylor 2006: 142–3; Jones 1981: 30; Christie 1852: 5; Thomson 1852: 12; *Remarks* 1852: 12.

14 Alborn 1991: 232–42; Horton and Macve 1994: 302–6, 315; Porter 1995: 106–12; Supple 1970: 141–3; *Hansard's Parliamentary Debates* 124 (1853): 1331. James Wilson, who chaired the 1853 committee, failed in his attempt to pass two insurance–related bills in 1857 and 1859; all that was accomplished was a one-clause bill in 1857 to fill a gap in a recent Companies Act that had exempted new life offices from registering under it.

15 *Return of Names* 1864–69; Ayres 1863: 3, 6; Smiles 1870: 24.

16 ASLOMB I (6 Feb. 1840, 25 June 1844, 21 Dec. 1855).

17 *Assurance Magazine* 1 (1850): 114–15; see Simmonds 1948: chapters 1– 3.

18 Alborn 1991: 232. On the Institute's role in training actuaries see chapter 3 below.

19 Davidson 1956: 208–19; CWP (Professional Life).

20 Soper 1847: [2]. See also *Account* 1839; Saint-Clair 1840; Bridges 1842; Pocock 1842; Young 1844; Sturrock 1846; Hutchison 1846; Hillman 1847; Jones 1847; Burt 1849; Scratchley 1851. Bridges, Hillman, Jones, Burt, and Scratchley all worked for recently formed companies.

21 See Ayres 1863; Walford 1867; *Insurance Register* (1869); Grahame 1869.

22 *Post Magazine* (9 Feb., 16 and 23 March, 13 April 1850) and 21 (1860): 393.

23 Walford VI: 15–16; *Post Magazine* (12 Oct. 1850).

24 Examples include the *Life Assurance Record* (1847–48), *Life Assurance Chronicle* (1846), and *Assurance Gazette* (1847). Rival almanacs included the *Annual Insurance Digest* (or *A.I.D.*), published from 1878, and the *Reporter's Almanac* (1850).

25 For exceptions see *Lawson's Merchant's Magazine* 1 (1852): 429, and *Policy-holder* 1 (1860): 264.

26 Moss 2000: 51, 62–3, 84–6, 94–8; Walford V: 429–30; Simpson 1936: 26, 41.

27 EMB VI (7 Dec. 1826); XI (14 July and 2 June 1847); *Insurance Record* 4 (1866): 204; Trebilcock I: 599–600.

28 EMB XI (1 Oct. 1847); XIII (24 July 1856), *passim.*

29 See, e.g., Globe 1857: 46–7.

30 These were the Empire (failed in 1867), English (1870), Mitre (1869), London & Glasgow (1871), National Widows' (1872), Norwich Provident (1874), and Provincial Union (1869).

31 *Economist* 27 (1869): 1014; Crawford 1871: 10.

32 *Times* (25 April 1864); Walford I: 48; III: 159; and LGBM XIX (23 May 1865); EMB XIV (5 Oct. 1859); Syed 1997: 30.

33 CWP (Professional Life); Walford I: 372–3, and III: 46–7; *Times* (14 Oct. 1869).

34 *Times* (4 Oct. 1869); *Insurance Record* 7 (1869): 238; Wilson 1871.

35 Macfadyen 1870: 10; Walford III: 51; S. De Morgan 1882: 279–80.

36 *Times* (14 Oct. 1869); Walford III: 48–52; *Economist* 27 (1869): 1250; *Times* (13–14 Aug. 1869). James was the 'Vacation Judge in Chancery'; the judge who later wound up the European was Richard Malins.

37 Walford I: 48–9, and III: 52–3; LGBM XXII (11 July 1871); AMB IX (13 July 1871); CEMB VI (6 Sept. 1869); Buley 1967: 270.

38 *Times* (11 Nov. 1872, 4 Aug. 1875, 5 Nov. 1877); Walford I: 48–9, and III: 55–63.

39 *Post Magazine* 47 (1886): 259; *Return of Payments* 1877; *Return of Sums* 1875.

40 Since the average policy issued by the European was for £279, customers would have paid around £8 per year in premiums: see *Insurance Register* (1867): 28. For an example of a surrender value paid for a policy that was still in force when the Albert went into liquidation see *Times* (27 Oct. 1874).

41 *Post Magazine* 41 (1880): 255; M'Lauchlan 1902: 241; Colquhoun 1883: 18; Gattie 1889: 498.

42 Hewat 1891: 2; *Report ... on Life Assurance Companies* 1906: 22.

43 ASLOMB II (19 and 24 March, 24 May, 28 July 1869); *Insurance Record* 7 (1869): 109, 124, 133, 172; Walford I: 474.

44 Ryan 1983: 243–4; Caverly and Bankes 1892: 224; ASLOMB II (4 and 18 March, 14 July 1870); IACMB III (11 March 1870).

45 Cox and Storr-Best 1962: 42–51. For criticism of the methods used in valuing the Albert, see Walford I: 47, and Tucker 1869: 11–14.

46 *Life Assurance Companies* 1869: 7; Boult 1870: 11; *Economist* 27 (1869): 1250.

47 *Times* (24 Feb. 1870); Sprague 1872: 10.

48 Malcolm and Hamilton 1875; *Insurance Record* 12 (1874): 405, and 13 (1875): 34, 86, 94, 133, 157, 181, 189–90; CMB VI (27 June 1877); Associated Scottish Life Offices 1895: 30.

49 *Statements* 1894: 347; *Bankers' Magazine* 50 (1890): 1037. The Board of Trade ceased this practice in 1898: *Assurance Agents' Review* 11 (1898): 92.

50 EdMB XV (2 Feb. 1872); WBP 30031.f.231 (De Ridder & Co. to William Blackwood and Sons, 29 Nov 1875); *Policy-holder* 4 (1886): 281.

51 Allen 1883: 3, 16; Freestone 1890. See Moss 2000: 125, 140, for a brief discussion.

52 IACMB IV (July 1882–June 1884); MPAC IV (14 March and 9 June 1884); LOAMB (12 Nov. 1888; private circular, 1894; *passim*); LOASB II (*passim*).

53 Low 1902: 8. On the Institute and Faculty mortality investigations see chapter 4. On interaction between the ASLO and the LOA see, e.g., LOAMB (30 March 1896), ASLORM I (30 April 1897), and LOASB V (21 Dec. 1908).

54 *Times* (9 Feb. 1882); *Post Magazine* 43 (1882): 208. Other failures after 1870 included the Sovereign, Albion, and Masonic & General.

55 Walford I: 391; *Times* (20 Feb. 1863) *Post Magazine* 46 (1885): 548.

56 *Post Magazine* 42 (1881): 243; *Insurance Record* 13 (1875): 276. For discussions of the BMG in 1874 see *Insurance Record* 12 (1874): 237, 261, 404, 413.

57 *Insurance Record* 13 (1875): 307–8; *Post Magazine* 38 (1877): 159, 174; 42 (1881): 243; 46 (1885): 64; 47 (1886): 89–90, 101–2, 124; 48 (1887): 172.

58 *Insurance Record* 12 (1874): 228, 261, 404, and 13 (1875): 20, 37; *Statements* 1875: 155–62; *Post Magazine* 47 (1886): 82.

59 *Post Magazine* 47 (1886): 455, 485; 53 (1892): 381; 43 (1882): 208; and *Statements* 1884: 195–204.

60 Supple 1970: 220. For outside critiques see Gattie 1889: 495; Welton 1889: 62–3.

61 *Report ... on Life Assurance Companies* 1906: q. 713.

62 NULMB XXVI (4 Nov. 1901); Rock 1906: 8.

63 *Policy-holder* 3 (1885): 265. See also *Insurance Record* 12 (1874): 277; MPAC III (1 April 1876).

64 Several companies had discovered this point prior to 1870 and converted to more aggressive sales tactics as a result: see LGBM XXI (Feb. 1869); CAB I (report by B. Hall Todd, 1870).

65 *Economist* 42 (1884): 747; *Post Magazine* 50 (1889): 551–2.

66 *Post Magazine* 39 (1878): 413. See also Star prospectus (1872): 20; English & Scottish Law prospectus (1879): 4; *Insurance Record* 7 (1869): 397 (Clerical Medical).

67 Schooling 1924: 29, 45–8; Trebilcock II: 309, 331–40; *Post Magazine* 52 (1891): 823; 51 (1890): 714; *Times* (4 Nov. 1909, 29 Oct. 1919, and 13 Dec. 1913); Supple 1970: 299.

68 Hendriks, cited in Supple 1970: 295; *Economist* 67 (1909): 1260; *Peeps* 1908: 3 and *passim*; Liveing 1961: 46–9, 84–92.

69 Trebilcock I: 486–8; Dickson, *Sun Fire*, 1960: 147–59; Ryan 1983: 394–5; Pearson 2004: 213–14.

70 Kent 1979; Westall 1997: 11.

71 *Times* (1 July 1910); Tapp 1986: 30; Raynes 1948: 358–64; Andras 1910: 118.

72 Skerman 1998: 61, 87; *Times* (2 July 1974); Horton and Macve 1994: 309, 317.

73 Dicksee 1909: 523–9, 545–8; Taylor 2006: 212–23; Wilson 1875: 273.

74 *Statements* 1872 *passim*; 1883: 266–70; 1911: 810, 812; see Figure 1.3. Ordinary business done by industrial offices is not included in this comparison because it was non-existent in 1872.

75 See Figure 1.2.

3 Doing Business

1 Hewat 1899: 3–4.

2 Williams 1973: 155.

3 Lawyers and surveyors are discussed (briefly) in chapter 6 and doctors are discussed in chapter 8. On clerks see Alborn 2008.

4 Francis 1853: 272–3; Cassis 1994: 124–5; Downes 1859: 15.

5 RLCB III (1 May 1816); Rock prospectus (1806): 2. See also CWP (Hope); AtMB I (3 Aug. 1808); Moss 2000: 23; Pearson 2004: 159, 246.

6 WBP 30044.f.5 (circular letter from J.M. McCandlish, 1 Jan. 1883); see also LGLB V (John Nettleton to Benjamin Adam, 19 July 1854); Pearson 2002: 852; YMB XVI (1 March 1853).

7 Pearson 2002: 854; Ryan 1985: 183–4; Ryan 1983: 312–19; Ogborn 1962: 178–82, 225–6; Jones 1877. Some joint stock life offices extended suffrage to at least some policyholders: Palladium prospectus (1827): 6; Star prospectus (1894): 21; *Northern Staff Magazine* 16 (1937): 221.

8 NLAR (30 June 1897); PCSB II (circular letter from Provident Clerks' Manchester branch secretary, 1857); Briton Life 1861: 31; PLPCA (circular letter from Samuel Beaumont, 6 April 1892).

9 AtST; AtPA; Medical Clerical & General prospectus (1824); Walford III: 25.

10 *Bankers' and Merchants' Almanack* 1813: 33–8; *Post Office London Directory* 1820: liii–lxv; *Post-Office Annual Directory* 1841: liv–lxxxiv; *Hand Book* 1856: 108–41; Clark 1818: 32; Babbage 1826: 53.

11 Supple 1970: 75–9, 352–3; Trebilcock I: 34, 529, 532–7; Liveing 1961: 10–13, 75; Cassis 1994: 153–6; *Post-Office Annual Directory* 1841: lix–lxxxiv; *Post-Office Glasgow Annual Directory* 1842: 160–70.

12 AtMB I (17 May 1808); Schooling 1924: 12–17; Campbell 1975: 16; Humpherson 1952: 21–2; Besant 1924: 191–4, 321–5; Leifchild 1859: 136; Sala 1865: 145.

13 *Insurance Record* 13 (1875): 83; RLMB I (12 Nov. 1812); Ryan 1983: 395.

14 Trebilcock I: 645; YMB XIV (2 Jan. 1850); LGBM XIV (24 Jan. 1860); EMB XVIII (5 July 1876) and XX (30 July 1884); *Insurance Record* 6 (1868): 74, and 40 (1902): 276.

15 *Report ... on Friendly Societies Act* 1889: 223; *Insurance Record* 5 (1867): 119; Trebilcock II: 597.

16 *First Report* 1844: 135, 150; Rock 1906: 44; Jones 1981: 30; ESLMB IX (26 April 1873); XI (29 March 1889); and Andras 1898: 163.

17 See, e.g., Docherty 1974: 15–16; Rock 1809: 11; EMB X (6 Oct. 1843); Low 1843: 9; Walford II: 150; *Insurance Record* 2 (1864): 71, 169.

18 Walford I: 93; PCPF; *Post Magazine* 15 (1854): 65; WBP 30063.f.157 (George Todd to William Blackstone, 19 Dec. 1893). On Scottish local boards see Moss 2000: 21, 32, 81; Worland and Paterson 1976: 128; Liveing 1961: 167; Steuart 1937: 20–1.

19 Tregoning and Cockerell 1982: 26; Supple 1970: 354.

20 SACR (2 Nov. 1883); CEMB I (23 Oct. 1846); RLMB I (12 Nov. 1812).

21 *Second Report* 1840: 95.

22 Ogborn 1962: 48, 57, 64–5, 79–81, 90–1, 100–2; Raynes 1948: 132.

23 Galloway 1841; Palladium 1825: i; De Morgan 1831: 106; Walford I: 542–3.

24 Alborn 2008: 46, 34–5, 51–2, 40; SLPM II (19 Sept. 1853); *Post Magazine* 46 (1885): 236.

25 See Alborn 1996; Ashworth 1994: 413–18, 424–9; Walker 1988: 12–22. Appointment information is from biographies in the *Post Magazine*, Walford's *Cyclopaedia*, the *Journal of the Institute of Actuaries*, and company histories.

26 *New Dictionary of National Biography* (Galloway); Parshall 1998: 2, 15; *Bankers' Magazine* 57 (1894): 808; Endelman 1984: 260–1; Eyler 1979: 74–6; AMB VIII (24 Jan. 1866); Van Sandau 1856; *Post Magazine* 52 (1891): 610.

27 Parshall 2006: 87, 139–40; FHP (Frend to Dawson Turner, 2 Sept. 1820); Minnitt 1985: 31.

28 Alborn 2008: 46–8; *Insurance Record* 38 (1900): 394; *Journal of the Institute of Actuaries* 52 (1921): 243; ESLMB XI (3 Dec. 1886); *Post Magazine* 47 (1886): 765.

29 *Journal of the Institute of Actuaries* 3 (1853): 333; Porter 1995: 106–13; 'Insurance as a Profession' 1893: 819.

30 *Economist* 68 (1910): 1121; Trebilcock II: 300–1; *Journal of the Institute of Actuaries* 75 (1948): 135.

31 Hewat 1906: 139–40; SAMBE (12–20 March and 3 May 1839); *Post Magazine* 41 (1880), 476; CWP (b/s James Moncrieff Wilson).

32 *Post Magazine* 51 (1890): 29; Marr 1883: 98; SAMB XV (22 Dec. 1891). Although T.B. Sprague at the Scottish Equitable was an exception to this rule, he spent his formative years in England and often rubbed his fellow Scottish actuaries the wrong way: see, e.g., *Commercial World* (15 April 1875).

33 *Post Magazine* 51 (1890): 12; HS 11.392 (Lubbock to Herschel, 30 Jan. 1861); SABMB III (8 Dec. 1870).

34 Ryan 1985: 192; Minnitt 1985: 20–1; Wood 1954: 297; Ogborn 1962: 212; Conder 1979: 266; Tregoning and Cockerell 1982: 16; Supple 1970: 366, 393; *Caledonian* 1905: 13; Lindsay 1987: 71; Withers 1951: 94; Walford I: 47, 209; *Comparison* 1850: 16–17, 46–9; and minute books from the Economic, Guardian, Clerical Medical, Alliance, Yorkshire, Eagle, Caledonian, Edinburgh, Atlas, Universal, Legal & General, Standard Life, Scottish Amicable, English & Scottish Law, and Westminster & General.

35 Ryan 1983: 387–8; Magnusson 1983: 40; Checkland 1975: 489; AMB IX (10 Jan. 1872); ESLMB XII (17 Feb. 1892); minute books as above plus Positive Government Security and Norwich Union.

36 Ogborn 1962: 161; Docherty 1974: 17, 56; Alliance, Eagle, Economic, Edinburgh, English & Scottish Law, Guardian, Legal & General, Standard Life, and University board minutes.

37 I was able to identify regular consulting work for 38% of actuaries with at least five years' service in the profession; the actual proportion is probably higher.

38 Philip 1992; Cordery 2003: 142–50, 156–7; *Post Magazine* 48 (1887): 511.

39 *Comparison* 1850: 18; Habakkuk 1994: 475.

40 Based on biographical information from Walford's *Insurance Cyclopaedia*, *Insurance Record*, *Post Magazine*, *Journal of the Institute of Actuaries*, and company minute books.

41 LGBM XIX (20–7 June 1865, 24–31 July 1866) and XXII (27 Dec. 1870); and *Post Magazine* 49 (1888): 742; RFMB XVIII (11 June 1872); RFBR (1884).

42 Alborn 2008: 41–3.

43 Supple 1970: 182, 285.

44 Marr 1886: 51; NLAR (30 June 1897). On advertising see Trebilcock I: 595, 604; LGBM XXI (Feb. 1869); Moss 2000: 83; Supple 1970: 182, 274.

45 Supple 1970: 181; RFMB XV (3 March 1857).

46 RFBR (6 March 1860); see also AMB VII (9 Sept. 1863); ESLMB IX (25 April 1873); LGBM XXI (20 April 1869); Supple 1970: 135, 288; AtMB X (28 July 1863).

47 CMC (Neate to J. Pinckard, 1 Feb. and 14 June 1825; Hillcoat to J. Pinckard, 6 Dec. 1825; Neate to G. Pinckard, 18 Dec. 1824).

48 Moss 2000: 81; Supple 1970: 289; *Post Magazine* 41 (1880): 360; EdMB XIII (1868, *passim*); CAB I.
49 Supple 1970: 287; Pearson 2004: 286; SAMB X (John E.C. Koch to William Spens, 12 Dec. 1849); Palladium 1825; Briton Life 1861: 23.
50 Browne 1878: 12–13; *Policy-holder* 1 (1883): 293; EdMB XVI (22 July 1873); SACR (28 Feb. 1880).
51 Moss 2000: 81–2; Walford I: 268; Brown 1898: 14; NMAGB (ca 1899); LUCLB (A. Mackay to A. Sullivan Fletcher, 11 Nov. 1901).
52 Median tenure taken from notices in the *Post Magazine* and lists of branches in the *Post Magazine Almanack*, covering appointments of 1,670 secretaries and 450 inspectors.
53 ESLMB IX (31 March 1871), X (14 March 1878), and XI (2 Jan. 1885); NLAR (14 Dec. 1891, 23 April 1902); SLPM I (20 Feb. 1844); Watson 1900: Table E; YBSS.
54 *Post Magazine* 59 (1898): 538; 48 (1887): 655; 51 (1890): 493; 55 (1894): 355; 58 (1897): 611; and NLAR; Moss 2000: 149, 181. In-house promotion is based on a sample of 1,566 inspectors and secretaries (same sources as above).
55 UlMB I (13 May 1835); WSLB (J.J. Duncan to W.D. Henderson, 10 July 1832); CMLB I (John Pinckard to Robert Ormiston, 27 Oct. 1824). Agents' gatekeeping duties are discussed in chapter 8.
56 Eagle and Protector 1847: 17; ESLMB IV (31 March 1848). For dismissals see EdR (Dec. 1855); LGBM XXI (Feb. 1869); SLSB XIV (May 1856).
57 AFLG I (5 Dec. 1843); SNMB I (20 Dec. 1844); SLPM IV (25 Feb. 1862); CAB I–II.
58 CAB I–II; NLAR; SAMB X (12 Dec. 1849); EcMB II–III.
59 Appendix 2.5.
60 See Appendices 2.1, 2.3, and 2.4 and sources cited therein. Judging from appointments recorded in minute books, the one major occupation of agents that is not accessible through trade directories is clerks.
61 Appendix 2.6; AtAAB.
62 SNMB I (1 Nov. 1844); Trebilcock I: 547; Digby 1999: 95; Supple 1970: 135–6. On lawyers see Stebbings 2002: 34–5; Garrard and Parrott 1998: 159.
63 ASLORM I (letter from Andrew Turnbull, Nov. 1900); Appendix 2.1 and sources cited therein.
64 Checkland 1975: 196–8, 379–81; *Bankers' Magazine* 49 (1889): 417.
65 SNMB I (20 Dec. 1844); Appendix 2.3; Holmes and Green 1986: 53–5, 69–78.
66 Jones 1981: 29–36, 80–2; CEMB II (6 Feb. 1852), IX–X *passim*; CMBM XIX (1863–66). Only three medical men in the Yorkshire sample were doctors (all surgeons), and just four out of 4,160 Scottish agents.

67 Appendix 2.1 (sources cited therein); WSLB (12 Oct. 1833).
68 AFLG II (25 March 1851); Hall 1992: 109; Digby 1994: 31–2; Appendices 2.2–2.4.
69 RLMB XV–XVIII; *Slater's* 1875; AtAAB; YPC (circular from Mrs J.E. Turner, 17 Sept. 1867); YMB XXVII (4 Sept. 1867); NULMB XXI (17 Feb. 1885); PGMB II (Sept. 1877); ESLMB XI (15 and 22 Jan., 26 Nov. 1891); Syed 1997: 85; Moss 2000: 185–7.
70 *Post Magazine* 55 (1892): 761 (interview with George King); Royal 1866: 5; Liverpool & London 1861: 30; North British & Mercantile 1873: 36.
71 *Insurance Record* 7 (1869): 273; *Caledonian Jottings* 1 (1892): 77; Herriot 1924: 34; *Bankers' Magazine* 33 (1873): 40; *Memoranda* 1880: 33; *Insurance Agent and Insurance Review* 39 (1904): 3; City of Glasgow prospectus (1910): 1; Morgan 1891: 12.
72 Walford II: 20; CMBM I (12 Jan. 1825); Palladium 1825; AMB I (19 May 1824); EcMB I (10 July 1829); WMB I (19 Sept. 1837).
73 Docherty 1974: 17; MPAC II (Feb. 1856); SLSB XIV (report of H.J. Williams, 29 Jan. 1855); Scottish Amicable 1887: 6–7; Worland and Paterson 1976: 36–7; Street 1980: 3; UMB XIII (31 Oct. 1888); Browne 1878: 13.
74 SLPM II (29 Jan. 1855); Docherty 1974: 56; EdMB XIII (9 Jan. 1868); ESLMB VIII (1 March 1867); LGMB XXI (Feb. 1869); Browne 1878: 10.
75 Spater 1951: 5; CAB I–II; Offer 1981: 15.
76 *Times* (21 March 1870); De Morgan 1838: 259; Baily 1810: 29; Babbage 1826: 132–41.
77 LOASB IV (20 July 1900) and V (2 April 1903, 19 March 1906, 21 Jan. 1907); ASLORM I (28 April 1903, 21 Dec. 1906). For context see Doig 1984: 69–77.
78 LGBM XXI (Feb. 1869); Rodger 1900: 37; Chapman 1906: 53.
79 Jackson 1910: 90; Rodger 1913–14: 37; Freud 1918: 77.
80 Dibdin 1884: 19; Alborn 2008: 51–6; *Insurance Record* 39 (1901): 73; Conder 1979: 224; Hewat 1893: 7; EWEG; *Post Magazine* 57 (1896): 202.
81 *Insurance Record* 16 (1878): 236; Zelizer 1983: 132–7; O'Malley 1999: 685–91; Freud 1918: 77.

4 Death and the Actuary

1 Chambers 1844: 331.
2 Bezobrazova 1878: 606.
3 Cullen 1975: 69–74; Porter 2000: 227.
4 *Life Assurance Premiums* 1910: 4–7.
5 Clark 1999: 76–81, 100–1; *Peeps* 1908: 58.
6 Daston 1988: chapter 3; Clark 1999: 115–27.

7 Ogborn 1962: 30, 109–12; Raynes 1948: 131–2; Buck 1982: 36–42; Trebilcock I: 578.
8 Ogborn 1962: 135; Babbage 1826: 177–9; *Norfolk Chronicle* 18 June 1808. The West of England lowered its premiums to approximate the Norwich Union's rates in 1818: Liveing 1961: 50.
9 *Report ... on the Laws respecting Friendly Societies* 1827: 5, 27, 35, 38; Milne 1815: 404–31; De Morgan 1837: 345; *Report ... on the Laws respecting Friendly Societies* 1825: 44.
10 De Morgan 1838: 271; Walford I: 42; Meikle 1872: 5.
11 Campbell-Kelly 1994: 7, 30; Davies 1825: v–vii; Walford III: 5.
12 GuMB II (15 July 1823) and X (7 April 1865); CAB I (21 Oct. 1874); Ryan 1983: 587; ELI (London & Provincial Law bonus report, 1860).
13 Trebilcock I: 578; Dickson, *Sun Life,* 1960: 18; Scottish National prospectus (1843): 7–8.
14 Walford V: 497–501, 513; Henry 1887: 11; *Report ... on the Laws respecting Friendly Societies* 1827: 8–9; EMB VI (31 Aug. 1826).
15 Clark 1818: 14, 18; Rankin 1830: ix–x; CMRS; CMC (Askew Hillcoat to John Pinckard, 13 March 1826).
16 Babbage 1826: xiv, 178–9; Saint-Clair 1840: 64; Sun Life prospectus (1823): 5.
17 Clark 1818: 19; Babbage 1826: 178; Walford V: 513; CMB III (20 Jan. and 6 Oct. 1841); Saint-Clair 1840: 61, 63, 68; Pocock 1842: 159.
18 Moss 2000: 45; CMB III (22 March 1843); Besant 1924: 331; Jones 1877: 52.
19 *Report ... on the Laws respecting Friendly Societies* 1827: 45; Morgan 1828: 41; Palladium prospectus (1827): 8.
20 Morgan 1834: iv, vii; Walford I: 85–7; Galloway 1841: Table V; Brown 1849: 19–24, 30, 15.
21 'Life Assurance Premiums' 1849: 138; J. Jones 1843: xxvii–xxx; GuMB V (letter of 6 April 1838); Cullen 1975: 96; Alborn 1994: 92.
22 Walford III: 94; GuMB V (6 April 1838); Ryan 1983: 240; ESLMB II (5 Oct. 1842); Woolhouse 1892: 139–40; Spens 1854: 2.
23 Recknell 1948, 18–21; J. Jones 1843: Table VIII.
24 Walford I: 551; Experience Life prospectus (ca 1846): 7; ExMB I (8 July 1844).
25 ExMB I (6 Dec 1843); Baylis et al. 1851: 2.
26 Murphy 2005: 28–51, 71–82; Walford III: 96–7; *Report of the Massachusetts Insurance Commissioners* 1859: 37–48, (1860): 54–5, 87–104.
27 *First Annual Report* 1839: 86; Evans 1998: 38–9; *Sixth Annual Report* 1845: 501; *Twelfth Annual Report* 1853: xii; Eyler 1979: 71–7; Hacking 1990: 118–19.
28 Morgan 1841: 28; ASLOMB I (8 Oct. 1841); Alborn 1991: 245.
29 *Twelfth Annual Report* 1853: viii; *Post Magazine* 40 (1879): 452, 460; Walford I: 382; Dennett 1998: 113; Eyler 1979: 85–90.

30 Higham 1851: 190–1, 202; *Post Magazine* (12 April 1851).

31 *Twelfth Annual Report* 1853: iii–vi; Eyler 1979: 84; Porter 1861: 282–8; *Insurance Record* 7 (1869): 10.

32 Bagehot XII: 349–50.

33 Brown 1852: 208; ASLOMB I (19 Jan. 1849, 2 Feb. 1852); *Insurance Record* 38 (1900): 16.

34 IACMB III (14 Jan. and 19 May 1862); Alborn 1994: 108; Downes 1857, and 1862: 5; ASLOMB II (26 May 1862); FASMB (5 Jan. 1864).

35 Aldcroft 1900: 369; FASMB (5 Jan. 1864); Meikle 1872: 5, 25, 50.

36 Aldcroft 1900: 380; Supple 1970: 253; AMB X (27 Oct. 1875); *Post Magazine* 37 (1876): 300, 388; YMB XLIII (21 Oct. 1885).

37 *Statements* 1872–76; *Post Magazine* 61 (1900): 538; Brown 1889: 1090; Supple 1970: 254; Aldcroft 1900: 381; ARAV (Marcus Adler, 11 Feb. 1879).

38 Valentine 1874: 240; see also *Insurance Record* 7 (1869); Curtis 1876: 229–30.

39 Paulin 1902: 222; Nicol 1895: 282–6; Cockburn 1905: 4.

40 King 1906: 3–4; Chisholm 1901: 186–7; Newman 1902: 290.

41 Davidson 1956: 78; *Insurance Record* 7 (1869): 10; Curtis 1876: 249; ASLORM II (11 Dec. 1912); Evans 1998: 34–5; *Continuous Investigation* 1933: v, xvi–xviii.

42 *Report ... on the Laws respecting Friendly Societies* 1825: 45; EMB VI (31 Aug. 1826); EPC (Eagle advertisement, ca. 1847).

43 YMB IV (11 May 1832); Yorkshire Fire & Life prospectus (ca 1834–35); LGBM I (26 July 1836); Royal Naval prospectus (1840); *Account* 1839: 28–9.

44 Walford III: 209; EMB XI *passim*; Brown 1852: 203.

45 J. Jones 1843: xvi, Table VIII; EMB XI (6 Sept. 1848, 27 Dec. 1848); Eagle advertisement (1850); Jellicoe 1854: 203–4. The Yorkshire waited until 1858 to abandon its lower female rates: Walford III: 230.

46 Aldcroft 1900: 370; Associated Scottish Life Offices 1895: 26–7; Metcalf 1967: 86; Lutt 1907: 473; Loudon 1992: 206–33.

47 NPAMI (2 Dec. 1862); *Post Magazine* 52 (1891): 43.

48 Woods 2000: 210–27; Hodgson 1864; *Insurance Record* 7 (1869): 383; Lutt 1907: 515.

49 Ibid., 515. Insurers more sporadically considered the problem of mortality among mariners and missionaries: see EdMB VIII (10 March 1853); ESLMB XI (4 Jan. 1889); Lindsay 1987: 53; UMB XIII (22 Oct. 1890).

50 Curtin 1989: 68–9, 169, 218; ASLOMB III (18 July 1882, 30 July 1883); Associated Scottish Life Offices 1895: 28.

51 ASLOMB III (20 May 1874, 15 Feb. 1879); Schooling and Rusher 1903: 24, 73–5; *Post Magazine* 43 (1882): 444; *Times* (15 Jan. 1900, 27 July 1911).

52 *Fourteenth Annual Report* 1855: xxi; *Supplement* 1864: xxxv; NPAMI (2 Dec. 1862, 23 Nov. 1883); *Post Magazine* 38 (1877): 70; 48 (1887): 246; 49 (1888): 213.

53 ASLOMB III (15 July 1896); ASLORM I (30 April 1897); LOAMB (26 Oct. 1896, 15 Feb. 1897).

54 Stewart 1861: 44; Pollock and Chisholm 1889: 163; NULRD (Robert Gardner to Thomas M. Grant, 30 Dec. 1881); LOASB III (15 July 1896); Deuchar et al. 1897: 248, 256, 261.

55 Aldcroft 1900: 370; ASLOMB I (29 Jan. 1847); *Times* (11 Feb. 1867). For examples of forfeiture see EMB XII (5 March 1851); CEMB IV (12 Nov. 1862).

56 Norman 1950: 21; ASLOMB I (4 Feb., 7 July and 24 Nov. 1846); *Assurance Magazine* 2 (1852): 169–70; PGMB II (24 July and 11 Dec. 1876); *Statements* 1872–80.

57 Alborn 1999: 66–8; Cullen 1975: 45–52; Walford I: 611–12.

58 See, e.g., Norman 1950: 292; SAER (4 Sept. 1888); RLCB II (28 June 1809).

59 Walford I: 615–16; Lutt 1907: 474–7; Winter 1909: 373–6; SACR (undated memo, ca 1886).

60 Eyler 1997: 32–33; Walford III: 301; ASLOMB III (18 Oct. 1878); *Insurance Record* 3 (1865): 77.

61 See, e.g., Laundy 1865; Oakes 1865.

62 Sang 1883: xv, xxi.

63 Warwick 1995: 321–2; FHP (card by J. Le Cappelain, 1862); Bell and Milne 1914: 50–3.

64 *Insurance Record* 3 (1865): 219; Walford I: 19, 24, 332, III: 296–7; *Hebrew National* 1 (1867): 1; Warwick 1995: 330; Davidson 1956: 30.

65 Sang 1883; Davidson 1956: 31.

66 Bryden 1997: 538; Stokes 1914: 156–60; Warwick 1995: 328–9; AMB X (8 Oct. 1873); ARAV (20 May 1903); Dennett 1998: 114–15; Henry 1887: xii.

67 Robertson 1896: 183; Carment 1880: 380.

68 EcMB I (4 July 1828); Sprague 1875: 414.

69 *Fifth Annual Report* 1843: 342; Clark 1999: 122; Price 1792: I: 308–9, 352. For instance, when the Northampton data revealed that more people died in their twenties than in their thirties, Price simply equalized the deaths for each decade.

70 King 1883: 204; Milne 1815: 101.

71 Gompertz 1825: 517–19; Edmonds 1832: v–vii; Alborn 1994: 101–3.

72 Campbell-Kelly 1994: 8; Galloway 1841: ix–x; Eyler 1979: 74–80; Woods 2000: 178–9.

73 Curtis 1876: 239, 248; Ansell 1874: 21; *Journal of the Institute of Actuaries* 31 (1894): 363–4.

74 King and Hardy 1880: 229; *Insurance Record* 7 (1869): 6; *Discussions* 1867: 44.

75 Makeham 1867: 335–7; Woods 2000: 172.

76 Woolhouse 1870: 408; *Journal of the Institute of Actuaries* 37 (1903): 439–2.

77 Rietz 1926: 13, 18–21; Sprague 1886: 305; *Insurance Record* 40 (1902): 374.

78 Baily 1810: 64–101; Davies 1825: xxxv–xl, Tables X and XIII–XIV.

79 Davies 1825: xxxix; Meikle 1861: 1. On the complicated history of the invention of D and N columns (variants of which date back to 1772), see Walford I: 618–23.

80 D. Jones 1843: xi–xiii; Walford III: 105, 114; ESLMB XIV (5 Aug. 1897); *Assurance Agents' Review* 10 (1897): 58; EMB XXIII (4 Aug. 1897).

81 EcMB I (7 Nov. and 23 Dec. 1828).

82 Hacking 1990: 63.

83 Alborn 1996; De Morgan 1838: xiii–xiv. See also De Morgan 1831, 1839, 1846; Herschel 1830: 58; Lubbock and Drinkwater 1830; D. Jones 1843.

84 Morgan 1841: iii, 27, 38; Blake 1958: 41.

85 Rock 1906: 12 (1806 prospectus); Standard Life prospectus (1839): 3; Alborn 1991: 142–3.

86 Bridges 1854: 29; Briton Life 1861: 5; *Post Magazine* 23 (1862): 330; HS 6.190 (De Morgan to Herschel, 30 Jan. 1844).

87 Aspland 1860: 60; SLPM IV (25 Feb. 1862); *Insurance Record* 12 (1874): 6; McCleery 1904: 10.

88 Clifford 1876: 12n; *Economist* 23 (1865): 341; Aspland 1860: 60; Raleigh 1864: 14. On Ted Porter's conception of 'trust in numbers' see the conclusion to this chapter.

89 Dickens 1854: 93–4; Carlyle 1840: 11.

90 *Journal of the Institute of Actuaries* 15 (1870): 460; Brown 1851: 31.

91 Pearson 2004: 213, 220–1, 320–2; Supple 1970: 215–17.

92 On the development of fire underwriting see Pearson 2002: 17–19.

93 *Report of the Massachusetts Insurance Commissioners* 1859: 5; Ryan 1985: 189; Knight 1921: 249; Experience Life prospectus (ca. 1846).

94 On the average clause see Supple 1970: 83–4; Dickson, *Sun Fire*, 1960: 80; YMB IV (1 March 1833). On fire prevention see Dickson, *Sun Fire*, 1960: 93, 160; Simpson 1936: 24; Liveing 1961: 73. On price fixing see above.

95 Walford III: 511; *Bankers' Magazine* 61 (1896): 144–5; Porter 1995: 104.

96 Walford I: 215, and II: 448; Conder 1979: 23; Blake 1958: 15–17.

97 Trebilcock I: 559–60; AMB II (29 June 1831, Sept.–Oct. 1831, 18 July 1832); Moss 2000: 32; BEMMB B (24 Oct. 1848); Christison 1853: 115; Fleming 1862: 25–6.

98 *Post Magazine* 53 (1892): 85, 763; 54 (1893): 416; and Rock 1906: 96; Blake 1958: 83; GMTS.

99 Weber 1946: 139; Smithson 1852: 7; *Economist* 40 (1882): 72.

100 Porter 1995: 32.
101 Hacking 1990: 119. Even industrial offices tended to reinforce behaviour (like expensive burials) that their working-class customers defined as 'normal' instead of trying to adjust that behaviour to middle-class norms: see Alborn, 'Senses,' 2001.
102 Farren, cited in Spens 1854: 7.

5 Death and the Salesman

1 *Chambers's Journal of Popular Literature, Science, and Arts* 333 (1860): 320 (to the tune of 'Ally Croker').
2 Standard Life prospectus (1839): 4.
3 Chisholm 1901: 186.
4 Smith 1851: 396.
5 Carlton 1955: 133–4. Dickens was accepted for £999 in July 1838 by the Britannia after being turned down by the Sun: Dickens 1965–2002, I: 352.
6 *Chambers's* 1857: 524.
7 Nisbet 1853: 4; Asylum prospectus (1838); Erith 1854: 15.
8 LGLPR.
9 CMRL 1824–95; Day 1887: 173; Sprague 1896: 383, 378.
10 Holcombe 1983: 46; Stebbings 2002: 11; Morris 2005: 127–30.
11 Simpson 1936: 33; Cox 1857: 9; Shepherd 1917: 16; Tosh 1991: 54.
12 Delany 2002: 142; *Dictionary of National Biography* (Lutyens).
13 Trollope 1861: 36.
14 McCarthy 2002: 411; PMDCF (policy on the life of Sarah Bellhouse).
15 Habakkuk 1994: 1–4, 62–5, 118–21.
16 Rock 1809: 16; *Times* (29 July 1892); Habakkuk 1994: 141, 637.
17 Daunton 1996: 137–8; *Bankers' Magazine* 58 (1894): 843; *Post Magazine* 58 (1897): 6; Tregoning and Cockerell 1982: 32.
18 Besant 1924: 237; Supple 1970: 223; Steuart 1937: 35; Powell 1896: 119.
19 Sources cited for Table 5.1.
20 LGNA.
21 Alborn, 'License,' 2008.
22 Bailey and Day 1861: 59; Pearson 1990: 241; LGLPR.
23 Habakkuk 1994: 340–4; Moss 2000: 18.
24 Habakkuk 1994: 263–5, 342, 636; Dickson, *Sun Fire,* 1960: 258–61; Ryan 1983: 748–9; Moss 2000: 45, 52; Supple 1970: 317; EMB X (18 May and 7 Sept. 1842).
25 Globe 1857: 61.

26 YMB XIX (3 Feb. 1858); Supple 1970: 175; EMB XX (31 Dec. 1887); EdMB XIV (23 March 1871).

27 Davidoff and Hall 1987: 207–11.

28 CWP (Mortgage Insurance); Fitzhugh 1863: 27; Emperor prospectus (1870): 7; *Post Magazine* 48 (1887): 154.

29 *Post Magazine* (26 April 1851), and 40 (1879): 414, 416, 435.

30 *Post Magazine* 44 (1883): 84; EdMB XIV (11 April 1871); Magnusson 1983: 57–8; Leigh-Bennett 1937: 93.

31 *Times* (19 Dec. 1856).

32 Bulwer-Lytton 1852: 339, 53–4; Thackeray 1848: 98, 669–71.

33 For examples of this kind of marketing in the United States, see Murphy 2005: 270–3.

34 Provident prospectus (1806): 4.

35 *Post Magazine* (10 Aug. 1850); Walford I: 220; Reliance Mutual 1850: 3; Lindsay 1987: 80; Saint-Clair 1840: 31.

36 Briton Life 1861: 5.

37 Walford III: 27; Star prospectus (1845): 16.

38 Smithson 1852, 7–8; Langley 1864: s. 225.

39 Dickens 1843: 83; Saint-Clair 1840: 39; *Insurance Record* 7 (1869): 412.

40 Lawrance 1843: 11–12; Reliance Mutual 1850: 7; Harris 1867: 9.

41 Sharman 1860 ('The Advantages of Promptitude'): 10–11; *Post Magazine* (18 Oct. 1851); Scottish Equitable 1887: 5.

42 Westall 1993: 196–7; Trebilcock II: 238; Pearson 2004: 283.

43 Hibberd 1855: 12; *Times* (11 July 1831); CMRL 1824–36; Ryan 1985: 183.

44 Babbage 1826: xv; *Lancet* (10 Feb. 1838); De Morgan 1838: 161.

45 *Memoranda* 1880: 12; *Uncle Tom's Twenty Reasons* 1860: 5; *To Parents* 1888: 5.

46 Ogborn 1962: 183; *Remarks* 1839: 6; *Insurance Record* 4 (1866): 195. On the standard representation of the Victorian breadwinner see Tosh 1999: 82–5.

47 Walford I: 38; Harris 1867: 10; Hilton 1884: 14.

48 Walford III: 158; *Insurance Record* 12 (1874): 335.

49 *Insurance Record* 3 (1865): 52; *Assurance Herald* 3 (1889): 633; Keating 1854: 18; Bate 1880: 55; Scratchley 1851: 67; Eagle sales brochure (ca 1870s).

50 *Assurance Gazette* 1 (1847): 3; Saint-Clair 1840: 42; Reliance Mutual 1850: 6.

51 Smithson 1852: 4; Cox 1857: 14–15; *Post Magazine* 23 (1862): 330. See also Alborn 2003: 81–3; Zelizer 1983: 79–84.

52 Hilton 1884: 10; *Account* 1839: 3; *Post Magazine* 15 (1854): 149.

53 *Insurance Record* 12 (1874): 300; Cox 1857: 13; Reliance Mutual 1850: 9. These depictions of destitute women resonated with the Victorian trope of the 'fallen woman,' on which see Anderson 1993, esp. 51–2.

54 Cansdell 1858: 15; Yorkshire Fire & Life prospectus (1824); Lawrance 1843: 34.
55 Kingsley 1882–83: 72; *Insurance Record* 12 (1874): 197, 371; *Life Agent's Mentor* 1890: 25.
56 Saint-Clair 1840: vii; *Weekly Notes* (1882): 354; *Post Magazine* (16 March 1850); *Notes and Queries* n.s. 3 (1862): 351. For Victorian attitudes about the evils of charity see Searle 1998: 16, 183–6.
57 Zelizer 1983: ix, 42–3; Richardson 1989: 105–15; Taylor 1983: 186–9; Laqueur 1983: 109–14; Church and Smith 1966: 621–6; Morris 1998: 113–14, and 2005: 79–109.
58 Scottish Equitable 1848: 14–15; *Once a Week* 1 (1880): 56; *Remarks* 1839: 5.
59 See, e.g., John Wesley's pronouncement that since the Fall, 'the air itself that surrounds us on every side is replete with the shafts of death,' reprinted in Lees 1843: 26.
60 Jalland 1996: 67; Brown 2001: 210; Walker 1991: 97–9.
61 Brown 2001; Tosh 1999: 54–7, 112–14.
62 Golby and Purdue 1999: 148–9; Brake 2001: 45.
63 *Policy-holder* 3 (1885): 297; *Insurance Record* 7 (1869): 204; Sharman 1860. Evangelicals and temperance reformers were similarly keen to exploit novels and short stories as a medium: see Brown 2001: 58–114, and Shiman 1988: 143–5.
64 Dickens 1853: 110, 160, 167, 464, 448–9; Welsh 1971: 59; Golby and Purdue 1999: 153–4.
65 Hadley 1995: 30–1.
66 Armstrong 1987: 5; Langland 1995: 46.
67 See esp. Gallagher 1985: 113–84.
68 In life insurance as well as other forms of insurance, there remain to this day substantial gaps between promise and practice that are apparently not inconsistent with commercial success: see (e.g.) Baker 1994.
69 Ryan 1985: 177; Saint-Clair 1840: 56–60.
70 *Post Magazine* 25 (1864); 37 (1876): 300; 42 (1881): 250. What 'immediate' payment meant in practice was that the company would pay as soon as it had verified the title, which could take up to three months: see *Post Magazine* 44 (1883): 183.
71 Scottish Equitable 1887: 6; CAB II (report by Joseph Mills, 19 June 1886).
72 Magnusson 1983: 55; EdMB XVIII (12 June 1880, 24 June 1880, 30 Sept. 1880).
73 *Insurance Record* 14 (1876): 231–2; 12 (1874): 420.
74 Peterson 1989: 125–30; Stebbings 2002: 6–9, 23–30; Morris 1994: 179–87.
75 *New Dictionary of National Biography* (Ann Alexander); *Times* (20 Oct. 1856).

76 Trollope 1859: 25–6, 83; *Household Words* 16 (1857): 38; Grey 1898: 35.
77 *New Dictionary of National Biography* (Walter Scott, Samuel Horsley).
78 Morris 1979: 92, 110; SLPM II (2 and 30 Aug. 1854); Jalland 1996: 237; *Return of Amount of Stamps* 1873: 365–6.
79 Murphy 2005: 159–67; *Post Magazine* 24 (1863): 65–6, 76; 28 (1867). An exception to the lack of British legislation enabling customers to settle policies on dependents concerned the several firms that registered under the 1834 Friendly Societies Act; their privilege of offering 'nomineeship' rights was revoked in 1850: see Supple 1974: 234; Hazell 1935: 24–8.
80 *Post Magazine* 39 (1878): 285–6; Bunyon 1868: xxxv.
81 *Post Magazine* 54 (1893): 785; Supple 1970: 255.
82 *Post Magazine* 43 (1882): 409; Holcomb 1983; Lindsay 1987: 110; English & Scottish Law prospectus (1885): 15.
83 *Post Magazine* 39 (1878): 54; 50 (1889): 663; 39 (1878): 54; and Sherriff 1940: 74–5.
84 *Policy-holder* 2 (1884): 13; Brown 1900: 409.
85 Jalland 1996: 199–200; Morley 1971: 76; Howarth 1997: 125; Dixon 1989: 149.
86 Tosh 1999: 170–94; Ormerod 1930: 3–4. For the marketing of life insurance to women see, e.g., Lutt 1907: 473; *Times* (27 May 1909, 29 April 1913); *Truth* (21 Sept. 1921).
87 Ewald 1991: 204; Orwell 1950: 191; Trebilcock II: 552; Syed 1997: 83.
88 Swaan 1990: 57.

6 Consuming Interest

1 ARAV (23 July 1867).
2 Clark 1999: 85–99; *Life Assurance Premiums* 1910: 4–7. The proportion of whole life policies issued by the Alliance rose from 77% in 1834 to 90% in 1867, and ranged between 87% and 93% at the Eagle between 1857 and 1892: ALCMB VI, XV; EMB.
3 *Twelfth Annual Report* 1853: xvi; *Economist* 27 (1869): 229.
4 Leigh 1916: 50; Supple 1970: 310, 332; Cassis 1994: 163; Checkland 1975: 530; *Statements* 1887: 370–4; 1914–16: 740–2.
5 Pearson 1990; Trebilcock I: 624–3.
6 Edinburgh Life prospectus (1885): 12.
7 Trebilcock I: 742, 755.
8 Supple 1970: 312–15; Trebilcock I: 620; Newmarch 1855: 264–7; Porter 1912: 617.
9 *Times* (13 April 1815 and 12 April 1825); Ryan 1983: 747, 751; Trebilcock I: 628.

10 *Economist* 61 (1903): 827; Trebilcock I: 633–9, 732; Ryan 1983: 748–50, 1134–5; Moss 2000: 34, 45, 52; Walford III: 42–4; Hewat 1896: 797.

11 Cannadine 1994: 42–3; CMB IV (7 May 1856); Ryan 1983: 1134–9; *Post Magazine* (8 Feb. 1851); Conder 1979: 143–4; Ryan 1983: 755–7; Thomson 1868: 15–16.

12 Supple 1970: 318; LGBM X (27 Dec. 1854); Ryan 1983: 378–82.

13 Cannadine 1994: 37, 44–7; Trebilcock I: 643; Habakkuk 1994: 64–5, 107.

14 Lane 1974: 67–81, 85–7; *Insurance Record* 4 (1866): 47; *Post Magazine* 47 (1886): 217; Day 1887: 175.

15 Lindsay 1987: 112; Ryan 1983: 774–6; Moss 2000: 110–12, 142; *Post Magazine* 51 (1890): 66.

16 Trebilcock II: 64; Ryan 1983: 761; Cannadine 1994: 50; *Journal of the Institute of Actuaries* 17 (1873): 296; *Statements* 1901: 370.

17 YMB XLVI (11 April 1888); Supple 1970: 344; Lindsay 1987: 116, 120; *Post Magazine* 47 (1886): 217–18; *Bankers' Magazine* 50 (1890): 1042, and 62 (1896): 664–5; Moss 2000: 114–16, 172.

18 Thomson 1868: 13; *Insurance Record* 5 (1867): 263; SACR (6 March 1878); *First Report* 1844: 152; Moss 2000: 70–1; Ryan 1983: 768, 771.

19 *Report ... on Friendly Societies Act* 1889: 223; WMB III (13 Jan. 1846); LGBM X (2 Jan. 1855); Supple 1970: 322; Trebilcock II: 29–31.

20 LGBM VII (10 Feb. 1852), IX (15 May 1854), XIII (4 Jan. and 28 June 1859), XV (18 Feb. 1862), XVI (25 March 1862), XXII (1 Aug. 1871), XXVII (28 June 1881).

21 GuMB VIII (6 Dec. 1855); Supple 1970: 324. Sixty per cent of loans to poor law unions in 1874, and 85% of loans to sanitary authorities, were repayable in 30 annual instalments: *Return of Monies* 1877.

22 Saltzman 2005: 186–7; YMB XIII (13 May 1848), XVI (31 Dec. 1851), XVII (22 March 1854); *Return of Amount* 1852.

23 *Return of Monies* 1877; Supple 1970: 340; *Journal of the Institute of Actuaries* 17 (1873): 296; *Economist* 61 (1903): 827; Finlaison 1895: 425; Supple 1970: 332; Appendix 3.1.

24 *Statements* 1872: 32, 41, 50, 130, 262, 267, 279, 313; Alborn 1998: 194–207; Coles 1869; Docherty 1974: 24–6; *First Report* 1844: 136.

25 Trebilcock II: 79–81, 87; Ryan 1983: 1167–8; Moss 2000: 98, 134, 170; Barrand 1899: 455–60; Appendix 3.1.

26 Page 1879: 739; Newman 1908: 302–3; Scott 2002: 79–83; Abbott 1998: 186–7; *Journal of the Institute of Actuaries* 61 (1929): 383–7.

27 Malcolm and Hamilton 1875: 392; Barrand 1899: 422; Appendix 3.2 and sources cited therein.

28 *Statements* 1896–1911; Ryan 1983: 1167–8; Moss 2000: 134, 171–4; Appendix 3.2. High yields did not always mean large bonuses for these exporters,

since (in the case of the Gresham and Standard Life) these were counteracted by heavier expenses.

29 Appendix 3.1; *Statements* 1891–1911.

30 *Statements* 1874 and 1911; Baker and Collins 2005: 154–5.

31 Raynes 1948: 134; Ryan 1985: 171.

32 Ogborn 1962: 122, 156–7, 164.

33 AtMB I (8 Jan. 1808); UlMB I (12 March 1835).

34 Rock 1906: 12; CWP (Provident Life); EMB VI (31 Aug. 1826); Supple 1970: 133; Minnitt 1985: 30–1.

35 Saint-Clair 1840: 56–60; Trebilcock I: 587; RFMB XV (15 Feb. 1875); Blayney 1848: 29; Walford I: 369; Ryan 1985: 172; YMB 20 (1 March 1858).

36 Ryan 1983: 235; Kelly 1835: 222.

37 Docherty 1974: 35; Standard Life prospectus (1839): 7–8; *Post Magazine* 55 (1894): 292; Cox and Storr-Best 1962: 25–6, 31; Scottish Widows' Fund prospectus (1842): 13–14; SAMB XII (18 April 1882); Walford II: 450; Rock 1809: 7.

38 Steuart 1937: 7; *Post Magazine* 42 (1881): 337–8.

39 *Bankers' Magazine* 53 (1890): 527; Walford 1867: 314–17. For examples of 'immediate bonus' offices see the Albion's and City of Glasgow's 1849 prospectuses.

40 Walford II: 462; *Times* (3 March 1910).

41 Ryan 1985: 187, 196; Moss 2000: 95–6.

42 *Bankers' Magazine* 55 (1893): 526; Cox and Storr-Best 1962: 39. On American deferred bonus policies see Ransom and Sutch 1987; Keller 1963: 56–8, 88.

43 GBL; Downes 1859: 10; *Post Magazine* 23 (1862): 9; Walford II: 434; *Economist* 44 (1886): 828, 856; Gattie 1889: 511. A handful of firms, most notably the London Life, required policyholders to receive bonuses in the form of reduced premiums: see Conder 1979: 51, 213.

44 Saint-Clair 1840: 56–60; Ogborn 1962: 231; Pocock 1842: 106–42.

45 Pelican prospectus (1842); Argus prospectus (ca. 1835): 3.

46 Cox and Storr-Best 1962: 29; Supple 1970: 173; Walford I: 586; Minnitt 1985: 36; *Statements* 1872. The two holdouts were the Friends' Provident and National Provident.

47 Jones 1877: 45; LGRA (report by Ernest Colquhoun, 1891).

48 ARAV; Downes 1859: 24; *Statements* 1872–91, 1901; LGRA (report by Ernest Colquhoun, 1891); GVS.

49 Richards 1990: 54; Poovey 2002; Searle 1998.

50 Schabas 1990; Collini, Winch, and Burrow 1983: 311–7 and *passim*.

51 Richards 1990: 58–9, 66; Rock 1906: 50. The other two elements are 'the transformation of the commodity into language [and] the figuration of a

consuming subject,' both of which also apply to life insurance but would take too much space to illustrate than is available here.

52 See, e.g., Besant 1924: 126; LGBM XXV (16 Jan. 1877); SMB XXII (31 Dec. 1903).

53 CAB I (reports by B. Hall Todd, 1870 and 1874); RFBR (24 March 1874); *Post Magazine* 37 (1876): 496.

54 CMVN.

55 Ogborn 1962: 124–5. For justifications see *Peeps* 1908: 60–1; Edinburgh Life prospectus (1842): 9.

56 Babbage 1826: 103; De Morgan 1838: 278; *Twelfth Annual Report* 1853: xxxi; Barrow 1827: 27; Hardy 1837: 240.

57 Cox and Storr-Best 1962: 17; EcMB IV (12 Dec. 1844); SAMB X (1847 bonus report); PLNCH 93; EMB XII (13 Aug. 1852).

58 *Insurance Record* 39 (1901): 575, and 40 (1902): 324; SUNMB (April 1905).

59 NMAGB (Dec. 1898 form letter).

60 Sprague 1884: 235; *Post Magazine* 47 (1886): 121 (on the Scottish Union & National).

61 EMB XIII (14 Aug. 1857); *Post Magazine* 43 (1882): 11.

62 *Times* (1 Nov. 1911); EdMB XV (24 Aug. 1871); WSLB (29 June 1833); Worland and Paterson 1976: 41, 124.

63 *Post Magazine* 42 (1881): 174; *Insurance Record* 13 (1875): 107, 110, 276.

64 Blake 1958: 31; Ryan 1983: 301, 312–34.

65 NULMB VI (30 June 1852; *Insurance Record* 5 (1867): 118–19; Ryan 1983: 370–2.

66 NULMB XXI (24 Nov. 1886), and XXVI (4 Nov. 1901).

67 GMTS (23 Oct. 1912); SLRV I: 181, 239–40, 293; Moss 2000: 149–53; *Pioneer* (8 Nov. 1906).

68 *Times* (21 and 25 Aug., 4 Oct. 1869); Walford I: 387, and III: 48–54.

69 Walford I: 331; ASLOMB II (24 and 31 May 1869).

70 Bailey 1878: 123; *Economist* 56 (1898): 614; Supple 1970: 336; Besant 1924: 232–3; *Post Magazine* 58 (1897): 20; SASB (H.J. Pearce to R. Stone, 18 July 1907).

71 SUNMB (April 1905); *Times* (2 April 1913).

72 LGRGM (memo by E. Colquhoun, ca 1918; T.E. Young, 4 Nov. 1918, recalling a speech from March 1889); *Bankers' Magazine* 48 (1888): 959.

73 See, e.g., AMB XV (11 Oct. 1893); Schooling 1924: 53; *Insurance Record* 7 (1869): 123; Worland and Paterson 1976: 86–7.

74 Moss 2000: 191–3; quoted in Supple 1970: 299.

75 Owen 1832: 52; Mill 1848: I: 246.

76 Another debate that focused on intergenerational issues concerned the financing of the Crimean War: see Anderson 1963.

77 Sturrock 1846: 24; 'Life Assurance Premiums and Policies' 1849: 141.
78 For examples of this argument see chapter 7.
79 Undated sales brochure (EA 6/1/1/1); *Insurance Record* 14 (1876): 370.
80 Appendix 1 and sources cited therein.
81 *Post Magazine* 49 (1888): 267; Brown 1856: 6; North British & Mercantile
     1873: 9; *Saturday Review* 93 (1902): 141.
82 Scottish Widows' Fund prospectus (1842): 16–17; Brown 1835: 19, 11.
83 Standard Life prospectus (1839): 7; NULMB VIII (1857 bonus report);
     Low 1843: 18; North British & Mercantile 1873: 15; *Bankers' Magazine* 56
     (1893): 641.
84 EMB XXIV (16 March 1898); Yorkshire prospectus (1900): 12; *Post Magazine*
     53 (1892): 448; Hendriks 1893: 274.
85 De Morgan 1838: 283; Brown 1889: 1092; Standard Life prospectus (1840): 15.
86 *Insurance Record* 16 (1878): 325, 332, 340.
87 *Post Magazine* 46 (1885): 415; SMB XII (28 May 1884); Whittall 1897: 10;
     Besant 1924: 275; ARAV (14 Aug. 1893).
88 Zelizer 1983: 94, 116.
89 Clark 1999: 57.
90 See, e.g., *Times* (7 July 1877, 8 July 1881 [Clergy Mutual], 10 Feb. 1890
     [Friends' Provident]); *Outlook* 2 (1899): 723.
91 Blake 1958: 25–6; *Statements* 1883: 270–1, and 1903: 436–7.
92 *Bankers' Magazine* 55 (1893): 523–4.
93 Bailey 1875: 9; NLAR (9 May 1891).
94 *Statements* 1892: 382–5, and 1893: 140; *Times* (4 March 1892).
95 *Statements* 1893: 131, 268.

7 Little Piles of Savings

1 Hewat 1892: 636.
2 Scratchley 1851: 63.
3 The exception to this rule were aristocratic debtors with large policies
    covering equally large loans; but in their case the creditor as opposed to
    the insurer exerted the discipline, by requiring premium payments as part
    of the interest.
4 Checkland 1975: 406; Holmes and Green 1986: 2–3.
5 Gosden 1973: 210–21; Supple 1974: 240–1; Alborn 1998: 137–9; *Return of
    Savings Banks* 1871: 38. The interest rate on savings bank deposits was
    reduced to 3.8% in 1828.
6 Commercial Life prospectus (1840): 8; Harrison 1992: 35 (Patriotic prospec-
    tus, 1856).

7 Hardy 1837: 244; Albion prospectus (1849): 13; Conder 1979: 25; Pelican prospectus (1814): 11; *Hand Book* 1856: 40.
8 WMB I (1 May 1839); WBP 30011.231 (F. Elderton to John Blackwood, 10 Aug. 1858).
9 Walford II: 451; V: 571; III: 101; and De Morgan 1838: 267; WMB I (12 and 19 Feb. 1839).
10 De Morgan 1838: 266–7.
11 Ibid., 266; Hardy 1837: 240; Ogborn 1962: 185.
12 Cited in Stalson 1942: 273; Smithson 1852: 8; Saint-Clair 1840: 35.
13 Commercial Life prospectus (1840): 8. See also Rhind 1839: 10; Saint-Clair 1840: 33–5; Low n.d.: 29. An additional incentive to employ life insurance as a savings mechanism appeared after 1853, when a new tax code enabled policyholders to deduct premium payments prior to reporting their taxable income: see Zimmeck 1985.
14 *Uncle Tom's Twenty Reasons* 1860: 4; Hannam 1860: 101; Nevins 1860–61: 66, 70.
15 Aytoun 1853: 107, 112; *Report of the Massachusetts Insurance Commissioners* 1859: 3.
16 Low 1843: 28–9; *Benefit Societies* 1822: 4–5; *Report ... on the Laws respecting Friendly Societies* 1825: 9.
17 National Loan Fund prospectus (1837): 4–5, 7; *Report ... on Friendly Societies* 1852: 44; Scratchley 1851: 16–18.
18 Walford II: 28, 150, and I: 397, 474; Robertson 1852: 47.
19 United Deposit prospectus (1845): 3–5; City of Glasgow prospectus (1846): 5–7; Soper 1847: 10–11; General Life prospectus (ca 1850); Deposit & General prospectus (1852); Walford I: 373. For deposit branches, see Walford I: 261; II: 28, 55; III: 26, 37; IV: 379; and Sovereign Life prospectus (undated).
20 City of Glasgow prospectus (1846): 6; United Deposit prospectus (1845): 5.
21 *Observations* 1838: 19–21; De Morgan 1846: 436; *Post Magazine* (2 Aug. 1851).
22 Supple 1970: 183; Eagle advertisement (1893); EMB XXII (6 Nov. 1889).
23 EcMB I (14 July 1826); Trebilcock I: 589–90; Walford I : 585; AtMB VI (25 Jan. 1839); SAMB X (1845–49); Tregoning and Cockerell 1982: 28; Harrison 1992: 38 (Patriotic prospectus, 1854).
24 Moss 2000: 79; Globe 1857: 72; Scottish Widows' Fund prospectus (1842): 47; CMB IV (7 May 1859); *Statements* 1884; ASLOMB III (21 Jan. 1874); AMB X (27 Oct. 1875).
25 *Post Magazine* 46 (1885): 79, 190, and 47 (1886): 275; *Policy-holder* 1 (1883): 8, 3 (1885): 117.
26 LOASB V (11 May 1905).

27 D. Jones 1843: 1159; *Times* (13 March 1911 and 25 Nov. 1913).
28 Walford I: 383, 461, 610, and II: 287 (Professional, British Nation, Colonial, Diadem); Baylis et al. 1851: 6 (Waterloo); *Daily News* (5 April 1851 [Trafalgar]).
29 NLAR (Francis Lamb to A.K. Tharp, 20 Sept. 1892); *Economist* 56 (1898): 232; *Times* (7 March 1907); Clough 1946: 266–7; GMTS (report by Harry Bearman, 13 May 1919).
30 *Post Magazine* 42 (1881): 36; 47 (1886): 712; 49 (1888): 839; and Ryan 1983: 611; *Economist* 61 (1903): 649–50, and 63 (1905): 1921.
31 Raynes 1948: 134; Ogborn 1962: 183; Hardy 1837: 240.
32 *Hand Book* 1856: 48; Nevins 1860–61: 80.
33 These companies were the Reversionary Interest (est. 1823), General Reversionary (1836), Norwich Reversionary (1836), National Reversionary (1837), and Law Reversionary (1853).
34 Sprague 1884: 232.
35 EcMB I (10 April 1829); Docherty 1974: 53; Life Association of Scotland brochure (1860); Walford II: 20; *Post Magazine* 37 (1876): 396.
36 *Economist* 50 (1892): 789; NLAR (16 Aug. 1892).
37 King 1896: 415; Higham 1851: 194–5; *Times* (12 Nov. 1880); *Economist* 43 (1885): 377; *Post Magazine* 47 (1886): 90; *Accountant* 24 (1898): 1193.
38 A sample of nineteen policies sold at three different auctions in 1878 netted just 11% more than their office valuations: *Insurance Record* 16 (1878): 188, 236–7, 309.
39 *Insurance Record* 14 (1876): 369; *Times* (22 July 1908); NLAR (13 June 1892).
40 Brewer 1990: 122, 125; Fairman 1802: 160; Porter 1912: 617; Levi 1862: 331.
41 Francis 1853: 157–68; Lewin 2003: 398–404.
42 Westminster Life prospectus (1792): 5; Supple 1970: 66–7, 118; Walford I: 145–6.
43 Walford I: 146, 159, 167; YLB (William Newman to R.W. Moxon, 12 Jan. 1825); Spater 1951: 17; SNMB I (5 Dec. 1843).
44 Provident prospectus (1806): 11; Scottish Widows' prospectus (1814): 18; Fernie 1822: 6; *Remarks* 1839: 22.
45 Alfred prospectus (1856); National Loan Fund prospectus (1838): 5, 2; Cordery 2003: 133.
46 Commercial Life prospectus (1840): 13–14; Walford I: 185, and II: 476–78; *Daily News* (5 April 1851); *Times* (11 Dec. 1863); Dowdeswell 1846: 129–32.
47 UlMB I (12 June 1834); Walford III: 164–5, and III: 158; Corbaux 1833: xvi, 117–19.
48 Bacon 1838: 47; Meikle 1872: 25.
49 *British Almanac* 1847: 164; Morris 2005: 172–7; Walford I: 55. The continued success of mutual pension plans among some professions (especially

lawyers) did probably divert some deferred annuity business from life insurance companies, but these were mostly limited to Scotland.
50 *Times* (21 Feb. 1911).
51 Pocock 1842: 100, 136; Spater 1951: 19; *Post-Office Annual Directory* 1841: lvii; Saint-Clair 1840: n.p. (National Endowment advertisement); AMB IV (29 March 1848); CEMB II (7 Dec. 1849); Supple 1970: 173; Minerva prospectus (1851): 6–7; ELI; Blake 1958: 42; Albion prospectus (1856); 11.
52 *Post-Office Annual Directory* 1841: lxxxvi; King 1876: 383.
53 Briton Life 1861: 20; *Policy-holder* 2 (1884): 310; *Lancet* (15 Nov. 1890); *Post Magazine* 53 (1892): 351, 371; Great Britain Mutual prospectus (1872): 5–7.
54 *Economist* 51 (1893): 411; *Post Magazine* 56 (1895): 157; *Statements* 1902: 43, 70, 309, 476; 1904: 12; 1911: 824–7.
55 Macnicol 1998: 7–12, 60–136; Paulin 1896: 14.
56 *Statements* 1911: 824–7; Moss 2000: 102; Walford II: 500; Supple 1970: 253; Besant 1924: 203; Lindsay 1987: 135; Andras 1895.
57 *Statements* 1911: 824–7. Based on median premiums in *Life Assurance Premiums* 1910: 4–5, 14.
58 Morgan 1891: 7; Newbatt 1891: 25; *Post Magazine* 53 (1892): 375.
59 Mills 1898: 177; *Post Magazine* 53 (1892): 411.
60 *Insurance Record* 40 (1902): 221; Moss 2000: 154–5; Ryan 1983: 251.
61 *Insurance Record* 40 (1902): 324; Westminster & General prospectus (1860): 9; PLPCA; *Policy-holder* 2 (1884): 13.
62 Briton Life 1861: 15; *Bankers' Magazine* 51 (1891): 905; Hannah 1988: 37. On the 'growing anxiety' of middle-aged men concerning their 'long–term financial stability' in the twentieth century, see Benson 1997: 126–8.
63 Morris 1979: 110.
64 On group pensions see Supple 1970: 436; Butt 1984: 164–7; Hannah 1988: 36–7; Dougharty 1920.

8 Victorian Gatekeeping

1 Harris 1867: 3.
2 North 1990: 30; Stone 2002: 52.
3 As discussed in chapter 7, life insurance practice regarding surrender values was also informed by the perceived moral hazard problem that healthy policyholders lapsed at higher rates.
4 Alborn forthcoming.
5 Clark 1999: 128–9.
6 Dickson, *Sun Fire*, 1960: 82; Pearson 2002: 15–16.
7 Trebilcock I: 141–8; Walford I: 6, 329, and III: 286.

8 Exceptional insurance-related murder cases included Thomas Wainewright, who killed his half-sister in 1830 after insuring her life for £18,000; William Palmer, who was suspected of killing sixteen people in the mid-1850s for insurance money; and Alfred Monson, who was charged but acquitted in 1893 for the murder of Cecil Hambrough. See Francis 1853: 213–25; Sweet 2001: 71–85; Roughead 2000: 379–464.

9 Burns 1873: 59–60; Walford II: 491; *Policy-holder* 4 (1886): 147, and 2 (1884): 30; Magnusson 1983: 25–34, 84.

10 NULRD (declaration forms from 1837, 1859, 1870, and 1879).

11 PCPF.

12 Walford II: 98; *Supplement* 1864: xvi ; Meikle 1872: 45; Walford I: 393; Smith 1862: 6; Morgan 1841: 81; Robertson 1865: 29–31.

13 Walford V: 584; Stewart 1861: 49; Brinton 1856: 25; NULRD; NULMB VIII (29 Oct. 1857).

14 Porter 1860: 105, 111; Alborn 2001: 414–23.

15 ASLOMB I ('Proposed Regulations for adoption ... in Cases of Consumptive Lives,' ca 1841); Manly 1892: 126.

16 Fleming 1862: 66. On the history of gout (an arthritic condition caused by a build-up of uric acid in the joints of fingers and toes) see Porter and Rousseau 1998.

17 Brockbank 1908: 155; Begbie 1853: 167; Meikle 1872: 50; Moinet 1876: 36; Williamson 1912: 24.

18 SLSB XIV (memo on hernia from H. Jones Williams, 2 May 1856); Meikle 1872: 50; see also Humphreys 1874: 187, 194. For examples of earlier penalties see RLCB II (26 May 1814); CMMB I (13 April 1825); WSLB (16 Nov. 1835).

19 Brockbank 1908: 238; ESLMB XIV (5 Aug. 1897); Hall 1896; LOASB V (circular letter from J.C. Wardrop, 3 Jan. 1906).

20 ESLMB I (3 March 1841); YMPF (friend's report to European, 7 June 1853); NULMB IX (19 April 1860); AFLG I (8 Oct. 1844).

21 Muirhead 1902: 31; Walford IV: 175; Mann 1865: 26, 74–5; Alborn forthcoming.

22 Mann 1865: 25; Smee 1871: 3; Begbie 1853: 151, 160, and 1860: 17.

23 *Fourth Annual Report* 1842: 163; Bury 1900–02: 12; Pruitt 1974: 94.

24 Rock 1906: 39.

25 Of 156 life offices in 1856, 119 met either at noon, 1:00, or 2:00; and 111 met on Tuesday, Wednesday, or Thursday: *Hand Book* 1856: 2–11.

26 LGBM I (20 Sept. 1836); WMB I (2 May 1837); Walford I: 182; Moss 2000: 29–30; ALCMB VI (1834).

27 Ogborn 1962: 102–3; Jureidini and White 2000: 198; Westminster Life prospectus (1792): 14; *Kent's* 1825: 406, 413; Trebilcock I: 530, 608.

28 Besant 1924: 155, 182–3, 303, 321; Kempe 1902: 68–74; Blake 1958: 72–3; NULMB XXII (24 July 1888).

29 *Kent's* 1825: 401–28; WSMBE (April 1837); SMB I (21 Feb. 1849).

30 SLPM V (16 July 1872); LGLB I (22 Feb. 1837); Eagle prospectus (1847): 4; PLPCA (1887); English & Scottish Law prospectus (1907): 4. For house calls see UlMB I (2 March 1837); LGLB II (8 Jan. and 29 March 1848).

31 Earnings are taken from Conder 1979: 266; Lindsay 1987: 39; *Equity and Law* (1994): 4; Magnusson 1983: 39; and board minutes of the Alliance, Caledonian, Church of England, Edinburgh, English & Scottish Law, Legal & General, Scottish Amicable, Scottish National, Scottish Union & National, Standard Life, Star, Universal, University, and Westminster & General.

32 *Medical Register* (1859–1910). The only hospital with more insurance doctors than St Thomas's was the Brompton Hospital for Consumption.

33 WMB I (23 Sept. 1839); Stoeckle 1987: 51.

34 *Medical Register* (1870–1910).

35 Alborn 2001: 414–16; Porter and Rousseau 1998: 192; *New Dictionary of National Biography* (Duncan, Gowers, and Peacock).

36 CMC (revised private friends' report, 1834); EFR; Moss 2000: 58; NULRD.

37 RLCB II (17 April 182); EFR (Henry Lindsell's responses concerning John Sydney Farrell, 1851); NULRD (James Healy; friend's report, 15 July 1839).

38 Dickens 1860: 400, and II: 494–5.

39 CMC (22 Nov. 1824); Christison 1850: 318; NULRD.

40 Metcalf 1967: 91; Christison 1850: 323.

41 CMC (R. Sherwood to John Pinckard, 8 July 1825; Charles C. Clark to George Pinckard, 21 Nov. 1826; Dr Hastings to George Pinckard, 25 March 1827).

42 AFLG 1 (8 Oct 1844); LGLB VI (31 March 1858).

43 Christison 1850: 326; *Lancet* (10 Feb. 1838); YMPF (European Life, 1859 medical attendant's report); NULRD (Law Union, ca 1879).

44 Marshall 1808: 782–83.

45 *Times* (31 July 1841); Taylor 1847: 52; Walford II: 449; Farren 1823: 175, 177, 189–90.

46 *Times* (6 Dec. 1831, 11 June 1833); Robertson 1848: 30.

47 For examples of out-of-court settlements see EdMB III (7 Feb. 1833); EMB VIII (1 April 1835); EcMB II (14 Feb. 1837); AtMB VI (10 Nov. 1838); *Post Magazine* 44 (1883): 321; CMB X (15 July 1890).

48 Robertson 1848: 14; *Times* (10 March 1846); Walford V: 458.

49 Villaronga 1976: 5; Scratchley 1851: 37; *Daily News* (5 April 1851); Walford I: 17, 185, 268, 388, 474, and II: 287, 490; Jopling 1854: 15.

50 SLSB XI (10 April 1851); CWP (Indisputable); North British & Mercantile 1873: 32; *Post Magazine* (24 May 1851).

51 Scottish Widows' prospectus (1842): 45.
52 Finn 2003: 289–314; Trebilcock I: 147; Walford 1879: 12; ESLMB I (5 Feb. 1840); ASLOMB I (20 April 1854); Associated Scottish Life Offices 1895: 75 (21 Dec. 1892); LOAMB I (9 Jan. 1893).
53 LOAMB I (19 June 1895); LOASB IV (6 Jan. 1899). The registry was modelled on a similar scheme designed by the Boston Library Bureau for North American offices: see LOASB I (23 Nov. 1892).
54 Pollock and Chisholm 1889: 175; Moxley 1903: 300.
55 See, e.g., *Times* (4 Aug. 1858, 18 Dec. 1862); *Insurance Record* 16 (1878): 235.
56 Taylor 1847: 265; Alborn forthcoming.
57 Amicable prospectus (ca. 1854): 12; MPAC III (2 Dec. 1876); *Times* (27 Sept. 1911); Kempe 1902: 32–3.
58 EcMB II (21 Sept. 1838); Withers 1951: 55; Nicoll 1904: 59.
59 Walford I: 175; National Loan Fund prospectus (1837): 7; Docherty 1974: 30.
60 Ryan 1985: 177; Walford I: 175 (Hope, 1807); Albion prospectus (1805); AtMB I (20 Dec. 1810).
61 Conder 1979: 165; LGLB I (31 Jan. 1837, 2 Jan. 1838); Walford I: 216.
62 See, e.g., AFLG I (18 May 1847); SAMBB (1 April and 6 May 1852).
63 Drew 1928: 60; AtMB I (24 Nov. 1808); Palladium 1825; Globe 1857: 64; CMC (undated form letter to agents, ca 1830).
64 De Morgan 1831: 94; NULRD. The Norwich Union forms are especially useful since they were multiple-choice in format.
65 AtMB V (6 March 1832); *Times* (13 Aug. 1896); Palladium 1825; Bignold 1948: 120.
66 Jellicoe 1895: 3; Walford 1880: 162.
67 See, e.g., ASLOMB I (8 Oct. 1834).
68 Chisholm 1901: 188; Rodger 1905: 54.
69 *Times* (27 Sept. 1911); Scottish Amicable 1887: 4; Langley 1864: s. 165.
70 EcMB II (3 Feb. 1837); *Lancet* (23 Sept. 1837, 18 Nov. 1848, 3 March 1849, 28 Aug. 1852, and 2 Nov. 1855); NULRD (16 Dec. 1858).
71 *Lancet* (27 Oct. 1849, 26 Oct. 1850); Sprigge 1897: 457.
72 Ibid. (9 Dec. 1848, 27 Jan. 1849, 23 and 28 May 1853, 30 Jan. 1858, 1 March 1862).
73 Ibid. (31 Aug. 1850, 21 March 1846).
74 ASLOMB I (15 Feb. 1850); *Lancet* (26 Oct. 1850, 14 March 1868); NULRD.
75 RLMB I (8 Dec. 1808); Blake 1958: 26; CWP (Medical Examination); AMB I (30 June 1824); Palladium 1825: 18–19; WSLB (J.J. Duncan to W.D. Henderson, 29 June 1833.
76 SAMB X (12 Dec. 1849); Loudon 1986: 278; Calwell 1911: 49; NULMB XIX (23 April 1880); Harris 1899: 164–5, 178; *Medical Examiner* 3/2 (1902): 5.

77 SNMB II (31 1847). See also WSLB (J.J. Duncan to W.D. Henderson, 29 June
.1833); UIMB I (31 July 1834); *Insurance Record* 6 (1868): 15; Langley 1864: s. 164.
78 Digby 1999: 79, 261–75; Marland 1987: 176-204.
79 *British Medical Journal* (25 Jan. 1896); 2 Jan. 1904. For examples of 10s 6d as
the normal fee, see AMB I (30 June 1824); Yorkshire Fire & Life 1848: 36.
80 *British Medical Journal* (2 Feb. 1901, 6 Feb. 1904, 21 Dec. 1901).
81 *Lancet* (29 Oct. and 5 Nov. 1898); *British Medical Journal* (24 April 1897 and
3 June 1899); Digby 1999: 23–32.
82 Walford 1880: 167–8; *British Medical Journal* (22 Feb. 1908).
83 Brinton 1856; Sieveking 1874; Pollock and Chisholm 1889; *British Medical
Journal* (30 Jan. 1892).
84 CMB VII (22 Nov. 1881); NULRD.
85 *Hand Book* 1856: 58.
86 Lyon 1901: 138, and 1895: 58.
87 Pollock and Chisholm 1889: 19; CAB I–II; Hughes 1899: 395.
88 *Insurance Record* 2 (1864): 395; *Policy-holder* 3 (1885): 142; Warner 1909: 76;
Sim 1888: 47; Saville 1872: 449.
89 *Medical Examiner* 5/3 (1904): 8.
90 Sutton 1890: 178–9; Minnitt 1985: 44; *Times* (9–11 and 15 Feb. and 7 Aug.
1890); *British Medical Journal* (22 Feb. 1890); *Lancet* (15 Feb. 1890).
91 CMB X (27 Jan., 24 Feb., 3 and 10 March 1891); *British Medical Journal*
(5 March 1892); *Caledonian Jottings* 1 (1891): 3–4, 12–13, 15. Sales figures
are from *Caledonian Jottings* and CMB X–XII, passim.
92 Minnitt 1985 44–5; *Insurance Record* 39 (1901): 168; Dickson, *Sun Life,* 1960:
26; *Medical Examiner* 4/3 (1903): 7; Prudential 1922: 37.
93 EMB XXII (3 Aug. 1892); *Post Magazine* 51 (1890): 714; PMDCF (1919 policy).
94 Thomson 1901: 293; *British Medical Journal* (14 March 1891); Gullan 1908–09:
37; *Medical Examiner* 5/2 (1904): 4.
95 *British Medical Journal* (21 Oct. 1905); Supple 1970: 280; Yorkshire prospectus (1908): 18; *Saturday Review* 110 (1910): 773–4; Metcalf 1967: 85.
96 Le Grys 1998: 171, 173; Conder 1979: 166; Metcalf 1967: 85.
97 Minnit 1985: 44; *Times* (8 Feb. 1945); Steeds 1964: 270 (comment by C.L.
Jaggers), 238; Le Grys 1998: 173.
98 Black 1861: 7; Birrell 1911: 74.
99 Titmuss 1976: 178–9.

9 Detecting Deviance

1 Mann 1865: 98.
2 Thompson 1879: 1; Fenwick 1873: 27; Bury 1894: 3.

3 Foucault 1975; Reiser 1978: 170.
4 Hutchinson 1852: 38.
5 Brinton 1856: 4; *Insurance Record* 13 (1875): 117; Williamson 1912: 10; Taylor 1909: 57.
6 Fox 1901: 132; Ward 1857: 67; Pollock and Chisholm 1889: 28; Glascott 1885–86: 15.
7 Risdon 1904: 56; Glascott 1885–86: 14; Davidson 1889; Fox 1901: 134.
8 Fox 1901: 134; Rickards 1901–2: 46; Bury 1900–02: 6–7; Gullan 1908–09: 35.
9 Sieveking 1874: 19, 40; Calwell 1911: 56; Williamson 1911: 16. Some forms of deception, including impersonation and lying about family history, needed to be guarded against in other ways – through an accurate description by the agent and confirmation with the GRO, respectively: see above.
10 *Medical Examiner* 2 (1901) nos. 6, 9; *Godey's Magazine* 18 (1839): 154.
11 Heron 1898: 103; Francis 1878: 786; Muirhead 1902: 43.
12 NULMB X (25 Nov. 1861); SABMB III (27 June 1872); Brockbank 1908: 60; *Insurance Record* 4 (1866): 246; Calwell 1911: 50; Muirhead 1902: 43.
13 Powell 1912: 503; Bramwell 1887: 23. Cf Horstman 1997: 75.
14 Chisholm 1901: 182, 187; Brockbank 1908: 20–1. For typical responses to rejected candidates' queries see RLMB I (1 Dec. 1808); NULMB IX (23 Jan. 1860); BEMMB (July 1848).
15 *Lancet* (6 Feb. 1904); Dawson 1907: 157; Muirhead 1902: 43.
16 Lawrence 1985: 507–10; Digby 1999: 188–9, 222; Digby 1994: 103.
17 Jureidini and White 2000: 191; Horstman 1997; Dupree 1997; Porter 2000.
18 *Post Magazine* 56 (1895): 51; Conder 1979: 199; Hutchinson 1852: 61.
19 *British Medical Journal* (5 Jan. 1884); Duckworth 1896: 134; Bramwell 1887: 6.
20 Risdon 1904: 56; Bruce 1900: 20.
21 NULRD (Scottish Equitable, 1880; Life Association of Scotland, 1880); NMAGB (National Mutual, 1898); PMDCF VI (Provident Clerks', 1897); PCPF (Royal Exchange, 1851); EP (Eagle, 1852). Strumous symptoms, in this context, would have referred to swollen lymphatic glands, indicating scrofula.
22 Thompson 1879: 30; Brinton 1856: 17; Williams 1904: 289–90; Brockbank 1908: 36.
23 PMDCF (Provident Clerks', 1897); SAMB XII (Scottish Amicable, 1877); Ward 1857: 6–7; Withers 1951: 55.
24 Mann 1865: 97; *Lancet* (6 Feb. 1904). See Jordanova 1993: 123–4.
25 Stewart 1861: 3; Ward 1857: 9; Mann 1865: 97.
26 Bruce 1900: 21; Ogilvie 1897: 86; Stashower 1999: 66; Dickens 1860: 397; Speight 1888: 584.
27 NULRD ; Bynum 1994: 35; Reiser 1978: 25–29, 40–3; Nicolson 1993: 136–39, 144–52; Christison 1853: 126; Powell 1878: 22.

28 Hutchinson 1852: 26–30; Lawrence 1985: 514; Powell 1878: 25; Thompson 1879: 51.
29 Glascott 1885–86: 15; Pollock and Chisholm 1889: 31; Bell 1903: 2; Calwell 1911: 52. The phrase 'sartorial dominance' is from Stoeckle 1987: 45.
30 NULRD (Norwich Union, 1897); Ogilvie 1897: 87.
31 Chisholm 1886: 411; Fox 1914: 1–2.
32 Hutchinson 1852: 56; Arthur Dingman, cited in Porter 2000: 240.
33 Hutchinson 1852: 56; *Assurance Magazine* 1 (1850): 88; Macaulay 1881: 62; *Journal of the Royal Statistical Society* 77 (1912): 577.
34 Brinton 1856: 31–2; Macaulay 1881: 64–5, and 1891: 289–93; Caddy 1912: 38–41; SLRV I (Oct. 1905 and Dec. 1908).
35 *Post Magazine* 58 (1897): 750.
36 *Assurance Magazine* 1 (1850): 87; Smith 1905: 17; Ward 1857: 8; Fairclough 1900–02: 76; Heron 1898: 110; Hall 1903: 47.
37 YMPF (European, 1859); LLSPF (London Life, 1892); Brockbank 1908: 49; NULRD.
38 Hutchinson 1852: 1–4, 11, 18, 74; Reiser 1978: 92–5; Brinton 1856: 46–8; Ward 1857: 64–5; *Post Magazine* 53 (1892): 847.
39 Gee 1877: 8–10; *British Medical Journal* (17 Dec. 1881); Powell 1886: 25; Ransome 1882: 4–17.
40 NULRD (Briton Medical & General, ca. 1870); 35/2 (Guardian, 1880); YMPF (European, 1859); PMDCF (Provident Clerks', 1897); YPF (Yorkshire, ca 1900); NULMB IX (7 Feb. 1861), XIX (7 Nov. 1881).
41 Hall 1903: 60; 'Section of Medicine' 1898: 760.
42 Reiser 1978: 105–6; Porter 2000: 241; Naqvi and Blaufox 1998: 43; *Standard Newsletter* (June 1922): 4–5.
43 Jennings 1883: 59; Bramwell 1883: 5; *Standard Newsletter* (June 1922): 5; 'Section of Medicine' 1898: 762; NULRD (12 Oct. 1880). On smoking as a risk see Turney 1913.
44 Reiser 1978: 127; Morgan 1841: 81; Hoar 1897: 185; Hudnut 1895: 391; Mackenzie 1900: 138.
45 *British Medical Journal* (24 Aug. 1889); CMB VII (14 Feb. and 21 Feb., 1882).
46 CMB VII (21 Feb., 1882); Williams 1904: 298; Pollock and Chisholm 1889: 115–18; Bedford 1904: 79–85.
47 Reiser 1978: 127–8, 135; Kauffmann 1900: 15; Bedford 1904: 14–21; Black 1895: 24, 30.
48 NULRD (Guardian, ca 1882); LLSPF (London Life, 1891); SAMB XV (Scottish Amicable, 1894); Chisholm 1886: 426; PMDCF (Provident Clerks', 1897).
49 Pollock and Chisholm 1889: 20, 105; Chisholm 1886: 426; Poore 1894: 24.

50 Stewart 1887: 250; *Post Magazine* 48 (1887): 331, 383; *British Medical Journal* (12 Dec. 1891); Dreschfield 1895–96: 20; Poore 1894: 27–9.
51 Brockbank 1908: 109; Bedford 1904: 77; Dawson 1907: 156–8; May 1914: 37, 45–7.
52 Kauffmann 1900: 13; Dawson 1907: 157; Hall 1903: 65; Ogilvie 1897: 85–6; May 1914: 52.
53 NULRD; Williams 1904: 275; *British Medical Journal* (24 Aug. 1889).
54 Poore 1894: 26; Pollock and Chisholm 1889: 31.
55 *Lancet* (22 April 1893); Mackenzie 1900: 144; *Medical Examiner* 6/1 (1905): 4; Pollock and Chisholm 1889: 111–12.
56 Stewart 1861: 38–40; Walford 1880: 170; Poore 1900: 46.
57 Young 1902: 2; Emanuel 1908: 1. See Alborn 2001: 424–32.
58 Hall 1903: 40; Fox 1914: 5.
59 *Post Magazine* 46 (1885): 568, 582.
60 Symes-Thompson 1899: 158.

10 Dealing with Deviance

1 *Post Magazine* 51 (1890): 580.
2 Lyon 1895: 57; Keller 1963: 59.
3 *Lancet* (26 Nov. 1887); Symes Thompson 1899: 154.
4 Meikle 1872: 5.
5 EdRP; Humphreys 1874: 178, 181; Walford V: 473; YMB IX (2 Dec. 1840); RLMB II (8 May 1817).
6 UlMB 1 (Christie to Bagshaw & Co., 23 Apr 1834).
7 EcMB I (24 May 1824); Farren 1826: 84; Asylum prospectus (1838); Walford I: 209–10; Humphreys 1874: 189, 192.
8 Besant 1924: 12; Medical, Clerical & General prospectus (1824).
9 Pinckard 1851: 274–6. The proportion of rated-up lives fell from 27% in 1824–33 to 17% in 1872. The company went from adding an average of 6.1 years to 'under–average' lives in 1824–33 to 10.4 years in 1868–73: CMRL (1824–33 and 1868–72).
10 Walford I: 584, and II: 332; Alborn 1991: 152; EMB VI (3 Jan. 1826).
11 Humphreys 1874: 188; Walford I: 36, 378, and II: 336–40; Metcalf 1967: 58.
12 Walford II: 335–6, and I: 393; Neison 1848: iii; *Post Magazine* 15 (1854): 50.
13 Medical Invalid prospectus (undated): 6; CWP (Medical Invalid).
14 EdMB VIII (5 Feb. 1852); CMB III (24 Dec. 1850); Walford III: 303; CMB VII–X (passim), X (23 April 1889), XII (14 Nov. 1893).
15 Metcalf 1967: 39–48; Le Grys 1998: 171.
16 Humphreys 1874: 181; AtMB V.

17 Chisholm 1886: 411; Lyon 1901: 140; Fox 1896: 177.
18 On risk classification in British fire insurance see Pearson 2002: 16; Pearson 2004: 59–61.
19 YPF (Yorkshire, ca 1900); Sunderland 1891: 437, 423–4.
20 Humphreys 1874: 181; Ward 1857: 70; Fox 1895: 251; Williams 1904: 278; Humphreys 1874: 192.
21 Mann 1865: 159; NULRD (28 May 1880); AFLG II (3 March 1858).
22 Chisholm 1886: 419; Moxley 1903: 296.
23 ESLMB XIV (23 March 1899). See also Watson 1900: 18; NLAR (23 April 1902).
24 NULMB XI (6 June 1864), XIX (17 Nov. 1880, 10 and 24 Jan., 25 April 1881), XXI (23 Jan., 2 Feb. 1885, 15 Nov. 1886); NULRD (12 March 1880).
25 *Post Magazine* 55 (1894): 376 (George Herschell, speech at Life Assurance Officers' Society). See also Pollock and Chisholm 1889: 21.
26 NULRD (W.H. Andersson to T. Muir Grant, 16 and 19 Oct. 1880; 3 Dec. 1885. In the event, the medical exam revealed 'a lupoid affection of the skin on the face' and 'a small quantity of albumin' in the man's urine and the extra apparently stayed in place.
27 NULRD (William H. Mabb to Charles Naismith, 5 Nov. 1880; Naismith to Grant, 6 and 16 Nov. 1880.
28 NULMB IX (4 Feb. 1861), X (16 Sept. and 24 Oct. 1861, 11 and 25 Aug. and 11 Dec. 1862); CAB I–II.
29 Jureidini and White 2000: 199–200.
30 Herzfeld 1992: 181.
31 *Insurance Record* 40 (1902): 579; Lyon 1892: 120; *Post Magazine* (2 Feb. 1850).
32 For exceptions see Walford III: 6, and V: 468; Morgan 1841: 81–2; Begbie 1847: 482; Neison 1850: 334–7.
33 In addition those mentioned below, see Walford I: 393 (Briton Medical & General); Stone and Helder 1873 (Clergy Mutual); EdMB XVI (4 June 1874); Walford V: 555–7 (Gresham); Burt 1862 (North British). Begbie's final report, which was the only one not published, is mentioned in Muirhead 1902: v.
34 Begbie 1847: 498–9; Neison 1850: 353; Fleming 1862: 14; Robertson 1865: 5; Walford III: 22–3. See also Mann 1865: 1–2; Walford I: 393; Smith 1862: 5.
35 *Seventh Annual Report*1846: 1–3; Begbie 1868: 968. For an example of death certificates initiated by life offices see SNMB II (31 March 1848). For an example of a life office relying on a GRO certificate see NULMB X (12 March 1863).
36 Christison 1853: 111; Begbie 1860: 8.
37 Christison 1853: 142; Robertson 1865: 9.

38 Begbie 1868: 979; SLSB XIV (memorandum by H.J. Williams, 2 May 1856).
39 Mann 1865: 40; Alborn 2001: 414–16; Lyon 1892: 121–4.
40 Stone and Helder 1873; Smith 1862: 10; Fleming 1862: 12–13; Robertson 1865: 4; Gillespie and Duffin 1874: 15.
41 Robertson 1865: 3; Fleming 1862: 5, 15; Stewart 1861: 46; MPAC II (6 Dec. 1856), and III (6 May 1876); Meikle 1872: 50.
42 Chisholm 1886: 414.
43 EMB XIV; CAB I–II.
44 Pollock and Chisholm 1889: viii; Chisholm 1886: 420; ASLOMB I (21 July 1843).
45 Muirhead 1902: v–vii; Rusher and Kenchington 1913: 434–38; Rock 1906: 91–140; Hoar 1897: 182–87.
46 Powell 1878: v; *Lancet* (13 Aug. 1898).
47 'Section of Medicine' 1898: 772; Hughes 1906: 26; Manly 1892: 130; Macfadyen 1872: 78.
48 Rusher and Kenchington 1913: 536; Humphreys 1874: 191.
49 From the customer's perspective, a third alternative to rating up (and the best one) was to join a group plan with one's employer; by 1900, British life offices sold these to some large companies and to the civil service (see chapter 1).
50 Metcalf 1967: 60; Younger 1862: 269–72. For other early examples of contingent debt plans see Black 1861: 7–8, 11–15; Walford I: 366, 547, and II: 345; London & Northern prospectus (1865): 5–6.
51 *Post Magazine* 23 (1862): 129; Black 1861: 29.
52 *Journal of the Institute of Actuaries* 10 (1863): 350; Lister 1901: 179–80; Fox 1895: 253–54.
53 Lutt 1907: 482; *Post Magazine* 37 (1876): 30; Lyon 1895: 57.
54 Fox 1895: 261; Sunderland 1891: 420; Fox 1895: 252; Lister 1901: 173.
55 Lister 1901: 164, 172; Lyon 1895: 69.
56 Lyon 1895: 69; *Post Magazine* 53 (1892): 847; Fox 1895: 253; Hall 1903: 12, 21, 32; 'Section of Medicine' 1898: 771–2; Lister 1901: 175.
57 Fackler 1902: 2–4; Le Grys 1998: 170; Oscar Rogers and Arthur Hunter (1919), cited in Metcalf 1967: 67–9. See also Porter 2000: 234–40.
58 *Journal of the Royal Statistical Society* 77 (1914): 575; Steeds 1965: 239, 244–5; Patton, cited in Porter 2000: 238.
59 Carruthers 1905: 306, 311; FACMB IV (6 Feb., 1 April, and 28 June 1912, 13 May 1913); Davidson 1956: 80–1. Carruthers's scheme was an adaptation of the Dewey decimal system, with 100 devoted to 'Family Longevity,' 200 to 'Diatheses and Zymoses,' and so on.
60 Carruthers 1905: 321–2; Pearson 1924–30, III: 537, 539.

61 Perks 1952: 205, 218, 223, 225; Davidson 1956: 111; Steeds 1965: 241.

62 Metcalf 1967: 63–4; Le Grys 1998: 170–2. On Steeds see the *Actuary* (Nov. 2005).

63 Steeds 1965: 239.

64 Davidson 1956: 111; Steeds 1965: 237–8.

65 CAB I. The new rates were 4% higher at age 30, 2.4% higher at age 45, and the same at age 50: *Accounts* 1872, 1881.

Conclusion

1 *Post Magazine* 44 (1883): 211.

2 Harvey 1990: 54; Jameson 1991: 27; Jones and Porter 1994; Burchill, Gordon and Miller 1991.

3 Douglas 1986: 108.

4 See Valenze 2006; Richards 1990.

5 Canguilhem 1989: 33; cf Rabinow 1989.

6 See Abbott 1988; Peterson 1978; Lenoir 1993: 79.

7 Sieveking 1874: 18–19; Hamlin 1998: 41, 68; Haley 1978: 20.

8 Pollock and Chisholm 1889: 15; Brockbank 1908: 8.

9 Symes Thompson 1899: 160; Williamson 1912: 4.

10 Mansel 1860: 274.

11 Hardy 1837: 229; De Morgan 1839: 415.

12 *Insurance Record* 5 (1867): 184; Hacking 1990: 48, 110–21.

13 Cited in Cooper 2007: 175; Porter 1986: 102; Hacking 1990: 119, 185.

14 *Insurance Record* 40 (1902): 316; Hambleton 1891: 36.

15 Cited in Pearson 1924–30, III: 73, 538.

16 Darwin 1906: 49–50; *Insurance Record* 40 (1902): 316; *British Medical Journal* (1 Feb. 1908).

17 *Assurance Magazine* 6 (1856): 111–12; *Guide to Health* 1919: 23.

18 Alborn, 'Insurance' 2001; Love 1979: 147–48; Orr 1913: 331.

19 Marr 1886: 48; Orr 1913: 332.

20 Pearson 1924–30, III: 73; *Post Magazine* 57 (1896): 491; Andras 1901: 328; O'Malley 1999: 685–91.

21 Ewald 1991: 198–201.

22 Clark 2002: 88, 93, and 1999: 22.

23 See, e.g., Thackeray 1849; Warren 1852; Dickens 1860 and above.

24 Wells 1910.

25 Freedgood 2000: 1.

26 Ibid.: 172; Appendix 1; *Oxford English Dictionary* (aegis, palladium).

27 *Life-Assurance* 1850: 9; *Short Account* 1835: 5.

28 *Insurance Record* 12 (1874): 53; *Policy-holder* 2 (1884): 266.
29 Zelizer 1983: 86; Alborn, 'License,' 2008.
30 *Times* (27 and 30 Aug., 2 and 3 Sept. 1907).
31 Bridges 1842: 42; *Twelfth Annual Report* 1853: xvi; De Morgan 1838: 1, 22.
32 *Weekly Notes* (1881): 236; *British Medical Journal* (1 Feb. 1908).
33 McCleery 1904: 16.
34 *Bankers' Magazine* 51 (1891): 580; Allen 1883: 20.
35 Fox 1895: 258; 'Gambling' 1852: 355–6.
36 Barnes 1986: 110–11.

References

Primary Sources

Manuscript Sources

Aviva plc, Norwich
  Edinburgh Life Assurance Co.
    EdMB Directors' minute books. 1829–86. CU 2727–44.
    EdRP Register of policies. 1823–48. CU 2770.
    EdR Reports read at the general court meetings of directors. 1853–66.
      CU 2768.
  Norwich Union Life Assurance Co.
    NULMB Board minutes. 1808–1902. NU 1375–1400.
    NULRD Referees' declarations. 1859, 1870, 1879–82. NU 446–7, 454,
      458–64.
  Scottish National Insurance Co.
    SNMB Board minutes. 1844–49. NU 1520–1.
  Scottish Union and National Insurance Co.
    SUNMB Board minutes. 1878–1910. NU 1524–31.
  Yorkshire Fire & Life Insurance Co.
    YBSS Branch staff salaries and administration register. 1903–19. GA 2707.
    YLB Secretary's correspondence. 1824–25. GA 2731.
    YMB Directors' minute books. 1831–92. GA 1069–89, 1223–32.
    YMPF Miscellaneous prospectuses and forms. GA 2903.
    YPC Printed circular. 1867. GA 2927.
    YPF Proposal forms. Ca 1900. GA 2811.
Cambridge University Library, Cambridge
  British Empire Mutual Life Assurance Co.

BEMMB Board minutes. 1848–58. Ms. Phoenix.
Positive Government Security Life Assurance Co.
PGMB Board minutes. 1875–91. Ms. Phoenix.
Chartered Insurance Institute, London
CWP Cornelius Walford Papers. Notes for unpublished volumes of *Insurance Cyclopaedia*, including biographical supplement (b/s) and entries in alphabetical order. Ms. 9.92.
Faculty of Actuaries in Scotland, Edinburgh
Associated Scottish Life Offices
ASLOMB Minute books. 1840–1909. Ms. 1/1/2/1–4.
ASLORM Reports, memoranda, etc. book. 1894–1914. Ms. 1/2/3/1–2.
FACMB Council minute book. 1856–1919. Ms. 4/1/4/1–5.
FASMB Sessional meeting minute book. 1856–1914. Ms. 4/1/3/1.
Guildhall Library, London
Alliance Assurance Co.
ALCMB Life Committee minute book. 1833–70. Ms. 30,672/6–15.
AMB Board minutes. 1824–93. Ms. 12,162/1–15.
ARAV Reports ... re actuarial valuations. 1829–1903. Ms. 14,980.
Atlas Assurance Co.
AtAAB Agency appointment book. 1897–1907. Ms. 16,176/1–4.
AtLD Life Department minute book. 1845–52. Ms. 16,171/1–4.
AtMB Court of Directors minutes. 1808–64. Ms. 16,170/1–10.
AtPA Particulars of assurance. 1808–70. Ms. 16,165.
AtST Lists of share transfers, 1814–40. Ms. 16,164/1–2.
Caledonian Insurance Co.
CMB Board minutes. 1840–95. Ms. 16,184/3–12.
Church of England Fire and Life Assurance Society
CEIMB Index to board minutes. 1840–93. Ms. 12,160E/1–12.
CEMB Board minutes. 1844–93. Ms. 12,160D/1–11.
Crown Life Assurance Co.
CAB Actuary's report books. 1870–90. Ms. 21,231/1–2.
Economic Life Assurance Society
EcMB Minutes of the Court of Directors. 1823–49. Ms. 14,065/1–42.
Gresham Life Assurance Society
GAH Reports ... regarding legislation in Austria, Hungary, Bosnia and Herzegovina. 1862–90. Ms. 17,905.
GBL Bonus list. 1848–85. Ms. 17,926A.
GIB Interim bonuses – various notes. 1880–1934. Ms. 17,926.
GMTS Miscellaneous typewritten statements. 1900–40. Ms. 17,899.

GSBE Summary of business and expenses. 1910–16. Ms. 17,923.

GVS Valuation summaries. 1888–1929. Ms. 17,921.

Guardian Assurance Co.

GuMB Board minutes. 1823–73. Ms. 14,281/2–12.

Industrial Life Offices' Association

ILOAMB Minute books. 1909–11. Ms. 29,802/3.

Law Union and Crown Insurance Co.

LUCLB General manager's private letter book. 1901–08. Ms. 21,266.

Law Union and Rock Insurance Co.

LURSA Papers relating to the Company's Activites in South Africa. 1910.
Ms. 21,267.

Legal and General Life Assurance Society

LGBM Board minutes. 1836–80. Ms. 33,437/1–26.

LGLB General letter books. 1836–66. Ms. 36,241/1–9.

LGLPR Life policy registers. 1836–91. Ms. 18,473/1–7.

LGNA Notices of assignment. 1839–70. Ms 18,477/1.

LGRA Report by the actuary and manager to the Finance Committee.
1891. Ms. 36,018.

LGRGM Reports to General Management Committee. 1886–1918. Ms. 36,017.

Life Offices' Association

LOAMB Committee meeting minute book. 1888–1904. Ms. 31,516.

LOASB Scrapbooks. 1890–1914. Ms. 28,376/1–7.

London Life Association

LLRM Register of members. 1860–1918. Ms. 19643/1–4.

LLSPF Scrapbook of printed forms. 1891–92. Ms. 19,645.

National Life Assurance Society

NLAR Agency reports scrapbook. 1891–1912. Ms. 34,413.

National Mutual Life Assurance Society

NMAGB Agency guard book. 1898–1900. Ms. 34,494/1.

National Provident Institution

NPAMI Actuaries' mortality investigations. 1835–1900. Ms. 20,291.

NPAR Actuaries' reports. 1836–1905. Ms. 20,290.

Provident Clerks' Mutual Life Assurance Association

PCPF Proposal forms of other offices. Ca. 1850. Ms. 20,939.

PCSB Scrapbooks relating to the association's activities. 1841–58.
Ms. 20,936/1–2.

Provident Life Office

PLNCH Notes on the company's history. 1923. Ms. 14,311.

PLPCA Copies of prospectuses, circulars and advertisements. 1885–99.
Ms. 30,647.

Provident Mutual Life Assurance Association
   PMDCF Death claim files. 1932–38. Ms. 20,928.
Royal Farmers and General Fire and Life Insurance Co.
   RFBR Board reports 1859–85. Ms. 14,991.
   RFMB Board minute books 1859–73. Ms. 14,989/15–18.
Rock Life Assurance Co.
   RLCB Committee minute book. 1806–45. Ms. 21,213/1–5.
   RLMB Minutes of directors 1807–17. Ms. 21,208/1–2.
University Life Assurance Society
   UMB Court of Directors minute books. 1880–92. Ms. 24,933/12–13.
Westminster and General Life Assurance Association
   WMB Board minutes. 1836–49. Ms. 14,283/1–3.
(Uncatalogued holdings from Eagle Star; original Eagle Star shelfmarks)
Eagle Insurance Co.
   EFR Friends' referee report. EA 4/1/3/2.
   ELI Papers relating to amalgamation with London Indisputable. EA 7/
      LN1/1/1.
   EMB Board minutes. 1807–1910. EA 1/5/1/1–26.
   EPC Press cuttings. EA 4/3/1/1.
   EWEG *West End Gazette*. March 1921. ES 6/5/1/2.
English and Scottish Law
   ESLMB Board minutes. 1839–1912. ESL 1/5/1/1/1–18.
Palladium Life Assurance Society
   PPF Proposal forms. PA 4/1/3/2.
Star Life Assurance Society
   SMB Board minutes. 1845–1909. ST 1/5/1/2–23.
HBOS plc, Edinburgh
   Clerical, Medical and General Life Assurance Society
      CMBM Board minutes. 1824–78. Acc. 2005/022 and 2006/063.
      CMC Incoming correspondence. 1824–1969. Acc. 2005/022 and 2006/063,
         boxes LD 299A and LD299B.
      CMLB Outgoing letter books (2 vols.), 1824-28. Acc. 2006/063.
      CMRL Renewal ledgers. 1824–1895. 1–10. 2006/063.
      CMRS Remarks on the State of the Society, 1841. Acc. 2006/063, box LD
         329.
      CMSB Salary books ('blue boks'), 2 vols, 1840s-1920s. Acc.2005/022.
      CMVN Valuation department notebook, 1906. Acc. 2006/063.
Institute of Actuaries, London
   IACMB Institute of Actuaries. Council minute book. 1848–96. Ms. MBK 925,
      958–62.
   MPAC Actuaries Club. Minutes of the proceedings. 1848–90. Ms. H 26a1.

M.E. Grenander Department of Special Collections and Archives, State University of New York at Albany
FHP Frederick Hendriks Collection. 1709–1891. Ms. 016.
Mitchell Library, Glasgow
Aberdeen Fire and Life Assurance Co.
AFLG Glasgow local board minute book. 1840–73. Ms. TD 446/1/1/1–3.
Universal Life Assurance Society
UlMB Minute book. Ms. TD 446/10/1.
National Library of Scotland, Edinburgh
WBP William Blackwood & Co. papers (ms. numbers individually cited in notes).
Royal Society, London
HS John F.W. Herschel papers (ms. numbers individually cited in notes).
Scottish Amicable Insurance Company Archives, Stirling (a unit of Prudential Assurance Company Limited)
Scottish Amicable Insurance Co.
SABMB Board room memorandum book. 1867–72. Ms. 1/3/1–3.
SACR Copy reports. 1878–88. Ms. 1/1/43.
SAER Memorandum book of extra rates. 1840–1920. Ms. 5/2/1.
SAMB Board minute books. 1834–99. Ms. 1/1/10–15.
SAMBB Manchester board book. 1850–55. Ms. 1/1/37.
SAMBE Extraordinary directors' minute book. 1834–39. Ms. 1/1/1.
SASB Scrap book. 1907–10. Unaccessed.
West of Scotland Insurance Co.
WSLB Letter book. 1832–36. Ms. 8/2/2
WSMBE Extraordinary directors' minute book 1827–33. Ms. 7/1/6.
Standard Life plc, Edinburgh
Experience Life Assurance Society
ExMB Board minutes. 1843–46. Ms. EX 1/1/1/1.
Standard Life Assurance Co.
SLPM Private minutes. 1846–91. Ms. A 1/3/1–5.
SLRV Reports and valuations. 1894–1913. Ms. A 3/3/1–3.
SLSB Sederunt books (Edinburgh). 1851, 1855–56. Ms. A 1/1/11, 14.

Company Prospectuses

Prospectuses without page references in footnotes are either broadsheets or unpaginated.

Aviva Group, Norwich
Asylum Life (1838). GA 2903.

City of Glasgow Life (1910).
Edinburgh Life (1885).
Sovereign Life (undated). GA 2901.
Yorkshire Fire & Life (1824, ca. 1834–35). GA 2895.
Yorkshire Fire & Life (1900, 1908). GA 2750.
Cambridge University Library, Cambridge
Sun Life (1823). Pam 5.82.9.
Chartered Insurance Institute, London
National Loan Fund (1837). 9.94 Box 150 Item 19.
Davis Library, St John's University, New York
Amicable Life (ca 1854). L 204 Am5.
Emperor Life and Fire (1870). L 204 Em68.
Great Britain Mutual (1872). L 204 G79.
Life Association of Scotland (1860). L 204 L62.
Westminster & General (1860). F 204.W525.
Guildhall Library, London (Eagle Star archives, uncatalogued; original shelfmarks)
Albion Life (1849, 1856). EA 7/AL/6/1.
Alfred Life (1856). EA 6/1/1/1.
City of Glasgow Life (1846, 1849). ESL 4/1/3/2/2.
Commercial Life (1840). ESL 4/1/3/2/1.
Deposit & General Life (1852). EA 6/1/1/1.
Eagle (ca 1830, 1847, 1850). EA 4/1/3/1/1.
Eagle sales brochure (ca 1870s). EA 6/1/1/1.
Eagle advertisement (1892). EA 4/3/1/1.
Edinburgh Life (1842). ESL 4/1/3/2/2.
English & Scottish Law (1839, 1851, 1879, 1885, 1907). 4/1/3/1/2,3,6,7; 4/1/3/2/1, 4.
Experience Life (ca 1846). ESL 4/1/3/2/2.
Minerva Life (1851). EA 6/1/1/1.
Palladium (1827). EA 6/1/1/1.
Royal Naval, Military & Honourable East India Company (1840). ESL 4/1/3/2/2.
Scottish National (1843). ESL 4/1/3/2/2.
Scottish Widows' Fund (1842). ESL 4/1/3/2/2.
Standard Life (1839, 1840). ESL 4/1/3/1/2.
Star Life (1845, 1872, 1894, 1910). ST 4/1/3/1/1/1, 3, 7, 14.
United Deposit Life (1845). ESL 4/1/3/2/2.
Guildhall Library, London (Provident Clerks' Mutual, proposal forms of other offices)
Pelican Life (1842). Guildhall Ms. 20,939.

HBOS plc Group Archives, Edinburgh
    Medical, Clerical & General Life (1824). Box LD 0520.
Institute of Actuaries Prospectus Collection, London
    General Life Assurance and Investment Society (ca 1850).
    Medical Invalid (undated).
Library of Congress, Washington, DC
    Argus Life (ca 1835). LC HG 9058.Z9 A25.
The Making of the Modern World (online database)
    Albion Fire & Life (1805).   ‘
    National Loan Fund (1838).
    Pelican Life (1814).
    Provident Institution (1806).
    Rock Life (1806).
    Scottish Widows' Fund (1814).
    Westminster Life (1792).
Scottish Amicable Insurance Company Archives, Stirling
    Scottish Amicable, Jamaican Prospectus (1876).

Other Primary Sources

Abstract Return of Assurance Companies completely Registered 1852–56. London:
    by order of the House of Commons, 1856.
Abstract Return of Assurance Companies completely Registered 1856–63. London:
    by order of the House of Commons, 1863.
An Account of the Various Societies or Companies established in London for the Pur-
    pose of Granting Assurances on Lives, with an Investigation of the Principles upon
    which they are Severally Grounded, and the Rates of Premium which they Charge.
    London: Strange, 1839.
Albion Life Assurance Company. *Instructions to Agents.* London: privately
    published, 1854.
Aldcroft, W.H. 'Characteristics of the Tables of Mortality.' *Journal of the Feder-*
    ated Insurance Institutes 3 (1900): 351–82.
Allen, Joseph. *Where Shall I Get the Most for my Money? An Inquiry concerning*
    all the Life Insurance Offices (British and Foreign) having Agencies in the United
    Kingdom. 10th ed. London: Smart and Allen, 1883.
Alliance British & Foreign Life & Fire Assurance Company. *For the Officials*
    of Her Majesty's Post Office: Special Prospects of the Alliance British &
    Foreign Life & Fire Assurance Company. London: privately printed,
    1860.
– *Instructions to Agents.* London: privately printed, 1874.
– *Instructions to Agents.* London: privately printed, 1896.

Andras, H.W. 'Endowment Assurance.' (1895). *Transactions of the Birmingham Insurance Institute* (1894–95). Unpaginated.
- 'Accountants and Life Assurance.' *Accountant* 24 (1898): 159–63.
- 'Life Assurance Prospects at the Opening of the Twentieth Century.' *Journal of the Federated Insurance Institutes* 4 (1901): 323–33.
- 'Returns of Life Assurance Companies to the Board of Trade.' *Insurance Institute Journal* 13 (1910): 93–120.
Ansell, Charles Jun. *On the Rate of Mortality at Early Periods of Life, the Age at Marriage, the Number of Children to a Marriage, the Length of a Generation, and other Statistics of Families in the Upper and Professional Classes.* London: Charles and Edwin Layton, 1874.
Aspland, Alfred. 'Hints on Life Insurance.' (1860). *Transactions of the Manchester Statistical Society* (1859–60): 58–81.
Associated Scottish Life Offices. *Resolutions and Proceedings, selected from the Records of the Association and printed for the use of Members.* Edinburgh: ASLO, 1895.
'Assurance and Insurance.' *London Saturday Journal* 2 (1839): 129–31.
Assurance Register. Being a Record of the Progress and Financial Position of various Life Assurance Associations in Great Britain, as reported in the year 1864. London: William Dawson and Sons, 1865.
Ayres, Henry. *The Balance Sheets of Insurance Companies; or, the Real Advantages of Publicity examined by reference to the Accounts of Companies presented to Parliament in June, 1863.* London: John Foss, 1863.
Aytoun, W.E. 'A Chapter on Life Assurance.' *Blackwood's Magazine* 74 (1853): 105–16.
Babbage, Charles. *Comparative View of the Various Institutions for the Assurance of Lives.* London: J. Mawman, 1826.
Bacon, Richard Mackenzie. *A Letter to the Insurers and Co–partners in the Norwich Union Life Office.* Norwich: Bacon, Kinnebrook, and Bacon, 1838.
Bagehot, Walter. *Collected Works.* 15 vols. Cambridge, Mass.: Harvard University Press, 1965–86.
Bailey, A.H. 'On the Rates of Extra Premium for Foreign Travelling and Residence.' *Journal of the Institute of Actuaries* 15 (1869): 77–94.
- 'On Insolvency in Life Assurance Companies.' *Journal of the Institute of Actuaries* 16 (1872): 389–408.
- 'The Expenses of Life Assurance Companies: How they affect the Assured.' *Journal of the Institute of Actuaries* 19 (1875): 1–11.
- 'The Pure Premium Method of Valuation.' *Journal of the Institute of Actuaries* 21 (1878): 115–26.
Bailey, Arthur Hutcheson, and Archibald Day. 'On the Rate of Mortality amongst the Families of the British Peerage, 1800–1855.' *Journal of the Statistical Society of London* 26 (1863): 49–61.

References 385

Baily, Francis. *Account of the several Life Assurance Companies established in London*. London: J. Richardson, 1810; 2nd ed. 1811.
Bankers' and Merchants' Almanack for 1814: to be Continued Annually. London: J. Souter, 1813.
Barnes, Julian. *Staring at the Sun*. London: J. Cape, 1986.
Barrand, Arthur Rhys. 'Debentures of Trading Companies as Investments for Life Assurance Funds.' *Journal of the Institute of Actuaries* 34 (1899): 421–74.
Barrow, John. 'Babbage on Life Assurance Societies.' *Quarterly Review* 35 (1827): 1–31.
Bate, George. *Life Assurance Agent's Pocket Handbook*. London: n.p., 1880.
Baylis, Edward. *Reply of the Professional Life Assurance Company to the Attacks of its Assailants; together with Remarks, Illustrative and Explanatory of the New System of Life Assurance*. 3rd ed. London: John Teulon, 1852.
– William Beresford, and Edwin Paul. *A Treatise on the New Application of the Principles of Life Assurance*. London: John Teulon, 1851.
Beaumont, John Augustus. *Thoughts and Details on Life Insurance Offices*. London: J. Ridgway, 1842.
Bedford, Charles H. *A Clinical Handbook of Urine Analysis*. 2nd ed. Edinburgh: Bell and Bradfute, 1904.
Begbie, James. 'Observations on the Mortality of the Scottish Widows' Fund and Life Assurance.' *Monthly Journal of Medical Science* 7 (1847): 481–500.
– 'Medical Statistics of Life Assurance.' *Monthly Journal of Medical Science* 17 (1853): 143–71.
– 'The Causes of Death in the Scottish Widows' Fund Life Assurance Society.' *Edinburgh Medical Journal* 6 (1860): 1–24.
– 'The Causes of Death in the Scottish Widows' Fund Life Assurance Society.' *Edinburgh Medical Journal* 13 (1868): 967–81.
Bell, Herbert, and J.R. Milne. 'A Working List of Mathematical Tables.' In E.M. Horsburgh (ed.), *Modern Instruments and Methods of Calculation: A Handbook of the Napier Tercentenary Exhibition*, 47–60. London: G. Bell and Sons, 1914.
Bell, Joseph. 'Some Hints by a Medical Examiner.' *Medical Examiner* 4/4 (1903): 1–3.
Benefit Societies versus Savings Banks and Insurance Companies: An Address to the Members of Benefit Societies and the Public in General. 2nd ed. London: J. Beswick, 1822.
Besso, Marco. 'Progress of Life Assurance throughout the World, from 1859 to 1883.' *Journal of the Institute of Actuaries* 26 (1887): 426–35.
Bezobrazova, Elizaveta. 'Contemporary Life and Thought in Russia.' *Contemporary Review* 33 (1878): 599–614.
Birrell, H. 'Climate and its Influence on the Human Constitution.' *Insurance Institute Journal* 14 (1911): 61–80.

Black, D. Campbell. *The Urine in Health and Disease, and Urinary Analysis Physiologically and Pathologically Considered*. London: Baillière, Tindall and Cox, 1895.

Black, Morrice A. *The Assurance of Diseased and Doubtful Lives on a New Principle, more Advantageous and Equitable to Policy–holders than the System hitherto Adopted*. London: W.S.D. Pateman, 1861.

Blayney, Frederick. *Life Assurance Societies Considered as to Comparative Merits*. London: William Stevens, 1848.

Boult, Swinton. *Observations on a Bill to Amend the law relating to Life Assurance Companies*. London: n.p., 1870.

Bramwell, Byrom. *Student's Guide to the Examination of the Pulse, and Use of the Sphygmograph*. Edinburgh: Maclachlan and Stewart, 1883.

– *Practical Medicine and Medical Diagnosis*. Edinburgh: Pentland, 1887.

Bridges, Wlliam. *The Hand-book for Life Assurers: Being a Popular Guide to the Knowledge of the System of Life Assurance*. London: John Mortimer, 1842.

– *The Prudent Man: or, How to Acquire Land, and Bequeath Money, By Means of Co-operation*. London: n.p., 1854.

Brinton, William. *On the Medical Selection of Lives for Assurance*. London: John Churchill, 1856.

British Almanac of the Society for the Diffusion of Useful Knowledge for the Year of Our Lord 1847. London: Charles Knight, 1847.

Briton Life Association. *A Few Words to the Agents of the Association, on the General Principles of Life Assurance, and the Peculiar Features introduced by the Briton*. London: W.H. Cox, 1861.

Brockbank, E.M. *Life Insurance and General Practice*. London: Henry Frowde, 1908.

Brown, Henry. 'Some Aspects of Sickness Insurance.' *Transactions of the Actuarial Society of Edinburgh* 4 (1900): 407–25.

Brown, James. *Report ... to the Directors of the Edinburgh Life Assurance Company, respecting the Division of the Company's Profits, 1835*. Edinburgh: privately published, 1835.

– *Report ... to the Directors of the Edinburgh Life Assurance Company, respecting the Division of the Company's Profits at 31st August 1856*. Edinburgh: Mould and Tod, 1856.

Brown, S. Stanley. 'Authorities on Life Assurance.' *Bankers' Magazine* 49 (1889): 1089–96.

Brown, Samuel. *A Few Thoughts on Commission, Divisions of Profit, Selection of Lives, the Mortality in India, and Other Subjects relating to Life Assurance*. London: W.S.D. Pateman, 1849.

– 'On the Fires in London during the 17 years from 1833 to 1849 inclusive, showing the numbers which occurred in different Trades, and the principal Causes by which they were occasioned.' *Assurance Magazine* 1 (1851): 31–62.

– 'On the Collection of Data in Various Branches of Assurance.' *Assurance Magazine* 2 (1852): 200–9.

Brown, Walter. 'Life Branch Work' (1877). *Journal of the Federated Insurance Institutes* 1 (1898): 9–17.

Browne, E.C. *Life Agencies: Thoughts and Suggestions concerning their Economic and Efficient Arrangement.* London: Charles and Edwin Layton, 1878.

Bruce, J. Mitchell. 'Inattention and Inexactness in Ordinary Diagnosis.' *Clinical Journal* 17 (1900): 17–23.

Bulwer-Lytton, Edward G. 'My Novel' (parts 22–24). *Blackwood's Magazine* 72 (1852): 49–70, 235–49, 331–53.

Bunyon, Charles John. *The Law of Life Assurance.* London: Charles and Edwin Layton, 1868.

Burns, Dawson. *The Bases of Temperance Reform: An Exposition and Appeal.* New York: National Temperance Society, 1873.

Burt, Alfred. *An Historical and Statistical Account of the Population, the Law of Mortality, and the Different Systems of Life Assurance.* London: Effingham Wilson, 1849.

Burt, John G.M. 'On the Causes of Death in the North British Insurance Company.' *Edinburgh Medical Journal* 7 (1862): 818–24.

Bury, Judson S. *Clinical Medicine: A Manual for the Use of Students and Junior Practitioners.* London: Charles Griffin, 1894.

– 'Habits and Occupations in Relation to Life Assurance.' *Report of the Insurance Association of Manchester* (1900–02): 5–16.

Caddy, Adrian. 'Life Insurance in India.' *Transactions of the Life Assurance Medical Officers' Association* (1912): 33–79.

Calwell, William. 'Some Observations on Medical Examination for Life Assurance.' *Insurance Institute Journal* 14 (1911): 47–59.

Cansdell, C.S. *A New Method of Life Assurance.* London: Mann Nephews, 1858.

Carlyle, Thomas. *Chartism.* London: James Fraser, 1840.

Carment, David. 'On the Application of the Arithmometer to the Construction of Tables of the Values of Endowment Insurance Policies.' *Journal of the Institute of Actuaries* 22 (1880): 368–80.

Carruthers, S.W. 'On the Importance and Practicability of a Standard Classification of Impaired Lives.' *Journal of the Institute of Actuaries* 39 (1905): 306–24.

Caverly, R.B., and G.N. Bankes. *Leading Insurance Men of the British Empire.* London: Index Publ., 1892.

Chambers, Robert. *Vestiges of the Natural History of Creation.* London: John Churchill, 1844.

Chambers's Information for the People. Philadelphia: J.B. Lippincott & Co., 1857.

Chapman, Robert. 'The Agency System of Insurance Companies.' *Transactions of the Insurance and Actuarial Society of Glasgow* 6 (1906): 43–55.

Chisholm, James. 'On the Assessment of Life Risks.' *Journal of the Institute of Actuaries* 25 (1886): 408–32.

– 'The Medical Examiner and the Insurance Company.' *Practitioner* 66 (1901): 181–99.

Christie, Robert. *Letter to the Right Hon. Joseph W. Henley ... regarding Life Assurance Institutions*. Edinburgh: Thomas Constable, 1852.

Christison, Robert. 'On the Claims of the Medical Profession on Assurance Companies.' *Monthly Journal of Medical Science* 11 (1850): 317–27.

– 'An Investigation of the Deaths in the Standard Assurance Company.' *Monthly Journal of Medical Science* 17 (1853): 104–42.

Clark, J. *Observations on the Nature of Annuities, Life Insurances, Endowments for Children, and Investment of Money for Accumulation*. London: John Tyler, 1818.

Clifford, George. *The Life Assurer's Handbook and Key to Life Assurance*. London: Effingham Wilson, 1876.

Cockburn, Henry. 'Opening Address by the President.' *Journal of the Institute of Actuaries* 39 (1905): 1–17.

Coles, John. 'Railway Debenture Stock as an Investment for the Funds of a Life Assurance Society.' *Journal of the Institute of Actuaries* 15 (1869): 1–18.

Colquhoun, E. *Notes on Life Assurance*. London: Wodderspoon and Co., 1883.

Comparison of the Emoluments of Persons in the Permanent Employment of Government with those of Persons in the Employment of Joint Stock Companies, Bankers, Merchants, &c. London: n.p., 1850.

Continuous Investigation into the Mortality of Assured Lives: Statistics for the Six Years 1924–1929. Cambridge: Cambridge University Press, 1933.

Corbaux, Francis. *The Natural and Mathematical Laws concerning Population, Vitality, and Mortality ...: with Tables of Mortality, applicable to Five Classes of Each Set*. London: privately published, 1833.

Cox, Jonathan. *How to Make a Fortune! Adapted to all Classes of the Community. An Essay on Life Assurance*. London: William Penny, 1857.

Crawford, R. *Letter to the Policy-holders and Annuitants of the European Assurance Society*. London: Charles and Edwin Layton, 1871.

Curtis. F.A. 'On the Collection of Data for Periodical Observation of Mortality among Lives Selected for Assurance.' *Journal of the Institute of Actuaries* 19 (1876): 229–49.

Dalgleish, W. Scott. 'Scotland's Version of Home Rule.' *Nineteenth Century* 13 (1883): 14–26.

Davidson, A. *On the Medical Selection of Lives for Life Assurance*. Liverpool: Adam Holden, 1889.

Davies, Griffith. *Tables of Contingencies; containing the Rate of Mortality among the Members f the Equitable Society, and the Values of Life Annuities, Reversions, &c., computed therefrom.* London: Longman & Co., 1825.

Dawson, Bertrand. 'Glycosuria and Life Insurance.' *Practitioner* 79 (1907): 156–60.

Day, Archibald. 'Opening Address by the President.' *Journal of the Institute of Actuaries* 26 (1887): 162–81.

De Morgan, Augustus 'Life Assurance.' *Companion to the Almanac*, 86–105. London: Charles Knight, 1831.

– 'Theory of Probabilities.' *Dublin Review* 2 (1837): 338–54.

– *An Essay on Probabilities, and on their Application to Life Contingencies and Insurance Offices.* London: Longman, Orme, Brown, Green, and Longmans, 1838.

– 'Mortality, Law of.' *Penny Cyclopaedia* 15 (1839): 413–19.

– 'The Necessity of Legislation for Life Assurance.' *Dublin Review* 9 (1840): 49–88.

– 'Reversion.' *Penny Cyclopaedia* 19 (1846): 430–6.

De Morgan, Sophia Elizabeth. *Memoir of Augustus De Morgan.* London: Longmans, Green, and Co., 1882.

Deuchar, David. 'On the Interpretation of the Statements required by the "Life Assurance Companies Act, 1870," with special reference to the question of Expenses.' *Journal of the Institute of Actuaries* 18 (1874): 323–35.

Dibdin, E. Rimbault. 'Agencies.' (1884). *Report of the Insurance Institute of Manchester* (1883–84): 13–27.

Dickens, Charles. 'A Christmas Carol' (1843). In *Christmas Books*, 1–90. New York: Oxford University Press, 1988.

– *Bleak House.* (1853). New York: New American Library, 1964.

– *Hard Times.* (1854). New York: Bantam Classic, 1981.

– 'Hunted Down.' *All The Year Round* 3 (1860): 397–400, 422–7.

– *The Letters of Charles Dickens.* Edited by Madeline House and Graham Storey. 12 vols. Oxford: Clarendon Press, 1965–2002.

Dicksee, Lawrence R. *Auditing: A Practical Manual for Auditors.* 8th ed. London: Gee and Co., 1909.

Discussions at the Institute of Actuaries. London: Institute of Actuaries, 1867.

Dougharty, Harold. *Pension, Endowment, Life Assurance, and other Schemes for Employees of Commercial Companies.* London: Sir Isaac Pitman and Sons, 1920.

Dowdeswell, George Morley. *The Law of Life and Fire Insurances: with an Appendix of Comparative Tables of Life Insurance.* London: William Benning, 1846.

Downes, James John. *Economic Life Assurance Society. Experience of Mortality from 1st June, 1823, to 31st December, 1855.* London: privately published, 1857.

– *Actuary's Report on the Seventh Quinquennial Investigation into the Affairs of the Economic Life Assurance Society*. London: privately published, 1859.
– *An Account of the Processes employed in getting out the Mortality Experience of the Economic Life Assurance Society*. London: privately published, 1862.
Dreschfeld, Julius. 'Notes on Life Assurance in Relation to Doubtful Cases.' *Report of the Insurance Association of Manchester* (1895–6): 13–20.
Duckworth, Dyce. *The Sequels of Disease ... together with Observations on Prognosis in Disease*. London: Longmans, Green, and Co., 1896.
Eagle and Protector Life Assurance Company. *Observations for the Use of the Agents*. London: privately published, 1847.
Edmonds, Thomas Rowe. *Life Tables founded upon the Discovery of a Numerical Law, Regulating the Existence of Every Human Being*. London: J. Moyes, 1832.
Emanuel, Joseph G. 'Tuberculosis and Insurance.' *Insurance Institute Journal* 11 (1908): 1–22.
Equitable Life Assurance Society of the United States. *A Statement and Opinions Thereon by Leading Actuaries*. London: Charles and Edwin Layton, 1873.
Erith, Francis Norton. *Stray Thoughts on Life Assurance, or The Great Principles of the Modern System Succinctly Explained, and Rendered Familiar: Life is Uncertain, Death is Sure*. London: William Tweedie, 1854.
Fackler, David Parks. 'Regarding the Mortality Investigation, instituted by the Actuarial Society of America and now in progress.' *Journal of the Institute of Actuaries* 37 (1902): 1–15.
Faculty of Actuaries in Scotland. *British Offices Life Tables, 1893*. London: Charles and Edwin Layton, 1902.
Fairclough, J.J. Kent. 'Medical Hints on Life Proposals.' *Report of the Insurance Association of Manchester* (1900–02): 72–80.
Fairman, William. *The Stocks Examined and Compared*. London: W.J. and J. Richardson, 1802.
Farren, George. *A Treatise on Life Assurance, in which the Systems of the Leading Institutions are Stated and Explained*. London: Butterworth and Son, 1823.
– *Observations on the Importance of Purchases of Land, and in Mercantile Adventures, of Ascertaining the Rates or Laws of Mortality among Europeans*.. London: Hessey and Richardson, 1826.
Fenwick, Samuel. *The Student's Guide to Medical Diagnosis*. 3rd ed. Philadelphia: H.C. Lea, 1873.
Fernie, Ebenezer. *Plan and Tables of the British Commercial Company ... for the Insurance of Lives*. London: n.p., 1822.
Fifth Annual Report of the Registrar-General of Births, Deaths, and Marriages in England. London: W. Clowes and Sons, 1843.

Finlaison, Alexander John. 'Opening Address by the President.' *Journal of the Institute of Actuaries* 31 (1895): 413–28.

First Annual Report of the Registrar-General of Births, Deaths, and Marriages in England. London: W. Clowes and Sons, 1839.

First Report of the Select Committee on Joint Stock Companies; together with the Minutes of Evidence (taken in 1841 and 1843), Appendix and Index. London: by order of the House of Commons, 1844.

Fitzhugh, John. *Hints on Life Assurance, with Selected Examples and Illustrations*. Liverpool: Webb and Hunt, 1863.

Fleming, J.G. *Medical Statistics of Life Assurance: Being an Inquiry into the Causes of Death among the Members of the Scottish Amicable Life Assurance Society, from 1826 till 1860 ... with remarks on the Medical Selection of Lives for Assurance*. Glasgow: Thomas Murray and Son, 1862.

Fourteenth Annual Report of the Registrar-General of Births, Deaths, and Marriages in England. London: George E. Eyre and William Spottiswoode, 1855.

Fourth Annual Report of the Registrar-General of Births, Deaths, and Marriages in England. London: W. Clowes and Sons, 1842.

Fox, R. Hingston. 'The Assurance of Impaired Lives, Chiefly with Reference to Special Forms of Assurance.' *Clinical Journal* 6 (1895): 249–68.

– 'Female Lives.' *Medical Examiner* 2/6 (1901): 1–12.

– 'A Review of the Progress of Life Assurance Medicine in the past 30 years.' *Transactions of the Life Assurance Medical Officers' Association* (1914): 1–26.

Fox, T. Colcott. 'Syphilis in Relation to Life Assurance.' *Transactions of the Life Assurance Medical Officers' Association* (1896): 125–81.

Francis, C.R. 'Life-Assurance and Residence in Hot Climates.' *Lancet* i (1878): 785–7.

Francis, John. *Annals, Anecdotes and Legends: A Chronicle of Life Assurance*. London: Longman, Brown, Green, and Longmans, 1853.

Freestone, John. *Where to Insure: An Impartial and Independent Guide with Comparative Tables, shewing the Security, Bonuses, and Expenses of the British Life Assurance Offices*. London: Simpkin, Marshall, Hamilton, Kent, and Co., 1890.

Freud, Sigmund. 'The Taboo of Virginity.' (1918). In *Sexuality and the Psychology of Love*, 70–86. New York: Collier, 1963.

Friend–in–Need Life, Fire, Guarantee and Accidental Assurance Company. *Instructions to Agents and Tables*. London: John Bedford Leno, 1864.

Galloway, Thomas. *Tables of Mortality Deduced from the Experience of the Amicable Society*. London: Samuel Bentley, 1841.

'Gambling, Betting, Lotteries, and Insurance.' *Chambers's Edinburgh Journal* 466 (1852): 353–6.

Gattie, Walter Montagu. 'Life Insurance in 1889.' *Universal Review* 3 (1889): 495–514.

Gee, Samuel. *Auscultation and Percussion: Together with the other Methods of Physical Examination of the Chest*. 2nd ed. London: Smith, Elder, 1877.

Gibson, James. *The Indicator for Industrial and Ordinary Life Assurance Agents*. Burnley: n.p., 1893.

Gillespie, James D., and A.B. Duffin. *Report on the Causes of Death among the Assured in the Scottish Union Insurance Co. from 1824 to 1870*. Edinburgh: R. and R. Clark, 1874.

Glascott, Charles E. 'Medical Examination for Life Insurance, with some remarks upon the presence of Albumin in the Urine of apparently Healthy Persons.' *Report of the Insurance Institute of Manchester* (1885–86): 11–28.

Globe Insurance Company. *Instructions to the Agents*. London: n.p., 1857.

Gompertz, Benjamin. 'On the Nature and Function of the Law of Human Mortality, and on a New Mode of Determining the Value of Life Contingencies.' *Philosophical Transactions of the Royal Society* 115 (1825): 513–85.

Grahame, James. *A Popular Survey of the Life Assurance Statistics of the Year 1868*. Edinburgh: Bell and Bradford, 1869.

Grey, Alice. 'A Commonplace Couple.' *London Society* 73 (1898): 24–35.

Grossmith, George, and Weedon Grossmith. *The Diary of a Nobody* (1892). Oxford: Oxford University Press, 1995.

Guide to Health: How to Keep Well. London: Queenhithe Publishing Co., 1919.

Gullan, A. Gordon. 'Some Aspects of Life Insurance from the Standpoint of (a) The Medical Examiner. (b) The Agent.' *Transactions of the Insurance Institute of Liverpool* 2 (1908–9): 31–41.

Hall, Francis de Havilland. 'Rupture in relation to Life Assurance.' *Transactions of the Life Assurance Medical Officers' Association* (1896): 280–8.

– *The Medical Examination for Life Assurance, with Remarks on the Selection of an Office*. Bristol: Wright, 1903.

Hambleton, G.W. 'Physical Development.' *Science* 18 (1891): 34–6.

Hand Book of Assurance, with Hints, Legal and Practical, and Characteristics of Every Company. London: Dean and Son, 1856.

Hannam, W. 'Life Assurance as an Investment.' *Transactions of the Manchester Statistical Society* (1859–60): 97–109.

Hardy, Peter. 'Popular Illustrations of Life Assurance.' *Saturday Magazine* 10 (1837): 212–13, 229–30; 11 (1837): 5–7, 99–101, 238–40, 244–5.

Harris, David. *An Address on the Principles, and Bonus Appropriations, of Life Assurance. Delivered at a Meeting of Policy–holders*. Edinburgh: Muir and Paterson, 1867.

Harris, Thomas. 'The Relationship of Provincial Medical Examiners to the Officials of the Head Office.' *Transactions of the Life Assurance Medical Officers' Association* (1899): 163–84.

'Hedging against Fate.' *Once a Week* 9 (1863): 584–6.

Hendriks, Augustus. 'Opening Address by the President.' *Journal of the Institute of Actuaries* 30 (1893): 265–91.

Henry, Jardine. *The Hand-book for Life Assurers, being a Popular Treatise on the System of Life Assurance and Life Annuities*. 2nd ed. Edinburgh: Maclachlan and Stewart, 1887.

Heron, G.A. 'Some Extra Ratings of Healthy Lives.' *Transactions of the Life Assurance Medical Officers' Association* (1898): 82–130.

Herriot, Walter. *Agency and Outside Work*. London: Post Magazine, 1924.

Herschel, John. *A Preliminary Discourse on the Study of Natural Philosophy*. London: Longman, Rees, Orme, Brown, and Green, 1830.

Hewat, Archibald. 'Life Assurance 1870–1890: Respice. Aspice. Prospice.' *Bankers' Magazine* 51 (1891): 161–79, 345–61.

– 'Life Assurance 'Features'.' *Bankers' Magazine* 53 (1892): 501–13, 633–46.

– *On Training for the Insurance Profession*. Dublin: n.p., 1893.

– 'Life Assurance Finance as affected by Rate of Interest and Rate of Expense.' *Bankers' Magazine* 82 (1896): 789–815.

– *The Stability of British Life Assurance*. Manchester: Policy-holder Journal, 1899.

– 'The Actuary in Scotland.' *Transactions of the Faculty of Actuaries* 3 (1906): 129–46.

Hibberd, Shirley. *We Are Never Safe: A Few Words on the Risks to which Life and Limb are Daily Exposed*. London: W.H. Collingridge, 1855.

Higham, John Adams. 'On the Value of Selection as exercised by the Policy-holder against the Company.' *Assurance Magazine* 1 (1851): 179–202.

Hill, Rowland, and George Birkbeck Hill. *The Life of Sir Rowland Hill ... and the History of Penny Postage*. 2 vols. London: Thos. De la Rue, 1880.

Hillman, W.E. *Familiar Illustrations of the Theory and Practice of Assurance*. London: W.S.D. Pateman, 1847.

Hilton, B.H. *Read Me Through*. London: n.p., 1884.

Hoar, C.E. 'The Registration of Completed Lives by means of Card Series.' *Transactions of the Life Assurance Medical Officers' Association* (1897): 182–95.

Hodgson, John. *Observations in reference to Duration of Life amongst the Clergy of England and Wales*. London: Charles and Edwin Layton, 1864.

Hogg, John. *London as It Is; Being a Series of Observations on the Health, Habits, and Amusements of the People*. London: John Macrone, 1837.

Horsell, William. *Hydropathy for the People: With Plain Observations on Drugs, Diet, Water, Air, and Exercise*. New York: Fowlers and Wells, 1850.

Hughes, William. 'On the Selection of Lives for Assurance.' *Journal of the Federated Insurance Institutes* 2 (1899): 383–96.
– 'The Assurance of Under–average Lives.' *Journal of the Federated Insurance Institutes* 9 (1906): 13–27.
Humphreys, George. 'On the Practice of the Eagle Company with regard to Lives classed as Unsound.' *Journal of the Institute of Actuaries* 18 (1874): 178–95.
Hutchinson, John. *The Spirometer, the Stethoscope, & Scale-Balance; their Use in Discriminating Diseases of the Chest, and their Value in Life Offices; with remarks on the Selection of Lives for Life Assurance Companies.* London: John Churchill, 1852.
Hutchison, John. *A Popular View of Life Assurance: Embracing a Sketch of its Origin and Progress, – its Principles, Objects, and Advantages.* Glasgow: William Lang, 1846.
Index to Statutes, Public and Private, from Union with Ireland to 1859, Part II, *Local and Personal Acts, Local Acts and Private Acts.* London: by order of the House of Commons, 1860.
Industrial Life Offices' Association. *Industrial Life Offices' Association, 1901–51.* London: The Association, 1951.
Institute of Actuaries. *Tables deduced from the Mortality Experience of Life Assurance Companies, as collected and arranged by the Institute of Actuaries of Great Britain and Ireland.* London: Charles and Edwin Layton, 1872.
'Insurance as a Profession.' *Bankers' Magazine* 55 (1893): 803–22.
Insurance Register: Being a Record of the Yearly Progress and the Present Financial Position of the Life Insurance Associations of Great Britain. 2nd ed. London: W. Kent and Co., 1869.
Jackson, Samuel. 'Popular Misconceptions regarding Life Assurance.' *Insurance Institute Journal* 13 (1910): 71–91.
Jellicoe, Charles. 'Rate of Mortality in the Eagle Insurance Company.' *Assurance Magazine* 4 (1854): 199–215.
– 'Data collected by the Council of the Institute, to determine Rates of Premium in Foreign Climates.' *Journal of the Institute of Actuaries* 7 (1857): 131–5.
Jellicoe, George R. *Eagle Insurance Company [Instructions to Agents].* London: privately printed, 1895.
Jennings, Hargrave. *The Childishness and Brutality of the Time: Some Plain Truths in Plain Language.* London, Vizetelly and Co., 1883.
Jones, David. *On the Value of Annuities and Reversionary Payments, with Numerous Tables.* London: Baldwin and Cradock, 1843.
Jones, G.W. *The Scottish Equitable Life Assurance Society: Analysis of the Schemes by which the Bonus has been Reduced from £2 to £1, and by which it is Attempted to Keep It at the Same Rate.* London: Davies and Co., 1877.

Jones, Jenkin. *A Series of Tables of Annuities and Assurances, Calculated from a New Rate of Mortality amongst Assured Lives*. London: Longman, Brown, Green, and Longmans, 1843.

– *What Is Life Assurance? Explained by Practical Illustrations of its Principles*. London: Longman, Brown, Green, and Longmans, 1847.

Kauffmann, O.J. 'The Urine in Its Bearing on Life Assurance.' *Transactions of the Birmingham Insurance Institute* (1899–1900): 13–23.

Keating, Michael G. *Life Assurance ... A Lecture*. London: n.p., 1854.

Kelly, James Birch. *A Practical Treatise on the Law of Life Annuities, with .... Observations on the Present System of Life Assurance, and a Scheme for a New Company*. London: A Maxwell, 1835.

Kempe, John Edward. *The Recollections of a Director*. Edinburgh: Ballantyne Press, 1902.

Kent's Original London Directory. London: Henry Kent Causton and Son, 1825.

King, George. 'On the Mortality amongst Assured Lives, and the requisite Reserves of Life Offices.' *Journal of the Institute of Actuaries* 19 (1876): 381–413.

– 'On the Method used by Milne in the Construction of the Carlisle Table of Mortality.' *Journal of the Institute of Actuaries* 24 (1883): 186–211.

– 'Insurance.' In R.H.I. Palgrave, ed., *Dictionary of Political Economy*, vol. 2, 409–16. London: Macmillan, 1896.

– 'On the Valuation in Groups of Whole-Life Policies by Select Mortality Tables.' *Journal of the Institute of Actuaries* 40 (1906): 1–11, 84–97.

King, George, and George F. Hardy. 'Practical Application of Mr Makeham's Formula to the Graduation of Mortality Tables.' *Journal of the Institute of Actuaries* 22 (1880): 191–231.

Kingsley, Francis. 'The Objects and Benefits of Fire and Life Insurance.' *Report of the Insurance Institute of Manchester* (1882–83): 48–72.

Kinnear, W.S. 'Insurance in the Twentieth Century.' *Royal Exchange Assurance Magazine* 3 (1910): 101–11.

Knight, F.H. *Risk, Uncertainty and Profit*. Boston: Houghton Mifflin, 1921.

Langley, J. Baxter. *The Life-Agent's Vade-Mecum, and Practical Guide to Success in Life Assurance Business*. London: Job Caudwell, 1864.

Laundy, Samuel Linn. *A Table of Products, by the Factors 1 to 9, of All Numbers from 1 to 100,000, by the Aid of which Multiplication may be Performed by Inspection*. London: Charles and Edwin Layton, 1865.

Lawrance, Frederick. *A Short Treatise on Life Assurance*. London: Pelham Richardson, 1843.

Lees, Frederic R. (ed.). *Standard Temperance Library*. London: W. Brittain, 1843.

Leifchild, J.R. 'Life Assurance Institutions.' *London Review* 13 (1859): 134–79.

Leigh, Samuel George. *Life Assurance: A Handbook of the Practical and Scientific Aspects of the Business*. London: Sir Isaac Pitman, 1916.

Levi, Leone. 'On the Progress and Economical Bearings of National Debts in this and other Countries.' *Journal of the Statistical Society of London* 25 (1862): 313–38.

Life Agent's Mentor, or Advantages versus Difficulties of an Assurance Agency. London: Boswell, 1890.

Life-Assurance, A Familiar Dialogue. London: n.p., 1850.

Life Assurance Companies: their Financial Condition Discussed. London: Effingham Wilson, 1869.

'Life Assurance Premiums and Policies.' *Bankers' Magazine and Statistical Register* 4 (1849): 138–46.

Life Assurance Premiums Charged by Various Companies. Arranged in Order of Magnitude. Newcastle-upon-Tyne: Mawson, Swan and Morgan, 1910.

Lightfoot, Thomas. *Stamps on Life Insurances*. London: HMSO, 1825.

Lister, Thomas D. 'A Graphic Expression of Extra Risk as Implied by an Addition of Years.' *Transactions of the Life Assurance Medical Officers' Association* (1901): 159–89.

Liverpool and London Fire and Life Insurance Company. *Instructions to Agents*. Liverpool: George M'Corquodale, 1861.

Livesay, Frank. *Insurer's Guide and Directory*. London: W. Kent and Co., 1884.

Low, Alexander. *The Principles and Practice of the Life Association of Scotland ... founded on the Original Model of the London Life Association*. Edinburgh: Neill and Co., 1843.

– *A Familiar Explanation of the Benefits and Practice of Life Assurance*. Edinburgh: Robert Inches, n.d.

Low, George M. 'The History and Present Position of the Faculty of Actuaries in Scotland.' *Transactions of the Faculty of Actuaries* 1 (1902): 1–16.

Lubbock, John William, and J.E. Drinkwater. *On Probability*. London: Baldwin and Cradock, 1830.

Lutt, Harold Edward William. 'On Extra Premiums.' *Journal of the Institute of Actuaries* 41 (1907): 461–527.

Lyon, T. Glover. 'Remarks on Consumption in relation to Life Assurance.' *Journal of the Institute of Actuaries* 30 (1892): 120–31.

– 'Some Medical Points of Difference between Life Assurance in the United States of America and in England.' *Transactions of the Life Assurance Medical Officers' Association* (1895): 51–69.

– 'Medical Examination Forms for Life Assurance.' *Practitioner* 66 (1901): 138–43.

Macaulay, T.B. 'On the Relation between the Height and Weight of Men.' *Journal of the Institute of Actuaries* 23 (1881): 62–4.

- 'Weight and Longevity.' *Publications of the American Statistical Association* 2 (1891): 287–96.
Macfadyen, James. *The Principles affecting the Solvency of a Life Assurance Company: and the Best Means of Protecting the Public against their Violation.* Glasgow: Philosophical Society, 1870.
- 'On "Extra Premium."' *Journal of the Institute of Actuaries* 17 (1872): 77–95.
- 'Does a Large New Business benefit the Policyholders of a Life Company?' *Assurance Magazine* 18 (1874): 335–43.
Mackenzie, Hector. 'Glycosuria and Diabetes in relation to Life Assurance.' *Practitioner* 65 (1900): 138–44.
Makeham, William. 'On the Law of Mortality.' *Assurance Magazine* 13 (1867): 325–49.
Malcolm, W.R., and R.G.C. Hamilton. 'Report to the Board of Trade upon the Accounts and Statements of Life Assurance Companies.' *Journal of the Institute of Actuaries* 18 (1875): 390–402.
Manly, H.W. 'An Attempt to measure the Extra Risk arising from a Consumptive Family History.' *Journal of the Institute of Actuaries* 30 (1892): 97–119.
Mann, John. *A Contribution to the Medical Statistics of Life Assurance wit Hints on the Selection of Lives.* London: J. Masters, 1865.
Mansel, Henry Longueville. *Prolegomena Logica: An Inquiry into the Psychological Character of Logical Processes.* 2nd English ed. Boston: Gould and Lincoln, 1860.
Marr, Thomas. 'Notes upon Insurance, and the Practical Working of a Life Assurance Fund.' *Transactions of the Insurance and Actuarial Society of Glasgow* 1 (1883): 93–104.
- 'The Future.' *Transactions of the Insurance and Actuarial Society of Glasgow* 2 (1886): 47–58.
Marshall, Samuel. *A Treatise on the Law of Insurance.* London: A. Strahan, 1808.
May, Otto. 'The Significance of (1) Diabetic Family History and (2) Temporary Glycosuria in Life Assurance.' *Transactions of the Life Assurance Medical Officers' Association* (1914): 27–53.
McCleery, J. Carlisle. *Some Insurance 'Don'ts' [mainly for Agents].* London: n.p., 1904.
McCormack, P.H. 'Group Insurance.' *Journal of the Institute of Actuaries* 51 (1919): 313–37.
Medical Register. London: Mackie and Co., 1859–1910.
Meikle, James. *The Rationale of Life Assurance Premiums.* Edinburgh: R. & R. Clark, 1861.

– *Observations on the Rate of Mortality of Assured Lives, as experienced by Ten Assurance Companies in Scotland, to December 31, 1863.* Edinburgh: William Blackwood and Sons, 1872.

Memoranda for Life Assurance Agents. London: n.p., 1880.

Mill, John Stuart. *Principles of Political Economy: With Some of their Applications to Social Philosophy.* 2 vols. London: John W. Parker, 1848.

Mills, D.Y. 'New Business and the Cost of its Extension.' *Transactions of the Insurance and Actuarial Society of Glasgow* 4 (1898): 167–79.

– 'The Value of New Business to a Life Office.' *Journal of the Federated Insurance Institutes* 7 (1904): 197–208.

Milne, Joshua. *A Treatise on the Valuation of Annuities and Assurances on Lives.* London: Longman, Hurst, Rees, Orme, and Brown, 1815.

M'Lauchlan, J.J. 'On the Book-keeping of a Life Office.' *Transactions of the Faculty of Actuaries* 1 (1902): 189–256.

Moinet, Francis. *Guide to Medical Examination for Life Insurance.* Edinburgh: Maclachlan and Stewart, 1876.

Morgan, A.H. 'Life Branch Work.' *Transactions of the Insurance and Actuarial Society of Glasgow* 3 (1891): 3–20.

Morgan, Arthur. *Tables showing the Total Number of Persons Assured in the Equitable Society.* London: Richard Taylor, 1834.

Morgan, Richard. *Familiar Observations on Life Insurance, and the causes affecting Population, etc. etc.* Norwich: Joseph Fletcher, 1841.

Morgan, William. *A View of the Rise and Progress of the Equitable Society, and of the Causes which have Contributed to its Success.* London: Longman, Rees, Orme, Brown, and Green, 1828.

Moxley, Vincent. 'Medical Examinations.' *Journal of the Federated Insurance Institutes* 6 (1903): 295–305.

Muirhead, Claud. *The Causes of Death among the Assured in the Scottish Widows' Fund and Life Assurance Society from 1874 to 1894 inclusive.* Edinburgh: R. & R. Clark, 1902.

Neison, F.G.P. *Prospectus of the Medical, Invalid, and General Life Assurance Society.* London: M. & W. Collis, 1848.

– 'Mortality of Master Mariners.' *Journal of the Statistical Society of London* 13 (1850): 193–209.

Nevins, J. Birkbeck. 'On Life Assurance: Regarded as an Investment.' *Proceedings of the Literary and Philosophical Society of Liverpool* (1860–61): 66–80.

Newbatt, Benjamin. 'Opening Address by the President.' *Journal of the Institute of Actuaries* 29 (1891): 1–27.

Newman, Philip L. 'The New Mortality Tables of the Institute of Actuaries and Faculty of Actuaries, 1893.' *Journal of the Federated Insurance Institutes* 5 (1902): 261–290.

– 'A Review of the Investments of Offices, with Notes on Stock Exchange Fluctuations.' *Journal of the Institute of Actuaries* 42 (1908): 294–337.

Newmarch, William. 'On the Loans raised by Mr Pitt, 1793–1801.' *Journal of the Statistical Society of London* 18 (1855): 104–40.

Nicol, William Smith. 'The New Combined Mortality Experience of British Life Assurance Companies.' *Transactions of the Insurance and Actuarial Society of Glasgow* 3 (1895): 257–86.

Nicoll, Jonathan. 'Life Assurance without Medical Examination.' *Transactions of the Faculty of Actuaries* 2 (1904): 57–89.

Nisbet, Harry C. *Prize Essay on Life Assurance.* Uxbridge: John Mackenzie, 1853.

North British and Mercantile Insurance Company. *Practical Hints for the Use of the Agents in the Life Department.* Edinburgh: R. & R. Clark, 1873.

Oakes, W.H. *Table of the Reciprocals of Numbers from 1 to 100,000, with their Differences, by which the Reciprocals of Numbers may be obtained up to 10,000,000.* London: Charles and Edwin Layton, 1865.

Observations on the National Loan Fund Life Assurance and Deferred Annuity Society. London: Hamilton, Adams, and Co., 1838.

Ogilvie, Leslie. 'Some Medical Aspects of Life Assurance.' *Transactions of the Actuarial Society of Edinburgh* 4 (1897): 81–114.

Ormerod, J. Redman. *The Practical Advocacy of Life Assurance and Other Reprinted Articles, Etc.* London: Stone and Cox, 1930.

Orr, Lewis P. 'Insurance Research and Eugenics.' *Eugenics Review* 4 (1913): 331–55.

Orwell, George. *Coming Up for Air.* New York: Harcourt, Brace, 1950.

Owen, Robert. *Report to the County of Lanark of a Plan for Relieving Public Distress and Removing Discontent by Giving Permanent, Productive Employment to the Poor and Working Classes.* London: Equitable Labour Exchange, 1832.

Page, Arnold. 'Assurance Investments.' *Fortnightly Review* 32 (1879): 732–54.

Palladium Life and Fire Assurance Company. *Life Department. Instructions to Agents.* London: privately published, 1825.

Paulin, David. 'Old Age Pensions and Pauperism: A Present-Day Problem.' *Transactions of the Actuarial Society of Edinburgh* 4 (1896): 1–32.

– '1801–1901: A Contrast.' *Transactions of the Insurance and Actuarial Society of Glasgow* 5 (1902): 221–46.

Pearson, Karl. *The Life, Letters and Labours of Francis Galton.* 3 vols. Cambridge: Cambridge University Press, 1924–1930.

Penman, William Jr. 'Special Policies (Life).' *Insurance Institute Journal* 12 (1909): 1–23.

Perks, Wilfred. 'The Treatment of Sub-standard Lives in Practice.' *Journal of the Institute of Actuaries* 78 (1952): 205–37.

Pinckard, George H. 'Practice and Experience of the Clerical, Medical, and General Life Assurance Society.' *Assurance Magazine* 1 (1851): 273–9.

Pocock, Lewis. *A Familiar Explanation of the Nature, Advantages, and Importance of Assurances upon Lives, and the Various Purposes to which they may be Usefully Applied.* London: Smith, Elder and Co., 1842.

Pollock, James Edward, and James Chisholm. *Medical Handbook of Life Assurance, for the Use of Medical and other Officers of Companies.* London: Cassell and Co., 1889.

Poore, G. Vivian 'The Relation of Slight Degrees of Albuminuria to Life Assurance.' *Transactions of the Life Assurance Medical Officers' Association* (1894): 24–39.

– 'Locality and Occupation in relation to Life Assurance.' *Transactions of the Life Assurance Medical Officers' Association* (1900): 16–46.

Porter, G.R. *The Progress of the Nation in its Various Social and Economic Relations from the Beginning of the Nineteenth Century.* Revised by F.W. Hirst. London: Methuen, 1912.

Porter, H.W. 'On some Considerations suggested by the Annual Reports of the Registrar-General.' *Assurance Magazine* 9 (1860): 89–112.

– 'Mr Finlaison's "Report and Observations on the Mortality of the Government Life Annuitants."' *Assurance Magazine* 9 (1861): 277–88.

Post Office Annual Directory, and Calendar, for 1841–42. Edinburgh: Ballantyne and Hughes, 1841.

Post Office Glasgow Annual Directory, for 1842 –43. Glasgow: John Graham, 1842.

Post Office London Directory for 1820. London: T. Maiden, 1820.

Powell, R. Douglas. *On Consumption and on Certain Diseases of the Lungs and Pleura.* London: H.K. Lewis, 1878.

– *On Diseases of the Lungs and Pleurae including Consumption.* 3rd ed. London: H.K. Lewis, 1886.

– 'Address delivered by the President.' (1896). *Transactions of the Life Assurance Medical Officers' Association* (1894–97): 115–24.

– 'On the Medical Aspects of Life Insurance.' *Practitioner* 88 (1912): 489–526.

Price, Richard. *Observations on Reversionary Payments; on Schemes for Providing Annuities for Widows, and for Persons in Old Age.* 5th ed., 2 vols. London: T. Cadell, 1792.

Pritchard, A.W.G. 'Insurance Work in South Africa.' *Transactions of the Birmingham Insurance Institute* (1898–99): 28–39.

Prudential Assurance Company. *Agents' Instructions.* London: privately published, 1868, 1922.

Raleigh, Samuel. *Address.* Edinburgh: Thomas Constable, 1864.

Rankin, Robert. *A Familiar Treatise on Life Assurance and Annuities, comprising a Historical Sketch of the Science, and of Life Assurance Offices.* London: Simpkin and Marshall, 1830.

Ransome, Arthur. *On the Relation of the Chest-Movements to Prognosis in Lung-Disease.* London: Macmillan, 1882

Reliance Mutual Life Assurance Society. *Life Assurance Explained.* London: n.p., 1850.

Remarks on a Letter by Robert Christie ... by an Official in One of the Registered Companies under the Joint-Stock Act. London: Pelham Richardson, 1852.

Remarks on the Constitution and Progress of the Dissenters' and General Life and Fire Assurance Company. Reprinted from the Eclectic Review of May, 1839. London: John Haddon, 1839.

Report from the Select Committee of the House of Lords on Children's Life Insurance Bill.. London: Herbert Hansard and Son, 1890.

Report from the Select Committee of the House of Lords on Life Assurance Companies. London: HMSO, 1906.

Report from the Select Committee on Friendly Societies. London: by order of the House of Commons, 1852.

Report from the Select Committee on Friendly Societies Act, 1875. London: Henry Hansard and Sons, 1889.

Report from the Select Committee on the Laws respecting Friendly Societies. London: by order of the House of Commons, 1825.

Report from the Select Committee on the Laws respecting Friendly Societies. London: by order of the House of Commons, 1827.

Report of the Royal Commission to Inquire into the Condition and Management of Lights, Buoys and Beacons on the Coast of the United Kingdom. London: by order of the House of Commons, 1861.

Return of Amount Expended out of Poor's Rate in Each County of England and Wales. London: by order of the House of Commons, 1852.

Return of Amount of Stamps for Policies of Life Assurance during the Years 1869 to 1872. London: by order of the House of Commons, 1873.

Return of Joint Stock Companies registered under Act 7 & 8 Victoria, chapter 110. London: by order of the House of Commons, 1845.

Return of Monies Borrowed by Vestries and Other Local Bodies. London: by order of the House of Commons, 1877.

Return of the Names, Places of Business, and Objects of all Assurance Companies completely Registered ... and also, of a Copy of every Account Registered by such Companies. London: by order of the House of Commons, 1849, 1852, 1857, and 1863.

Return of Names, Places of Business, Date of Registration, Nominal Capital and Number of Shares of Joint Stock Companies; Number of Shareholders and Number

of Companies registered in City of London. London: by order of the House of
Commons, 1864–1897.

*Return of Number of Private Bills introduced and brought from House of Lords, and
of Acts*. London: by order of the House of Commons, 1847–1891.

Return of Payments for Services in Albert Life Assurance Company Arbitration.
London: by order of the House of Commons, 1877.

*Return of Savings Banks in United Kingdom, showing Number of Officers, Accounts
open, Amount owing to Depositors ... 1869–70*. London: by order of the House
of Commons, 1871.

*Return of Sums paid to Arbitrators, Assessors, Liquidators and Solicitors under European
Society Arbitration Act, 1872*. London: by order of the House of Commons, 1875.

Rhind, Henry. *Proposals and Rates of the Glasgow Insurance Company*. Glasgow:
Scottish Guardian, 1839.

Rickards, E. 'A Plea for Uniformity of Forms of Medical Officers' Reports.'
Transactions of the Birmingham Insurance Institute (1901–2): 46–52.

Rietz, H.L. 'On Certain Applications of the Differential and Integral Calculus
in Actuarial Science.' *American Mathematical Monthly* 33 (1926): 9–23.

Risdon, W.E. 'Notes on the Medical Examination for Life Insurance.' *St Bartholomew's Hospital Journal* 11 (1903–4): 28–9, 56–8, 112–14.

Robertson, Alexander. *Defects in the Practice of Life Assurance, and Suggestions
for their Remedy*. London: W.S. Orr, 1848.

– *Periodical Savings, applied to Provident Purposes ... suggesting a Plan of Self-
Protecting Life Insurance*. London: W.S. Orr, 1852.

Robertson, J.A. 'On a New Method of Performing Approximately Certain
Operations in Multiplication and Division.' *Journal of the Institute of Actuaries* 32 (1896): 160–84.

Robertson, William. *Report on the Causes of Death among the Assured in the Scottish Equitable Life Assurance Society from 1831 to 1864*. Edinburgh: privately
printed, 1865.

Rock Life Assurance Company. *The Principles of Life Assurance Explained:
together with New Plans of Assurance and Annuities adapted to the Prudent of All
Classes, Civil and Military*. London: J. Lambert, 1809.

Rodger, A.K. 'The Race for Records.' *Transactions of the Insurance and Actuarial
Society of Glasgow* 5 (1900): 21–43.

Rodger, John. 'Proposal, Medical, and Other Forms in Connection with Life
Assurance.' *Journal of the Federated Insurance Institutes* 8 (1905): 39–61.

– 'New Business Difficulties – Past and Present.' *Report of the Insurance Institute of Bristol* (1913–14): 30–44.

Roughead, William. *Classic Crimes: A Selection from the Work of William Roughead*.
New York: New York Review of Books, 2000.

Royal Insurance Company. *Instructions to the Agents*. London: Truscott, Son and Simmons, [1866].

Rusher, Edward A., and Charles William Kenchington. 'On the Effects of Family and Personal History in various Classes of Life Assurance Risks.' *Journal of the Institute of Actuaries* 47 (1913): 433–523.

Saint-Clair, William. *Popular View of Life Assurance*. London: Jones and Causton, 1840.

Sala, George Augustus. *Quite Alone: A Novel*. New York: Harper and Bros., 1865.

Sang, Edward. *A New Table of Seven-Place Logarithms of all Numbers Continuously up to 200 000*. 2nd ed. London: Williams and Norgate, 1883.

Saville, Walter. 'Curiosities of Life Assurance.' *Gentleman's Magazine* n.s. 8 (1872): 445–50.

Schooling, Frederick ,and Edward A. Rusher. *The Mortality Experience of the Imperial Forces during the War in South Africa, 11 October 1899 to 31 May 1902*. London: Charles and Edwin Layton, 1903.

Scottish Amicable Life Assurance Society. *Private Instrucions to the Agents ... with Tables of Rates*. Glasgow: privately published, 1887.

Scottish Equitable Assurance Society, on the Model of the London Equitable. Edinburgh: Thomas Constable, 1835.

Scottish Equitable Life Assurance Society. *Report of the Proceedings of the Seventeenth Annual General Court*. Edinburgh: Thomas Constable, 1848.

– *Report of the Proceedings of the Fifty-sixth Annual general Court*. Edinburgh: privately published, 1887.

Scratchley, Arthur. *Observations on Life Assurance Societies, and Savings Banks*. London: John W. Parker, 1851.

Scudamore, Frank Ives. *Life Insurance by Small Payments: A Few Plain Words concerning It*. London: Emily Faithfull and Co., 1861.

Second Report from the Select Committee on the Act for the Regulation of Mills and Factories. London: by order of the House of Commons, 1840.

'Section of Medicine in Relation to Life Assurance.' *British Medical Journal* (17 Sept. 1898): 757–74.

Seventh Annual Report of the Registrar-General of Births, Deaths, and Marriages in England. London: W. Clowes and Sons, 1846.

Sharman, H. Riseborough. *Life Assurance Leaflets*. London: G.J. Stevenson, 1860.

Short Account of the Mutual Life Assurance Society. London: H. Barnett, 1835.

Sieveking, Edward H. *The Medical Adviser in Life Assurance*. London: Churchill, 1874.

Sim, R.A. *Life Assurance. Objections Answered*. Edinburgh: n.p., 1888.

Sixth Annual Report of the Registrar-General of Births, Deaths, and Marriages in England. London: W. Clowes and Son, 1845.

Slater D.M. *Life Assurance in India: Its Origin and Development*. Bombay: Canton Steam Printing Works, 1893.

Slater's Royal National Commercial Directory of the Counties of Cumberland, Durham, Northumberland, Westmoreland, and the Cleveland district. Manchester: Slater, 1877.

Slater's Royal National Commercial Directory of Scotland. Manchester: Slater, 1878.

Slater's Royal National Commercial Directory of ... Yorkshire. Manchester: Slater, 1875.

Smee, A.H. Jun. *Gresham Life Assurance Society: The Causes of Death*. London: privately published, 1871.

Smiles, Samuel. 'Life Assurance Companies.' *Quarterly Review* 128 (1870): 18–49.

Smith, David. *Report on the Causes of Death among the Assured in the North British Insurance Company, from the Commencement of the Business in 1823, up to 31st December 1860*. Edinburgh: Thomas Constable, 1862.

Smith, J.B. 'The Responsibilities of Actuaries.' *Accountant* 33 (1905): 618–21.

Smith, William Henry. 'Southey.' *Blackwood's Magazine* 69 (1851): 385–405.

Smithson, T.C. *Ten Minutes Advice to the Thoughtful and Prudent. Being a Prize Essay on the Importance and Duty of Life Assurance*. Uxbridge: John Mackenzie, 1852.

Soper, George Isabell. *On the Life Assurance Offices: Their National and Social Advantages, Their Principles and Practice*. London: W.S.D. Pateman, 1847.

Speight, T.W. 'Bolsover Brothers.' *Chambers's Journal of Popular Literature, Science and Arts* 5 (1888): 553–56, 567–70, 584–8, 600–2.

Spens, William. 'On the Inadequacy of Existing Data for Determining Mortality among Select Lives.' *Assurance Magazine* 4 (1854): 1–9.

Sprague, A.E. 'An Investigation as to how far Life Insurance is of a Provident Nature ... and how far it is of a merely Financial Character.' *Transactions of the Actuarial Society of Edinburgh* 3 (1896): 375–90.

Sprague, Thomas Bond. *Life Insurance in 1872*. London: Layton, 1872.

– 'On the Usefulness of Mathematical Studies to the Actuary.' *Journal of the Institute of Actuaries* 18 (1875): 403–16.

– 'Opening Address by the President.' *Journal of the Institute of Actuaries* 24 (1884): 229–42.

– 'Opening Address by the President.' *Journal of the Institute of Actuaries* 25 (1886): 293–313.

Sprigge, S. Squire. *The Life and Times of Thomas Wakley*. London: Longmans, Green and Co., 1897.

Star Life Assurance Society ... and Its Intimate Connection with the Wesleyan Methodist Society. London: privately published, 1900.

Star Life Assurance Society. *Souvenir.* Appended to Wesleyan Methodist Conference, *Official Programme of Meetings & Services.* London: Methodist Publishing House, 1907. 51–95.

Statements and Abstracts of Reports deposited with the Board of Trade, under 'The Life Assurance Companies Act, 1870.' London: by order of the House of Commons, 1872–80.

Statements of Account and of Life Assurance and Annuity Business, and Abstracts of Actuarial Reports deposited with the Board of Trade under ... the Life Assurance Companies Act, 1870.' London: by order of the House of Commons, 1882–83; Hansard, 1884–91; HMSO, 1892–1910.

Statements of Account and of Life Assurance and Annuity Business, and Abstracts of Actuarial Reports deposited with the Board of Trade under the Life Assurance Companies Act, 1870,' and ... the 'Assurance Companies Act, 1909.' London: HMSO, 1910–20.

Steeds, A.J. 'Some Considerations Affecting the Selection of Risks.' *Journal of the Institute of Actuaries* 91 (1965): 231–85.

Stevenson, Robert Louis. *The Letters of Robert Louis Stevenson to His Family and Friends.* Edited by Sidney Colvin, vol. 2. New York: Charles Scribner's Sons, 1899.

Stewart, A.P. *Observations on the Characteristics of Assurable and Non–assurable Lives.* London: W.S.D. Pateman, 1861.

Stewart, John Watson (comp.). *The Gentleman's and Citizen's Almanack ... for the Year of Our Lord 1825.* Dublin: Stewart and Hopes, 1825.

Stewart, Thomas Grainger. 'On the Discharge of Albumen from the Kidneys of Healthy People.' *Proceedings of the Royal Society of Edinburgh* 14 (1887): 240–50.

Stokes, G.D.C. 'The Slide Rule.' In E.M. Horsburgh (ed.), *Modern Instruments and Methods of Calculation: A Handbook of the Napier Tercentenary Exhibition,* 155–80. London: G. Bell and Sons, 1914.

Stone, W.H., and Stewart Helder. *On Some Points in the Medical History of the Clergy Mutual Assurance Society.* London: privately published, 1873.

Stout, Robert. 'Notes on the Progress of New Zealand for Twenty Years, 1864–84.' *Journal of the Statistical Society of London* 49 (1886): 539–80.

Sturrock, John. *The Principles and Practice of Life Assurance.* Dundee: W. Middleton, J. Chalmers, and F. Shaw, 1846.

Sunderland, A.W. 'On a Method frequently adopted of treating Under-average Lives for Assurance Purposes, by making Temporary Deductions from the Sums Assured.' *Journal of the Institute of Actuaries* 29 (1891): 419–44.

Supplement to the Twenty–fifth Annual Report of the Registrar-General of Births, Deaths, and Marriages in England. London: George E. Eyre and William Spottiswoode, 1864.

Sutton, William. 'Opening Address by the President.' *Journal of the Institute of Actuaries* 28 (1890): 169–84.

Symes-Thompson, Edward. 'Extra Rating of Unhealthy Lives.' *Transactions of the Life Assurance Medical Officers' Association* (1899): 135–62.

Tait, P.M. 'The Prospectuses of the Indian Life Assurance Offices.' *Assurance Magazine* 6 (1855): 15–45.

– *Anglo-Indian Vital Statistics. A Paper read before the East India Association.* London: East India Association, 1874.

Tarn, Arthur Wyndham. 'Some Notes on Life Assurance in Greater Britain.' *Journal of the Institute of Actuaries* 34 (1899): 517–61.

Taylor, Alfred S. 'A Course of Lectures on Medical Jurisprudence.' *London Medical Gazette* 39 (1847): 45–52, 265–71, 661–9.

Taylor, Tom R. 'Undesirables.' *Insurance Institute Journal* 12 (1909): 57–67.

Thackeray, William Makepeace. *Vanity Fair.* (1848). New York: Airmont Publishing Co., 1967.

– *The History of Samuel Titmarsh and the Great Hoggarty Diamond.* London: Bradbury and Evans, 1849.

Thompson, Reginald E. *The Physical Examination of the Chest in Health and Disease.* London: Henry Renshaw, 1879.

Thomson, J. Stitt. 'Glycosuria and Life Assurance.' *Journal of the Federated Insurance Institutes* 4 (1901): 293–8.

Thomson, William Thomas. *On the Present Position of the Life Assurance Interest of Great Britain.* Edinburgh: Blackwood, 1852.

– *The Rates of Interest on Landed Securities in Scotland.* Edinburgh and London: William Blackwood and Son, 1868.

To Parents with Marriageable Daughters, and to the Ladies Themselves. (A Brochure in Favour of Life Assurance.) London: n.p., 1888.

Trollope, Anthony. *The Bertrams.* (1859). Harmondsworth: Penguin, 1993.

– *The Family Parsonage.* (1861). New York: Viking, 1985.

Tucker, Robert. *On Causes which lead to the Insolvency of Life Assurance Companies.* London: Kent, 1869.

Turney, Horace G. 'The Habit of Smoking in its Relation to the Insurance Examiner.' *Transactions of the Life Assurance Medical Officers' Association* (1913): 151–82.

Twelfth Annual Report of the Registrar-General of Births, Deaths, and Marriages in England. London: George E. Eyre and William Spottiswoode, 1853.

Uncle Tom's Twenty Reasons why Life Assurance should be Universal. Manchester: Kennedy and Watson, 1860.

Valentine, James. 'A Comparison of Reserves brought out by the Use of Different Data in the Valuation of the Liabilities of a Life Office.' *Journal of the Institute of Actuaries* 18 (1874): 229–42.

Van Sandau, Andrew. *An Exposition of the Author's Experience as one of the Assured in the 'Alliance' British & Foreign Life & Fire Assurance Company.* London: C.A. Bartlett, 1856.

Walford, Cornelius. *The Insurance Guide and Hand Book, dedicated especially to Insurance Agents.* 2nd ed. London: Charles and Edwin Layton, 1867

– *The Insurance Cyclopaedia.* 6 vols. London: Charles and Edwin Layton, 1871–80.

– 'A Suggestion towards adding a New Feature of Usefulness to the Institute of Actuaries.' *Journal of the Institute of Actuaries* 22 (1879): 1–20.

– 'The Position of Life and Other Insurance Associations in Relation to their Local Medical Examiners.' *Journal of the Institute of Actuaries* 22 (1880): 153–90.

Ward, Stephen H. *On the Medical Estimate of Life for Life Assurance.* London: John Churchill, 1857.

Warner, S.G. 'Twenty Years' Changes in Life Assurance.' *Insurance Institute Journal* 12 (1909): 67–86.

– 'The Effect on British Life Assurance of the European War (1914–1918).' In Norman Hill et al. (eds.), *War and Insurance,* 99–168. London: Oxford University Press, 1927.

Warren, Samuel. *Confessions of an Attorney.* London: Cornish, Lamport, 1852.

Watson, J. Douglas *Report upon the Expenses of the Association* [English and Scottish Law]. London: Waterlow and Sons, 1900.

Watson, James. *American Life Offices in Great Britain: Remarks on Reply of the Equitable Life Assurance Society of the United States, to the Memorandum for Agents and Policyholders of the Scottish Provident Institution.* Edinburgh: Bell and Bradfute, 1884.

Weber, Max. *From Max Weber: Essays in Sociology.* New York: Oxford University Press, 1946.

Weekly Notes from Correspondence ... A Private and Confidential Weekly Communication to the Agents of the British Equitable Assurance Company. London: British Equitable, 1881–82.

Wells, H.G. *The History of Mr Polly.* (1910). London: J.M. Dent, 1993.

Welton, Thomas. 'Hints on Life Assurance.' *Universal Review* 6 (1889): 60–70.

Whittall, W.J.H. *Clerical, Medical and General Life Assurance Society. A Short Address to the Agents of the Society and some other Connections.* London: privately published, 1897.

Williams, C. Theodore. 'Medical Examination of Candidates for Life Assurance.' *Clinical Journal* 24 (1904): 273–80, 289–99.

Williamson, George. *The Medical Report: Its Place in the Selection of Lives.* Aberdeen: Central Press, 1911.
– *The Assurance of Sub-Standard Lives.* Aberdeen: Central Press, 1912.
Wilson, James. *The Albert Life Office Libel Case. How It Arose, and How It Was Settled.* Calcutta: n.p., 1871.
Wilson, Roland Knyvet. *History of Modern English Law.* London: Rivingtons, 1875.
Winter, A.T. 'Notes on Mortality and Life Assurance in India.' *Journal of the Institute of Actuaries* 43 (1909): 365–407.
Woolhouse, W.S.B. 'Explanation of a New method of Adjusting Mortality Tables.' *Journal of the Institute of Actuaries* 15 (1870): 389–410.
– 'Some Practical Observations relating to Tables of Mortality.' *Bankers' Magazine* 53 (1892): 137–42.
Young, Alexander. *A Guide to Life Assurance containing an Account of the Origin and Progress, and Explanation of the System, and Pointing Out the benefits of Life Assurance.* London: R. Groombridge, 1844.
Young, Norwood. 'Betting.' *Badminton Magazine* 3 (1896): 708–16.
Young, W. McGregor. 'Some Problems in Medical Examination for Life Assurance.' *Medical Examiner* 3/4 (1902): 1–5.
Younger, Samuel. 'On a Plan for making Conditional the Payment of extra Premium in the case of a Life supposed to be Diseased or more than ordinarily Hazardous.' *Assurance Magazine* 10 (1862): 268–72.

Secondary Sources

Company Histories

Besant, Arthur Digby. *Our Centenary: Being the History of the First Hundred Years of the Clerical, Medical & General Life Assurance Society.* London: Clerical, Medical and General Life Assurance Society, 1924.
Bignold, Sir Robert. *Five Generations of the Bignold Family 1761–1947 and their connection with the Norwich Union.* London: B.T. Batsford, 1948.
Blake, Robert. *Esto Perpetua: Norwich Union Life Insurance Society 1808–1958.* Norwich: Newman Neame, 1958.
Buley, R. Carlyle. *The Equitable Life Assurance Society of the United States 1859–1964,* vol 1. New York: Appleton-Century-Crofts, 1967.
Butt, John. 'Life Assurance in War and Depression: The Standard Life Assurance Company and Its Environment, 1914–39.' In O.M. Westall (ed.), *The Historian and the Business of Insurance,* 155–72. Manchester: Manchester University Press, 1984.

Caledonian Insurance Company. History of a Hundred Years 1805 to 1905. Edinburgh: T. and A. Constable, 1905.

Campbell, Alan E. (comp.). *University Life Assurance Society 1825–1975.* London: privately published, 1975.

Champness, Arthur. *A Century of Progress.* London: General Life Assurance Company, 1937.

Clough, Shepard B. *A Century of American Life Insurance: A History of the Mutual Life Insurance Company of New York 1843–1943.* New York: Columbia University Press, 1946.

Conder, William S. *The Story of the London Life Association Limited.* London: privately published, 1979.

Dennett, Laurie. *A Sense of Security: 150 Years of Prudential.* Cambridge: Granta Editions, 1998.

Dickson, P.G.M. *The Sun Fire Insurance Office 1710–1960: The History of Two and a Half Centuries of British Insurance.* London: Oxford University Press, 1960.

– *Sun Life Assurance Society, 1810–1960. An Account of the Society during its First One Hundred and Fifty Years.* London: Sun Life, 1960.

Docherty, Elizabeth R. 'The Minerva Life Assurance Company 1836–1864.' University of Strathclyde B.A. dissertation, 1974.

Drew, Bernard. *The London Assurance: A Chronicle.* Oxford: Kemp Hall Press, 1928.

Equity & Law: 150 Anniversary 1844–1994. High Wycombe: AXA Equity & Law, 1994.

Francis, E.V. *London and Lancashire History: The History of the London and Lancashire Insurance Company Limited.* London: Newman Neame, 1962.

Hazell, Stanley. *A Record of the First Hundred Years of the National Provident Institution 1835–1935.* Cambridge: Cambridge University Press, 1935.

Henham, Brian. *The Insurance Offices of Shrewsbury.* Chichester: Braidwood Books, 2002.

Hudnut, James M. *Semi-Centennial History of the New-York Life Insurance Company 1845–1895.* New York: The Company, 1895.

Humpherson, L.H. *The First Hundred Years of the Marine and General Mutual Life Assurance Society.* London: Adprint, 1952.

Karch, Ceclia, with Henderson Carter. *The Rise of the Phoenix: The Barbados Mutual Life Assurance Society in Caribbean Economy and Society 1840–1990.* Kingston: Ian Randle, 1997.

Leigh-Bennett, E.P. *On this Evidence: A Study in 1936 of the Legal and General Assurance Society since its Formation in 1836.* London: Baynard Press, 1937.

Lindsay, Maurice. *Count All Men Mortal: A History of Scottish Provident 1837–1987.* Edinburgh: Canongate, 1987.

Liveing, Edward. *A Century of Insurance: The Commercial Union Group of Insurance Companies 1861–1961*. London: H. F. & G. Witherby, 1961.

Magnusson, Mamie. *A Length of Days: The Scottish Mutual Assurance Society 1883–1983*. London: Henry Melland, 1983.

McAfee, David (comp.). *One Hundred Years Ago and Today: A Centenary Souvenir of the Gresham Life Assurance Society, Limited*. London: The Company, 1948.

Minnitt, Jack. *The Sun Life Story 1810–1985*. Bristol: Sun Life Assurance Society plc, 1985.

Moss, Michael. *Standard Life 1825–2000: The Building of Europe's Largest Mutual Life Company*. Edinburgh: Mainstream Publishing, 2000.

Norman, G.A.S. *The Overseas History of the Standard Life Assurance Company*. Edinburgh: The Company, 1950.

Ogborn, Maurice Edward. *Equitable Assurances: The Story of Life Assurance in the Experience of the Equitable Life Assurance Society 1762–1962*. London: George Allen and Unwin, 1962.

Peeps into the Past: A Souvenir of the... Centenary of the Norwich Union Life Office. Norwich: Jarrold and Sons, 1908.

Rock Life Assurance Company. *Centenary 1806–1906*. London: privately published, 1906.

Ryan, Roger. 'A History of the Norwich Union Fire and Life Assurance Societies from 1797 to 1914.' Doctoral dissertation, University of East Anglia, 1983.

– 'The Early Expansion of the Norwich Union Life Insurance Society, 1808–37.' *Business History* 28 (1985): 166–96.

Schooling, William. *Alliance Assurance 1824–1924*. London: The Company, 1924.

Shepherd, A.F. *Links with the Past: A Brief Chronicle of the Public Service of a Notable Institution*. London: Eagle and British Dominions Insurance Co., 1917.

Sherriff, F.H. *From Then ... Till Now, being a Short History of the Provident Mutual Life Assurance Association 1840 ... 1940*. London: Nissen and Arnold, 1940.

Short History of the Oriental Government Security Life Assurance Company, Ltd. Bombay: privately published, 1924.

Simpson, J. Dyer. *The Liverpool and London and Globe Insurance Company. Our Century Year*. London: n.p., 1936.

Spater, Ernest. *Box 1299*. London: Eagle Star Insurance Co., 1951.

Steuart, M.D. *The Scottish Provident Institution 1837–1937*. Edinburgh: privately published, 1937.

Street, Eric (comp.). *The History of the National Mutual Life Assurance Society 1830–1980*. London: The Company, 1980.

Supple, Barry. *The Royal Exchange Assurance: A History of British Insurance 1720–1970*. Cambridge: Cambridge University Press, 1970.

Syed, Isabel (comp). *Eagle Star: A Guide to Its History and Archives*. Cheltenham: Eagle Star Holdings, 1997.

Tarn, A.W., and C.E. Byles. *A Record of the Guardian Assurance Company Limited: 1821–1921*. London: Blades, East and Blades, 1921.

Topliss, John. 'Taking Thought for the Morrow: The Catholic Law and General Life Assurance Company.' *London Recusant* 6 (1976): 105–11.

Trebilcock, Clive. *Phoenix Assurance and the Development of British Insurance*, 2 vols. Cambridge: Cambridge University Press, 1985, 1999.

Tregoning, David, and Hugh Cockerell. *Friends for Life: Friends' Provident Life Office 1832–1982*. London: Henry Melland, 1982.

Van Selm, R. *History of the South African Mutual Life Assurance Society 1845–1945*. Cape Town: South African Mutual Life Assurance Society, 1945.

Westall, Oliver M. 'The Making of Eagle Star.' In I. Syed (comp.), *Eagle Star: A Guide to Its History and Archives*, 1–16. Cheltenham: Eagle Star Holdings, 1997.

Withers, Hartley. *Pioneers of British Life Assurance*. London: Staples Press, 1951.

Worland, H.S., and M.D. Paterson (eds.). *SALAS 150: A History of Scottish Amicable Life Assurance Society 1826–1976*. Glasgow: The Company, 1976.

Other Secondary Sources

Abbott, Andrew. *The System of Professions: An Essay on the Division of Labor*. Chicago: University of Chicago Press, 1988.

Alborn, Timothy L. 'The Other Economists: Science and Commercial Culture in Victorian England.' Doctoral dissertation, Harvard University, 1991.

– 'A Calculating Profession: Victorian Actuaries among the Statisticians.' In M. Power (ed.), *Accounting and Science: Natural Inquiry and Commercial Reason*, 81–119. Cambridge: Cambridge University Press, 1994.

– 'The Business of Induction: Industry and Genius in the Language of British Scientific Reform, 1820–1840.' *History of Science* 34 (1996): 191–221.

– *Conceiving Companies: Joint-Stock Politics in Victorian England*. London: Routledge, 1998.

– 'Age and Empire in the Indian Census.' *Journal of Interdisciplinary History* 30 (1999): 61–89.

– 'Senses of Belonging: The Politics of Working-Class Insurance in Britain, 1880–1914.' *Journal of Modern History* 73 (2001): 561–602.

– 'Insurance against Germ Theory: Commerce and Conservatism in Late-Victorian Medicine.' *Bulletin of the History of Medicine* 75 (2001): 406–45.

- Review of Clive Trebilcock, *Phoenix Assurance and the Development of British Insurance. Connecticut Insurance Law Journal* 7 (2001): 657–63.
- 'The First Fund Managers: Life Insurance Bonuses in Victorian Britain.' *Victorian Studies* 45 (2002): 67–92.
- 'Postnational Insurance on the Eve of Destruction.' *Connecticut Insurance Law Journal* 10 (2003): 73–101.
- 'Quill-Driving: British Life Insurance Clerks and Occupational Mobility, 1800–1914.' *Business History Review* 82 (2008): 31–58.
- 'A License to Bet: Life Insurance and the Gambling Act in the British Courts.' *Connecticut Insurance Law Journal* 14 (2008): 1–20.
- 'Dirty Laundry: Exposing Bad Behavior in Life Insurance Trials, 1830–1890.' In M.J. Lobban, J.C.B. Taylor, and M.C. Finn (eds.), *Spurious Issues: Legitimacy and Illegitimacy in Law, Literature and History*. London: Palgrave Macmillan, forthcoming.
Anderson, Amanda. *Tainted Souls and Painted Faces: The Rhetoric of Fallenness in Victorian Culture*. Ithaca, NY: Cornell University Press, 1993.
Anderson, Olive. 'Loans versus Taxes: British Financial Policy in the Crimean War.' *Economic History Review* 16 (1963): 314–27.
Armstrong, Nancy. *Desire and Domestic Fiction*. Oxford: Oxford University Press, 1987.
Ashworth, William J. '"The Calculating Eye": Baily, Herschel, Babbage and the Business of Astronomy.' *British Journal of the History of Science* 27 (1994): 409–41.
Austrian, Geoffrey D. *Herman Hollerith: Forgotten Giant of Information Processing*. New York: Columbia University Press, 1982.
Baker, Mae, and Michael Collins. 'The Asset Portfolio Composition of British Life Insurance Firms, 1900–1965.' *Financial History Review* 10 (2005): 137–64.
Baker, Tom. 'Constructing the Insurance Relationship: Sales Stories, Claims Stories, and Insurance Contract Damages.' *Law and Social Inquiry* 21 (1994): 229–64.
Beckles, Hilary M. *A History of Barbados: From Amerindian Settlement to Nation-State*. Cambridge: Cambridge University Press, 1990.
Benson, John. *Prime Time: A History of the Middle Aged in Twentieth-Century Britain*. London: Longman, 1997.
Best, Paul J. 'Insurance in Imperial Russia.' *Journal of European Economic History* 18 (1989): 139–69.
Biddle, Gordon. 'Insurance.' In J. Simmons and G. Biddle (eds.), *The Oxford Companion to British Railway History*, 226–7. Oxford: Oxford University Press, 1997.
Brake, Laurel. *Print in Transition, 1850–1910: Studies in Media and Book History*. London: Palgrave Macmillan, 2001.

Brewer, John. *The Sinews of Power: War, Money and the English State, 1688–1783.* Cambridge, Mass.: Harvard University Press, 1990.

Brewer, John, and Susan Staves (eds.). *Early Modern Conceptions of Property.* New York: Knopf, 1996.

Burchill, Graham, Colin Gordon, and Peter Miller (eds.). *The Foucault Effect: Studies in Governmentality.* Chicago: University of Chicago Press, 1991.

Brown, Callum G. *The Death of Christian Britain: Understanding Secularisation 1800–2000.* London: Routledge, 2001.

Bryden, D.J. 'Slide Rule.' In Robert Bud (ed.), *Instruments of Science: An Historical Encyclopedia,* 536–8. London: Routledge, 1997.

Buck, Peter. 'People Who Counted: Political Arithmetic in the Eighteenth Century.' *Isis* 73 (1982): 28–45.

Bynum, W.F. *Science and the Practice of Medicine in the Nineteenth Century.* Cambridge: Cambridge University Press, 1994.

Campbell-Kelly, Martin. 'Charles Babbage and the Assurance of Lives.' *IEEE Annals of the History of Computing* 16 (1994): 5–14.

Canguilhem, Georges. *The Normal and the Pathological.* New York: Zone Books, 1989.

Cannadine, David. *Aspects of Aristocracy: Grandeur and Decline in Modern Britain.* London: Penguin, 1994.

Carlton, William J. 'Dickens's Insurance Policies.' *Dickensian* 51 (1955): 133–7.

Cassis, Youssef. *City Bankers, 1890–1914.* Cambridge: Cambridge University Press, 1994.

Checkland, S.G. *Scottish Banking: A History, 1695–1973.* Glasgow: Collins, 1975.

Church, R.A., and Barbara M.D. Smith. 'Competition and Monopoly in the Coffin Furniture Industry, 1870–1915.' *Economic History Review* 19 (1966): 621–41.

Clark, Geoffrey. *Betting on Lives: The Culture of Life Insurance in England 1695–1775.* Manchester: Manchester University Press, 1999.

– 'Embracing Fatality through Life Insurance in Britain.' In T. Baker and J. Simon (eds.), *Embracing Risk: The Changing Culture of Insurance and Responsibility,* 80–96. Chicago: University of Chicago Press, 2002.

Cockerell, Hugh A.L., and Edwin Green, *The British Insurance Business: A Guide to Its History and Records.* Sheffield: Sheffield Academic Press, 1994.

Collini, Stefan, Donald Winch, and John Burrow. *That Noble Science of Politics: A Study in Nineteenth-Century Intellectual History.* Oxford: Oxford University Press, 1983.

Cooksey, W.J. *Morrice Alexander Black (1830-1890): Some Notes on his Contribution to the Theory and Practice of Life Assurance.* Sydney: A.M.P. Central Printing Unit, 1981.

Cooper, Brian P. *Family Fictions and Family Facts: Harriet Martineau, Adolphe Quetelet, and the Population Question in England, 1798–1859*. London: Routledge, 2007.

Cordery, Simon. *British Friendly Societies, 1750–1914*. New York: Palgrave Macmillan, 2003.

Corfield, P.J. *Power and the Professions in Britain, 1700–1850*. London: Routledge, 1995.

Cox, Peter R., and R.H. Storr-Best. *Surplus in British Life Assurance: Actuarial Control Over Its Emergence and Distribution during 200 Years*. Cambridge: Cambridge University Press, 1962.

Cullen, Michael J. *The Statistical Movement in Early Victorian Britain: The Foundations of Empirical Social Research*. New York: Barnes and Noble, 1975.

Curtin, Philip D. *Death by Migration: Europe's Encounter with the Tropical World in the Nineteenth Century*. Cambridge: Cambridge University Press, 1989.

Daston, Lorraine J. *Classical Probability in the Enlightenment*. Princeton: Princeton University Press, 1988.

Daunton, M.J. *Royal Mail: The Post Office since 1840*. London: Athlone Press, 1985.
– 'The Political Economy of Death Duties: Harcourt's Budget of 1894.' In N. Harte and R. Quinault (eds.), *Land and Society in Britain, 1700–1914: Essays in Honour of F.M.L. Thompson*, 137–71. Manchester: Manchester University Press, 1996.

Davidoff, Leonore, and Catherine Hall. *Family Fortunes: Men and Women of the English Middle Class, 1780–1850*. Chicago: University of Chicago Press, 1987.

Davidson, Andrew Rutherford. *The History of the Faculty of Actuaries in Scotland 1856–1956*. Edinburgh: Faculty of Actuaries, 1956.

Defert, Daniel. '"Popular Life" and Insurance Technology.' In G. Burchell et al. (eds.), *The Foucault Effect*, 211–33. Chicago: Chicago University Press, 1991.

Delany, Paul. *Literature, Money and the Market: From Trollope to Amis*. London: Palgrave Macmillan 2002.

Digby, Anne. *Making a Medical Living: Doctors and Patients in the English Market for Medicine, 1720–1911*. Cambridge: Cambridge University Press, 1994.
– *The Evolution of British General Practice, 1850–1948*. Oxford: Oxford University Press, 1999.

Dixon, Diana. 'The Two Faces of Death: Children's Magazines and Their Treatment of Death in the Nineteenth Century.' In Ralph Houlbrooke (ed.), *Death, Ritual and Bereavement*, 136–50. London: Routledge, 1989.

Dohrn, Susanne. 'Pioneers in a Dead-End Profession: The First Women Clerks in Banks and Insurance Companies.' In Gregory Anderson (ed.), *The White-Blouse Revolution: Female Office Workers since 1870*, 48–66. Manchester: Manchester University Press, 1988.

Doig, Alan. *Corruption and Misconduct in Contemporary British Politics.* Harmondsworth: Penguin, 1984.

Douglas, Mary. *How Institutions Think.* Syracuse: Syracuse University Press, 1986.

Dow, J.B. 'Early Actuarial Work in Eighteenth-Century Scotland.' *Transactions of the Faculty of Actuaries* 33 (1975): 193–229.

Dupree, Marguerite W. 'Other Than Healing: Medical Practitioners and the Business of Life Assurance during the Nineteenth and Early Twentieth Centuries.' *Social History of Medicine* 10 (1997): 79–104.

Endelman, Todd. *The Jews of Georgian England, 1714–1830: Tradition and Change in a Liberal Society.* Philadelphia: Jewish Publication Society of America, 1984.

Ericson, Richard V., Aaron Doyle, and Dean Barry. *Insurance as Governance.* Toronto: University of Toronto Press, 2003.

Evans, Jillian. 'Mortality, Behold and Fear.' In Derek Renn (ed.), *Life, Death and Money: Actuaries and the Creation of Financial Security,* 29–42. Oxford: Blackwell, 1998.

Ewald, François. 'Insurance and Risk.' In G. Burchell et al. (eds.), *The Foucault Effect: Studies in Governmentality,* 197–210. Chicago: University of Chicago Press, 1991.

Eyler, John. *Victorian Social Medicine: The Ideas and Methods of William Farr.* Baltimore: Johns Hopkins University Press, 1979.

– *Sir Arthur Newsholme and State Medicine, 1885–1935.* Cambridge: Cambridge University Press, 1997.

Finn, Margot. *The Character of Credit: Personal Debt in English Culture, 1750–1914.* Cambridge: Cambridge University Press, 2003.

Foucault, Michel. *The Birth of the Clinic: An Archaeology of Medical Perception.* New York: Vintage, 1975.

– 'On Governmentality.' *Ideology and Consciousness* 6 (1979): 5–22.

Freedgood, Elaine. *Victorian Writing about Risk: Imagining a Safe England in a Dangerous World.* Cambridge: Cambridge University Press, 2000.

Gallagher, Catherine. *The Industrial Reformation of English Literature: Social Discourse and Narrative Form 1832–1867.* Chicago: University of Chicago Press, 1985.

Garrard, John, and Vivienne Parrott. 'Craft, Professional and Middle-Class Identity: Solicitors and Gas Engineers c. 1850–1914.' In Alan Kidd and David Nicholls (eds.), *The Making of the British Middle Class? Studies of Regional and Cultural Diversity since the Eighteenth Century,* 148–68. Stroud: Sutton, 1998.

Golby, J.M., and A.W. Purdue. *The Civilisation of the Crowd: Popular Culture in England 1750–1900.* 2nd ed. Stroud: Sutton, 1999 [1984].

Gosden, P.H.J.H. *Self-Help: Voluntary Associations in Nineteenth-Century Britain*. London: Batsford, 1973.

Gray, A.C. *Life Insurance in Australia: An Historical and Descriptive Account*. Melbourne: McCarron Bird, 1977.

Habakkuk, John. *Marriage, Debt, and the Estates System: English Landownership 1650–1950*. Oxford: Clarendon Press, 1994.

Hacking, Ian. *The Taming of Chance*. Cambridge: Cambridge University Press, 1990.

Hadley, Elaine. *Melodramatic Tactics: Theatricalized Dissent in the English Marketplace, 1800–1885*. Stanford: Stanford University Press, 1995.

Haley, Bruce. *The Healthy Body and Victorian Culture*. Cambridge, Mass.: Harvard University Press, 1978.

Hall, Catherine. *White, Male and Middle Class: Explorations in Feminism and History*. New York: Routledge, 1992.

Hamlin, Christopher. *Public Health and Social Justice in the Age of Chadwick: Britain, 1800–1854*. Cambridge: Cambridge University Press, 1998.

Hannah, Leslie. *Inventing Retirement: The Development of Occupational Pensions in Britain*. Cambridge: Cambridge University Press, 1988.

Harris, Ron. *Industrializing English Law: Entrepreneurship and Business Organization, 1720–1844*. Cambridge: Cambridge University Press, 2000.

Harrison, Richard S. *Irish Insurance: Historical Perspectives, 1650–1939.* Cork: privately printed, 1992.

Harvey, David. *The Condition of Postmodernity*. Oxford: Blackwell, 1990.

Heimer, Carol A. 'Insurers as Moral Actors.' In R.V. Ericson and A. Doyle (eds.), *Risk and Morality*, 284–316. Toronto: University of Toronto Press, 2003.

Herzfeld, Michael. *The Social Production of Indifference: Exploring the Symbolic Roots of Western Bureaucracy*. Chicago: University of Chicago Press, 1992.

Holcombe, Lee. *Wives and Property: Reform of the Married Women's Property Law in Nineteenth-Century England*. Toronto: University of Toronto Press, 1983.

Holmes, A.R., and Edwin Green. *Midland: 150 Years of Banking Business*. London: B.T. Batsford, 1986.

Horstman, Klasien. 'Chemical Analysis of Urine for Life Insurance: The Construction of Reliability.' *Science, Technology and Human Values* 22 (1997): 57–78.

Horton, Joanne, and Richard Macve. 'The Development of Life Assurance Accounting and Regulation in the U.K.: Reflections on Recent Proposals for Accounting Change.' *Accounting, Business and Financial History* 4 (1994): 295–320.

Howarth, Glennys. 'Professionalising the Funeral Industry in England 1700–1960.' In Peter C. Jupp and Glennys Howarth, *The Changing Face of Death:*

Historical Accounts of Death and Disposal, 120–34. New York: St Martin's Press, 1997.

Industrial Life Offices' Association, 1901–1951. London: The Association, 1951.

Jalland, Pat. *Death in the Victorian Family*. Oxford: Oxford University Press, 1996.

Jameson, Frederic. *Postmodernism: Or, the Cultural Logic of Late Capitalism*. Durham, NC: Duke University Press, 1991.

Jones, Colin, and Roy Porter (eds.). *Reassessing Foucault: Power, Medicine and the Body*. New York: Routledge, 1994.

Jones, Edgar. *Accountancy and the British Economy 1840–1980: The Evolution of Ernst & Whinney*. London: Batsford, 1981.

Jordanova, Ludmilla. 'The Art and Science of Seeing in Medicine: Physiognomy 1780–1820.' In William Bynum and Roy Porter (eds.), *Medicine and the Five Senses*, 122–33. Cambridge: Cambridge University Press, 1993.

Jureidini, Ray, and Kevin White. 'Life Insurance, the Medical Examination and Cultural Values.' *Journal of Historical Sociology* 13 (2000): 190–214.

Keller, Morton. *The Life Insurance Enterprise, 1885–1910: A Study in the Limits of Corporate Power*. Cambridge, Mass.: Harvard University Press, 1963.

Kent, Tim. 'The Accident Offices Association.' *CII Journal* 4 (1997): 16–19.

Kwolek-Folland, Angel. *Engendering Business: Men and Women in the Corporate Office, 1870–1930*. Baltimore: Johns Hopkins University Press, 1994.

Lane, Padraig G. 'The Management of Estates by Financial Corporations in Ireland after the Famine.' *Studia Hibernica* 14 (1974): 67–89.

Langland, Elizabeth. *Nobody's Angels: Middle-Class Women and Domestic Ideology in Victorian Culture*. Ithaca, NY: Cornell University Press, 1995.

Laqueur, Thomas. 'Bodies, Death, and Pauper Funerals.' *Representations* 7 (1983): 109–31.

Lawrence, Christopher. 'Incommunicable Knowledge: Science, Technology and the Clinical Art in Britain 1850–1914.' *Journal of Contemporary History* 20 (1985): 503–20.

Le Grys, Desmond. 'Life Underwriting and Reassurance.' In Derek Renn (ed.), *Life, Death and Money: Actuaries and the Creation of Financial Security*, 165–77. Oxford: Blackwell, 1998.

Lenoir, Timothy. 'The Discipline of Nature and the Nature of Disciplines.' In E. Messer-Davidow, D.R. Shumway, and D.J. Sylvan (eds.), *Knowledges: Historical and Critical Studies in Disciplinarity*, 70–102. Charlottesville: University Press of Virginia, 1993.

Lewin, C.G. *Pensions and Insurance before 1800*. East Linton: Tuckwell Press, 2003.

Loudon, Irvine. *Medical Care and the General Practitioner 1750–1850*. Oxford: Oxford University Press, 1986.

– *Death in Childbirth: An International Study of Maternal Care and Maternal Mortality 1800–1950*. Oxford: Clarendon Press, 1992.

Love, Rosaleen. '"Alice in Eugenics-Land": Feminism and Eugenics in the Scientific Careers of Alice Lee and Ethel Elderton.' *Annals of Science* 36 (1979): 145–58.

Macnicol, John. *The Politics of Retirement in Britain, 1878–1948*. Cambridge: Cambridge University Press, 1998.

Marland, Hilary. *Medicine and Society in Wakefield and Huddersfield, 1780–1870*. Cambridge: Cambridge University Press, 1987.

McCarthy, Fiona. *Byron: Life and Legend*. New York: Farrar, Straus and Giroux, 2002.

Metcalf, H.A., et al. *History of Life Assurance Underwriting*. London: Insurance Institute of London, 1967.

Morley, John. *Death, Heaven and the Victorians*. London: Studio Vista, 1971.

Morris, R.J. 'The Middle Class and the Property Cycle during the Industrial Revolution.' In T.C. Smout (ed.), *The Search for Wealth and Stability*, 91–113. London: Macmillan, 1979.

– 'Men, Women and Property: The Reform of the Married Women's Property Act, 1870.' In F.M.L. Thompson (ed.), *Landowners, Capitalists and Entrepreneurs: Essays for Sir John Habakkuk*, 171–92. Oxford: Oxford University Press, 1994.

– 'Reading the Will: Cash Economy Capitalists and Urban Peasants in the 1830s.' In Alan Kidd and David Nicholls (eds.), *The Making of the British Middle Class? Studies of Regional and Cultural Diversity since the Eighteenth Century*, 113–29. Stroud: Sutton, 1998.

– *Men, Women, and Property in England, 1780–1870: A Social and Economic History of Family Strategies amongst the Leeds Middle Classes*. Cambridge: Cambridge University Press, 2005.

Murphy, Sharon Ann. 'Security in an Uncertain World: Life Insurance and the Emergence of Modern America.' Doctoral dissertation, University of Virginia, 2005.

Naqvi, N.H., and M.D. Blaufox. *Blood Pressure Measurement: An Illustrated History*. New York: Parthenon, 1998.

New Dictionary of National Biography. Oxford: Oxford University Press, 2004.

Nicolson, Malcolm. 'The Introduction of Percussion and Stethoscopy to Early Nineteenth-Century Edinburgh.' In William Bynum and Roy Porter (eds.), *Medicine and the Five Senses*, 134–53. Cambridge: Cambridge University Press, 1993.

North, Douglass C. *Institutions, Institutional Change and Economic Performance*. Cambridge: Cambridge University Press, 1990.

Offer, Avner. *Property and Politics, 1870–1914: Landownership, Law, Ideology, and Urban Development in England.* Cambridge: Cambridge University Press, 1981.

O'Malley, Pat. 'Imagining Insurance: Risk, Thrift, and Industrial Life Insurance in Britain.' *Connecticut Insurance Law Jounral* 5 (1999): 675–705.

Parshall, Karren Hunger. *James Joseph Sylvester: Life and Work in Letters.* New York: Oxford University Press, 1998.

– *James Joseph Sylvester: Jewish Mathematician in a Victorian World.* Baltimore: Johns Hopkins University Press, 2006.

Pearson, Robin. 'Thrift or Dissipation? The Business of Life Assurance in the Early Nineteenth Century.' *Economic History Review* 43 (1990): 236–54.

– 'Towards an Historical Model of Services Innovation: The Case of the Insurance Industry, 1700–1914.' *Economic History Review* 50 (1997): 235–56.

– 'Moral Hazard and the Assessment of Insurance Risk in Eighteenth- and Early-Nineteenth-Century Britain.' *Business History Review* 76 (2002): 1–35.

– 'Shareholder Democracies? English Joint-Stock Companies and the Politics of Corporate Governance during the Industrial Revolution.' *English Historical Review* 117 (2002): 840-66.

– *Insuring the Industrial Revolution: Fire Insurance in Great Britain, 1700–1850.* Aldershot: Ashgate, 2004.

Peterson, M. Jeanne. *The Medical Profession in Mid-Victorian London.* Berkeley: University of California Press, 1978.

– *Family, Love, and Work in the Lives of Victorian Gentlewomen.* Bloomington: Indiana University Press, 1989.

Philip, George C. 'Actuarial Investigations up to the Amalgamation of the Schemes in 1930.' In A. Ian Dunlop (ed.), *The Scottish Ministers' Widows' Fund, 1743–1993,* 105–17. Edinburgh: Saint Andrew Press, 1992.

Poovey, Mary. *A History of the Modern Fact: Problems of Knowledge in the Science of Wealth and Society.* Chicago: University of Chicago Press, 1998.

– 'Writing about Finance in Victorian England: Disclosure and Secrecy in the Culture of Investment.' *Victorian Studies* 45 (2002): 17–41.

Porter, Roy, and G.S. Rousseau. *Gout: The Patrician Malady.* New Haven: Yale University Press, 1998.

Porter, Theodore M. *The Rise of Statistical Thinking 1820–1900.* Princeton: Princeton University Press, 1986.

– *Trust in Numbers: The Pursuit of Objectivity in Science and Public Life.* Princeton: Princeton University Press, 1995.

– 'Life Insurance, Medical Testing, and the Management of Mortality.' In L. Daston (ed.), *Biographies of Scientific Objects,* 226–46. Chicago: University of Chicago Press, 2000.

Pruitt, Amy A. 'Approaches to Alcoholism in Mid-Victorian England.' *Clio Medica* 9 (1974): 93–101.

Rabinow, Paul. *French Modern: Norms and Forms of the Social Environment.* Cambridge, Mass.: MIT Press, 1989.

Ransom, Roger L., and Richard Sutch. 'Tontine Insurance and the Armstrong Investigation: A Case of Stifled Innovation, 1868–1905.' *Journal of Economic History* 47 (1987): 379–90.

Raynes, Harold E. *A History of British Insurance.* London: Pitman, 1948.

Recknell, G.H. *The Actuaries' Club 1848–1948.* London: Actuaries Club, 1948.

Reiser, Stanley Joel. *Medicine and the Reign of Technology.* Cambridge: Cambridge University Press, 1978.

Richards, Thomas. *The Commodity Culture of Victorian England: Advertising and Spectacle, 1851–1914.* Stanford: Stanford University Press, 1990.

Richardson, Ruth. 'Why Was Death So Big in Victorian Britain?' In Ralph Houlbrooke (ed.), *Death, Ritual and Bereavement,* 105–17. London: Routledge, 1989.

Robb, George. *White-Collar Crime in Modern England: Financial Fraud and Business Morality 1845–1929.* Cambridge: Cambridge University Press, 1992.

Saltzman, Steven H. 'The Middle Class and Debt Financing of Municipal Trading: A Case Study in 19th Century Glasgow and Birmingham.' Doctoral dissertation, City University of New York, 2005.

Schabas, Margaret. *A World Ruled by Number: William Stanley Jevons and the Rise of Mathematical Economics.* Princeton: Princeton University Press, 1990.

Scott, Peter. 'Towards the "Cult of Equity"? Insurance Companies and the Interwar Capital Market.' *Economic History Review* 55 (2002): 78–104.

Searle, G.R. *Morality and the Market in Victorian Britain.* New York: Oxford University Press, 1998.

Shiman, Lilian Lewis. *Crusade against Drink in Victorian England.* New York: St Martin's Press, 1988.

Simmonds, Reginald Claude. *The Institute of Actuaries 1848–1948: An Account of the Institute of Actuaries during its First One Hundred Years.* Cambridge: Cambridge University Press, 1948.

Simon, Jonathan. 'The Ideological Effects of Actuarial Practices.' *Law and Society Review* 22 (1988): 771–800.

Skerman, Ronald. 'Actuaries and Life Insurance.' In Derek Renn (ed.), *Life, Death and Money: Actuaries and the Creation of Financial Security,* 61–103. Oxford: Blackwell, 1998.

Stalson, J. Owen. *Marketing Life Insurance: Its History in America.* Cambridge, Mass.: Harvard University Press, 1942.

Stashower, Daniel. *Teller of Tales: The Life of Arthur Conan Doyle.* New York: Holt, 1999.

Stebbings, Chantal. *The Private Trustee in Victorian England.* Cambridge: Cambridge University Press, 2002.

Stern, Rebecca. 'Proleptic Economies: Time Bargains, Futures, and the Logic of Regret.' Paper delivered at the North American Conference on British Studies, San Francisco, November 2007.

Stoeckle, John D. 'Introduction.' In J.D. Stoeckle (ed.), *Encounters between Patients and Doctors: An Anthology,* 1–129. Cambridge, Mass.: MIT Press, 1987.

Stone, Deborah. 'Beyond Moral Hazard: Insurance as Moral Opportunity.' In T. Baker and J. Simon (eds.), *Embracing Risk: The Changing Culture of Insurance and Responsibility,* 52–79. Chicago: University of Chicago Press, 2002.

Supple, Barry. 'Legislation and Virtue: An Essay on Working Class Self Help and the State.' In N. McKendrick (ed.), *Historical Perspectives,* 211–54. London: Europa, 1974.

– 'Corporate Growth and Structural Change in a Service Industry: Insurance, 1870–1914.' In B. Supple (ed.), *Essays in British Business History,* 69–87. Oxford: Oxford University Press, 1977.

Swaan, Abram de. *The Management of Normality: Critical Essays in Health and Welfare.* London: Routledge, 1990.

Sweet, Matthew. *Inventing the Victorians.* New York: St Martin's Press, 2001.

Tapp, Julian. 'Regulation of the U.K. Insurance Industry.' In Jörg Finsinger and Mark V. Pauly (eds.), *The Economics of Insurance Regulation: A Cross–National Study,* 27–61. New York: St Martin's Press, 1986.

Taylor, James. *Creating Capitalism: Joint-Stock Enterprise in British Politics and Culture 1800–1870.* London: Boydell Press, 2006.

Taylor, Lou. *Mourning Dress: A Costume and Social History.* London: Allen and Unwin, 1983.

Titmuss, Richard. *Commitment to Welfare.* 2nd ed. London: Allen and Unwin, 1976.

Tosh, John. 'Domesticity and Manliness in the Victorian Middle Class: The Family of Edward White Benson.' In M. Roper and J. Tosh, *Manful Assertions: Masculinities in Britain since 1800,* 44–73. London: Routledge, 1991.

– *A Man's Place: Masculinity and the Middle-Class Home in Victorian England.* New Haven: Yale University Press, 1999.

Trebilcock, Clive. 'The City, Entrepreneurship and Insurance: Two Pioneers in Invisible Exports – the Phoenix Fire Office and the Royal of Liverpool, 1800–90.' In N. McKendrick and R.B. Outhwaite (eds.), *Business Life and Public Policy,* 137–72. Cambridge: Cambridge University Press, 1986.

Valenze, Deborah. *The Social Life of Money in the English Past.* Cambridge: Cambridge University Press, 2006.

Vernon, James. 'The Ethics of Hunger and the Assembly of Society: The Techno-Politics of the School Meal in Modern Britain.' *American Historical Review* 110 (2005): 693–725.

Villaronga, Luis M. *The Incontestable Clause: An Historical Analysis*. Philadelphia: S.S. Huebner Foundation, 1976.

Walker, Pamela. '"I Live but Not Yet I for Christ Liveth in Me": Men and Masculinity in the Salvation Army, 1865–90.' In M. Roper and J. Tosh (eds.), *Manful Assertions: Masculinities in Britain since 1800*, 92–112. London: Routledge, 1991.

Walker, Stephen P. *The Society of Accountants in Edinburgh, 1854–1914: A Study of Recruitment to a New Profession*. New York: Garland, 1988.

Warwick, Andrew. 'The Laboratory of Theory or What's Exact about the Exact Sciences?' In M.N. Wise (ed.), *The Values of Precision*, 311–51. Princeton: Princeton University Press, 1995.

Welsh, Alexander. *The City of Dickens*. Cambridge, Mass.: Harvard University Press, 1986 [1971].

Westall, Oliver M. 'Entrepreneurship and Product Innovation in British General Insurance, 1840–1914.' In J. Brown and M.B. Rose (eds.), *Entrepreneurship, Networks and Modern Business*, 191–208. Manchester: Manchester University Press, 1993.

Williams, Raymond. *The Country and the City*. Oxford: Oxford University Press, 1973.

Wood, Alexander. *Thomas Young, Natural Philosopher 1773–1829*. Cambridge: Cambridge University Press, 1954.

Woods, Robert. *The Population History of Britain in the Nineteenth Century*. Cambridge: Cambridge University Press, 1995.

– *Demography of Victorian England and Wales*. Cambridge: Cambridge University Press, 2000.

Yates, JoAnne. *Control through Communication: The Rise of System in American Management*. Baltimore: Johns Hopkins University Press, 1989.

– *Structuring the Information Age: Life Insurance and Technology in the Twentieth Century*. Baltimore: Johns Hopkins University Press, 2005.

Zelizer, Viviana A. Rotman. *Morals and Markets: The Development of Life Insurance in the United States*. New Brunswick, NJ: Transaction Books, 1983.

Zimmeck, Meta. 'Gladstone Holds His Own: The Origins of Income Tax Relief for Life Insurance Policies.' *Bulletin of the Institute of Historical Research* 58 (1985): 167-188.

Zunz, Olivier. *Making America Corporate, 1870–1920*. Chicago: University of Chicago Press, 1990.

Index

Rogers, O., 292
routinization, 11, 83, 87, 244–5, 284
Royal Exchange Assurance, 4, 12–13,
22, 28, 47–8, 55–6, 70, 86, 88–9, 93,
112, 145, 171, 177, 188, 247, 259,
290, 313, 318, 327
Royal Farmers Fire & Life, x, 14, 87,
89, 96, 177, 320, 327
Royal Insurance, 25, 92, 318, 324–5
Royal Naval & Military Life, 36, 318
Royal Society, 83, 124
Russell, F., 160
Ryan, R., 13

Sala, G., 79
salesmen: see agents
Salvation Army, 155, 163, 318
Sang, E., 122–3
saving, 7, 12, 16–17, 54, 73, 102, 129,
136, 189, 196–219, 362
savings banks, 12, 22, 38, 167, 199–
200, 202–5, 219, 361
Sceptre Life, 71, 318
Scotland, 4, 19, 21, 24–9, 33–4, 43–5,
47–9, 54–5, 58, 65–7, 70–1, 74, 79–
83, 85–6, 93–8, 126, 167, 172, 199,
229, 275–6, 322–5, 328, 340, 346, 364
Scott, W., 138, 161
Scottish Amicable Life, ix, 14, 26, 31,
47, 49, 85–6, 88, 90, 93, 96, 133, 173,
184, 229, 255, 285, 303, 318
Scottish Equitable Life, 26, 47, 49, 51,
57, 65, 68, 84, 92, 150, 154, 180, 183,
216, 225, 259, 318, 347
Scottish Imperial Insurance, 71, 318
Scottish Indisputable Life, 67
Scottish Life, 303, 318
Scottish Metropolitan Life, 207, 318
Scottish National Fire & Life, 14, 49,
92, 95, 107, 207, 229, 243, 318

Scottish Provident Institute, 26–7,
47, 49, 51, 86, 109, 162, 179, 190–1,
230, 319
Scottish Provincial Fire & Life, 14,
281, 320
Scottish Temperance (later Scottish
Mutual) Life, 40, 146, 158, 229, 240,
319, 321
Scottish Union (later Scottish Union
& National) Fire & Life, 14, 26, 49,
85, 258, 277, 314, 318–19, 321
Scottish Widows' Fund, 25–7, 45, 47,
49, 51, 100, 111, 129, 156, 171, 190,
212, 226, 235, 253, 255, 285, 287,
319
Scratchley, A., 161, 184–5, 197, 214,
342
Scudamore, F., 42
Sea Fire & Life, 23, 59
selection, effect of, 104, 110, 112–15,
285
self-help, 12, 22, 34, 38, 197, 203
shareholders, 20, 35–6, 43, 46–7, 57,
61–2, 77–80, 168–9, 177; as critics,
56, 83
Sheffield, 44, 149, 317
shopkeepers, 56, 152; as agents, 6,
88, 93–4, 96, 322–8; as policyholders, 139, 142–3
Sieveking, E., 243, 299
Smee, A., 19, 284
Smiles, S., 58
Smith, D., 85
Smith, G., 93
Smithson, T.C., 133
Solicitors' & General Life, 35, 319
solidarity, 22, 34, 173, 193–5, 305–7
South Africa, 29, 31–3, 120
Southey, H., 138
Southey, R., 138